Peasant Life in China

—A Field Study of Country Life in the Yangtze Valley

江村经济

——中国农民的生活

费孝通 著　戴可景 译

英汉对照

外语教学与研究出版社
FOREIGN LANGUAGE TEACHING AND RESEARCH PRESS
北京 BEIJING

图书在版编目 (CIP) 数据

江村经济 ：中国农民的生活 ＝ Peasant Life in China: A Field Study of Country
Life in the Yangtze Valley ：英汉对照 / 费孝通著 ；戴可景译. — 北京 ：外语教学
与研究出版社，2010.10（2022.7 重印）
　　ISBN 978-7-5135-0268-9

　　Ⅰ . ①江… 　Ⅱ . ①费… ②戴… 　Ⅲ . ①农村－社会调查－吴江市－英、汉
②农村－社会调查－禄丰县－英、汉 　Ⅳ . ①D668

中国版本图书馆 CIP 数据核字 (2010) 第 202498 号

出 版 人　王　芳
系列策划　吴　浩
责任编辑　易　璐
执行编辑　蒲　瑶
装帧设计　视觉共振设计工作室
出版发行　外语教学与研究出版社
社　　址　北京市西三环北路 19 号（100089）
网　　址　http://www.fltrp.com
印　　刷　三河市北燕印装有限公司
开　　本　650×980　1/16
印　　张　30
版　　次　2010 年 10 月第 1 版 2022 年 7 月第 8 次印刷
书　　号　ISBN 978-7-5135-0268-9
定　　价　60.00 元

购书咨询：（010）88819926　电子邮箱：club@fltrp.com
外研书店：https://waiyants.tmall.com
凡印刷、装订质量问题，请联系我社印制部
联系电话：（010）61207896　电子邮箱：zhijian@fltrp.com
凡侵权、盗版书籍线索，请联系我社法律事务部
举报电话：（010）88817519　电子邮箱：banquan@fltrp.com
物料号：202680001

记载人类文明
沟通世界文化
www.fltrp.com

"博雅双语名家名作"出版说明

    1840 年鸦片战争以降，在深重的民族危机面前，中华民族精英"放眼看世界"，向世界寻求古老中国走向现代、走向世界的灵丹妙药，涌现出一大批中国主题的经典著述。我们今天阅读这些中文著述的时候，仍然深为字里行间所蕴藏的缜密的考据、深刻的学理、世界的视野和济世的情怀所感动，但往往会忽略：这些著述最初是用英文写就，我们耳熟能详的中文文本是原初英文文本的译本，这些英文作品在海外学术界和文化界同样享有崇高的声誉。

    比如，林语堂的 *My Country and My People*（《吾国与吾民》）以幽默风趣的笔调和睿智流畅的语言，将中国人的道德精神、生活情趣和中国社会文化的方方面面娓娓道来，在美国引起巨大反响——林语堂也以其中国主题系列作品赢得世界文坛的尊重，并获得诺贝尔文学奖的提名。再比如，梁思成在抗战的烽火中写就的英文版《图像中国建筑史》文稿（*A Pictorial History of Chinese Architecture*），经其挚友费慰梅女士（Wilma C. Fairbank）等人多年的奔走和努力，于 1984 年由麻省理工学院出版社（MIT Press）出版，并获得美国出版联合会颁发的"专业暨学术书籍金奖"。又比如，1939 年，费孝通在伦敦政治经济学院的博士论文以 *Peasant Life in China—A Field Study of Country Life in the Yangtze Valley* 为名在英国劳特利奇书局（Routledge）出版，后以《江村经济》作为中译本书名——《江村经济》使得靠桑蚕为生的"开弦弓村"获得了世界性的声誉，成为国际社会学界研究中国农村的首选之地。

    此外，一些中国主题的经典人文社科作品经海外汉学家和中国学者的如椽译笔，在英语世界也深受读者喜爱。比如，艾恺（Guy S. Alitto）将他 1980 年用中文访问梁漱溟的《这个世界会好吗——梁漱溟晚年口述》一书译成英文（*Has Man a Future? —Dialogues with the Last Confucian*），备受海内外读者关注；

此类作品还有徐中约英译的梁启超著作《清代学术概论》（*Intellectual Trends in the Ch'ing Period*）、狄百瑞（W. T. de Bary）英译的黄宗羲著作《明夷待访录》（*Waiting for the Dawn: A Plan for the Prince*），等等。

有鉴于此，外语教学与研究出版社推出"博雅双语名家名作"系列。

博雅，乃是该系列的出版立意。博雅教育（Liberal Education）早在古希腊时代就得以提倡，旨在培养具有广博知识和优雅气质的人，提高人文素质，培养健康人格，中国儒家六艺"礼、乐、射、御、书、数"亦有此功用。

双语，乃是该系列的出版形式。英汉双语对照的形式，既同时满足了英语学习者和汉语学习者通过阅读中国主题博雅读物提高英语和汉语能力的需求，又以中英双语思维、构架和写作的形式予后世学人以启迪——维特根斯坦有云："语言的边界，乃是世界的边界"，诚哉斯言。

名家，乃是该系列的作者群体。涵盖文学、史学、哲学、政治学、经济学、考古学、人类学、建筑学等领域，皆海内外名家一时之选。

名作，乃是该系列的入选标准。系列中的各部作品都是经过时间的积淀、市场的检验和读者的鉴别而呈现的经典，正如卡尔维诺对"经典"的定义：经典并非你正在读的书，而是你正在重读的书。

胡适在《新思潮的意义》（1919年12月1日，《新青年》第7卷第1号）一文中提出了"研究问题、输入学理、整理国故、再造文明"的范式。秉着"记载人类文明、沟通世界文化"的出版理念，我们推出"博雅双语名家名作"系列，既希望能够在中国人创作的和以中国为主题的博雅英文文献领域"整理国故"，亦希望在和平发展、改革开放的新时代为"再造文明"、为"向世界说明中国"略尽绵薄之力。

外语教学与研究出版社

人文社科出版分社

著者前言

　　本书是 1939 年英国 Routledge 书局出版我所写 *Peasant Life in China* 一书的中译本，原书扉页有《江村经济》中文书名，今译本即沿用此名。这书的翻译工作原应由我自己动笔，但在该书有条件翻译时，我一直忙于其它事务，无暇及此。今由戴可景同志译出，无任感激。应译者要求，我在书前说一说这书写作和翻译的经过。

　　这本书的写成可说是并非出于著者有意栽培的结果，而是由于一连串的客观的偶然因素促成的。话要从 1935 年我从清华大学研究院毕业时说起。我毕业后由该校社会学及人类学系推荐，取得该校公费留学资格。按惯例应于该年暑假出国，但出于指导我研究工作的导师史禄国教授的主张，在出国前应到少数民族地区实地调查一年，因偕前妻王同惠赴广西大瑶山。该年冬，在瑶山里迷路失事，妻亡我伤。经医治后，我于翌年暑期返乡休息，准备出国。在此期间，我接受家姊费达生的建议，去吴江县庙港乡开弦弓村参观访问，她在该村帮助农民建立生丝精制运销合作社。我被这个合作社所吸引，在该村进行了一个多月的调查，在出国前夕才离开该村。这次调查并不是有计划的，是出于受到了当时社会新事物的启迪而产生的自发行动。

　　我去英国，乘坐一艘意大利的邮轮"白公爵"，从上海到威尼斯航程要两个多星期。我在船上无事，趁我记忆犹新，把开弦弓调查的资料整理成篇，并为该村提了个学名叫"江村"。到了英国，进入伦敦经济学院人类学系。最初见到该系 Reader[①] 弗思 (Raymond Firth) 博士，他负责指导我选择论文题目。我原来打算以"花蓝瑶社会组织"作底子编写论文。随后我谈到曾在江村进行过调查，他看了我已经整理出来的材料，主张编写"江村经济"这篇论文。不久该系教授马林诺夫斯基 (B. Malinowski) 从美国讲学返英，我向他汇报了江村调查经过和内容，他决定直接指导我编写这

[①]　Reader 是英国大学教职体中独有职位，低于教授，高于副教授。

篇论文的工作。该论文中主要的几章都在他主持的有名的"今天的人类学"讨论班上宣读、讨论、修改、重写过的。1938年春季，我申请论文答辩，通过后，由伦敦大学授予我博士学位。博士证明书上所标明的论文题目是："开弦弓，一个中国农村的经济生活"。

论文通过的那天晚上，由导师马林诺夫斯基把这篇论文介绍给Routledge书局出版。书局编辑阅后建议书名改为《中国农民的生活》。我看过该书清样后，离英返国，已是1938年的初秋。我记得，由于在轮船上得到广州沦陷的信息，所以临时决定在西贡登陆，直奔云南昆明。到了云南，不久就开始我的内地农村调查。

该书是1939年出版的，其时欧洲已发生战事。全球战乱连年，我已把这书置之脑后。我仿佛记得直到战后我回到清华园，才接到书店寄给我的这本书。当时届解放前夕，时局紧张，我哪里有闲情来想到翻译此书。解放后，我参加民族调查工作，此书的译事提不到日程上来。1956年英伦老同学格迪斯(W. R. Geddes)博士，澳大利亚悉尼大学教授，参加该国文化代表团访华，得到周恩来总理的同意，访问了江村。他引起了我重访江村的兴趣。翌年成行，在调查工作进行过程中，有事返京，适逢"反右"斗争。在《新观察》发表的《重访江村》连载报告尚未结束，我已遭殃及，被错划右派。在被批判中，即使这本书并未译成中文发行，它还是作为一项"流毒深远"的"罪证"。

"文革"后期，我国对外开放，不断有西方学者来华访问，从他们的口上，我才知道，该书已重印了三次。在许多大学的人类学课程中把它列为必读参考书。还有不少现已成名的人类学者告诉我，这本书启发了他们研究人类学和研究中国社会的兴趣。我当时不免担心，深恐其"流毒"太广，增加我的"罪行"。这种历史条件排除了翻译该书的可能性。

这一页历史终于翻过去了。1981年我得到老师弗思的来信，他告诉我：英国皇家人类学会将在1981年授我赫胥黎奖章。这是这门学科中最高的荣誉。他并说《中国农民的生活》又重印发行，建议我在接受奖章时要宣读的论文，最好是叙述江村在四十多年中的变化。我因此又到江村进行了短期的访问，写了《三访江村》这篇文章。

从伦敦回国，我又回江村继续我的农村调查。1982年就从江村作为起点"更上一层楼"开始研究作为农村政治、经济、文化中心的小城镇。从吴江县各镇入手，逐步扩大研究范围，包括苏州、无锡、常州、南通四个市。1984年又扩大到苏北及南京、镇江两市。小城镇的研究，从我个人来说是江村研究的继续。在这段工作中，我已感到有需要把《江村经济》翻译出来给一起调查的同仁们作参考之用，而且江苏人民出版社已约定出版这个译本。但是我自己这几年恢复了学术活动，任务较重，实在抽不出时间和精力来做这项翻译工作，所以只能委托戴可景同志代劳。她在1984年就已经完成译稿，又请潘乃穆同志校阅过一遍。她把译稿交给了我，搁在我书架上，一搁几乎有一年。我应该对译者表示歉意。

屈指一算，离我最初在江村调查时，明年是整整半个世纪了。我自幸在今生能看到这项偶然形成的研究成果取得了国际上的承认，又在国内恢复了名誉。另一方面，经过这将近五十年的阅历，自己对这本早年的著作，总觉得有许多不能惬意之处。作为我个人在人生道路上的一个脚印，自当珍惜；作为国家社会历史的一些历史记录，固然也有它存在的价值；但是我既然还活着，而且尚能工作，自觉有责任再把江村在这半个世纪里的变化写下来，作这本书的续编，并当尽力把这段时期自身的长进来补足早年的不足。因而，我决定和上海大学社会学系合作进行为期两年的江村再调查，编写一本《江村五十年》。在准备这项研究计划时，我才挤出时间，把译稿重读了一遍，做了些必要的修正后，交付出版。至于它的续编在两年之后是否能出世，目前还是难于预知之事，但是我自己是有决心去完成这个自己给自己规定的任务。

以上是本书中译本诞生的经过，就以此作为前言，写在译本的前面。

费孝通

1985年4月15日

译者说明

为了满足社会学研究工作者和广大读者的需要，我利用业余时间完成了本书的翻译工作。初稿供当时去吴江县调查的研究人员参考。后来，译稿由北京大学社会学系潘乃穆同志帮助校阅，又承蒙费孝通先生亲自过目修改，谨在此向他们表示衷心的感谢。

有关译文中的一些技术问题，说明如下：

一、对度量衡单位未作换算，如 mile 直接译作英里（1 英里 = 1.609 公里），bushel 译为蒲式耳（1 蒲式耳〔英〕= 36.368 升）。

二、修正了原文中的一些数字。农业用田改按该村土地总面积的 90% 计算，户数改按 274 户农业户计算，每户按平均四口人计算；这样，对第三章第三节、第七章第五节、第十章第四节以及第十二章第二节中的其他有关数字也作了相应的修改。[①]

三、附录中关于中国亲属称谓仍用原音符表示，仅译出其解释部分。

此外，我根据费老的意见又将澳大利亚悉尼大学人类学系主任 W. R. 格迪斯著的《共产党领导下的中国农民生活》一文附录于后，以供读者参照阅读。[②]

限于译者水平，译文有不妥之处，望读者指正。

1985年4月

---

① 译者还对第二章第二节、第五章第四节中的数字作了修改。另，编者对译文中太平天国运动（第三章第八节）和宋朝（第六章第五节）的起止年代以及两处关于节气时刻的换算（第九章第二节）作了修改，特此说明。

② 因篇幅有限，本书未收入此文。

The Author and Village Girls

作者和农村姑娘

1 4
2 5
3

❶ A Bridge 木桥

❷ Houses along the Stream (1) 沿河的房屋（1）

❸ Houses along the Stream (2) 沿河的房屋（2）

❹ The Stove and the Palace of the Kitchen God 炉灶和灶王爷的神龛

❺ Small Wooden Pavilion Keeping the Tablet of the Newly Dead Ancestor 新近过世的祖宗牌位神龛

Above-Ground Burial 地上葬

Sailing 运输航船

1 2
3 4

❶ A Village Woman in Summer Dress 穿夏装的农村妇女.
❷ A Typical Front View of a House 典型的房屋正面图
❸ Carpenter's House 木匠的房屋
❹ Sheep Hut 羊圈

Diving Birds for Fishing 鱼鹰

Shrimp Traps 捕虾篓

Rich Rice-Fields 茂盛的稻田

Collective Drainage 集体排水

The Co-operative Silk Factory 合作丝厂

Bargaining with Sellers on the Stream 与河上的售货者在进行交易

A Village Store
村庄店铺

An Agent Boat on its Way to the Town
驶往城镇的航船

TO MY WIFE TUNG-WEI WANG

献给我的妻子王同惠

ACKNOWLEDGEMENTS

I have to thank all those who have encouraged and helped me in my field investigation and in my preparation of this book. Above all, I must acknowledge my indebtedness to the following teachers and friends:

To Professors Wu Wen-tsao and S. M. Shirokogoroff I owe my early training in sociology and ethnology, and encouragement in introducing the intensive field investigation in studying Chinese culture. My sister, whose devotion to the rehabilitation of the livelihood of the villagers has actually inspired me to take up this investigation, had introduced me to the village and financed my work. Later, I was awarded a scholarship by Tsing Hua University, which enabled me to pursue my study in England and, so to speak, "to enter under the door" of Professor B. Malinowski. His intellectual inspiration and paternal affection during the past two years has imposed on me a life-long filial duty—a duty, as I understand, to share his heavy burden in building up a science of man, and in realizing a genuine co-operation among all civilizations.

I must thank Mr. G. F. A. Wint, Dr. and Mrs. Raymond Firth, Dr. M. H. Read, Mr. C. Wrong and Miss M. Wrong for their kindness in reading my manuscript and in correcting my English. I was also assisted in various ways by members of the Seminar in the London School of Economics, especially Mr. P. L. Haksar and L. K. Hsü.

Finally, let me remember my wife, who died for Anthropology in our expedition to the Yao Mountains in 1935. Her solemn sacrifice leaves me no alternative but to follow her always. To her this book is dedicated.

致　谢

我由衷地感谢所有鼓励我并帮助我进行实地调查和撰写此书的人。首先，我必须对以下的老师和朋友表示谢意：

吴文藻教授和史禄国教授是我早年攻读社会学和人类学的老师，他们鼓励我用深入实地调查的方法来研究中国文化。我的姐姐把我介绍给这个村庄并资助我工作；她那为改善农民生计的热忱，确实激励了我从事这项调查研究工作。后来，清华大学授予我一笔奖学金，使我有可能到英国去求学，也就是说，进入了布·马林诺夫斯基教授的"门下"。过去两年来，他对我知识上的启示和亲长般的情谊使我感到对他一生具有承上启下的责任——以我所理解的说，我必须在建立一门研究人的科学以及在使一切文明之间真正合作上分担他那沉重的负担。

我一定要感谢 G. F. A. 温特先生、雷蒙德·弗思博士和夫人；感谢 M. H. 里德博士、C. 朗先生和 M. 朗小姐，感谢他们阅读了我的手稿并润色了我的英文。伦敦经济学院讨论班成员，特别是 P. N. 哈克塞先生和许烺光先生也为我提供了各方面的帮助。

最后，请允许我以此书来纪念我的妻子。1935 年，我们考察瑶山时，她为人类学献出了生命。她的庄严牺牲使我别无选择地永远跟随着她。谨以此书献给我的妻子。

序 iii

壹 前言 3

贰 调查区域 11
一、调查区域的界定 11
二、地理状况 13
三、经济背景 17
四、村庄 23
五、村里的人 29
六、选择这个调查区域的理由 33

叁 家 37
一、家，扩大的家庭 37
二、『香火』绵续 39
三、人口控制 43
四、父母和子女 45
五、教育 51
六、婚姻 53
七、家中的儿媳妇 61
八、表亲婚姻与『小媳妇』 67

肆 财产与继承 75
一、所有权 75
二、家产 77
三、财产的传递 83
四、继承对婚姻和继嗣的影响 91
五、赡养的义务 95
六、新的继承法 105

伍 亲属关系的扩展 109
一、父系亲属关系的扩展 109
二、母系亲属关系的扩展 113
三、名义上的收养 115
四、村庄的亲属关系基础 117

陆 户与村 125
一、户 125
二、邻里 127
三、宗教和娱乐团体 129
四、村政府 139
五、保甲——强加的行政体制 143

PREFACE *ii*

CHAPTER I   INTRODUCTION *2*

CHAPTER II   THE FIELD *10*
    ❶ *Delimitation of Field* *10*
    ❷ *Geographical Foundation* *12*
    ❸ *Economic Background* *16*
    ❹ *The Village Site* *22*
    ❺ *The People* *28*
    ❻ *Reasons for Selecting the Field* *32*

CHAPTER III   THE CHIA *36*
    ❶ *Chia as an Expanded Family* *36*
    ❷ *Continuity of "Incense and Fire"* *38*
    ❸ *Population Control* *42*
    ❹ *Parents and Children* *44*
    ❺ *Education* *50*
    ❻ *Marriage* *52*
    ❼ *The Daughter-in-Law in the Chia* *60*
    ❽ *Cross-Cousin Marriage and* Siaosiv *66*

CHAPTER IV   PROPERTY AND INHERITANCE *74*
    ❶ *Ownership* *74*
    ❷ *Property of the Chia* *77*
    ❸ *Transmission of Property* *82*
    ❹ *Effects of Inheritance on Marriage and Descent* *90*
    ❺ *Obligation of the Young* *95*
    ❻ *New Legislation on Inheritance* *104*

CHAPTER V   KINSHIP EXTENSIONS *108*
    ❶ *Paternal Extension* *108*
    ❷ *Maternal Extension* *112*
    ❸ *Pseudo-Adoption* *114*
    ❹ *Kinship Basis of the Village* *116*

CHAPTER VI   THE HOUSEHOLD AND VILLAGE *124*
    ❶ *Household* *124*
    ❷ *Neighbourhood* *127*
    ❸ *Religious and Recreative Groups* *129*
    ❹ *The Village Government* *138*
    ❺ *The Imposed Administrative System, Pao Chea* *142*

柒　生活　155
一、文化对于消费的控制　157
二、住房　159
三、运输　161
四、衣着　163
五、营养　165
六、娱乐　169
七、礼仪开支　173
八、正常生活的最低开支　177

捌　职业分化　183
一、农业——基本职业　183
二、专门职业　185
三、渔业　189

玖　劳作日程　191
一、计时系统　191
二、三种历法　197
三、经济活动和其他社会活动时间表　201

拾　农业　207
一、农田安排　207
二、种稻　213
三、科学与巫术　219
四、劳动组织　225

拾壹　土地的占有　231
一、湖泊、河流及道路　231
二、农田的所有权　235
三、雇农及小土地出租　237
四、不在地主制　239
五、完全所有制　251
六、继承与农业　255

拾贰　蚕丝业　259
一、变迁过程图解　259
二、促进工业变迁的条件　259
三、变革的力量及其意图　271
四、当地对变革的支持　279

CHAPTER VII   LIVELIHOOD *154*

❶ *Cultural Control on Consumption* *156*
❷ *Housing* *158*
❸ *Transportation* *161*
❹ *Clothing* *162*
❺ *Nutrition* *164*
❻ *Recreation* *168*
❼ *Ceremonial Expenses* *172*
❽ *Minimum Expenditure* *176*

CHAPTER VIII   OCCUPATIONAL DIFFERENTIATION *182*

❶ *Agriculture as the Basic Occupation* *182*
❷ *Special Occupations* *184*
❸ *Fishing* *188*

CHAPTER IX   CALENDAR OF WORK *190*

❶ *Systems of Time-Reckoning* *190*
❷ *Three Calendars* *196*
❸ *Time-Table of Economic and Other Social Activities* *200*

CHAPTER X   AGRICULTURE *206*

❶ *Lay-out of the Farm* *206*
❷ *Rice Cultivation* *212*
❸ *Science and Magic* *218*
❹ *Organization of Labour* *224*

CHAPTER XI   LAND TENURE *230*

❶ *Lakes, Streams, and Roads* *230*
❷ *Ownership of Farm-Land* *234*
❸ *Farm Labourers and Land Leasing* *236*
❹ *Absentee Landlordship* *238*
❺ *Full-Ownership* *250*
❻ *Inheritance and Agriculture* *254*

CHAPTER XII   THE SILK INDUSTRY *258*

❶ *Scheme of the Process of Change* *258*
❷ *Conditions Working for Industrial Change* *258*
❸ *Agents of Change and Their Intentions* *270*
❹ *Local Support for Change* *278*

拾肆 贸易 319

一、交换方式 319

二、内外购销 323

三、小贩 325

四、零售店 329

五、航船，消费者的购买代理 331

六、航船，生产者的销售代理 337

七、其他收集方式 341

八、贸易区域和集镇 341

九、销售与生产 345

拾叁 养羊与贩卖 313

五、养蚕的改革计划 281

六、合作工厂 287

七、政府的支持 299

八、改革中的困难 303

九、对亲属关系的影响 309

拾陆 中国的土地问题 373

附录 关于中国亲属称谓的一点说明 381

一、对话时的称呼 381

二、间接称谓 391

三、描述亲属关系用的称谓 395

注释 400

后记 重读《江村经济·序言》 412

拾伍 资金 349

一、积蓄与亏空 349

二、互助会 353

三、航船，信贷代理 363

四、高利贷 365

五、信贷合作社 371

❺ *Programme of Change in Raising Silkworms* 280

❻ *The Co-operative Factory* 286

❼ *Government Support* 298

❽ *Difficulties in Change* 302

❾ *Effects on Kinship Relations* 308

CHAPTER XIII   SHEEP RAISING AND TRADE VENTURES 312

CHAPTER XIV   MARKETING 318

❶ *Types of Exchange* 318

❷ *Internal and External Marketing* 322

❸ *Pedlars* 324

❹ *Retail Stores* 328

❺ *Agent Boats as Consumers' Buying Agent* 330

❻ *Agent Boats as Producers' Selling Agent* 336

❼ *Other Types of Collecting* 340

❽ *Marketing Areas and the Town* 340

❾ *Marketing and Production* 344

CHAPTER XV   FINANCE 348

❶ *Saving and Deficiency* 349

❷ *Financial Aid Society* 352

❸ *Agent Boats as Credit Agent* 362

❹ *Usury* 364

❺ *Co-operative Credit Society* 370

CHAPTER XVI   AGRARIAN PROBLEMS IN CHINA 372

APPENDIX   A NOTE ON CHINESE RELATIONSHIP TERMS 380

❶ *Terms of Address* 380

❷ *Terms of Reference* 391

❸ *Terms to Describe Relationships* 394

NOTES 400

PREFACE

I venture to foretell that *Peasant Life in China* by Dr. Hsiao-Tung Fei will be counted as a landmark in the development of anthropological field-work and theory. The book has a number of outstanding merits, each of them marking a new departure. Our attention is here directed not to a small, insignificant tribe, but to the greatest nation in the world. The book is not written by an outsider looking out for exotic impressions in a strange land; it contains observations carried on by a citizen upon his own people. It is the result of work done by a native among natives. If it be true that self-knowledge is the most difficult to gain, then undoubtedly an anthropology of one's own people is the most arduous, but also the most valuable achievement of a field-worker.

The book, moreover, though it takes in the traditional background of Chinese life, does not remain satisfied with the mere reconstruction of the static past. It grapples fully and deliberately with that most elusive and difficult phase of modern life: the transformation of traditional culture under Western impact. The writer is courageous enough to cast away all academic pretence at scientific detachment. Dr. Fei fully realizes that knowledge is indispensable to the right solution of practical difficulties. He sees that science, in rendering real service to mankind, is not degraded. It indeed receives the acid test of its validity. Truth will work, because truth is nothing else but man's adaptation to real facts and forces. Science becomes only prostituted when the scholar is forced, as in some countries of Europe, to adapt his facts and his convictions to the demands of a dictated doctrine.

Dr. Fei as a young Chinese patriot is fully alive, not only to the present tragedy of China, but to the much bigger issues involved in the dilemma of his great Mother-country to Westernize or to perish. And since as an anthropologist he knows how difficult a process is that of readaptation; how this process must be built on the old foundations, and built slowly, gradually, and wisely, he is deeply concerned that all change should be planned, and that the planning be based on the solid foundation of fact and knowledge.

序

　　我敢于预言费孝通博士的《中国农民的生活》（又名《江村经济》——译注）一书将被认为是人类学实地调查和理论工作发展中的一个里程碑。此书有一些杰出的优点，每一点都标志着一个新的发展。本书让我们注意的并不是一个小小的微不足道的部落，而是世界上一个最伟大的国家。作者并不是一个外来人，在异国的土地上猎奇而写作的；本书的内容包含着一个公民对自己的人民进行观察的结果。这是一个土生土长的人在本乡人民中间进行工作的成果。如果说人贵有自知之明的话，那么，一个民族研究自己民族的人类学当然是最艰巨的，同样，这也是一个实地调查工作者的最珍贵的成就。

　　此外，此书虽以中国人传统的生活为背景，然而它并不满足于复述静止的过去。它有意识地紧紧抓住现代生活最难以理解的一面，即传统文化在西方影响下的变迁。作者在科学研究中勇于抛弃一切学院式的装腔作势。他充分认识到，要正确地解决实际困难，知识是必不可少的。费博士看到了科学的价值在于真正为人类服务。对此，科学确实经受着严峻的考验。真理能够解决问题，因为真理不是别的而是人对真正的事实和力量的实事求是。当学者被迫以事实和信念去迎合一个权威的教义的需要时，科学便被出卖了。在欧洲某些国家里就有这种情况。

　　费博士是中国的一个年轻爱国者，他不仅充分感觉到中国目前的悲剧，而且还注意到更大的问题：他的伟大祖国，进退维谷，是西方化还是灭亡？既然是一个人类学者，他毕竟懂得，再适应的过程是何等的困难。他懂得，这一过程必须逐步地、缓慢地、机智地建立在旧的基础之上。他深切地关注到，这一切改变应是有计划的，而计划又须是以坚实的事实和知识为基础的。

Some passages of this book can indeed be taken as a charter of practical sociology and anthropology. "The need of such knowledge has become more and more urgent in China because the country cannot afford to waste any more of her wealth and energy in making mistakes." Dr. Fei sees clearly that with the best intentions and the most desirable end clearly in view, planning must remain faulty if the initial situation of change be misconceived. "An inaccurate definition of a situation, either due to deliberate aberration or to ignorance, is dangerous for a group," because it presupposes forces which do not exist, and ignores obstacles which obstruct the way of progress.

I feel I have to quote one more paragraph from the Introduction. "An adequate definition of the situation, if it is to organize successful actions and attain the desired end, must be reached through a careful analysis of the functions of the social institutions, in relation to the need that they purport to satisfy and in relation to other institutions on which their working depends. This is the work of a social scientist. Social science therefore should play an important rôle in directing cultural change." This expresses well the greatest need, not only of the Chinese but of our own civilization, the need, that is, to recognize that even as in mechanical engineering only a fool or a madman would plan, design, and calculate without reference to scientific physics and mathematics, so also in political action, reason and experience must be given the fullest play.

Our modern civilization is perhaps now facing its final destruction. We are careful to use only the most qualified specialists in all mechanical engineering. Yet as regards the control of political, social, and moral forces, we Europeans are yielding more and more to madmen, fanatics, and gangsters. A tremendous arraignment of force, controlled by individuals without a sense of responsibility or any moral obligation to keep faith is accumulating on the one side of the dividing line. On the other side, where wealth, power, and effectives could still be made overwhelmingly strong, we have had during the last few years a consistent and progressive display of weakness, lack of unity, and a gradual whittling down of the sense of honour and of the sanctity of obligations undertaken.

I have read Dr. Fei's clear and convincing arguments as well as his vivid and well-documented accounts with genuine admiration, at times not untinged with envy. His book embodies many of the precepts and

此书的某些段落确实可以被看作是应用社会学和人类学的宪章。"中国越来越迫切地需要这种知识,因为这个国家再也承担不起因失误而损耗任何财富和能量。"费博士清晰地看到,纵然有最好的意图和理想的目的,如果一开始对变化的环境有错误的理解和看法,那么,计划也必定是错误的。"对形势或情况的不准确的阐述或分析,不论是由于故意的过错或出于无知,对这个群体都是有害的",因为这会造成这样的错误:预先假设了不存在的力量或是忽视了前进道路上的障碍。

我感到,还必须引述前言中的一段话,"如果要组织有效果的行动并达到预期的目的,必须对社会制度的功能进行细致的分析,而且要同它们意欲满足的需要结合起来分析,也要同它们的运转所依赖的其他制度联系起来分析,以达到对情况的适当的阐述。这就是社会科学学者的工作。所以社会科学应该在指导文化变迁中起重要的作用。"这充分表达了中国文化和我们自己的文化的最大需要,也就是说,我们必须认识到,即使在机械工程中,只有傻子或疯子才会不顾科学的物理和数学而作出规划、设计或计算,故在政治行动中同样需要充分发挥理智和经验的作用。

我们的现代文明目前可能正面临着最终的毁灭。我们只注意在机械工程中使用最合格的专家。但在政治、社会和道德力量控制方面,我们欧洲人越来越依从于疯子、狂人和歹徒。在界线的一边,一种审讯的力量被一些既无责任感又无道德义务的人控制着,正在逐渐强大,而在另一边我们尽管仍然可以在财富、权力和实力上具有压倒的优势,近数年来却始终不断地暴露出软弱、涣散以及对荣誉、对所负的神圣义务的忽视。

我怀着十分钦佩的心情阅读了费博士那明确的令人信服的论点和生动翔实的描写,时感令人嫉妒。他书中所表露的很多箴言和原则,

principles which I have been preaching for some time past, without, alas, having the opportunity of practising them myself. Most of us forward-looking anthropologists have felt impatient with our own work for its remoteness, exoticism, and irrelevancy—though perhaps these may be more apparent than real. But there is no doubt that my own confession that "Anthropology, to me at least, was a romantic escape from our over-standardized culture," was essentially true.

The remedy, however, is at hand. If I may be allowed to quote some of my other reflections, "the progress of anthropology towards a really effective analytic science of human society, of human conduct, and of human nature, cannot be staved off." To achieve this, however, the science of man has first and foremost to move from so-called savagery into the study of more advanced cultures of the numerically, economically, and politically important peoples of the world. The present book and the wider work in China and elsewhere, of which it is a part, justifies my forecast: "The anthropology of the future will be...as interested in the Hindu as in the Tasmanian, in the Chinese peasants as in the Australian aborigines, in the West Indian negro as in the Melanesian Trobriander, in the detribalized African of Haarlem as in the Pygmy of Perak." In this quotation is implied another important postulate of modern field-work and theory: the study of culture change, of the phenomena of contact, and of present-day diffusion.

It was therefore a great pleasure when some two years ago I received the visit of a distinguished Chinese sociologist, Professor Wu Wen-Tsao of Yenching University, and learnt from him that independently and spontaneously there had been organized in China a sociological attack on the real problems of culture change and applied anthropology, an attack which embodies all my dreams and desiderata.

Professor Wu and the young scholars whom he was able to train and inspire had realized first of all that to understand the civilization of their great country and to make it comprehensible to others, it was necessary to read in the open book of Chinese life, and learn how the live Chinese mind works in reality. Just because that country has had the longest unbroken tradition, the understanding of Chinese history must proceed from the appreciation of what China is to-day. Such an anthropological approach is indispensable as a supplement to important historical work carried out by modern Chinese scholars, and by a body of sinologists

也是我过去在相当一段时间里所主张和宣扬的，但可惜我自己却没有机会去实践它。我们中间绝大多数向前看的人类学者，对我们自己的工作感到不耐烦，我们厌烦它的好古、猎奇和不切实际，虽然这也许是表面上的，实际并不如此。但我的自白无疑是真实的，我说过："人类学，至少对我来说是对我们过分标准化的文化的一种罗曼蒂克式的逃避。"

然而补救办法近在咫尺，如果允许我再引述我的一些其他看法的话，我认为"那面向人类社会、人类行为和人类本性的真正有效的科学分析的人类学，它的进程是不可阻挡的"。为达到这一目的，研究人的科学必须首先离开对所谓未开化状态的研究，而应该进入对世界上为数众多的、在经济和政治上占重要地位的民族的较先进文化的研究。本书以及在中国和其他地方开展的广泛的工作，证实了我的预言："未来的人类学不仅对塔斯马尼亚人、澳洲土著居民、美拉尼西亚的特罗布里恩德群岛人和霹雳的俾格米人有兴趣，而且对印度人、中国农民、西印度群岛黑人、脱离部落的哈勒姆非洲人同样关注。"这一段引语中还包含着对现代实地调查和理论工作提出的重要的基本要求：研究文化变迁、文化接触的现象、现代文化的传播。

因此，约两年前，当我接待了燕京大学杰出的中国社会学家吴文藻教授来访，感到极大的欣慰，从他那里得知，中国社会学界已独立自发地组织起一场对文化变迁和应用人类学的真正问题进行学术上的攻关。这一学术进攻表达了我梦寐以求的愿望。

吴教授和他所培育的年轻学者首先认识到，为了解他们的伟大祖国的文明并使其他的人理解它，他们需要去阅读中国人生活这本公开的书本，并理解中国人在现实中怎样思考的。正因为那个国家有着最悠久的没有断过的传统，要理解中国历史还必须从认识中国的今天开始。这种人类学的研究方法对于现代中国学者和欧洲的一些汉学家

in Europe, on the basis of written records. History can be read back, taking the present as its living version, quite as much as it can be read forward, starting with the archæological remains of the dimmest past and the earliest written records. The two approaches are complementary and they must be used concurrently.

The principles and the substance of Dr. Fei's book reveal to us how sound are the methodological foundations of the modern Chinese School of Sociology. Take the main subject-matter of the book. It is a field-study of country life on one of those riverine plains which for thousands of years have nourished the Chinese people both materially and spiritually. It is axiomatic that the foundation of an essentially agrarian culture will be found in village life, in rural economy, and in the needs and interests of a peasant population. By becoming acquainted with the life of a small village, we study, under a microscope as it were, the epitome of China at large.

Two main motives dominate the story of this book: the exploitation of the soil, and the reproductive processes within the household and the family. In this book, Dr. Fei limits himself to the fundamental aspects of peasant life in China. He proposes, I know, in his subsequent studies, to give a fuller account of ancestor-worship; of the more complicated systems of belief and knowledge which flourish in village and township alike. He also hopes sooner or later to make a wider synthesis of his own works and that of his colleagues, giving us a comprehensive picture of the cultural, religious, and political systems of China. For such a synthesis, monographic accounts such as the present one are the first step. Dr. Fei's book and the contributions of his fellow-workers will become valuable pieces for the mosaic which it will be possible to construct from them.[1]

It is not the task of a preface writer to retell a story so admirably told as the one of this book. The reader will find himself introduced into the setting: the charming riverine village of Kaihsienkung. He will be able to visualize its lay-out with its streams and bridges, its temples, ricefields, and mulberry trees. In this the excellent photographs will prove an additional help. He will appreciate the good balance of concrete, at times numerical data, and the clear descriptions. The account of agricultural life, of the means of livelihood, and the typical occupations of the villagers; the excellent seasonal calendar, and the precise definition of land tenure, give a type of intimate and at the same time tangible information not to be found anywhere else in the literature on China.

所进行的以文字记载为依据的重要历史工作，是一种不可缺少的补充。研究历史可以把遥远过去的考古遗迹和最早的记载作为起点，推向后世；同样，亦可把现状作为活的历史，来追溯过去。两种方法互为补充，且须同时使用。

费博士著作中的原理和内容向我们揭示了现代中国社会学派的方法论基础是多么结实可靠。本书的主要题材是对湖泽地带的平原乡村生活的一次实地考察。那水道纵横的平原是数千年来在物质上和精神上抚育中国人民的地方。不言而喻，在乡村生活、农村经济、农业人口的利益和需要中找到的主要是农业文化基础。通过熟悉一个小村落的生活，我们犹如在显微镜下看到了整个中国的缩影。

贯穿此书的两个主题是：土地的利用和农户家庭中再生产的过程。在本书中，费博士集中力量描述中国农民生活的基本方面。我知道，他打算在他以后的研究中说明关于崇祀祖先的详细情况以及在村庄和城镇中广为流传的关于信仰和知识等复杂的体系。他还希望终有一日将自己的和同行的著作综合起来，为我们展示一幅描绘中国文化、宗教和政治体系的丰富多彩的画面。对这样一部综合性著作，像本书这样的专著当是第一步。费博士的书和他同行的贡献将成为他们可能完成的精雕细琢的镶嵌品中的一件件珍品。[1]

序言作者的任务并不是再来复述一番本书已经动人地描述过的内容。随着本书的描述，读者本身将自然地被带入故事发生的地点：那可爱的河流，纵横的开弦弓村。他将看到村庄的河流、桥梁、庙宇、稻田和桑树的分布图，此外，清晰的照片更有助于了解这个村庄。他将欣赏到具体资料、数据和明晰的描述三者之间很协调的关系。对农村生活、农民生活资料、村民的典型职业的描述以及完美的节气农历和土地占有的准确定义等都为读者提供了一种深入的确实的资料，这在任何有关的中国文献中都是十分罕见的。

I am allowed to quote from a statement by Sir E. Denison Ross, who read the book in manuscript, and thus defined its position in scientific literature: "I regard this treatise as quite exceptional. I know of no other work which describes at first hand and with intimate understanding the full story of life in a Chinese village community. We have had works dealing with statistics, economic studies, and novels full of local colour— but in no book have I found the answer to every kind of inquiry which the curious stranger might make." The "curious stranger," when he appears in the person of Sir Denison Ross, is a man of science, a historian, and one of the world's experts in Oriental Studies.

To me personally, the chapter on the silk industry is perhaps the most significant achievement of the book. It is an account of a planned change from domestic industry into a readaptation to co-operative work compatible with modern conditions. It vindicates some of the claims of sociology to be a practical and relevant study for social engineering. It raises a number of collateral questions, and will become, I think, the starting point of other inquiries both in China and elsewhere.

In the argument of this chapter and in many other passages we can discover a moral quality of the book which I may be allowed to underline. There is no trace of special pleading or self-justification, although the book is written by a Chinese to be placed before Western readers. It is rather a criticism or self-criticism. Thus in the chapter on "Agrarian Problems in China" we read "The national government with all its promises and policies on paper was not able to carry out any practical measures owing to the fact that most of the revenue was spent in its anti-communist campaign, while, as I have pointed out, the real nature of the communist movement was a peasant revolt due to their dissatisfaction with the land system. Despite all kinds of justification on either side, one thing is clear: that the conditions of the peasants are getting worse and worse. So far no permanent land reform has been accomplished in any

part of China since the recovery of the Red Area by the government."
That a type of sociological work which openly criticizes the inadequacy
of government action is yet carried on with the encouragement of the
government speaks for itself. It proves on the one hand the integrity
of the young sociologists in China and on the other the goodwill and
wisdom of their official patrons.

　　我已得到允许，引述 E. 丹尼森·罗斯爵士在读了该书手稿以后的
一段话，他阐明了该书在科学文献中的地位："我认为这篇论文是相
当特殊的。据我所知，没有其他作品能够如此深入地理解并以第一手
材料描述了中国乡村社区的全部生活。我们曾经有过统计报告、经济
研究和地方色彩浓厚的小说——但我未曾发现有一本书能够回答好奇
的陌生人可能提出的各种问题。"这里所说的"好奇的陌生人"就是
丹尼森·罗斯爵士，他恰是一个科学家、历史学家和世界知名的东方
学专家。

　　我个人认为或许有关蚕丝业的这一章是本书最成功的一章。它向
我们介绍了家庭企业如何有计划地变革成为合作工厂，以适应现代形
势的需要。它证明，社会学需要研究社会工程的有关实际问题。它提
出了一些附带的问题，我想这些问题将成为中国和其他地方的另一些
研究的起点。

　　在这一章和其他很多章节的论据中，我们能够发现著书的道德品
质，请允许我强调提出这一点。虽然这本书是一个中国人写给西方读
者看的，文字中没有特殊的辩护或自宥的流露。相反倒是一种批评和
自我批评。在"中国的土地问题"这一章中我们可以读到："国民党
政府在纸上写下了种种诺言和政策。但事实上，它把绝大部分收入都
耗费于反共运动，所以它不可能采取任何实际行动和措施来进行改
革，而共产主义运动的实质，正如我所指出的，是由于农民对土地制
度不满而引起的一种反抗。尽管各方提出各种理由，但有一件事是清
楚的，农民的境况是越来越糟糕了。自从政府重占红色区域以来到目
前为止，中国没有任何一个地区完成了永久性的土地改革。"这样一
种公开批评政府不当行为的社会学工作，现在仍然进行着，想必得到
政府的鼓励，这一方面证明了中国青年社会学家的正直和团结，另一
方面也说明了官方的善意和明智。

A dispassioned, detached, and dignified attitude characterises all the Author's observations. That a Chinese must to-day have bitter feelings against Western civilization and the political rule of Western nations, is understandable. Yet no trace of this will be found in the present book. In fact, throughout my personal acquaintance with Dr. Fei and some of his colleagues, I had to admire the absence of national prejudice and national hatred—a moral attitude from which we Europeans could learn a great deal. The Chinese seem to be able to distinguish between nationhood and the political system. There is no hatred even of the Japanese as a people. On the first page of this book the Author refers to the invading country only in terms of dispassionate appreciation of its rôle in consolidating the Chinese nation and forcing it to build up a united front, and to readjust some of its fundamental problems, economic and social. The very village which we have learnt to know, to appreciate, to which we have almost become attached, has probably now been destroyed. We can only echo the writer's prophetic desire that in the ruin of that village and many others, "the internal conflicts and follies should find their last resting-place" and that "from the ruin a new China shall emerge."

B. MALINOWSKI

DEPARTMENT OF ANTHROPOLOGY,
UNIVERSITY OF LONDON,
15th October, 1938

作者的一切观察所具有的特征是，态度有尊严、超脱、没有偏见。当今一个中国人对西方文明和西方国家的政治有反感，这是可以理解的。但本书中未发现这种迹象。事实上，通过我个人同费博士和他的同事的交往，我不得不羡慕他们不持民族偏见和民族仇恨——我们欧洲人能够从这样一种道德态度上学到大量的东西。看来中国人是能够区别民族和政治制度的。日本作为一个民族来说，他们对它甚至不怀仇恨。在本书第一页上，作者提到这个侵略国，冷静地评价它的作用在于迫使中国建立起一条统一战线并调整它的某些基本的经济和社会问题，从而巩固了中国。我们所了解、评价甚至逐渐依恋的那个村庄，现在可能已被破坏。我们只能回想着作者预言式的愿望：在这个村庄和其他许多村庄的废墟中，"内部冲突和耗费巨大的斗争最后必将终止"，"一个崭新的中国将出现在这个废墟之上"。

布·马林诺夫斯基
1938 年 10 月 15 日于伦敦大学人类学系

CHAPTER I INTRODUCTION

This is a descriptive account of the system of consumption, production, distribution and exchange of wealth among Chinese peasants as observed in a village, Kaihsienkung, south of Lake Tai, in Eastern China. It aims at showing the relation of this economic system to a specific geographical setting and to the social structure of the community. The village under investigation, like most Chinese villages, is undergoing a tremendous process of change. This account, therefore, will show the forces and problems in a changing village economy.

An intensive investigation of a small field of this kind is a necessary supplement of the broad surveys made of present-day economic problems in China. It will exemplify the importance of regional factors in analysing these problems and will provide empirical illustrations.

This type of study will enable us to realize the importance of the background of the traditional economy, and the effect of the new forces on the everyday life of the people.

To stress the equal importance of the traditional and the new forces is necessary because the real process of change of Chinese economic life is neither a direct transference of social institutions from the West nor a mere disturbance of a traditional equilibrium. The problems arising from the present situation are results of the interaction of these two forces. In the village under our examination, for instance, the financial issues can only be understood by taking into consideration the decline of the price of silk due to the world industrial development on the one hand, and on the other, the importance of domestic industry in the family budget based on the traditional system of land tenure. Underestimation of either aspect will distort the real situation. Moreover, the product of the interaction of these two forces, as we shall see in the later description, cannot be a reproduction of the West or a restoration of the past. The result will depend on how the people solve their own problems. A correct understanding of the existing situation based on empirical facts will assist in directing the change towards a desired end. Herein lies the function of social science.

Culture is a set of material equipment and a body of knowledge. It is man who uses the equipment and the knowledge in order to live. Culture is changed by men for definite purposes. When a man throws away a tool to acquire a new one, he does so because he believes that

壹 前言

这是一本描述中国农民的消费、生产、分配和交易等体系的书，是根据对中国东部太湖东南岸开弦弓村的实地考察写成的。它旨在说明这一经济体系与特定地理环境的关系，以及与这个社区的社会结构的关系。同大多数中国农村一样，这个村庄正经历着一个巨大的变迁过程。因此，本书将说明这个正在变化着的乡村经济的动力和问题。

这种小范围的深入实地的调查，对当前中国经济问题宏观的研究是一种必要的补充。在分析这些问题时，它将说明地区因素的重要性并提供实事的例子。

这种研究也将促使我们进一步了解传统经济背景的重要性及新的动力对人民日常生活的作用。

强调传统力量与新的动力具有同等重要性是必要的，因为中国经济生活变迁的真正过程，既不是从西方社会制度直接转渡的过程，也不仅是传统的平衡受到了干扰而已。目前形势中所发生的问题是这两种力量相互作用的结果。例如对我们观察的这个村庄的经济问题，只有在考虑到两方面的情况时才能有所理解：一方面是由于世界工业的发展，生丝价格下跌，另一方面是以传统土地占有制为基础的家庭副业在家庭经济预算中的重要性。对任何一方面的低估都将曲解真实的情况。此外，正如我们将在以后的描述中所看到的，这两种力量相互作用的产物不会是西方世界的复制品或者传统的复旧，其结果如何，将取决于人民如何去解决他们自己的问题。正确地了解当前存在的以实事为依据的情况，将有助于引导这种变迁趋向于我们所期望的结果。社会科学的功能就在于此。

文化是物质设备和各种知识的结合体。人使用设备和知识以便生存。为了一定的目的人要改变文化。一个人如果扔掉某一件工具，又去获取一件新的，他这样做，是因为他相信新的工具对他更加适用。

the new tool suits his purpose better. Therefore in any process of change, there is an integration of his past experience, his understanding of the present situation and his expectation of the future consequences. Past experiences are not always a real picture of past events because they have been transformed through the selective process of memory. The present situation is not always accurately comprehended because it attracts attention only in so far as interest directs. The future consequences do not always come up to expectations because they are the products of many other forces besides wishes and efforts. So the new tool may at last prove not to be suitable to man's purpose.

It is more difficult to achieve successful changes in social institutions. Even when an institution has failed to meet the need of the people, there may be no substitute. The difficulty lies in the fact that since a social institution consists of human relations, it can be changed only through concerted actions which cannot readily be organized. Moreover, the social situation is usually complicated and expectation varies among the individuals involved. Therefore in the process of social change, it is always necessary in order to organize collective actions to have a more or less accepted definition of the situation and a formulated programme. Such preparatory activities generally take a linguistic form. It can be seen in its simplest form in the command of a captain to his crew when directing the course of a ship. It can also be observed in the well staged debates in parliament or congress. Different definitions of the situation and varying expectations about the results form the centre of the debates. Nevertheless, such preparatory activities are always present in an innovation in socially organized activities.

An inaccurate definition of situation, either due to deliberate aberrations or to ignorance, is dangerous for the group because it may lead to an undesired future. There are many instances in the present account to illustrate the importance of an empirical definition of the situation. In anticipation of the following pages, I shall mention a few of them. In kinship organization, the present practice of inheritance is defined by the legislature as an instance of inequality between sexes. Since the situation is so defined, once the idea of sex equality has been accepted, the resultant actions would involve a revision of the unilateral kinship principle. As I shall show, the transmission of property is a part of the reciprocal relation between generations; the obligation of supporting the old, in a society where that responsibility falls upon the children,

所以，任何变迁过程必定是一种综合体，那就是：他过去的经验、他对目前形势的了解以及他对未来结果的期望。过去的经验并不总是过去实事的真实写照，因为过去的实事经过记忆的选择已经起了变化。目前的形势也并不总是能得到准确的理解，因为它吸引注意力的程度常受到利害关系的影响。未来的结果不会总是像人们所期望的那样，因为它是希望和努力以外的其他许多力量的产物。所以，新工具最后也可能被证明是不适合于人们的目的。

对社会制度要完成一个成功的变革是更加困难了。当一种制度不能满足人民的需要时，甚至可能还没有替代它的其他制度。困难在于社会制度是由人际关系构成的，只有通过一致行动才能改变它，而一致行动不是一下子就组织得起来的。另外，社会情况通常是复杂的，参与改革的一个个人，他们的期望也可以各不相同。所以在社会变革的过程中，为组织集体行动，对社会情况需要有一个多少为大家所接受的分析和定义以及一个系统的计划。这种准备活动一般都需要一种语言形式。最简单的形式如一个船长在指挥一条船航行时，对他的船员们发出命令；又如在议会或国会里进行一场有准备的辩论。对形势或情况的不同解释和关于结果的各种期望形成辩论的中心。无论如何，这样的准备活动总是会在有组织的革新活动中出现的。

对形势或情况的不准确的阐述或分析，不论是由于故意的过错或出于无知，对这个群体都是有害的，它可能导致令人失望的后果。本书有许多例子说明了对情况或形势的实事求是的阐述或分析的重要性。下面我想先举几个例子：在亲属组织中，目前法律对财产继承问题的规定似已成为两性不平等的实例。一旦男女平等的思想被接受，这样的规定将产生一种修改单方亲属原则的行动。正如我要说明的，财产的继承是两代人之间相互关系的一部分。供养老人的义务，落在

cannot be equally shared by sons and daughters under the present system of patrilocal marriage. Therefore the bilateral inheritance combined with unilateral affiliation creates inequality between the sexes. Seen in this light, the consequences of the legislation are obviously contrary to expectation (IV–6).

A definition of situation sometimes may be accurate but not complete. In the silk industry, for instance, the reformers have defined the situation mainly in technical terms. The omission of the factor of international trade in the decline of the price of silk had resulted in their failure for many years to fulfil their promise to the villagers of big incomes from the industry (XII–8).

An adequate definition of situation, if it is to organize successful actions and attain the desired end, must be reached through a careful analysis of the functions of the social institutions, in relation to the need that they purport to satisfy and in relation to other institutions on which their working depends. This is the work of a social scientist. Social science therefore should play an important rôle in directing cultural change.

The need of such knowledge has become more and more urgent in China because the country cannot afford to waste any more of her wealth and energy in making mistakes. The fundamental end is evident; it is the satisfaction of the basic requirements common to every Chinese. This should be recognized by all. A village which stands on the verge of starvation profits nobody, not even the usurers. In this sense there should be no political differences among the Chinese upon these fundamental measures. Where differences exist, they are due to misrepresentation of facts. A systematic presentation of the actual conditions of the people will convince the nation of the urgent policies necessary for rehabilitating the lives of the masses. It is not a matter for philosophical speculation, much less should it be a matter for dispute between schools of thought. What is really needed is a common-sense judgment based on reliable information.

The present study is only one of the initial attempts of a group of young Chinese students who have realized the importance of this task. Similar studies have been carried out in Fukien, Shantung, Shansi, Hopei, and Kwangsi and will be pursued in the future by more extensive and better organized efforts. I am reluctant to present this premature account, premature because I have been deprived of chances of further field investigation in the immediate future on account of the Japanese

子女身上的社会里，在目前父居家庭的婚姻制度下，女儿和儿子不能分担同等的义务。因此，双系继承与单方立嗣相结合将形成两性的不平等。从这一点来看，立法的后果显然与期望是背道而驰的（第四章第六节）。

有时，对情况或形势的阐明或分析可能是正确的，但不完整。例如，在缫丝工业中，改革者主要从技术方面来分析情况，忽略了在丝价下降中国际贸易的因素，这就导致多年来，对村民许下的从工业中增加收入的诺言，未能实现（第十二章第八节）。

如果要组织有效果的行动并达到预期的目的，必须对情况有细致的阐述，而这种阐述需要对社会制度的功能进行细致的分析，而且要同它们意欲满足的需要结合起来分析，也要同它们的运转所依赖的其他制度联系起来分析。这就是社会科学者的工作。所以社会科学应该在指导文化变迁中起重要的作用。

中国越来越迫切地需要这种知识，因为这个国家再也承担不起因失误而损耗任何财富和能量。我们的根本目的是明确的，这就是满足每个中国人共同的基本需要。大家都应该承认这一点。一个站在饥饿边缘上的村庄对谁都没有好处，即使对放贷者也是如此。从这个意义上说，对这些基本措施，在中国人中间应该没有政治上的分歧。分歧之处是由于对事实的误述或歪曲。对人民实际情况的系统反映将有助于使这个国家相信，为了恢复广大群众的正常生活，现在迫切地需要一些政策。这不是一个哲学思考的问题，更不应该是各学派思想争论的问题。真正需要的是一种以可靠的情况为依据的常识性的判断。

目前的研究，仅仅是一群懂得了这一任务的重要性的中国青年学生们的初步尝试。在福建、山东、山西、河北和广西都开展了同样的研究。将来还会有更广泛的、组织得更好的力量，继续进行研究。我不太愿意把这本不成熟的书拿出来，它之所以不成熟，是因为日本人占领并破坏了我所描述的村庄，我被剥夺了在近期作进一步的实地

occupation and destruction of the village here described. But I am presenting this study in the hopes that it may give a realistic picture to Western readers of the huge task that has been imposed on my people and the agony of the present struggle. Without being pessimistic, let me assure my readers that the struggle is evidently to be a long and grave one. We are ready for the worst and it may be a thousand times worse than the Japanese bombs and poisonous gas. I am, however, confident that, despite the past errors and present misfortunes, China will emerge once more a great nation, through the unswerving effort of her people. The present account is not a record of a vanished history but a prelude to a new chapter of the world history that will be written not in ink but in the blood of millions.

调查的机会。但我还是要把本书贡献出来，希望它能为西方读者提供一幅现实的画面，这就是：我的人民肩负重任，正在为当前的斗争付出沉痛的代价。我并不悲观，但肯定地说这是一场长期而严酷的斗争。我们已作了最坏的准备，准备承受比日本的炸弹和毒气还会更坏的情况。然而我确信，就算有过去的错误和当前的不幸，通过人民坚持不懈的努力，中国将再一次以一个伟大的国家屹立在世界上。本书并不是一本消逝了的历史的记录，而是将以百万人民的鲜血写成的世界历史新篇章的序言。

CHAPTER II   THE FIELD

❶ Delimitation of Field

To carry out intensive study of the life of the people, it is necessary to confine oneself to the investigation of a small social unit. This is due to practical considerations. The people under investigation must be within easy reach of the investigator in order that the latter can observe personally and intimately. The unit of study, on the other hand, should not be too small. It should provide a fair cross-section of the social life of the people.

This general problem has been discussed by Professor A. Radcliffe-Brown, Dr. Wu Wen-tsao, and Dr. Raymond Firth.[2] It is agreed that in the first stage of such a study, a village would be the most appropriate unit. "To start with a single village as a centre," says Dr. Firth, "investigate the relationships of the persons composing it, in terms of kinship, the distribution of authority, economic organization, religious affiliations, and other social ties, and try to see how these relationships affect one another and determine the co-operative life of the small community. From this centre the investigation will radiate out following the personal relationships into other units in adjacent villages, economic linkage and social co-operation."[3]

A village is a community characterized by its being an aggregate of households on a compact residential area, separated from other similar units by a considerable distance (this may not hold good in some parts of China where households are scattered), organized in various social activities as a group, and possessing a special name of its own. It is a *de facto* social unit recognized by the people themselves.

A village as such does not enter formally into the new administrative system in China—Pao Chea[*]—which is artificially created for certain specific purposes (VI–5). Since this system was introduced to Kaihsienkung only in 1935, it is very difficult to say when these *de jure* units, through increasing administrative function, will cause a shift in the existing *de facto* groupings. But at present, in actual practice, the Pao Chea system is still largely a formality. Thus the unit of our study, the aim of which is to understand the life of the people, must follow the real existing functioning unit—the village.

贰 调查区域

一、调查区域的界定

为了对人们的生活进行深入细致的研究，研究人员有必要把自己的调查限定在一个小的社会单位内来进行。这是出于实际的考虑。调查者必须容易接近被调查者，以便能够亲自进行密切地观察。另一方面，被研究的社会单位也不宜太小，它应能提供人们社会生活的较完整的切片。

A. 拉德克利夫－布朗教授、吴文藻博士和雷蒙德·弗思博士[2]曾经讨论过这个基本问题。他们一致认为，在这种研究的最初阶段，把一个村子作为单位最为合适。弗思博士说："应当以一个村子作研究中心来考察村民们相互间的关系，就亲属关系而言，考察权力的分配、经济的组织、宗教的皈依以及其他种种社会联系，并进而观察这种种社会关系如何相互影响，如何综合以决定这社区的合作生活。从这研究中心循着亲属系统、经济往来、社会合作等路线，推广我们的研究范围到邻近村落以及市镇。"[3]

村庄是一个社区，其特征是：农户聚集在一个紧凑的居住区内，与其他相似的单位隔开相当一段距离（在中国有些地区，农户散居，情况并非如此），作为一个群体组织各种社会活动，具有其特定的名称，而且是一个为人们所公认的事实上的社会单位。

这样一个村庄并没有正式进入保甲制。保甲制是中国的一种新的行政体制，是为了某种特殊目的而人为地设置的（第六章第五节）。开弦弓村在 1935 年才有这种制度，因此很难说得清，这种法律上的保甲单位，究竟到什么时候才能以其不断增长的行政职能取代现存的事实上的群体。但目前，在实施过程中，保甲制仍然大多流于形式。因此，我们所研究的单位必须是实际存在的职能单位——村庄。我们研究的目的在于了解人民的生活。

To take the village as the unit of study at the present stage of investigation, does not mean that it is a self-contained unit. The inter-dependence of territorial groups, especially in economic life, is very close in China. It can even be said that the Chinese people have during the last half century entered into the world community. Western goods as well as ideas have reached very remote villages. The economic and political pressure of the Western powers is the prime factor in the present change of Chinese culture. In this connection, one can ask what understanding of these changes and of the external forces causing them can be gained by a field investigation in a small area, such as a village.

It is obvious that the investigator in the village cannot analyse the outside forces in their wide perspective. For instance, the decline of the price of native silk in the world market as a result of the world economic depression and of the technical improvement of the silk industry in general, has produced such effects in the village as deficiency in the family budget, shortage of food, postponement of marriage and the partial break-down of the domestic industry. The field investigator in this case must record as fully as possible the forces that affect village life but he will of course leave the further analysis of these forces themselves to other sciences. He will take these facts for granted and limit himself to tracing the effects which can be directly observed in the life of the village.

Generalizations made from such an intensive study of a small social unit may not be applicable to other units. But they can be used as hypotheses and as comparative material for further investigation in other fields. This is the soundest way to obtain really scientific generalizations.

❷ Geographical Foundation

The village chosen for my investigation is called Kaihsienkung, locally pronounced *kejiug'on*. It is situated on the south-east bank of Lake Tai, in the lower course of the Yangtze River and about eighty miles west of Shanghai. It is in the geographical region of the Yangtze Plain. The geographical foundation of this region has been described by G. B. Cressey: "The Yangtze Plain is a land of rivers and canals. Probably nowhere else in the world is there an area with so many navigable waterways. The Yangtze Kiang, the Hwai Ho, and their tributaries provide a splendid highway through the length of the region. In addition

在目前阶段的调查中，把村庄作为一个研究单位，这并不是说村庄就是一个自给自足的单位。在中国，地方群体之间的相互依存，是非常密切的，在经济生活中尤为如此。甚至可以说，在上半个世纪中，中国人民已经进入了世界的共同体中。西方的货物和思想已经到达了非常边远的村庄。西方列强的政治、经济压力是目前中国文化变迁的重要因素。在这一点上有人可能会问，既然如此，那么在这样一个小的地区，在一个村庄里搞实地调查，对于这种外来力量及其所引起的变迁会取得什么进一步的了解呢？

显然，身处村庄的调查者不可能用宏观的眼光来观察和分析外来势力的各种影响。例如，由于世界经济萧条及丝绸工业中广泛的技术改革引起了国际市场上土产生丝价格的下跌，进而引起农村家庭收入不足、口粮短缺、婚期推迟以及家庭工业的部分破产。在这种情况下，实地调查者必须尽可能全面地记录外来势力对村庄生活的影响，但他当然应该把对这些势力本身的进一步分析留给其他学科去完成。调查者应承认这些事实，并只专注于跟踪那些可以从村庄生活中直接观察到的影响。

对这样一个小的社会单位进行深入研究而得出的结论并不一定适用于其他单位。但是，这样的结论却可以用作假设，也可以作为在其他地方进行调查时的比较材料。这就是获得真正科学结论的最可靠方法。

二、地理状况

我所选择的调查地点叫开弦弓村，坐落在太湖东南岸，位于长江下游，在上海以西约80英里的地方，其地理区域属于长江三角洲。G. B. 克雷西曾经这样描述该区域的地理概况："在长江平原的土地上，布满了河流与运河。世界上大概再也没有其他地区会有那么多可通航的水路。长江、淮河及其支流形成了一条贯穿这个区域的通道，

to the many rivers there are a series of great lakes, chief among which are Tungting, Poyang, Tai, and Hungtse Hu. It is the canals, however, which give the most characteristic note to the landscape. These canals are the very arteries of life. In the region of Yangtze Delta they form an intricate network and serve as an artificial drainage system which takes the place of rivers. Their length in the south delta alone is estimated by F. H. King, at twenty-five thousand miles.

"This region is compound alluvial plain, the accumulation of sediment laid down by the rivers during long ages. There are a few isolated hills, but for the most part the land is level. The country is flat, but innumerable grave mounds and the trees about the villages break the view. Both rural and urban settlement is more congested than in the region of the North, but factors of climate and location combine to make this the most prosperous part of China.[4]

"The Yangtze Plain is...distinctly influenced by summer-monsoon conditions... Here, too, are felt the greatest effects of continental cyclonic storms.

"Owing to the southernly latitude, the summers are subtropical with temperatures which frequently rise to 38℃. (100℉.)... The average (rainfall) for the entire region is about 1,200 mm. (45 in.).... Most of the rain falls during the spring and summer, with June the rainiest month. The period from October to February is comparatively dry with clear skies and stimulating temperatures, making this the most pleasant season of the year.

"Winter temperatures seldom remain below freezing for more than a few days at a time. Ice forms only in thin sheets on the colder nights and there is little snow.... The average of summer maximum temperature for Shanghai is 37℃. (91℉.), and the average of winter minimum is −7℃. (19℉.).

"The Yangtze Plain has climate conditions which are favourable for agriculture during most of the year so that the growing season lasts for about 300 days."**5**

The commanding position of this region in Chinese economy is due partly to its superior natural environment and partly to its favourable position in the system of communications. It is located at the crossing point of the two main water routes: namely, the Yangtze River and the Grand Canal. They connect this region with the immense territory of western and northern China. Being a coastal region, it has become more

颇为壮观。这里不但河流多，而且还有许多大小湖泊，其中主要有洞庭、鄱阳湖、太湖、洪泽湖。然而赋予这个地貌以最显著的特征的是人工河渠。这些河渠正是生活的命脉。在长江三角洲地区，河渠形成了错综复杂的网络，起着人工水系的作用，取代了河流。据 F. H. 金的估计，仅三角洲南部的河渠长度就有 25,000 英里左右。

"这个地区是复合冲积平原，由长期以来河流带来的泥沙淤积而成，只有少数孤立的山丘，大部地区是平川。乡下土地平坦，但是无数的坟墩和村子周围的树林遮住了视线。这里，无论是乡村或城市的居住区都比北方地区人口密集。但由于气候、地理位置等因素的共同作用，这里成为了中国最繁荣的地方。**4**

"长江平原　　显然受夏季季节风的影响　　也经受大陆性旋风的巨大威力。

"由于纬度偏南，夏季呈亚热带气候，气温经常升至 38℃（100 ℉）。　　整个地区平均降雨量约为 1,200 毫米（45 英寸）春、夏季多雨，6 月份的雨量最多。自 10 月至来年 2 月，气候较为干燥，天空晴朗，气温宜人，这时候是一年中最爽快的季节。

"冬天的气温，难得一连数日都在零下，在较冷的夜间才结薄冰，很少下雪。　　在上海，夏季平均最高气温 37℃（91℉），冬季平均最低气温为 –7℃（19℉）。

"长江平原一年四季，大部分时间的气候条件都有利于农业，生长季节约持续 300 天。"**5**

这个地区之所以在中国经济上取得主导地位，一方面是由于其优越的自然环境，另一方面是由于它在交通上的有利位置。该地区位于长江和大运河这两条水路干线的交叉点上。这两条水路把这个地区与中国西部和北部的广大疆土联结起来。作为沿海地区，自从通过远洋

and more important since the development of international trade by ocean transport. Shanghai, the seaport of this region, has developed into the biggest metropolis in the Far East. The railway system in this region is also well developed. From Shanghai, two important lines have been built, one to Nanking, passing Soochow, and one to Hongchow, passing Chianhsing. Recently in 1936 a new line between Soochow and Chianhsing was added to form a circuit between the above-mentioned two main lines. Motor roads have been built for the intra-regional communication; and besides there is an extensive use of the canals and canalized streams.

This region has supported a very dense population, most of which is resident in villages. A bird's-eye view shows a cluster of villages. Each village is separated from its neighbour by only a walking distance of, on an average, twenty minutes. Kaihsienkung is but one of these thousands of villages crowding on this land.

In the centre of several tens of villages there is a town. The town is the collecting centre of the basic produce from the surrounding villages and the distributing point for manufactured goods brought from the outside cities. The town on which Kaihsienkung depends is called Chên Tsê, about four miles south of the village. It takes about two and a half hours for a single trip by boat. Chên Tsê lies about six miles south-east of Lake Tai and eight miles west of the Grand Canal and the Soochow-Chianhsing line. At present it is connected with the nearest station, Ping Wang, both by motor boat and bus services. By the existing railway lines, one can reach Shanghai from the town within eight hours. The geographical position of Kaihsienkung in relation to the above-mentioned towns and cities is shown in the accompanying maps (Map I and II).

❸ Economic Background

Here the human geographer will be right in inferring the occupation of the people from the natural conditions of the land they occupy.

A traveller in a train, passing through that region, would not lose sight of the rice fields for more than intervals of a few minutes. In Kaihsienkung, according to estimates, more than ninety per cent. of the land is used for rice cultivation. This single village produces, on the average, eighteen thousand bushels of rice every year (X–2). Only a little more than half of the produce is consumed by the people themselves (VII–5). Very few households in the village are entirely free from agricultural work. About seventy-six per cent. of the total number of households are engaged

运输发展国际贸易以来，它的重要性与日俱增。该地区的港口上海现已发展成为远东的最大城市。这里的铁路系统也很发达，已经修建了两条重要线路，一条从上海经苏州至南京；另一条由上海经嘉兴至杭州。最近，也就是在 1936 年，苏州与嘉兴之间又增加了一条新线路，与上述两条干线形成环行铁路。为了便利地区内的交通，还修建了汽车路；除此之外，还广泛利用了运河及改成运河的河道进行交通运输。

该地区人口密集，大多数人口居住在农村。如从空中俯视，可以看见到处是一簇簇的村庄。每个村子仅与邻村平均相隔走 20 分钟路的距离。开弦弓只不过是群集在这块土地上成千上万个村庄之一。

在数十个村庄的中心地带就有一个市镇。市镇是收集周围村子土产品的中心，又是分配外地城市工业品下乡的中心。开弦弓所依傍的市镇叫震泽，在开弦弓以南约四英里，坐手摇船单程约需两个半小时。震泽地处太湖东南约六英里，大运河及苏嘉线以西约八英里。目前，可乘轮船或公共汽车到达苏嘉线的平望站。通过现有的铁路线，可在八小时以内从震泽到达上海。开弦弓与上述各城市及集镇间的位置关系，详见所附地图（见地图 I、II）。

三、经济背景

在这里，人文地理学者会正确地从人们所占据的土地的自然条件推论人们的职业。一个旅客，如果乘火车路经这个地区时，将接连不断地看到一片片的稻田。据估计，开弦弓 90% 以上的土地都用于种植水稻。该村每年平均产米 18,000 蒲式耳（第十章第二节）。仅一半多一点的粮食为人们自己所消费（第七章第五节）。村里极少有完全不干农活的人家。占总户数约 76% 的人家以农业为主要职业

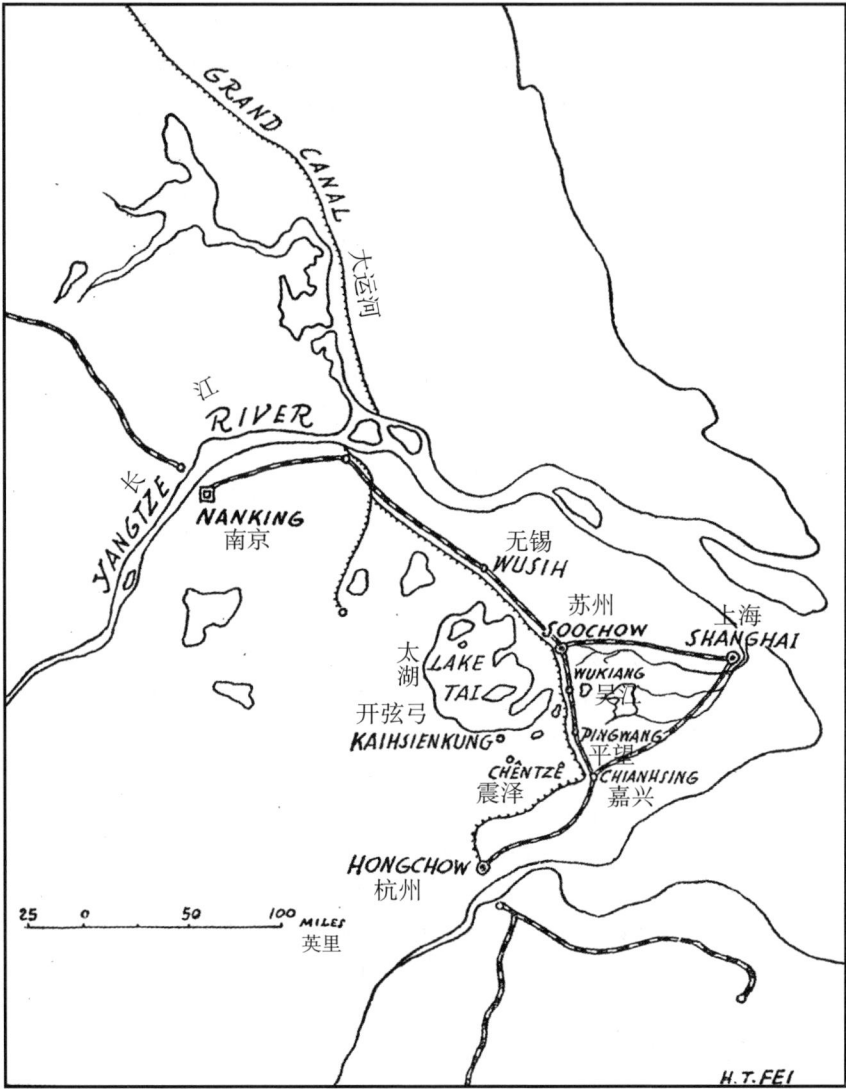

Map I The Lower Yangtze Valley
地图 I 长江下游流域

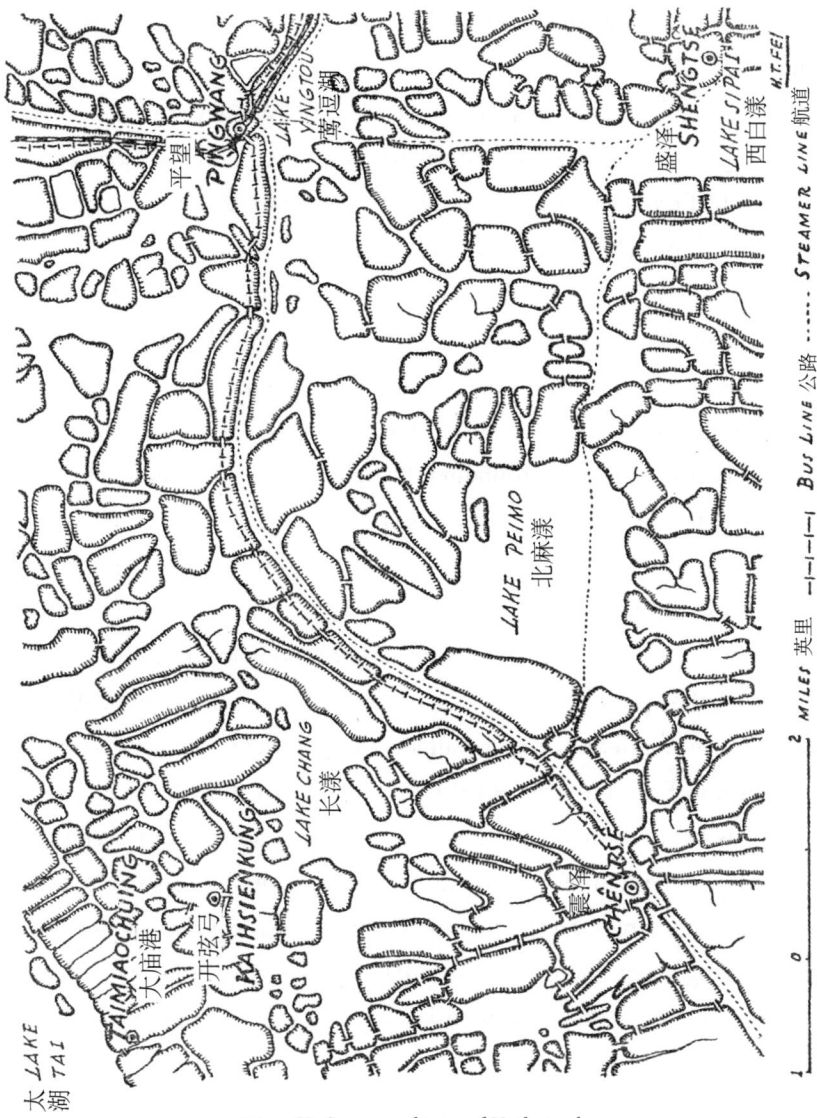

MAP II Surroundings of Kaihsienkung

地图 II 开弦弓周围的环境

in agriculture as their main occupation (VIII–1). The time spent in cultivating rice amounts to six months in the year (IX–3). From this crop the people earn more than half of their income (XII–2). Thus from any angle, rice is of primary importance.

But rice is not the only produce of the land. Wheat, rapeseeds and various vegetables are grown too, although they are insignificant as compared with the chief crop. Moreover, the water provides fish, shrimps, crabs, and different kinds of water plants which are all used locally as food.

The mulberry tree plays an important part in the economic life of the villagers. It enables them to develop their silk industry. Wright wrote early in 1908, "Raw white silk, the *tsatlee* silk of European markets, is produced by the hand reeling of the Chinese silkworm farms... The best white silk comes from the district surrounding Shanghai, which contributes by far the greatest proportion of the value exported."[6]

Silk industry is common to the whole region but it is specially well developed in the villages around Lake Tai. This specialization is due, according to the local people, to the good quality of the water. It is said that the so-called *tsatlee* silk is produced only in the area about four miles in diameter around Kaihsienkung. How far this statement is true is another question, but the importance of the village in rural industry is beyond doubt. During its prosperous period, this area not only contributed a large part of China's silk export but also supplied the demand for raw material for the domestic weaving industry of the neighbouring town Sheng Tsê (Map II). The weaving industry of that town before its decline had been known to be able to produce "ten thousand pieces a day."

The rural silk industry began to decline when the modern factory for silk manufacturing with its improved technique of production was introduced both into Japan and China. This industrial revolution changed the fortunes of the domestic rural industry.

"Previous to 1909... the quantity of Chinese silk exported had been larger than that of Japanese silk. In 1907, for instance, the two were almost the same. It was only in 1909, however, that Japanese silk export began to exceed that of China, and this advantage the former has been able to keep up ever since. In fact, in recent years, the Japanese export was nearly three times that of this country. From the point of view of our foreign trade, silk also decreased in significance since 1909. Before that date it used to constitute from 20 to 30 per cent. of our total exports, but the average for the years 1909—1916 fell to 17 per cent." [7]

（第八章第一节）。一年中，用于种稻的时间约占六个月（第九章第三节）。人们靠种稻挣得一半以上的收入（第十二章第二节）。因而，从任何一个角度看，种植水稻的重要性是居于首位的。

此地不仅产米，人们还种麦子、油菜籽及各种蔬菜，尽管它们与主要作物相比是无足轻重的。此外，江河里尚有鱼、虾、蟹及各种水生植物等，这些都是当地的食物。

桑树在农民的经济生活中起着重要的作用。人们靠它发展蚕丝业。赖特早在 1908 年写道："白色生丝，即欧洲市场中的'辑里丝'，是中国养蚕农家用手抽制的。　最佳生丝产自上海附近地区，该地区出口的丝占出口额的绝大部分。" [6]

蚕丝业在整个地区非常普遍，在太湖周围的村庄里尤为发达。据当地人说，它之所以成为该地特产是由于水质好。据说，所谓的"辑里丝"仅产于开弦弓周围方圆四英里的地带。这一说法的真实性暂且不论，但这个村庄在当地乡村工业中的重要地位确是毫无疑问的。在繁荣时期，这个地带的丝不仅在中国蚕丝出口额中占主要比重，而且还为邻近的盛泽镇（见地图 II）丝织工业的需要提供原料。在丝织业衰退之前，盛泽的丝织业号称"日产万匹"。

现代制丝业的先进生产技术引进日本、中国之后，乡村丝业开始衰退。这一工业革命改变了国内乡村手工业的命运。

"1909 年以前　中国蚕丝出口量比日本大。例如 1907 年，两国出口量几乎相同。但到 1909 年，日本蚕丝出口便超过了中国，而且从此以后，日本一直保持优势。事实上近年来，日本的出口量几近中国的 3 倍。从我国外贸角度来看，自从 1909 年以来，蚕丝的重要性也降低了。以前，蚕丝通常占我国出口总额的 20% 至 30%，而从 1909 年至 1916 年的平均数下降至 17%。" [7]

The amount of produce, however, had been increasing although irregularly up to 1923. But owing to the fall in price, the increasing amount of export did not mean necessarily an increase of return. The amount of export has declined steadily ever since that time. During 1928 to 1930, the percentage of decrease was about twenty.[8] The rate of decrease was more rapid in the period between 1930 to 1934. "As Japanese silk was dumped on the American market in the latter part of the year (1934), China's silk export dropped to the lowest point accordingly. The volume of silk exported amounted to only one-fifth of that in 1930, a fact which is indicative of the depression of the Chinese silk trade.

"The price of raw silk dropped to a new low level in 1934.... The 1934 price level for the same quality of silk was only one-third of the 1930 price level."[9]

The internal market for silk has shrunk at the same time due to the same forces of industrial revolution affecting the weaving industry. The consequence of the shrinkage of the market is the break-down of the traditional domestic silk industry in the rural district. The traditional specialization in the silk industry and its recent decline form the background of the economic life of the village in the present analysis.

❹ The Village Site

Let us examine the village itself. The land occupied by the people in this village consists of eleven *yu*. *Yu* is the local term for the unit of land surrounded by water. Each *yu* has its own name. Its size is determined by the distribution of streams and thus varies. The total area of land of this village is 3,065 *mow* or 461 acres. The names and sizes of these eleven *yu* are given in the following table, according to the official survey of 1932. Two of the *yu* belong in part to other villages, and, since there are no clear boundaries, I can only make a rough estimate of the portion belonging to Kaihsienkung.

Hsi Chang *yu*	.	.	.	.	986.402 *mow*
Ch'eng Kioh Hsi Tou *yu*		.	.	.	546.141
Kuei Tsǔ *yu*	.	.	.	.	458.010
Ch'eng Kioh *yu*	.	.	.	.	275.110
Liang Kioh *yu*	.	.	.	.	261.320
Hsi Tou *yu*	.	.	.	.	174.146

　　尽管如此，一直到 1923 年，蚕丝的产量一直是在增加的，虽然增长的幅度并不固定。由于蚕丝价格下跌，出口量的增长并不一定意味着收入的增加。从 1923 年以后，出口量便就此一蹶不振。1928 年至 1930 年间，出口量下降率约为 20%。[8] 1930 年至 1934 年间，下降得更为迅速。"1934 年下半年，由于日本向美国市场倾销蚕丝，中国蚕丝出口量随之降到最低水平。出口蚕丝量共计仅为 1930 年的五分之一。这一事实，说明了中国蚕丝贸易的不景气。

　　"1934 年生丝价格跌到前所未有的更低的水平。　　同样质量的丝，1934 年的价格水平仅为 1930 年的三分之一。"[9]

　　工业革命影响丝织业的力量同样使国内蚕丝市场缩小。市场缩小的结果带来了农村地区传统家庭蚕丝手工业的破产。传统的专业化蚕丝丝业及其近年来的衰落就形成了我们目前所分析的开弦弓村的经济生活背景。

四、村庄

　　现在让我们来观察一下村庄本身。村里的人占有土地共 11 圩。圩是土地单位，当地人称一块环绕着水的土地为一"圩"。每个圩有一个名字。圩的大小取决于水流的分布，因此各不相等。该村土地的总面积为 3,065 亩（或 461 英亩）。据 1932 年官方勘测，各圩的名称及面积如下表所示，其中有两圩部分属于其他村子，由于无明显的界限，我只能粗略地估计属于开弦弓那部分土地的面积：

西长圩	986.402 亩
城角西多圩	546.141 亩
龟字圩	458.010 亩
城角圩	275.110 亩
凉角圩	261.320 亩
西多圩	174.146 亩

P'an Hsiang Pa	.	.	.	.	.	173.263
Tou Tsŭ *yu*	.	.	.	.	.	70.540
Wu Tsŭ *yu*	.	.	.	.	.	56.469
Peh Cheng Kioh	.	.	.	.		55.858
Hsin Tien *yu*	.	.	.	.	.	8.545

TOTAL	.	.	.	.	.	3,065.804
	or	.	.	.		461.12 acres

The land can be roughly divided into two parts: namely, that used for cultivation and that used for dwellings. The residential area occupies rather a small portion. It is found at the junction of three streams and the houses are distributed on the margin of four *yu*. Names of these *yu* and number of houses on each are given in the following table:

I. Ch'eng Kioh *yu*	.	.	.	.	.	133
II. Liang Kioh *yu*	.	.	.	.	.	95
III. Hsi Chang *yu*	.	.	.	.	.	75
IV. T'an Chia Têng (Wu Tsŭ *yu*)		.	.	.		57

TOTAL	.	.	.	.	.	360

The plan of the residential area must be studied in relation to the communication system of the village. In this region, boats are extensively used for heavy and long-distance traffic. The land routes connecting different villages and towns are mainly used for pulling the boats against unfavourable currents and winds. People usually come to the village by boats, except a few pedlars. Nearly every household possesses at least one boat. The importance of the boat in communication means that the houses must be near the water and consequently determines the plan of the village. Villages grow up along the streams; at the junction of several streams, bigger villages are found. As we can see from the accompanying map, the backbone of Kaihsienkung village is formed by three streams, designated here as A, B, and C. Stream A, the main one, runs like an arc, and from this the village gets its name. Kaihsienkung literally means open-string-bow.

Boats are not convenient for short distances or very light traffic inside the residential area. Roads are built for communication between the houses. In this case, the streams represent obstacles to communication and the separated *yu* must be connected by bridges.

潘乡背	173.263 亩
多字圩	70.540 亩
吴字圩	56.469 亩
北城角	55.858 亩
新添圩	8.545 亩
总计	3,065.804 亩
	或 461.12 英亩

土地可略分为两部分：庄稼用地及居住用地。住宅区仅占相当小的部分，就在三条小河的汇集处，房屋分散在四个圩的边缘。这四个圩的名称及每个圩边的房屋数目如下：

I. 城角圩	133
II. 凉角圩	95
III. 西长圩	75
IV. 谈家墩（吴字圩）	57
总计	360

研究住宅区的规划必须同村子的交通系统联系起来。在这个地区，人们广泛使用船只载运重物进行长途运输。连接不同村庄和城镇的陆路，主要是在逆流、逆风时拉纤用的，即所谓塘岸。除了一些担挑的小商人之外，人们通常乘船来往。几乎家家户户都至少有一条船。由于船只在交通运输上的重要位置，为便利起见，房屋必须建筑在河道附近，这就决定了村子的规划。河道沿岸，大小村庄应运而生；一些的村子都建在几条河的岔口。正如我们可以从附图上看到，开弦弓的"脊梁骨"系由三条河组成，暂且定名为 A、B 和 C。河 A 是主流，像一张弓一样流过村子，开弦弓便由此而得名。字面上的意思就是："拉开弦的弓"。

在住宅区内，用船装载轻便的东西，或作短距离运输，不甚方便。因此在住房之间修起了道路以利往来。在这种情况下，河流就成了交通的障碍。各圩被河流所分割，必须用桥来连接。

The road system of this village does not form a complete circle. In the northern part of *yu* III, a large part of the land is used for farming. In that part, there are only small paths among the farms, and they are not convenient for walking, especially during wet weather. Owing to this fact the bridge at the west end of Stream A is the central point in the system. Small shops are concentrated largely around the bridges, especially the bridge at the west end (XIV–8).

Nevertheless, in the village plan, there is no special place where the public life of the people is concentrated. Except for the informal gatherings in the summer evenings around the bridges, there has been no organized public gathering for more than ten years, since the annual opera performance was suspended.

The headquarters of the village headmen is at the east end in the co-operative silk factory. The position of the factory was selected for technical reasons. The current of Stream A runs from west to east. To avoid adding the dirt of the factory to the stream which provides the daily water supply of the people along the stream, the factory was built at the lower course.

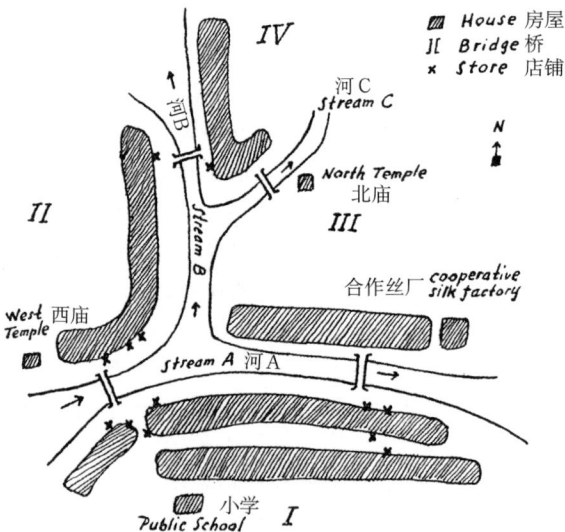

MAP III The Village Plan
地图 III   村庄详图

Two temples are found on the outskirts of the residential area: one at the west end and the other at the north end. But the position of the temples does not mean that the religious life of the people is concentrated on the outskirts. In fact, their religious life is largely carried on in their own houses. It would be more correct to regard the temples as the residences of priests and gods, who are not only segregated some distance apart from the ordinary people but are also separated from everyday community life except on special ceremonial occasions.

The public school is at the south end. The building was originally used as the office of the silk reform bureau. It was given to the school when the factory was established.

The residential area is surrounded by farming land, which is low owing to the irrigation system (X–1). The area suitable for buildings has been covered by houses and for a long time has not expanded.

这个村的陆路系统不能形成完全的环行路。在圩 III 的北部，大部分土地用来耕种，田间仅有小路，不便于行走，雨天尤其如此，因此，河 A 西端的桥便成了交通中心。小店铺大多集中在各桥附近。特别是集中在村子西边的桥旁（第十四章第八节）。

虽然如此，村庄的规划中却没有一个人们集中起来进行公共活动的专用场所。自从一年一度的唱戏停止演出后，除了夏天夜晚人们随意地聚集在桥边乘凉以外，十多年来，从未有过组织起来的公众集会。

村长的总部设在村子东端合作丝厂里面。厂址的选择是出于技术上的原因。河 A 的水自西向东流。由于河 A 供给沿岸居民的日常用水，所以把厂子建在下游，以免污染河水。

在住宅区外围有两座庙，一个在村西，一个在村北。这并不意味着人们的宗教活动都集中在村外边进行。实际上，他们的宗教活动多数都在自己家里开展。比较确切地说，庙是和尚及菩萨的住所。和尚、菩萨不仅同普通的人隔开一段距离，而且也与社区的日常生活隔开，但进行特殊仪式时除外。

公办小学在村的南端。校舍原先用作蚕丝改进社的办公室。合作丝厂建立以后便把房子给了学校。

住宅区周围都是农田，由于灌溉系统的缘故，农田地势较低（第十章第一节）。适宜于建筑的地区都已盖满了房屋，而且长期没有扩大。

The newly introduced public institutions such as the school and the silk factory could only find their location at the outskirt of the old residential area. Their location is an expression of the process of change in the community life.

❺ The People

A census of the village was taken in 1935. Because no continuous registration of births and deaths has been properly carried out, I can take this census only as the basis for my analysis. In the census, all the residents in this village, including those temporarily absent, are recorded. The figures are summarized in the following table:

Age	Male	Female	Total
71+	4	15	19
66–70	10	19	29
61–65	14	32	46
56–60	30	39	69
51–55	40	38	78
46–50	26	29	55
41–45	45	38	83
36–40	69	55	124
31–35	64	45	109
26–30	75	61	136
21–25	63	52	115
16–20	68	54	122
11–15	72	61	133
6–10	73	59	132
–5	118	87	205
?	—	—	3
TOTAL	771	684	1,458

Those temporarily residing in the village but living in definite households are recorded in the census in a special class called "Persons living together"; these are not included in the above table. The total number in this class is 25.

The density of population (excluding surface of water in computation) is about 1,980 per square mile. This cannot be compared with the average density of the province. The latter is calculated from the general area of

新的公共机构，例如学校和合作丝厂，只有在老的住宅区外围找到地盘。它们的位置说明了社区生活的变化过程。

五、村里的人

1935 年该村的人口有过一次普查。因为出生、死亡情况一直没有连续的登记，所以我只能把这次普查结果作为分析的基础。这次人口普查对村里的所有居民，包括暂时不在村里的人口，都做了记录。统计数字见下表：

年龄	男	女	总计
71+	4	15	19
66—70	10	19	29
61—65	14	32	46
56—60	30	39	69
51—55	40	38	78
46—50	26	29	55
41—45	45	38	83
36—40	69	55	124
31—35	64	45	109
26—30	75	61	136
21—25	63	52	115
16—20	68	54	122
11—15	72	61	133
6—10	73	59	132
—5	118	87	205
?	—	—	3
总计	774	684	1,458

对那些暂时寄居在村里农户家里的人口，普查记录专设了一栏。这些人口未包括在上表中。这一栏的总人数为 25 人。

人口密度（计算时不包括水面面积）约为每平方英里 1,980 人。这个数字不能与本省的平均人口密度相比，因为省人口密度是根据全省

the province which includes the surface of water and uncultivated land; it is a gross density. My figure represents the actual ratio between men and land used. The gross density of the province (Kiangsu), as quoted by Professor Tawney, is 896 per square mile.[10]

Not all those who reside in the village are indiscriminately considered as villagers. If the inhabitants are asked which are the people who belong to the village, we shall discover that distinction is made locally between natives and outsiders. This is not a legal distinction; from the legal point of view those who reside in a district for more than three years become members of the local community.[11] But this does not constitute, in the people's eyes, real membership of the village.

To analyse this distinction, it may be better to take concrete cases of those who are considered as outsiders in the village. There are ten such households, and their professions and birth-places are as follows:

Barber	2 Chenkiang (Kiangsu)
Miller and shoemaker . . .	1 Tanyang (Kiangsu)
Grocer	1 Hengshan (A village in the same district)
Spinner	1 Wuchiashen (A village in the same district)
Priest	1 Chên Tsê
Operator of the pumping machine .	1 Ningpo (Chekiang)
Silversmith	1 Shaohsing (Chekiang)
Bamboo artisan	1 Chinhua (Chekiang)
Medicine dealer	1 Wuchen (Chekiang)

Their common characters are (1) that they are immigrants and (2) that they are engaged in special professions. But I have no information about the necessary period of residence in order to attain the status of being a native villager. I have, however, known cases of children of the "outsiders" born in the village being treated like their parents. It appears that the distinction is not made solely on the consideration of period of residence.

On the other hand, the fact that none of the outsiders are farmers is significant. Although not all special professions are filled by them, they constitute one-third of the whole group (VIII–2). It prevents them from quick assimilation.

The villagers as a group possess certain cultural peculiarities. One of my informants mentioned three outstanding items to me: (1) that the villagers tend to palatalize the words such as *gon, jeu,* etc., in speech,

---

总面积（包括水面及非耕地）来计算的，那是一个总密度。我的数字代表着人和被使用的土地之间的比率。托尼教授所引述的江苏省的人口总密度是每平方英里 896 人。[10]

人们并不认为所有住在村里的人一律都是本村人。如果问本村居民，哪些人是本村的，我们就会发现当地对于本村人和外来人有着明显的区别。但这种区别并不是法律上的；从法律观点看，一个人只要在某地居住三年以上，他就成为当地社区的一名成员。[11] 可是在人们的眼里，这样的人并不是真正的本村人。

为说明这种区别，不妨举一些具体的例子：那些被当作外来户的村里人。这样的外来户共有 10 家，其职业和本籍分述如下：

理发匠	2 镇江（江苏）
磨工兼鞋匠	1 丹阳（江苏）
杂货商	1 横塥（同区—村庄）
纺织工	1 吴家村（同区—村庄）
和尚	1 震泽
水泵操作者	1 宁波（浙江）
银匠	1 绍兴（浙江）
篾匠	1 金华（浙江）
药商	1 邬镇（浙江）

他们的共同特点是：（1）都是移民，（2）从事某种特殊职业。我未听说一个外来人究竟需要在本村住多久才能算作本村人，但是我却听说过：外来人的孩子，虽生于本村，仍像其父母一样，被视作外来人。由此看来，并非完全根据居住期的长短来确定这种区别的。

另一方面，值得研究的是这样一个事实：凡是外来户都不是农民。虽然并非所有特殊的职业都是外来人干的，但他们仍构成了这类人的三分之一（第八章第二节），从事特殊职业使他们不会很快被同化。

作为一个群体，本村人具有一定的文化特色。一个提供资料的本地人向我提到过三个显著特点：（1）本村人说话时，吐字趋于腭音化，

(2) their women do not work on the farm, and (3) their women always wear skirts even in the hot summer. In these respects, they differ even from the people from the nearest town, Chên Tsê.

Those who are regarded as outsiders have not been culturally assimilated. I noticed their non-native accent in speech and non-native way of dressing; for instance, the women in the medicine shop did not wear skirts.

As long as the outsiders preserve their own linguistic and cultural difference, and those are noticed by the natives, they will live on more or less symbiotically in the community. The distinction of natives and outsiders is significant because it has been translated into social relations. The fact that outsiders are all engaged in special professions and possess no land is alone sufficient to indicate that the distinction has far-reaching economic consequences.

❻ Reasons for Selecting the Field

The village as described is of interest in the following respects.

(1) It has been one of the important centres of domestic silk industry in China. The village can therefore be taken as a representative case of the process of change in Chinese industry; the change has been chiefly concerned with the substitution of the factory for the domestic system and the social problems rising therefrom. This is a general process, still going on in China, and also has parallels in different parts of the world. The problem of industrial development in China has its practical significance, but has never been studied intensively with a full knowledge of the social organization of the village. Moreover, in this village an experiment at industrial reform has been made during the past ten years. The social reform activities are of great relevance to the social changes in China; they should be carefully analysed in an objective way. It is possible that through such an analysis certain important but hitherto unnoticed problems may be revealed.

(2) Kaihsienkung is located in an area where, owing to superb natural resources, agriculture has been developed to a very high degree. The institution of land tenure also has here peculiar elaborations. The village would provide a good field for the study of land problems in China.

例如"讲"、"究"等等；(2)妇女不下田干活；(3)妇女总是穿裙子，甚至在炎热的夏天也穿着。在这几方面，本村人甚至与最近的震泽镇人都不相同。

那些被视为外来户的人，在生活上一直未被同化。我注意到他们的非本地口音及非本地穿着方式，例如，药店里的妇女不穿裙子。

只要外来户保留着他们自己的语言和文化差别，而且本村人注意到这些差别，那么，在这个社区内，外来户总是过着多少有所见外的生活。对本村人及外来户作出区别是颇有意义的，因为这种区别已经具有广泛的社会意义。外来户全部从事特殊职业，没有土地，仅这一事实就足以说明，区别是有其深远的经济后果的。

六、选择这个调查区域的理由

这个村庄有下列值得注意和研究之处：

(1) 开弦弓是中国国内蚕丝业的重要中心之一。因此，可以把这个村子作为在中国工业变迁过程中有代表性的例子；主要变化是工厂代替了家庭手工业系统，并从而产生的社会问题。工业化是一个普遍过程，目前仍在我国进行着，世界各地也有这样的变迁。在中国，工业的发展问题更有其实际意义，但至今没有任何人在全面了解农村社会组织的同时，对这个问题进行过深入的研究。此外，在过去十年中，开弦弓村曾经进行过蚕丝业改革的实验。社会改革活动对于中国的社会变迁是息息相关的；应该以客观的态度仔细分析各种社会变迁。通过这样的分析，有可能揭示或发现某些重要的但迄今未被注意到的问题。

(2) 开弦弓一带，由于自然资源极佳，农业发展到很高水平。有关土地占有制度在这里也有特殊的细节。开弦弓将为研究中国土地问题提供一个很好的实地调查的场地。

(3) The extensive use of water communication in that region, with its net-like distribution of water ways, has led to a special relation between town and village, which is different from that found in North China. We are thus able to study a typical case of a marketing system based on water transport.

Besides these considerations, I had special facilities in investigating this village. My investigation had to be limited to a period of two months. It would have been impossible in this short time to carry out any intensive study, if I had worked in an entirely unfamiliar field. Kaihsienkung is a village belonging to the district of Wukiang of which I am a native. I thus started with certain linguistic advantages. Differences in Chinese dialect is one of the practical difficulties in carrying out field investigation. The people in villages usually cannot understand any other dialect besides their own. Being a native of the district, it was not necessary for me to spend time in learning the local dialect. The community feeling of being a native of the same district also enabled me to penetrate into more intimate life without arousing suspicion.

Above all, in this village I could fully utilize the personal connections of my sister, who, being responsible for the silk reform, had gained the confidence of practically every person in the village. I could without any difficulty secure the best possible co-operation of the villagers in general and the village heads in particular. Having understood my intention, they not only supplied me with all possible material, but made very intelligent and valuable suggestions and explanations to facilitate my investigation. Furthermore, I had visited the village several times before and had been kept continuously informed by my sister about the conditions there. Thus I could go directly into the problem without wasting my time in preliminary work.

My investigation covered the two months of July to August, 1936. Within this time limit, I was naturally not able to follow the complete annual cycle of social activities. However, these two months are significant in their economic life. They cover the last part of the silk industry and the first part of the agricultural work. Supplemented by oral information and my past experiences, the material so far gathered concerning their economic life and the related social institutions is enough for a preliminary analysis.

（3）这个地区广泛使用水上交通，有着网状分布的水路，因而城乡之间有着特殊的关系，这与华北的情况截然不同。这样我们就能够通过典型来研究依靠水上运输的集镇系统。

除去这些考虑之外，我调查开弦弓村还具备特殊便利的条件。由于时间有限，我的调查必须在两个月之内完成。如果我在一个全然不熟悉的地方工作，要在这样短的时间内进行任何细致的研究是不可能的。开弦弓村属于吴江县，而我就是吴江人，我首先在语言上就有一定的有利条件。中国各地方言的差别是进行实地调查的实际困难之一。村里的人们除自己的方言外，一般不懂得任何其他方言。作为一个本地人，就不必再花费时间去学习当地方言。而且同乡的感情使我能够进一步深入到人们的生活中去，不致引起怀疑。

尤其是在这个村里，我可以充分利用我姐姐个人的联系。我姐姐负责蚕丝业的改革，村里的人确实都很信任她。我能够毫无困难地得到全村居民的通力合作，特别是村长们的帮助。他们理解我的意图，不仅尽一切可能提供材料，而且还提出一些可行的办法和有价值的建议，这使我的调查得以顺利进行。此外，我以前曾多次访问过该村，姐姐也继续不断地向我提供该村的情况。因此，我一开始就能直接进入调查本身，无须浪费时间去做那些初步的准备工作。

我的调查历时两个月，是在 1936 年的 7 月至 8 月进行的。在这有限的时间内，我自然不能对完整的一年为周期的社会活动进行调查。然而，这两个月在他们的经济生活中是有重要意义的，包括了一年中蚕丝业的最后阶段及农活的最初阶段。以我过去的经验及人们口头提供的资料作为补充，到目前为止，我所收集到的关于他们的经济生活及有关社会制度的材料，足以进行初步的分析。

CHAPTER III   THE CHIA

The basic social group in the village is the Chia, an expanded family. The members of this group possess a common property, keep a common budget and co-operate together to pursue a common living through division of labour. It is also in this group that children are born and brought up and material objects, knowledge, and social positions are inherited.

Larger social groups in the village are formed by combining a number of Chia for various purposes and along kinship or territorial principles. Associations based on individual membership are few and secondary. The following four chapters will provide a social background of the village for our study of its economic life.

❶ Chia as an Expanded Family

The term family, as commonly used by anthropologists, refers to the procreative unit consisting of parents and immature children. A Chia is essentially a family but it sometimes includes children even when they have grown and married. Sometimes it also includes some relatively remote patrilineal kinsmen. We can call it an expanded family, because it is an expansion of a family due to the reluctance of the sons to separate from their parents after marriage.

Chia emphasizes the inter-dependence of parents and children. It gives security to the old who are no longer able to work. It tends to ensure social continuity and co-operation among the members.

In a given economy, the indefinite expansion of the group may not be advantageous. In the process of expansion social friction among the members increases. As we shall see presently, the Chia will divide whenever the division proves to be advisable. The size of the group is, therefore, maintained by the balance of the opposing forces working for integration on the one hand and for disintegration on the other. We shall analyse these two forces in the following sections.

Some quantitative data about the size of the Chia in the village may be helpful for our further discussion. In spite of the fact that most studies of China have stressed the importance of the large-family system in China, curiously enough, in this village a large-family is rare. In less than ten per cent. of the total number of Chia do we find more than one married couple.

叁 家

农村中的基本社会群体就是家，一个扩大的家庭。这个群体的成员占有共同的财产，有共同的收支预算，他们通过劳动的分工过着共同的生活。儿童们也是在这个群体中出生、养育并继承了财物、知识及社会地位。

村中更大的社会群体是由若干家根据多种不同目的基于亲属、地域等关系组成的。由个人成员组成的社团很少且占次要地位。以下四章将提供该村的社会背景以便我们研究其经济生活。

一、家，扩大的家庭

"家庭"这个名词，人类学家普遍使用时，是指一个包括父母及未成年子女的生育单位。中国人所说的"家"，基本上也是一个家庭，但它包括的子女有时甚至已成年或已婚。有时，它还包括一些远房的父系亲属。之所以称它是一个扩大了的家庭，是因为儿子在结婚之后并不和他们的父母分居，因而把家庭扩大了。

家，强调了父母和子女之间的相互依存。它给那些丧失劳动能力的老年人以生活的保障。它也有利于保证社会的延续和家庭成员之间的合作。

在一定的经济条件下，这个群体本身无限的扩展很可能是不利的。在扩展进程中，其成员之间的磨擦增加了。我们即将看到，家是会分的，即所谓"分家"。而且，分家只要较为可取，它就分。因此，家的规模大小是由两股对立的力量的平衡决定的：一股要结合在一起的力量，另一股要分散的力量。在下面几节里，我将分析这两股力量。

关于这村里家的规模，有一些定量的数据可以帮助我们进一步开展讨论。尽管大部分对中国的研究强调中国大家庭制度的重要性，但非常奇怪，在这个村里，大家庭很少。在家的总数中，我们发现有一对以上已婚夫妇的家不到十分之一。

The most common type is that which consists of a nucleus of a married couple and several dependent patrilineal relatives. In fact, more than half, or 58 per cent. of the total, are of this type. But there is not a married couple in every Chia. Sometimes, for instance, after the death of her husband, a woman lives with her children without joining another unit. It may also be the case that a father lives with his son without a woman in the house. These are cases resulting from social disorganization, mainly due to the death of working members of the group; they are consequently unstable. Either the widower will remarry or the child will marry in the earliest possible future so that a normal functioning of the group can be restored. This type of unstable Chia amounts to 27 per cent. of the total.[12]

An average Chia in the village consists of four persons. This is by no means an exception, and indicates the smallness of the group. Evidences from other rural districts in China give a similar conclusion. The variation lies between six to four persons per family.[13] The so-called large-family is chiefly found in towns and evidently has a different economic basis. For the present material, it can be said that in the village here described, the Chia is a small kinship group consisting of a family as its nucleus and several dependent relatives.

❷ Continuity of "Incense and Fire"

The parent-child and the husband-wife relations are two fundamental axes in the family organization. But in the Chia the former seems more important. The essential character of the Chia is that married sons do not always leave their parents, especially when either father or mother is dead. Furthermore, to find a bride for a young man is regarded as part of the parental obligation. Mates are selected and ceremonies arranged by the parents. On the other hand, the legal act of marriage, although preceding the birth of the child, always anticipates the realization of parenthood. The main purpose of marriage, in the village, is to secure the continuity of descent. To ensure posterity is the chief consideration in the selection of a daughter-in-law and this is explicitly expressed in the consultations which are held with the fortune-tellers. The incapacity of a daughter-in-law to fulfil her obligations may be taken as a strong ground for her repudiation without compensation. Again, the full status of a woman is acquired after the birth of her child. Similarly, the affinal relation

最常见的类型是：以一对已婚配偶为核心，再包括几个依赖于此家的父系亲属。事实上，超过一半的家，准确地说，占总数 58% 的家都属于此类。但并不是每一个家都有一对已婚配偶。有时候，在一个妇女丧夫之后，她就和她的子女在一起生活，而不去加入另一个单位。也有这样的情况，一个父亲和他儿子居住在一起，家中没有女人。这些都是社会解组的结果，主要是由于这个群体中从事劳动的成员死亡所致，因而它们是不稳定的。鳏夫会再结婚，孩子也会在不久的将来，一有可能就结婚。任何一种情况都能使一个不正常的家庭得到恢复。这一类不稳定的家占总数的 27%。[12]

村中，一个家的成员平均为 4 人。这说明这种群体是很小的，而且这绝不是一种例外的情况，从中国其他农村地区的材料也可以得出同样的结论。中国农村家庭，平均的人数大约是在 4 至 6 人之间。[13] 所谓大家庭，看来主要存在于城镇之中，很明显，它们具有不同的经济基础。就现有材料看，可以说，这个村里的家是一个小的亲属群体，以一个家庭为核心，并包含有几个依靠他们的亲属。

二、"香火"绵续

父母与子女、夫与妻这两种关系是家庭组织的基本轴心。但在中国所谓的"家"中，前者的关系似乎更为重要。家的基本特征是已婚的儿子中往往有一个不离开他们的父母，父母之中如有一人亡故，更是如此。此外，为儿子找一个媳妇被视为父母的责任。配偶由父母选就，婚礼由父母安排。另一方面，婚姻的法定行为尽管先于生孩子，但结婚总是为了有后代。生孩子的期望先于婚姻。在农村中，结成婚姻的主要目的是为了保证传宗接代。选聘媳妇的主要目的是为了延续后代，保证生育男儿是向算命先生明白提出的要求。如果当媳妇的没有能力来完成她的职责，夫家就有很充足的理由将她遗弃而无需任何赔偿。妇女在生育了孩子之后，她的社会地位才得到完全的确认。

remains impotent unless a child is born. It is, therefore, justifiable to start our description of the organization of Chia from the parent-child relation.

The importance of the posterity is conceived in religious and ethical terms. The local term for the continuity of descent is "continuity of incense and fire"; this means a continuity of ancestor worship. Beliefs connected with the relation of living descendants to the spirits of their ancestors are not clearly and systematically formulated among the people. The general view is that the spirits live in a world very similar to ours, but that economically they are partially dependent on the contributions of their descendents which are made by periodically burning paper money, paper clothes, and paper articles. Therefore it is essential to have someone to look after one's well-being in the after-world.

Some explain the importance of having children on purely ethical grounds. They conceive it to be their duty because it is through their children that they can pay back their debt to their own parents. Thus the desire to have children is backed up by a two-fold motive: it ensures, in the first place, the continuity of the line of descent; and, in the second place, it is a concrete expression of filial piety by the future father towards his ancestors.

These beliefs, while undoubtedly connected with religious and ethical ideas, have also practical value. In later sections I shall show how the child helps the development of intimate relations between husband and wife, who are little acquainted with one another before marriage. The child stabilizes the relations in the domestic circle. The economic value of the child is also important. A child starts contributing very early to the family welfare, often before he is ten years of age, in such tasks as collecting grass to feed sheep. A girl is specially useful in the daily house work and in the silk industry. Moreover, when a boy grows up and gets married, his parents are relieved by the young couple of the full burden of work on the land and in the house. When the parents are old and unable to work, they are supported by their sons. This is illustrated by the following fact: there are 145 widows in this village who are unable to live on their own resources, but this does not constitute a serious social problem because most of them are supported by their adult children. Children in this sense are insurance for old age.

Social continuity in kinship is complicated by the unilateral emphasis of affiliation. Membership and property of a person is not transmitted equally to the son and daughter. Emphasis is on the male side.

同样，姻亲关系只有在她生育孩子以后才开始有效。因此，先从父母与孩子的关系着手来描述和研究家的组织是有根据的。

传宗接代的重要性可以从宗教和伦理角度加以理解。传宗接代，用当地的话说就是"香火"绵续，意思是，不断有人继续祀奉祖先。关于活着的子孙和他们祖先鬼魂之间联系的信仰，在人们中间不太明确，也没有系统的说法。大致的观点是：这些祖宗的鬼魂生活在一个和我们非常相像的社会中，但在经济方面他们部分地依靠子孙所作的奉献，这就是定时地烧纸钱、纸衣服和其他纸扎的模拟品。因此，看来死者在阴间的福利还是要有活人来照管的。

有人用纯伦理的观点来解释生育子女的重要性。他们认为这是一种做人的责任，因为只有通过他们的子女才能向自己的父母偿还他们对自己的抚育之恩。因此，要有子女的愿望是出于双重的动机：首先是传宗接代；第二是向祖宗表示孝敬。

这些信仰，无疑地和宗教及伦理观念联系在一起，同时也有实际的价值。在以后的章节里我将说明子女如何有助于建立夫妇间亲密的关系，因为丈夫和妻子在结婚前是互不相识的。子女还起着稳定家庭群体里各方关系的作用。子女的经济价值也是很重要的。孩子很早就开始给家庭福利作出贡献，常常在十岁之前，就打草喂羊。女孩在日常家务劳动及缫丝工业方面是非常有用的。再者，孩子长大结婚后，年轻的夫妇代替父母担负起在田地上及家庭中的重担。当父母年老而不能劳动时，他们就由儿子们来赡养。这些可以由以下的事实来说明：这个村子中有 145 名寡妇，她们不能靠自己的经济来源维持生活，但这并没有形成一个严重的社会问题，因为她们之中的绝大多数都由成年子女赡养。从这个意义上来说，孩子是老年的保障，即所谓"养儿防老"。

亲属关系的社会延续问题，由于强调单系的亲属关系而变得复杂起来。一个人的身份和财产并不是平等地传递给子女的。总是把重点

During childhood both male and female children are cared for by their parents. Both assume their father's surname, but when they grow up, and get married, the son will continuously live in the parents' house before division while the daughter will leave her parents and live with her husband. She will add her husband's surname to her own. She has no claim on the property of her parents except what she gets as dowry. She also has no obligation to support them except by offering periodical gifts and occasional financial help as their affinal relations (XV–2). Property is inherited by the son whose obligation it is to support the old (IV–3). In the third generation, only the children of the son carry on the continuous line of affiliation. The children of the daughter are regarded as affinal relatives, and assume their father's surname. Therefore, in the village, the principle of descent is patrilineal.

This principle, however, can be modified in case of need. By agreement, a daughter's husband may add his wife's surname to his own and their children will carry their mother's line. Sometimes the husband and wife may carry both lines of their parents. These however are minor obliterations of the general principle and appear only in specific circumstances (IV–4). The present legal system has attempted to alter the traditional unilateral emphasis of kinship affiliation owing to the new conception of sex equality (IV–6). We will discuss these obliterations later.

❸ Population Control

In spite of the fact that the villagers recognize the importance of posterity, there is a limiting factor for population. It is true that children can contribute labour to the domestic economy, but there must be enough work on which it can be utilized. With land holdings of limited size, and with limits to the extent of silkworm raising, surplus members of a Chia will be merely a burden to the unit. This brings us to an examination of the average size of a land holding in the village.

The total area of cultivated land is 3,065 *mow* or 461 acres. If this area were equally allotted to 360 households, it would mean that each household could only occupy a piece of land about 9.5 *mow* or 1.2 acres in size. Each *mow* of land can produce in a normal year six bushels of rice. About twenty-seven bushels of rice is needed for the consumption of one man, one woman, and one child (VII–5). In other words, to obtain sufficient food, a family group needs a piece of land of about five *mow*.

放在男性这一边。在幼年时期，男孩和女孩都由父母抚养。他们都用父亲的姓氏。但当他们长大成亲后，儿子在分家前还继续住在父母的房屋里，而女儿则离开父母去和自己的丈夫住在一起。她在自己的姓名前要加上丈夫的姓氏。她除了能得到自己的一份嫁妆外，对自己父母的财产不能提出什么要求。出嫁的女儿，除了定时给父母送礼品及有时给父母一些经济帮助外，她也没有赡养自己父母的责任（第十五章第二节）。财产由儿子继承，他的责任是赡养其父母（第四章第三节）。在第三代，只有儿子的儿子接续他的家系。女儿的孩子则被视为亲戚关系，他们使用自己父亲的姓氏。因此，在村子中，传代的原则是父系的。

然而，这个原则有时也可以根据需要加以修改。经过协议，女儿的丈夫也可以在自己的姓名前面加上他妻子的姓，他们的孩子则接续母亲的家系。也有时夫妇双方各自接续双方的家系。总之，这些是总的原则在特定条件下的次要变动（第四章第四节）。由于男女平等的新概念，现行的法律制度企图改变这种传统的偏重单系的亲属制度（第四章第六节）。关于这些变化，留到以后再加以讨论。

三、人口控制

尽管村中的人认识到后代的重要性，但现实中还存在着必须限制人口的因素。儿童的劳动能对家庭经济作出贡献，这是事实，但必须要有足够的劳动对象来利用这些劳动力，由于拥有土地的面积有限，能养多少蚕也有限度，家中多余的成员，成了沉重的负担。有鉴于此，让我们先来观察一下这个村平均的土地拥有量情况。

该村的总面积为 3,065 亩，农地占 90%，如果将 2,758.5 亩农田平均分配给 274 家农户，则意味着每户只能有一块约 10.06 亩大的土地。正常年景，每亩地能生产 6 蒲式耳稻米。一男、一女和一个儿童一年需消费 33 蒲式耳稻米（第七章第五节）。换句话说，为了得到足够的食物，每个家庭约需有 5.5 亩地。目前，即使全部土地都用于

The present size of land holdings is hardly sufficient to provide an average household with a normal livelihood which requires sufficient food and other necessities. The pressure of population on the land is thus a strong limiting factor on the number of children. For example, a family, with a small holding of nine *mow*, will face a serious problem if a second boy is born. According to local custom, the children when grown up will divide the estate. This will mean poverty for both sons. The usual solution is infanticide or abortion. The people do not attempt to justify these practices and admit that they are bad. But there is no alternative except poverty and "crime." The result can be seen in the figures of the total number of children in the village: there are only 470 children under sixteen years of age, 1.3 per Chia.

The practice of infanticide is more often for the female children. The patrilineal descent and the patrilocal marriage have effected the social status of women. A girl is of less value in the eyes of the parents because she cannot continue the "incense and fire" and because as soon as she is mature, she will leave her parents. In consequences, the ratio of females in the age group 0–5 is unusually low. There are only 100 girls to 135 boys (II–5). Only in 131 Chia, or 37 per cent. of the total, are there girls (under sixteen) among their children (excluding *siaosiv*), and in only fourteen Chia is there more than one girl.

Since population control is considered as a precaution against poverty, families with comparatively large estates are free to have more children. They are proud of their numerous children, and these are taken as a sign of their wealth in the eyes of the people. The desire for posterity, the dislike of infanticide and abortion, and economic pressure—these factors work together to equalize land holdings (XI–6).

❹ Parents and Children

Before the birth of a child, the mother has already definite obligations toward it. During pregnancy, the mother must abstain from violent emotion, from looking at abhorrent things, and from eating certain types of food. There is an idea that the foetus needs education. Good behaviour by the mother is expected to affect the future personality of the child. No special obligations are, however, incurred by the father, except perhaps abstaining from sex relations with his wife, since this is considered unfavourable to the physiological development of the child and may lead to its early death.

粮食生产，一家也只有大约 60 蒲式耳的稻米。每户以 4 口人计算，拥有土地的面积在满足一般家庭所需的粮食之后仅能勉强支付大约相当于粮食所值价的其他生活必需品的供应。因此，我们可以看到，这个每家平均有 4 口人的村子，现有的土地已受到相当重的人口压力。这是限制儿童数量的重要因素。按照当地的习惯，孩子长大后就要分家产。有限的土地如果一分为二，就意味着两个儿子都要贫困。通常的办法是溺婴或流产。人们并不为这种行为辩护，他们承认这是不好的，但是有什么别的办法以免贫穷呢？从这个村子中儿童的总数可以看到这个结果：16 岁以下儿童，总共只有 470 名，平均每家 1.3 个。

杀害女婴就更为经常。父系传代及从父居婚姻影响了妇女的社会地位。在父母亲的眼中，女孩的价值是较低的，因为她不能承继"香火"，同时，她一旦长成，就要离开父母。结果 0～5 岁年龄组的性比例是：100 个女孩比 135 个男孩（第二章第五节）。只在 131 家中，即占总数 37% 的家中，有 16 岁以下的女孩（不包括"小媳妇"），只在 14 家中，有一个以上的女孩。

正因为人口控制是为了预防贫穷，一些有着较大产业的家庭就不受限制地有更多的子女。他们对自己有为数众多的子女感到自豪，而在人们的眼中，又视之为富裕的象征。有后嗣的愿望、厌恶杀婴与流产及经济上的压力等等，这些因素同时发生作用使土地的拥有量趋向平均化（第十一章第六节）。

四、父母和子女

孩子出生之前，当母亲的已经有了明确的责任。在妊娠期间，当母亲的要避免感情冲动，避免观看令人憎恶的事物，禁忌吃某些食物等。人们已经有了胎教的观念。人们认为母亲的良好行为会影响到孩子将来的性格。对父亲则无特殊的要求，只是认为他应避免和妻子同房，因为这被认为对孩子的生理发育不利，甚至可能导致夭亡。

Expectation and fear cause a general tension in the house. The pregnant woman is recognized to be in a special position and is exempted from her various household duties. The exemption is associated with the sense of uncleanliness of sex matters. Her own parents share the tension. Shortly before the child is delivered, they will offer a kind of medical soup to their daughter. Her mother will stay in her room for several days to look after her. It is also the duty of her own mother to clean all the soiled clothes and wait on her daughter after delivery.

It is not customary for the mother to take a long period of rest after the child is born. She resumes her work in the household within a week. This practice was regarded by my informant as the cause of the high death rate of women after childbirth. The actual death rate is not known. But in the population statistics, there is an apparent fall in numbers in the age group of females of 26–30 and 41–45 (II–5); this indicates the fact.

Infantile mortality is also high. If we compare the number of individuals in the age group 0–5 with that in the age group 6–10, a big decrease is observed. The difference between the groups is 73 individuals, or 33 per cent. of the group. This phenomenon is also reflected in the belief in "spirit sadism." In the ceremony of *menyu*, literally "child-reaching-full-month," the child will be shaved and given a personal name by his maternal uncle. This is usually a name of abuse, such as dog, cat, or monk. The people believe that the lives of the children, particularly those who are specially regarded by their parents, are sought by devil spirits. A way of protecting the child is to show the spirits that there is no one interested in it; the theory is that spirits, being sadists, will then discontinue their intervention. This is sometimes carried so far that children are nominally given for protection to somebody who is considered to have greater influence, or even to gods. This pseudo-adoption will be described later (V–3). The parents' outward expression of love of their children is thus carefully concealed.

The attitude of the parents and elder relatives towards children must be understood in relation to these factors—the need for population control due to economic pressure, the small number of children, the high infant mortality, the belief in spirit sadism, the desire for posterity and the connected religious and ethical ideas. As a result of these factors, we can see that the children who survive are highly valued, even though there is an outward show of indifference.

　　对生育的期待与恐惧，使家庭充满了紧张的气氛。怀孕的妇女被认为处于特殊地位并免除了她各项家务劳动。这是因为人们对性有一种不洁净的意识。她自己的父母也分担了这种紧张。小孩快出生之前，娘家的父母给她喝药汤。母亲要在女儿房里陪住几天，以便照顾她。她的母亲也有责任去洗涤污脏的衣服，并在产后，守在她身边。

　　孩子出生后，按习惯，当母亲的不长期休息。她在一个星期之内便恢复家务劳动。当地向我提供情况的人认为，这种做法是造成妇女产后高死亡率的原因。真实的死亡率还不得而知，但在人口统计中，26～30岁及41～45岁两年龄组妇女人数的明显下降（第二章第五节）说明了这个问题。

　　婴儿的死亡率也是高的。如果把年龄组0～5岁与6～10岁相比较，会发现人数有很大的下降。两组数字相差为73人，占这个组总数的33%。这种现象也反映在当地人迷信"鬼怪恶煞"。孩子"满月"时要剃头，并由孩子的舅父起一个小名。这通常是一个带贬义的名字，如阿狗、阿猫、和尚等等。人们迷信孩子的生命会被鬼怪追索，受父母宠爱的孩子尤其如此。保护孩子的一种办法，就是向鬼怪表示，没人对这孩子感兴趣；其理由是鬼怪性喜作恶，看父母溺爱孩子，就要进行打击；孩子既然受到冷淡，鬼怪就不再继续插手了。甚至有时采取这样一些方法，名义上把孩子舍给那些被认为大有影响、甚至在神道面前也是很有影响的人物，以求得保护。这种假的领养孩子的办法以后还会讲到（第五章第三节）。因此，父母原来在表面上表露出来的对孩子的珍爱，被小心地掩藏起来了。

　　关于父母以及长亲对孩子的态度问题，必须联系下述各种因素来加以理解。这些因素是：由于经济压力需要控制人口；儿童为数很少；婴儿死亡率高；迷信鬼怪恶煞；要子嗣的愿望及有关的宗教伦理观念。从这众多因素的结合中可以看到，活下来的孩子便受到高度的珍爱，虽然从表面上看，对待孩子的态度是淡漠的。

The children in the village cling to their mothers all the day long. The cradle is little used if there are arms available for nursing the babies. The period of suckling lasts three or more years. The time of feeding is not fixed. Whenever the child cries, the mother will at once put her nipple into the child's mouth to keep the child quiet. Moreover, women in the village do not go to the farm, but work almost all the day in the house. Contact between mother and child is thus in ordinary circumstances almost uninterrupted.

The relation between the father and the child is slightly different. The husband has no special duties during his wife's pregnancy and child delivery. For more than half the year, men are at work outside the house. They go out in the early morning and come back in the evening, the chance of contact between them and the children is relatively less. During the child's infancy, so far as the child is concerned, its father is only an assistant of its mother and sometimes an occasional playmate. The husband will take over a part of his wife's work, even in the kitchen, to relieve his wife when she is nursing the child. I have seen young husbands holding their babies awkwardly in their arms in the evening when enjoying their leisure after hard work in the daytime.

As the child grows, the father's influence over the child increases. In the case of boys, the father is the source of discipline; less so in the case of girls. The mother is more or less indulgent; when a child is mischievous the mother often will not punish him directly but threaten to tell his father. The method adopted by the father is usually beating. Very often in the evening a big storm will burst out in a house and show that a child is being beaten by a bad-tempered father. As a rule this is ended by the mediation of the mother. Sometimes, the result is a dispute between husband and wife.

Children more than six years old are usually engaged in collecting grass to feed the sheep. This job is congenial to them because it permits a free run in the wild with their companions without any interference from the elders. Girls above twelve generally stay at home with their mothers and are engaged in household work and silk reeling, keeping apart from the children's group.

It is only through a gradual process that a dependent child becomes a full member of the community and it is also by a gradual process that the old retire to a dependent position. These two processes are actually two phases of a general process, that is, the transmission of social functions

村里的孩子整天依恋着他们的母亲。只要有可能，孩子总是被抱在手里，很少用摇篮。孩子吃奶要吃到 3 岁或更长的时间。喂奶无定时。每当孩子哭闹，母亲立刻就把奶头塞到孩子的嘴里，使他安静下来。村里的妇女不到田里劳动，整天在家中忙碌。因此在平常的环境里，母子的接触几乎是不间断的。

孩子与父亲的关系稍有不同。在妻子怀孕和生孩子时，丈夫并没有什么特殊的责任。在一年之中，男人有半年以上的时间在户外劳动。他们早出晚归，父子之间的接触相对地比较少。在孩子的幼年，就孩子来说，父亲只是母亲的一个助手，偶尔还是他的玩伴。在妻子养育孩子时，丈夫会接过她的一部分工作，甚至是厨房里的工作。我曾经看到，一些年轻的丈夫，经过一天忙碌的劳动，在傍晚余暇的时候，笨拙地把孩子抱在手里。

孩子大一些以后，父亲对孩子的影响就增加了。对男孩来说，父亲或为执行家法的主要人物，对女孩子，则管得较少些。母亲对孩子总有点溺爱。当孩子淘气时，母亲往往不惩罚他而只吓唬说要告诉他的父亲。而父亲经常用敲打的办法来惩罚他。傍晚时分，常常听到一所房子里突然爆发一阵风暴，原来是一个坏脾气的父亲在打孩子。通常这阵风波往往由母亲调解而告平息。有时，也在夫妻之间引起一场争辩。

孩子过了 6 岁就参加打草、喂羊的劳动。孩子们对这种劳动很感兴趣，因为可以和同伴们在田野里随便奔跑而不受大人的任何干涉。女孩子过了 12 岁，一般都耽在家中，和母亲共同操持家务和缫丝，不再和孩子们在一起了。

只有通过这样一个过程，一个依赖别人的孩子才逐渐成为社区的一个正式成员，同样，通过这种逐渐的变化，老年人退到了一个需要依靠别人的地位。这两个过程是总的过程的两个方面，这就是社会

from one generation to the other—whereby social continuity is secured in spite of biological discontinuity. The social functions of the newcomers, owing to the limited material environment of the community, cannot be acquired without displacing the old. It is specially true in the village where material expansion is very slow. For instance, the total amount of labour required for the land, under the unchanged technique of production, is more or less constant. The introduction of a young man to the land means the displacement of an old man in the working team.

This process is gradual but nevertheless the older generation is retreating step by step. In the process, knowledge and material objects are transmitted from the old to the young, and the latter gradually takes over at the same time his obligation towards the community and the older generation. Here we find the problems of education, inheritance and filial obligation.

❺ Education

Children receive their education from their families. Boys of fourteen begin to learn the technique of agriculture from their fathers by practical instruction and participation in the farm work. They become full workers before they are twenty. Girls learn the technique of the silk industry, sewing and other household work from their mothers.

A few words may be added on the school education in the village. The public school is conducted according to general prescriptions of the Minister of Education. The total term for attendance is six years. Instruction is exclusively literary. If a child starts his school days at six, he will still have enough time to learn his main occupations, in agriculture and the silk industry, after twelve. But in the past ten years, sheep raising has become an important domestic industry. As I shall describe later, these sheep are kept in huts and their food must be collected for them (XIII). This has become the children's job. Thus the village economy comes into conflict with the school curriculum.

Furthermore, literary training has not been proved to be very useful in community life. Illiterate parents do not take school education very seriously. Without the help of the parents, primary school education is not very successful. The enrollment is more than a hundred but the actual attendance as some students told me, rarely exceeds twenty, except when the inspector visits the school. Vacations are long. My stay in the

职能逐代的继替。虽然在生物学上一代代的个体是要死亡的，但社会的连续性却由此得到了保证。由于社区的物质条件有限，老的不代谢，新生力量的社会功能就得不到发挥。农村中物质基础的扩大尤其缓慢。例如，在生产技术不改变的情况下，土地所需要的劳力总量一般来说是不变的。一个年轻人的加入便意味着生产队伍里要淘汰一个老人。

虽然这个过程是缓慢的，但老的一代在逐步隐退。在这一过程中知识和物质的东西从老的一代传递给青年一代，同时，后者便逐步承担起对社区和老一代的义务。因此，也就产生了教育、继承和子女义务等问题。

五、教育

孩子们从自己的家庭中受到教育。男孩大约从 14 岁开始，由父亲实际指导，学习农业技术，并参加农业劳动。到 20 岁时，他成为全劳力。女孩子从母亲处学习蚕丝技术、缝纫及家务劳动。

另外还要讲几句村里的学校教育。公立学校根据教育部的教学大纲进行教学。学生就学的时间为六年，是单纯的文化教育。如果孩子在六岁开始上学，在 12 岁以后还有足够的时间来学习他的主要职业技能——蚕丝业或农业劳动。但在最近的十年里，养羊开始成为一种重要的家庭副业。以后我们还要讲到这个问题。羊是饲养在羊圈里的，因此要为羊打饲草（第八章）。打草就成了孩子们的工作。因此，村子里的经济活动与学校的课程发生了矛盾。

再说，文化训练并不能显示对社区生活有所帮助。家长是文盲，不认真看待学校教育；而没有家长的帮助，小学校的教育是不易成功的。学校里注册的学生有 100 多人，但有些学生告诉我，实际上听课的人数很少，除了督学前来视察的时间外，平时上学的人很少超过 20 人。学校的假期很长。我这次在村中停留的时间比学校正式的

village covered a period longer than the official vacation, but I had had no opportunity to see the school at work. The literary knowledge of the students, so far as I could test, is surprisingly poor.

Chen, a village head, who had himself been a schoolmaster, complained to me that the new school system could not work in the village. His reasons are worth quoting here: Firstly, the school terms are not adjusted to the calendar of work in the village (IX–3). Students in the school are generally about twelve years old, and have reached the age when practical education must be started. The leisure periods in the calendar of work are two: from January to April and from July to September. But during these periods, the school is closed for the vacation. While the people are busy at the silk industry and agriculture, the school is open. Secondly, the system of education in the school is the so-called "collective" method, that is, the giving of lessons one after another without considering individual absence. Since absence is frequent, the student who has been absent cannot follow the class when he comes back. In consequence students cannot keep up their interest and this causes further absence. Thirdly, the present girl teacher does not command prestige in the village.

I cannot go into the problem in detail here but it is clear that there is a maladjustment of the present educational system to the general social condition in the village. A field study of the educational system in a district in Shantung by Mr. Liao Taichu[14] shows that the maladjustment is not limited to this village but is a general phenomenon in Chinese villages. This deserves further systematic investigation from which practical suggestions may be drawn.

❻ Marriage

The problems of inheritance and filial obligation do not arise in normal conditions until the children grow up and get married. Therefore, we can come to the problem of marriage first.

In the village, sons and daughters give their parents a free hand in arranging their marriage affairs and will obey accordingly. It is considered as improper and shameful to talk about one's own marriage. Therefore there is no such thing as courtship. The parties to this transaction are not acquainted with one another; and after the engagement is fixed, must avoid each other.

放假时间长，但我仍没有机会看到村中的学校上课。学生的文化知识，就作文的测验看，是惊人的低下。

姓陈的村长，他曾经当过村中的小学校长，向我诉说，认为这种新的学校制度在村中不能起作用。在这里，他的理由值得引述一下：第一，学期没有按照村中农事活动的日历加以调整（第九章第三节）。村中上学的学生大多数是 12 岁的孩子，他们已到了需要开始实践教育的年龄。在农事活动的日历中有两段空闲的时间，即从 1 月至 4 月及 7 月至 9 月。但在这段时间里，学校却停学放假。到了人们忙于蚕丝业或从事农作的时候，学校却开学上课了。第二，学校的教育方式是"集体"授课，即一课接着一课讲授，很少考虑个人缺席的情况。由于经常有人缺席，那些缺课的孩子再回来上课时，就跟不上班。结果，学生对学习不感兴趣，并造成了进一步的缺课。第三，现在的女教员在村中没有威信。

在这里，我不能就此问题更深入一步进行讨论，但明显的是，村中现有的教育制度与总的社会情况不相适应。廖泰初先生[14] 在山东地区对教育制度进行了实地调查。从他的材料中可以看到，不适应的情况不限于这个村子，而是中国农村中的普遍现象。应当进一步进行系统的调查以便提出更为实际的建议。

六、婚姻

关于继承问题和子女的义务问题，在通常情况下并不会提出来，要到孩子长大成人并且要结婚的时候才会提出来。因此，我们首先要提到婚姻问题。

在这个村子里，儿女将婚姻大事完全交由父母安排并且服从父母的安排。谈论自己的婚姻，被认为是不适当的和羞耻的。因此，这里不存在求婚这个说法。婚配的双方互不相识；在订婚后，还要互相避免见面。

Arrangements for marriage are made early in the child's life, usually when it is six or seven years of age. This is necessary if there is to be a large range for selection, because children of good families are usually promised very early. My informants repeatedly observed that if a girl is engaged too late, she will not be able to make a good match. But it is improper for a girl's mother to initiate a proposal. Moreover, as mentioned, the relation between mother and daughter is very strong. Marriage means the separation of a girl from her parents, and the mother is therefore usually reluctant to contemplate it. Indeed the girl cannot be retained too long in her parents' house. Under the patrilineal system, a woman has no rights of inheritance to the property of her parents. Her future, even a proper livelihood, can only be received through marriage. A third party is thus needed for making arrangements for the marriage. The villagers state that match-making is a good job, because the service is well paid.

The first step by the match-maker is to ascertain the time of birth of the girl. This is written on a red paper with eight characters defining the year, month, date, and hour of the birth. The parents will not object to anyone to whom these papers are sent by the match-maker—at least so they pretend. The match-maker carries the paper to the family of an eligible boy and lays it before the kitchen god. She then explains her mission. A boy of an ordinary family usually receives more than one such red paper at a time. Thus his parents are able to make a choice.

The next step is for the boy's mother to bring the red papers to a professional fortune-teller, who will answer questions (according to a special system of calculation based on the eight characters) as to the compatibility of the girls in question and the members of the boy's Chia. He will suggest the relative merits of each girl, tactfully leaving his client to express her real attitude, and give a decision accordingly. Even if the fortune-teller gives a judgment against his client's wishes, which are usually uncertain, the latter is not bound to take this as final. She can seek a further consultation with the same fortune-teller or with another.

A rational selection of a daughter-in-law is a very difficult matter. No girl is perfect, but everyone seeks the best. It is easy to be mistaken. If no other reason for error can be found, the selector will be blamed. The fortune-teller thus serves not only as a means of reaching a decision, but also for shifting responsibility for human error to the supernatural will.

婚姻大事，在孩子的幼年，经常在6～7岁时就已安排了。如果要在较大的范围内进行选择，这是必要的，因为好人家的孩子往往很早就定了婚。村中向我提供情况的人曾多次说到，如果女孩订婚过晚，她就不能找到好的婚配对象。但由女孩的母亲来提亲也是不合适的。而且前面讲过，母亲和女儿之间的关系是极为紧密的。结婚意味着女儿和她父母的分离，因而当母亲的总是很勉强地来办这件事。女儿留在父母的家中时间过长也是不可能的。在父系社会里，女人没有权利继承她父母的财产。她的前途，即使是一个安定的生活，也只有通过她的婚姻才能得到。因此，需要有第三者来为双方的婚姻作出安排。村里的人说作媒是一件好差使，因为媒人从中说合可以得到很好的报酬。

媒人的第一件事是弄清楚女方的生日。就是在红帖上写明女孩的八字，即诞生的年、月、日及时辰。当父母的对媒人送红帖子到哪一家男方去从来不表示反对，至少是假装不反对。媒人把红帖送到有合适男童的家庭时，把红帖供在灶神前面，然后媒人说明来意。一个普通家庭的男孩，同时会收到几张帖子，因而他的父母可以进行选择。

下一个步骤是男孩的母亲拿着红帖去找算命先生。他将根据生辰八字的一种特殊推算办法，来回答一些问题，即这个女孩的命与男孩家里人是否和谐。他要对每个女孩命中的优点加以介绍，并圆滑地让他的顾客来表示她的真实态度，并依此作出决定。即使算命先生的判断和顾客的意愿不一致，虽然顾客的愿望通常是犹豫不定的，她不一定要把算命先生的话当作最后决定。她可以找这位算命先生再商量，或者另找一位算命先生。

用理智选择儿媳妇是一件很难的事情。没有一个女孩子是完美无缺的，但每户人家都想找到最好的。因此很容易出错。如果找不到其他出错的原因，那就要归罪于挑选的人了。因此，算命先生不仅是充当作出决定的一种工具，同时，也被用作把错误的责任推卸给上天意志

If the marriage turns out to be an unhappy one, it is fate. This attitude is a very practical aid in the adjustment of husband and wife. But it must be clearly understood that the real factor in the selection is the personal preference of the boy's parents, as specially seen in cross-cousin marriage (III–8), although this is disguised under the cover of a supernatural judgment.

The chief considerations in the selection are two: physical health that insures posterity, and skill in the silk industry. These represent the two main functions that are expected from a daughter-in-law: the continuity of the family, and the economic contribution to the household.

When in the manner described a candidate has been selected, the match-maker will go to persuade the girl's parents to accept the match. The custom is first to refuse the proposal. But a diplomatic match-maker will not find very much difficulty in obtaining consent if there is no competition. Lengthy negotiation is needed to determine the marriage settlement. The negotiation between the parties involved is carried out through the third party—the match-maker—and the villagers remarked that at this period the principals behave to each other like enemies. The girl's parents will make exorbitant demands for gifts; the boy's parents will bargain; and the match-maker goes between them. The marriage gift, including money, dress, and ornaments, will be sent on three ceremonial occasions. The total amount of a proper marriage gift varies from two to four hundred dollars.[15]

It is far from correct to regard the bargaining as a kind of economic transaction. It is not a compensation to the girl's parents. All the gifts, except that offered to the girl's relatives, will be returned to the boy's Chia as the dowry, to which the girl's parents will add nearly as much as the marriage gift. How much the girl's parents will add it is difficult to estimate, but according to the rule generally accepted, they will be disgraced if they cannot match at least the marriage gift, and the girl's position in her new Chia will be an embarrassing one.

The keen bargaining, hotly carried on, has a twofold meaning. It is a psychological expression of the conflict between mother-love and patrilineal descent. As the people put it, "We cannot let them have our girls without making a fuss." On the sociological side, it is important because the marriage gifts and dowry are, in fact, the contribution of the parents on both sides to provide the material basis for the new family, and a periodic renewing of the material basis of the household for each generation.

的一个办法。如果婚姻不美满，那是命运。这个态度实际上有助于维持夫妻关系。但必须明白，真正起作用的挑选因素，首先是男孩父母的个人喜好，在表亲婚配时尤其如此（第三章第八节），但这都被假装说成为天意的决定。

挑选时主要考虑到两点：一是身体健康，能生育后代；二是养蚕缫丝的技术。这表明了对一个儿媳妇所要求的两个主要职能，即：能绵续家世，及对家中的经济有所贡献。

当一个对象被选中之后，媒人就去说服女方的父母接受订婚。按照风俗习惯，女方应当首先拒绝提亲。但只要不出现其他竞争者，一个会办事的媒人，不难使对方答应。为了作好以后的婚事安排，要进行长时间的协商，双方的协议要经过第三者即媒人来达成。村里的人说，在协商的阶段双方家长相持如同对手一般。女孩的父母提出极高的聘礼要求，男孩的父母表示要求过高，难于接受，媒人则在中间说合。聘礼包括钱、衣服、首饰等，聘礼分三次送去。聘定所花的钱，总数约在 200 至 400 元之间。[15]

如果把双方的争议看成一件经济交易是完全不正确的。财礼并不是给女孩父母的补偿。所有的聘礼，除了送给女方亲属的那部分外，这些聘礼都将作为女儿的嫁妆送还给男家，而其中还由女方父母增添了一份相当于聘礼的财物。究竟女方的父母增添多少嫁妆，是较难估计的，但按照一般能接受的规则来说，增添的财物如果抵不上聘礼，那就是丢脸的事，女儿在新的家中的地位也将是尴尬的。

尖锐而热烈的协商本身具有双重的意义。它是母爱与父系继嗣这两者之间斗争的心理反映。就像人们所说的，"我们可不能随随便便地把女孩子给人家"。从社会学方面看，它的重要性在于，这些聘礼与嫁妆事实上都是双方父母提供新家庭的物质基础，同时也是为每一家物质基础定期的更新。

The point must be made clear that from the economic point of view the marriage is disadvantageous to the girl's parents. The girl, as soon as she is mature and can assume her full share of work, is taken from her own parents, who have had all the expense of her upbringing. The marriage gifts do not belong to them, but are returned to the daughter in the form of a dowry with an addition which nominally is at least equal in amount. Since the bride will live and work at her husband's house, this means a net loss to her parents. Furthermore, when the girl is married, her parents and brothers assume a new series of obligations towards their relatives, specially to the children of their girls. In actual life, interest is taken in a child by relatives both on the father's and mother's side. But descent is unilateral, and the child has fewer obligations to its relatives on the mother's side (IV–5 and V–2). The immediate reaction on the side of the girl's parents towards their disadvantages in their girl's marriage is reflected in the whole process of arrangement and wedding ceremony and also in the high rate of female infanticide and its resulting unbalanced sexual ratio.

The wedding ceremony takes as a rule the following forms. The bridegroom goes in person to meet his bride, travelling by a special "meeting-boat" used for this purpose. He puts on a humble and self-deprecating air, and he must face a crowd of the bride's relatives whose attitude to him is usually by no means friendly. He must behave strictly according to custom, and there are experts in this who direct him. A mistake will lead to the suspension of the proceedings. Sometimes the ceremony lasts for a whole night. The culminating scene is when the bride makes a final effort at resistance and buries herself in tears before leaving her father's house. This is ended by the ritual of "throwing the bride" by her father, or, if she has no father, by her nearest male relative on her father's side, into the sedan chair. As soon as the bride enters the chair, the bridegroom's party leaves very quickly and quietly, and no music is played until they are clear of the village. The symbolic expression of antagonism on the part of the girl's relatives often causes unpleasant feelings between the newly established affinal relatives, especially if they have not a sense of humour.

The next stages of the procedure are the transporting of the bride by "the meeting-boat," the act of union, the ritual recommendation of the bride to her husband's relatives, and the worshipping of her husband's ancestors; these I cannot describe here. A big feast is prepared by the

应当明确，从经济观点来看，女儿的婚姻对女方父母是不利的。女孩一旦长成，能分担一部分劳动之后，却又被人从她的父母手中夺走，而父母为了把她抚育成人，是花了不少钱的。所收下的聘礼并不属于父母，这些聘礼要作为嫁妆陪嫁；此外，还要加上一份至少和聘礼相等的嫁妆在内。新娘婚后将要在她丈夫家里生活和劳动，这对她父母来说，是一种损失。再说女儿结婚后，她的父母和兄弟又对这门亲戚承担了一系列新的义务，特别是对女儿生的孩子将承担更多的义务。在现实生活中，不论父方还是母方的亲戚，都对孩子很上心，但由于是单系继嗣，因而孩子对他母亲方面的亲戚承担的义务较小（第四章第五节及第五章第二节）。在女方父母方面，对女儿出嫁受到的损失所作出的反应，首先表现在整个安排过程及举行婚礼方面；同时，也表现为大量溺死女婴，从而造成人口的男女性别比例失调的现象。

婚礼照例有如下的一些程序。由新郎去迎亲，乘坐一条特备的"接亲船"。他要做到很谦逊而不惹事，他要面对的是新娘家的一群亲戚，他们对他的态度通常都是装得不友好的。他的一举一动必须严格按照习惯行事，一些专门管礼仪的人在旁进行指导。发生的任何一个错误都会使整个进程停下来。有时，这种仪式要延续整整一夜。最后结束的场面是新娘作出表示拒绝的最后努力。她在离开她父母的房子之前痛哭流涕，于是由她父亲进行"抛新娘"的仪式，把新娘送进轿子。如果她没有父亲，则由父方的最近男亲来代替。一旦新娘上了船，男方的迎亲队伍马上安静地离去，乐队默默无声，直到离开村庄。女方亲属的这种象征性的对抗，往往会引起男家亲戚们不愉快的感觉，如果他们缺乏幽默感的话。

下一步的程序是用"接亲船"接新娘、两人拜堂、新娘向丈夫的亲戚见礼以及向男方的祖先祭拜等等。这些，我在这里就不详加描写了。

bridegroom's parents for their relatives and friends. This is one of the occasions for the kinship group to assemble, and the ties of relationship between them are thus reinforced. Each relative or friend offers a gift in cash, the amount of which is determined by the proximity of kinship and friendship. The expenses of the ceremony amount to two to four hundred dollars.

❼ The Daughter-in-Law in the Chia

The girl has now entered her husband's house. She finds herself among strangers, but in the most intimate relations with them. Her position is dictated by custom. At night, she sleeps with her husband and she must respond submissively to him. With him alone she can have sexual relations. By day, she shares in the housework under the supervision of her mother-in-law, who has authority over her. She must treat her father-in-law with respect but not with intimacy. She must deal tactfully with her husband's sisters and brothers or they will intrigue against her. She will undertake the cooking and at meals will take the lowest place at table—or even not appear at the table at all.

It must be remembered that in her own family, she enjoyed a rather free life, and one can then imagine what a new world she has now entered. This is her time for discipline. Occasionally, she is allowed to go back to her mother and sob for comfort, as every newly married girl will do. But as the traditional verse runs, "Spilled water cannot be gathered up"; so no one can help her. She accepts her position. This is facilitated by religious beliefs. Human marriage is believed to be held together by the old man in the moon, *yulou*, with invisible red and green threads. This knitting together is symbolically performed in the wedding ceremony. The paper inscription of the god is in evidence in every marriage ceremony. Human helplessness breeds such religious beliefs and they help to relieve the situation. At least in this case they mitigate the tendency of the bride to rebel.

The process of adjusting herself in her husband's house does not in ordinary conditions last very long. She is useful in the house especially in the silk industry, which, as will be shown later, is of great importance in domestic economy (XII–2). In the first spring after marriage, a new daughter-in-law must pass a kind of test. Her mother sends her a sheet of

新郎的父母为亲友准备了盛宴，这是亲属会集的一个场合，他们之间的联系因而也得到了加强。每门亲朋都要以现钱作贺礼，至于送多少钱，由他们之间的关系亲疏而定。举行婚礼的开支，在 200 至 400 元之间。

七、家中的儿媳妇

女孩子终于到了她丈夫的家中。她发现自己处在陌生人的中间，但这些人又属于和她有着最亲密的关系的人。她的地位是由习俗来支配的。夜间，她和丈夫睡在一起，她必须对丈夫十分恭顺。她只能和丈夫发生两性关系。白天，她在婆婆的监督下从事家务劳动，受她婆婆的管教。她必须对她的公公很尊敬但又不能亲近。她必须灵活机敏地处理她和小姑子、小叔子的关系，否则他们将同她捣乱。她要负责烧饭，而在吃饭的时候，她只能坐在饭桌的最低下的位置，甚至不上桌吃饭。

必须记住，她在娘家的时候，生活是相当自由的，因此，可以想象她进入了一个什么样的新环境。这是她要严守规矩的时候了。她偶尔也被允许回家去看望她的母亲，并向她的母亲哭诉一番以解心头之闷，差不多所有的新娘都是这样做的。但正如俗话所说："泼水难收"，没有人再能帮助她。她只能接受她的地位和处境。宗教信仰在此也起着促进的作用。人们相信，人间的姻缘是由月下老人用肉眼看不见的红线绿线牵在一起的。在结婚仪式上也象征性地用红绿绸带来表示这种结合。每一个结婚典礼中都可看到刻印在纸上的"月老"神像。人类本身无能为力的感觉，引起了这种宗教信仰，并借此减轻现实的压力。至少在这种情况下，可以缓和新娘的反抗倾向。

一般说来，新娘适应她夫家的状况并不需要很长的时间。她在家中，特别对从事蚕丝生产是很有用的。后面还要讲到，蚕丝业在家庭经济中占有很重要的地位（第七章第二节）。在结婚之后的第一个春天，新的儿媳妇必须经过这样的一种考试。新娘的母亲送给她一张

specially selected good silkworm eggs. She will raise these worms entirely by herself. If as a result she proves her skill, she will, so to speak, win the favour of her mother-in-law. This is considered an important event in the life of a girl and on it depends her position in her husband's house.

Similarly her position will be strengthened if she bears a child, especially a boy. Before the birth of the child, her husband, at least overtly, is indifferent to her. He will not mention her in conversation. Even in the house, in anyone's presence, if he shows any intimate feeling for his wife it will be considered improper and consequently will become a topic for gossiping. Husband and wife do not sit near each other and very seldom talk to each other in that situation. Rather they talk through a third party and they have no special terms for addressing one another. But when a child is born, the husband can refer to his wife as the mother of his child. Thereafter, they can converse freely and behave naturally towards each other. It is the same with other relatives. It is the child that actually admits a woman to her husband's household. The care of the child is an integrative force in the domestic circle.

There are, however, difficulties in the adjustment of relations between a bride and her new relatives. She may not take a quick liking to her husband with whom she has had no previous acquaintance. The people are prejudiced against any intimate relations of a woman with men outside wedlock. To prevent such a possibility prenuptial chastity is strictly maintained by social disapproval of any intimate association between grown-up girls and boys. Any lapse of this code on the girls' side may lead to invalidating their marriage arrangement and difficulties in making other arrangements. Adultery of married women is still more grave. Husbands, in theory, can murder the adulterers with impunity. But in practice it is seldom done. The expense of marriage prevents people even from repudiating a misbehaved daughter-in-law. Sexual intrigues are talked about without seriousness in the evening gatherings. In one case, as my informant told me, the husband indulges his wife in holding a man for economic purposes. But unfaithfulness of a wife is undoubtedly a factor for domestic conflict.

Domestic conflicts are more frequently found between the daughter-in-law and her mother-in-law. It comes to be taken more or less for granted that the mother-in-law is a potential enemy of the daughter-in-law.

特殊挑选出来的好蚕种。她完全靠自己的能力来养这批蚕。如果她养得好，显示了她的技能，就能赢得她婆婆的好感。这被认为是女孩子一生中的重要时刻，据此可以确定她在丈夫家中的地位。

同样，她如果能生一个孩子，特别是一个男孩，她的地位也可以得到提高。在生孩子之前，丈夫对她的态度是冷淡的，至少在公开场合是如此。在讲话的时候，丈夫都不会提到她。甚至在家中，只要有别人在场，她的丈夫如果表示出对她有一些亲密的感情都会被认为是不妥当的，结果会成为人们背后议论的一个话题。在这种情况下，夫妻之间坐也不挨得很近，而且彼此极少交谈。他们宁愿通过第三者来交谈，而且彼此还没有一个专门名词来称呼对方。但一旦生了孩子，当丈夫的就能称他的妻子为孩子的妈。从此之后，他们能比较自由地交谈，彼此之间也能较自然地相处。对于其他亲属来说，情况也是相同的。真正使丈夫的家接受一个妇女的，是那个孩子。对孩子的关怀是家中的一种结合力量。

然而，新娘和她的新的亲属之间的关系，要调整得好，总是有困难的。她对自己的丈夫，由于过去并不熟悉，也许不会很快就喜欢他。人们对一个妇女与婚姻之外的任何一个男性比较亲密的关系都存在着偏见。为了防止这种可能性，社会上绝不允许成年的女孩和男孩有亲密的关系，以严格保持女孩婚前的贞洁。女方的任何失检将导致原定婚约无效，并亦为其他的婚事安排带来困难。对已婚妇女的通奸，看得更为严重。从理论上说，当丈夫的可以杀死奸夫而不受惩罚，然而在实际上很少这样做。由于结婚花费很贵，人们甚至不会轻易遗弃有不轨行为的儿媳。晚上人们聚拢在一起时，也会很随便地谈到私通的事。我的情况提供者告诉我，有那么一个例子，有一个丈夫因经济上的原因纵容妻子另有一个男人。但毫无疑问的是，妻子的不忠实始终是家庭中发生争吵的一个因素。

但家庭纠纷更经常地发生在媳妇和婆婆之间。人们理所当然地认为婆婆是媳妇的潜在对手。她们之间发生摩擦是司空见惯的，

Friction between them is taken as usual and harmony as worth special praise. Anyone who has listened to gossips among the elder women, will confirm this statement. They are never tired of cursing their daughters-in-law. The potential conflict between them can be understood considering the daily life of the household. The husband and father-in-law do not spend their whole time in the house, but work outside. But the mother-in-law is always there. The daughter-in-law starts with no affection for her. When she comes into the house, she finds herself being watched by her, criticized and constantly scolded. She must obey her, otherwise she may be beaten by her husband on behalf of her mother-in-law. The mother-in-law represents authority.

Similarly from the point of view of the old woman, the daughter-in-law is not always pleasant. I have pointed out in the above section that the tie between parent and child is strong. The relation between husband and wife is in a certain sense a disturbing factor in the parent-child relation. If there is any conflict between the daughter-in-law and the mother-in-law, the husband cannot keep entirely aloof. If he takes sides with his mother, as is usually the case at the beginning of married life, the quarrel becomes one between husband and wife. If he takes side with his wife, the conflict becomes one between mother and son. I witnessed a case where the son became so furious with his mother, owing to a conflict between her and his wife, that he beat his mother. With this triangular relation in the house it is often very difficult to maintain harmony.

If the conflict becomes intolerable, the daughter-in-law may be repudiated. Repudiation is usually on the initiation of the mother-in-law even against the will of her son. If she could find any recognized ground of such action, such as adultery or sterility of the daughter-in-law, no compensation would be asked; otherwise, sixty to seventy dollars must be given to the repudiated party. The daughter-in-law has no right of redress against such action, but she may be able to persuade her husband to stand firm for her. In the latter case, a division of Chia will result.

The daughter-in-law has no right to request a divorce. The positive action open to her is desertion of the home. She may run away to the town, where she can find a job to maintain herself until a compromise becomes possible. If her husband supports his mother too firmly and there is no hope of reconciliation, she may take a more desperate course: committing suicide. According to popular belief she then becomes a spirit and is able to revenge herself; furthermore her own parents and brothers

因而关系和睦就会得到特殊的赞扬。有人如果听到老年妇女的私下议论，就会证实我的说法。那些老年的妇女总是喋喋不休地咒骂她们的儿媳。如果考虑到日常的家庭生活，婆媳之间存在的潜在冲突是可想而知的了。丈夫和公公白天不在家中，终日外出劳动，但婆婆总是在家。儿媳对婆婆本来毫无感情基础，来到这个家之后，感到自己被婆婆看管着，且经常受到批评和责骂。但她必须服从婆婆，否则，丈夫会替婆婆来打她。婆婆就代表着权力。

老年妇女都有类似的观点，认为儿媳妇总是不合意。我在前面已经指出过，父母和孩子之间的联系是紧密的。夫妻之间的关系，在一定的意义上说，是父母与儿女关系中的干扰因素。如果婆媳之间发生纠纷，当丈夫的不能完全置身事外。如果他站在母亲一边，这往往是结婚后不久发生的情况，夫妻之间将发生争吵。如果他站在妻子一边，就成为母子纠纷。我曾亲眼看到过这样一个例子，由于婆媳之间的纠纷，儿子对母亲大发雷霆以致打了母亲。家庭中的这种三角关系使家庭很难保持和睦相处。

如果纠纷闹得忍无可忍，儿媳妇就可能被休弃。休妻通常是由婆婆提出，甚至违背自己儿子的意愿。如果婆婆能为采取这种行动找到一些站得住脚的理由，如儿媳通奸、不育等，则儿媳不能要求赔偿，否则必须给离弃的女方 60 至 70 元。当儿媳的没有权利来改变这种行动，但她可能说服她的丈夫坚定地站在她一边。如果发生后一种情况，就要闹分家。

媳妇无权提出离婚。她唯一可以采取的有效行动是放弃家庭。她可以逃奔到城里去，在那里找些事干来维持生活，直到有可能和家庭慢慢达成和解。如果她丈夫坚决地支持他的母亲，以致夫妻和好无望时，她可能采取更加绝望的行动，即自杀。人们普遍都迷信她将变成鬼为自己报仇。此外，她自己的父母、兄弟将要求赔偿，

will seek redress, sometimes even destroying part of her husband's house. Therefore the mere threat of suicide is enough for practical purposes to effect a reunion. Moreover, since the mother-in-law has to face this possibility, she will usually not drive the daughter-in-law so far as to provoke the result she so much fears.

Disharmony in the Chia should not be exaggerated. In the group, cooperation is essential. It is true that the mother-in-law has a privileged position, so long as she is supported by her husband and her son, but the educational value of her discipline should also be taken into consideration. The discipline which a boy receives from his father, a girl gets from her mother-in-law. And, as the people themselves say, in the long run justice is done; for when the girl's own son takes a wife, the mother will enjoy the same privilege as her own mother-in-law. The economic value of a daughter-in-law, and the common interest in the child, make for a harmonious give and take.

❽ Cross-Cousin Marriage and *Siaosiv*

I have now briefly reviewed the parent-child relation and the husband-wife relation. I have brought out the fact that there is an apparent lack of economic reciprocity between the boy's and girl's families, and that owing to the marriages being arranged without regard for the inclinations of husband and wife, there is the possibility of domestic disharmony which may lead to the instability of the Chia. Admittedly in the long run, there is a reciprocity of economic advantage, and this is the fundamental stabilizing force in the kinship institutions; but the temporary grievances of the daughter-in-law are not favourable to the smooth working of the group. Cross-cousin marriage is one of the solutions.

In the village, two kinds of "cross-cousin" marriage can be distinguished. A girl married to the son of her father's sister is called *saonseodiu*, meaning a girl going up the hill. "Up the hill" signifies the prosperity of the family. A girl married to the son of mother's brother is called *wesienodiu,* meaning a girl going back to the native place. This is interpreted as a sign of ruin of the family. As these terms show, the people prefer the up-hill type and dislike the "reverting" type.

Let us see what is the real difference between these two types. If family A in the first generation gives a girl to family B to be the latter's

有时甚至把丈夫的房子部分拆毁。因此，仅仅是自杀的威胁，实际上已足以使人们重新言归于好。另一方面，当婆婆的由于害怕面临这种可能性，因而她通常还不敢把媳妇逼到这种地步，以免激起她自己都十分害怕的后果。

家中的不和睦也不应当加以夸张。在这群体中，基本的情况是合作的。当婆婆的有特权，这是事实，只要她得到她的丈夫和儿子的支持。但也应当考虑到她维护家规所具有的教育作用。男孩从父亲那里受到的管教，媳妇从婆婆处得到。而且正像人们所说的那样，日久天长总有公道。因为当这个女孩自己有了一个儿子并娶了妻，她自己也能享受当婆婆的特权。一个媳妇的经济价值和对小孩的共同兴趣，使家庭中得失相抵，大致上得到了和谐。

八、表亲婚姻与"小媳妇"

我已扼要地叙述了父母与子女的关系及夫妻关系，并提出了这样的事实，在男方和女方亲家之间，很明显地缺少经济的互惠关系。而且婚姻的安排很少考虑到丈夫和妻子的爱好，因而存在着家庭不和睦的可能性，它会导致家的不稳定。从长远看来，经济互惠还是存在的，它是亲属制度基本稳定力量；但在短时期内，媳妇的处境不利于这个群体的和睦相处。因此，表亲联婚成了一种解决问题的办法。

在村中可以看到有两种不同的"表亲"婚姻。一个女孩子嫁给她父亲的姊妹的儿子，叫做"上山丫头"，"上山"意味着家庭的兴旺。一个女孩子嫁给她母亲的兄弟的儿子，叫做"回乡丫头"，就是一个女孩又回到她的本地。这被认为对这家不利的。可以从这字面上表达的意思看出，人们都喜欢"上山"的一类，而不喜欢"回乡"的一类。

让我们来看看这两种类型之间有哪些真正的不同。如甲家庭在第一代将一个女孩给乙家庭，成为乙家的儿媳妇；到了第二代，又重复

daughter-in-law, and in the next generation the process is repeated, the process is an "up-hill" one. If the process is reversed in the next generation, the girl is the "reverting" type. In the first case the girl will be the daughter-in-law of her father's sister, who is from the father's Chia and still stands in an intimate relation to her father; while in the second case, the girl will be the daughter-in-law of her mother's brother's wife, who has suffered from her own mother-in-law who is the girl's mother's mother. An intimate relation of a mother towards her married daughter is usually jealously resented by her son's wife. When the girl comes under her control, she will take her as a target for revenge.

In this family situation, we can see that the psychological factor is stronger than the economic factor, because from the economic point of view the second type is much preferable for a balancing of obligations.

I could not ascertain the actual number of cases of each type of cross-cousin marriage. But my informant admitted that if there is an opportunity of a suitable match of the up-hill type, it will usually be made. In a neighbouring village, there is only one case of the "reverting" type, and that was cited as fresh evidence of its unhappy results. Furthermore, comparative materials from South China confirms the conclusion here suggested. The same type of patrilineal family system and the potential conflict between the mother-in-law and daughter-in-law is found, together with the same preference for the up-hill type of cross-cousin marriage.[16]

The economic burden of girl children has led to a high rate of female infanticide. This I have already shown in the previous section. The sex ratio which results actually makes it difficult for poorer boys to get a mate. If we take 16 as the lower age limit for marriage, we find that there are 128 marriageable men, or 25 per cent. of the total, who are still single. On the other hand there are only 29 women above 16, or 8 per cent. of the total, who are unmarried. Not a single woman above 25 is a spinster. But there are still 43 bachelors above 25.

The unbalanced sex ratio also affects the age difference between husband and wife. The average difference is as seen in 294 cases 4.9 years while the husbands are older than wives by an average of 3.65 years. We must remember that very young wives are not looked upon with favour, because they are unable to perform their share of the labour of

了这个过程，这种婚姻就叫做"上山"型。如果这个过程在第二代向相反方向发展，这女孩子的婚姻就成了"回乡"型。在第一种情况下，这女孩子成为她父亲的姊妹的儿媳，她的婆婆是从她的父亲的家中来的，和儿媳的父亲还有着亲密的关系；而在第二种情况下，一个女孩成为她母亲的兄弟的妻子的儿媳。兄弟的妻子曾在婆婆手里受过苦的。兄弟的妻子的婆婆正是女孩的母亲的母亲。当母亲的总和她出嫁的女儿之间存在着一种亲密的关系，而这种亲密的关系往往被她的儿媳所忌恨。当这个女孩子落到了她母亲的兄弟的妻子手上当儿媳，而她的婆婆正是她母亲的母亲的儿媳，她正好成了她婆婆报复的对象。

在这种家庭情况下，可以看到心理上的因素往往超过了经济上的因素。因为从经济观点来看，第二种情况更利于两家在承担义务问题上取得平衡。

我不能证实每类表亲婚姻的准确数字。但向我提供情况的人认为，如果有合适的上山型婚配机会，往往就办成了。在邻村，只有一对"回乡"型的婚姻，恰好成为被引用来作为结局不愉快的最新证据。此外，从中国南部得到的对比材料也证明了这里所提出的结论。在那里，一样存在父系家庭制度以及婆媳之间潜在冲突，同样，也存在着偏爱上山型表亲婚姻中的情况。[16]

女孩带来的经济负担导致了大量的溺女婴，这在前面的章节里已有所述。现存的两性比例的情况，使一些贫穷的男孩子难以找到对象。如果以 16 岁为结婚的最低年龄，我们发现有 128 个婚龄男子（占总数的 25%）仍是单身汉；另一方面，超过 16 岁的妇女只有 29 名（占总数的 8%）没有结婚。25 岁以上的妇女没有一个是未婚的，但村里却有 43 个 25 岁以上的单身汉。

两性比例的不平衡也影响到夫妻之间的年龄差别。在 294 例中，夫妻之间的平均年龄差别为 4.9 岁，其中，丈夫比妻子平均大 3.65 岁。应当知道，在农村里娶年龄太小的妻子并没有什么好处，因为她们

the household. There are many cases where the wife is older than the husband. Indeed in one case the wife was eleven years older than her husband.

I must add that the figures given above were confined to this village; but marriage is, in most cases, inter-village. Thus, I am assuming a similarity of conditions in other villages. Such an assumption is justified by the fact that the marriage area is identical with the industrial area, and that the silk industry in this area makes identical demands upon girls. In the town conditions are different. The sex ratio in the town is unknown. But the villagers, instead of practising infanticide often send their girls to the town as foster maids in big families as well as to special philanthropic institutions. Moreover, in the town, I found that infanticide was less practised. In consequence it is to be expected that the sex ratio will be higher than in the village. The difference in the sex ratio between town and village has led to the practice of women being supplied from the town to the village. For instance, when a maid servant in the town comes of age, her master will arrange a marriage for her with villagers. In the village, I know eleven such cases (representing 2.5 per cent. of the married women).

Late marriage is also due to the high expense of the ceremony. Though I could not discover a definite figure for such expenses, a rough estimate is about five hundred dollars (VII–7). This amount is equivalent to the total yearly family expenditure. During the past few years of depression, marriage has been entirely suspended. The depression of rural industry has fundamentally challenged the existing marriage proceedings. But since marriage cannot be postponed indefinitely, another type of marriage is found. This is the so-called *siaosiv* system: *siaosiv* meaning small daughter-in-law or more precisely the foster daughter-in-law.

The parents of the boy will take a girl as foster-child at a very early age, the future mother-in-law even feeding her at her breast, and will take care of her up to marriage. All the elaborate proceedings such as match-making, marriage gifts, the sending of the meeting-boat and sedan chair, will not be needed, if the daughter-in-law has been brought up in her husband's house. Some of the *siaosiv* even do not know their own parents. Those who have still maintained contact with their own parents, owing to early separation, will not be of special interest to them. The wedding ceremony can be curtailed to cost less than one hundred dollars.

还不能分担家务劳动。有许多例妻子的年龄大于丈夫，事实上，有一对夫妻，女的比男的大 11 岁。

我必须进一步说明，这些数字仅限于这个村子，而大部分婚姻是本村与外村之间的。因此，我假定在别的村子中也存在着相同的情况。这种假设是由以下的事实来证明的，即进行婚配的地区与从事某种家庭工业的地区是相同的，而这地区的蚕丝业对女孩子的需求也是相同的。在城市中，情况可以不同，城市中的两性比例尚不清楚。但农村中的人，常把女孩送到城里去给大家庭作养女，或把她们送到慈善机构里去，以代替溺婴。此外，我发现在城中较少溺婴。因此，可以预期在城市中女性的比例比农村中为高。由于农村和城市中两性比例的不同，导致了从城市中把妇女送到农村的现象。例如，在城里的年轻女佣，到了结婚的年龄，她的主人就为她安排一门农村的亲事。在这个村子中，我知道有 11 对（占已婚妇女的 2.5%）就属于这种情况。

晚婚也是由于婚事费用过高而造成的。虽然我还没有找到这种开支的一个肯定的数字，粗略地估计，大约需 500 元（第七章第七节）。这个数字相当于一个家庭一年的开支。由于近几年来经济萧条，村里几乎中止办婚事。农村工业的不景气从根本上向现存的婚姻程序进行了挑战。但由于成婚是不可能无限期推迟的，所以出现了另一种结婚的方式，这就是所谓的"小媳妇"制度，"小媳妇"的意思是年幼的儿媳妇，即别的地方所说的"童养媳"。

在女孩很小的时候，男孩的父母领养了她。她未来的婆婆甚至还要给她喂奶，并一直要抚养她到结婚。如果这女孩是在她丈夫家中养大的，那么婚姻的一切复杂程序如做媒、行聘、接亲船、轿子等等都不再需要了。有些"小媳妇"甚至不知道她自己的父母。而那些与自己父母还保持联系的女孩，由于早期即与父母分离，父母对她们也就没有特别的兴趣。婚事的费用，可以缩减到少于 100 元。

The relations among the members of the Chia and between the affinal relatives are greatly modified by the new institution. The girl brought up from an early age by her future mother-in-law, becomes, as I have observed in many cases, very closely attached to the latter and feels towards her just like a daughter, especially in the frequent cases where there is no real daughter. Even those who are badly treated by the future mother-in-law become used to their position and do not thus experience a crisis after marriage. Thus the conflict between the mother-in-law and the daughter-in-law is often not so acute, even if not entirely avoided. Affinal relation is very loose, and in many cases is entirely eliminated.

The number of *siaosiv* has increased during the last decade. Among the married women, 74 out of 439, or 17 per cent. had been *siaosiv* before marriage. But among the unmarried girls, there are 95 *siaosiv* against 149 non-*siaosiv*. This amounts to 39 per cent. On the average there is one *siaosiv* for each 2.7 households. This figure is very instructive. But it is too early to predict the further development of the institution. Traditional marriage is still the predominant institution, both in frequency of occurrence and in the regard of the people. The *siaosiv* system is despised, since it develops at times of economic depression and is usually practised by poorer families. Moreover, its effect in loosening ties of affinal relationship, affects the normal working of kinship organization. It is also unfavourable to the status of women and to the possibility of the young couple forming an independent family, since they lack the contribution of their parents in marriage gifts and dowry. It is significant that, according to my informants, this type of marriage had in rather similar circumstances become very popular after the Taiping Rebellion (1848—1865), which was followed by a general economic depression. But it had given way to the traditional type as soon as normal conditions had been recovered.

由于这种新的制度，家中的成员之关系和姻亲之间的关系起了很大的变化。我曾观察到，有许多从幼年起就被未来的婆婆带领大的女孩子，十分依附于她的婆婆，就像一个女儿对母亲一样。特别是，如果这家真的没有女儿，情况就更是如此。甚至那些受到未来婆婆虐待的人，逐渐习惯于自己的地位，在婚后也不至于经受不起。故婆媳之间的纠纷，即使不能完全避免却常常不是那么尖锐。姻亲关系是松散的，在许多情况下它已经消失了。

　　在最近的 10 年里，"小媳妇"的数字增加了。在已婚的 439 名妇女中，有 74 人（即 17%）在婚前是"小媳妇"。但在未婚的妇女中，"小媳妇"有 95 人，而非小媳妇有 149 人，"小媳妇"占 39%。平均起来，每 2.7 户人家就有一个"小媳妇"。这个数字是非常有意义的。但现在就来预测这种制度进一步发展的情况，为时尚早。从成婚率和人们关心的程度来看，传统的婚姻仍然是主要的制度。"小媳妇"制度是受到轻视的，因为它是在经济萧条的时候产生的，而且通常是贫困的人家才这么做。此外，它使姻亲联系松散，影响亲属结构的正常功能。它对妇女的地位、甚至对年轻夫妇建立一个独立的家庭都有不利的影响，因为他们缺少双方的父母供给的聘礼和嫁妆。有意思的是，据提供情况者说，此类型的婚姻，在太平天国运动（1851～1864 年）之后，曾在很相似的情况下流行过。太平天国运动以后接着是普遍的经济萧条。但一旦情况恢复正常，传统婚姻就取代了这种类型的婚姻。

CHAPTER IV　PROPERTY AND INHERITANCE

❶ Ownership

Before we proceed to discuss the problems of property and inheritance, it is necessary to add a section on ownership in this chapter. I will reserve the problem of land ownership to a later chapter.

Ownership is a certain relation between an object and an individual or a group of individuals. The owner can use, enjoy the benefits of, and dispose of the object under the prescription of custom and law. There are three subjects to be studied, namely: the owner, the object, and the relation between them. From the villagers, we can get a classification of property based on the nature of the owner.

(1) "No man's property." Everyone without discrimination has free access to such property—air, road, water ways, etc. But free access is qualified by the essential fact that one individual should not deprive another of its use. Take the example of water routes: everyone can use the village streams, but they are not allowed to use the route to the detriment of the villagers. The streams are closed during the night. No one can then pass unless he gets permission from the night guards. Again, even in daytime, boats are not allowed to block the passage. When a boat stops, it must be close to the bank and must leave room for others to pass.

(2) Village property. The inhabitants of the village have equal rights to use and to be benefited by such property—the water products in the surrounding lakes and streams, the grass on the public roads and on the "tomb-land." But the right of disposing of such property is in some cases in the hands of the village heads. This kind of property will be described more fully in the chapter on land tenure (XI–1).

Objects belonging to other territory groups are few. Perhaps we may mention the idol of *luiwan* which is "owned" by the group *de* (VI–3).

(3) Property of extended kinship groups. The clan in the village does

not own any common property. But among brothers, after the process of division of Chia, they may still use the same front room of the house (VII–2). The ancestral tombs do not come under property in the real sense because they cannot be used for any benefit of the descendants, but the descendants are on the contrary obliged to keep them in repair. The obligation is shared among the sibling Chia.

肆 财产与继承

一、所有权

在开始讨论财产和继承问题以前，有必要在本章加述一节所有权的问题。关于土地所有权问题，我将在以后章节中论述。

所有权是一物与个人或一组人之间的一定关系。所有者根据惯例和法律规定，可以使用、享有和处理某物。关于这一问题有下列三方面需要研究：所有者、物、所有者与物之间的关系。我们从村里的人了解到他们对财产的一种分类办法。他们是根据所有者的性质来分类的。

（1）"无专属的财产"。每个人可以无例外地自由享用此类财产——如空气、道路、航道等。但自由享用必须是在不侵犯别人享用的条件下进行。以航道或水路为例：每个人均能享用村里的河流，但不允许其在使用时做出对当地居民有害的事。夜间停止使用河流，除得到守夜人许可外，任何人不得通过。又如，即使在白天，船只不得堵塞航道，船只停留时，必须靠岸以使他人通过。

（2）村产。凡该村居民，均有同等权利享用此类财产，如：周围湖泊河流的水产品、公共道路和"坟地"上的草。但在某些情况下，此类财产的处理权在村长手中。这将在土地占有这一章（第十一章第一节）中作更详细的描述。

属于其他地域群体的物很少，也许我们可以提到刘皇的偶像，它属于"段"这个群体所有（第六章第三节）。

（3）扩大的亲属群体的财产。村里的氏族没有任何共同的财产。但兄弟之间分家后，仍然可共用一间堂屋（第七章第二节）。祖坟不列入真正的财产，因为它对子孙后代没有任何用处，相反，后代有修缮祖坟的义务。同一祖宗的各家均有这种义务。

(4) Chia property. This category will be the main subject of the next section.

These four categories have exhausted those about which a villager will inform you, and with them all the objects in the village can be classified accordingly. It may be surprising to note the essential omission of individual ownership. The fact is that individual ownership is always included under the name of Chia ownership. For instance, when you ask a person whether his pipe belongs to him or to his Chia, he will answer that it belongs to both. When he says the pipe belongs to his Chia he is trying to exclude members of other Chia from using it; and when he says it is his personal belonging, he is trying to indicate that his fellow members in the Chia do not use it. These two types of ownership do not seem to him mutually exclusive. Everything owned by an individual is recognized as a part of the property of his Chia. Members of a Chia are under an obligation to protect any article belonging to any particular member in the group. This does not mean that there is no discrimination in the rights over the object of the different members of the group. What it really indicates is only a title under which there is a wide range of intermediary gradations between property jointly owned by the group and individually owned by each member.

Objects may be classified again by types of use.

(1) Those used as a means of production, such as the land, the house so far as it is used for the silk industry, the hut used for raising sheep, the implement, the kitchen, etc.

(2) Those used for consumption.

> (a) Those not destroyed or exhausted after being used, such as rooms, clothes, furniture, ornaments, etc.

> (b) Those destroyed and exhausted after being used, such as food, etc.

(3) Those immaterial objects, such as purchasing power (as represented by money), credit, services, and, on the negative side, liabilities, and debts.

❷ Property of the Chia

Among the property-owning groups, the Chia is the fundamental one. It is the basic social unit of production and consumption and thus becomes the basis of the collective aspect of ownership. But, as mentioned, the collective aspect of ownership of the Chia does not entirely rule out the group. It is therefore necessary to analyse how different kinds

（4）家产。此类财产是下一节要讨论的主要题目。

村里的人告诉你的都可包括在这四类财产之中。村里全部东西也可依据这四类来分类。可能有人会惊奇地注意到，没有列出个人的所有权。实际上，个人所有权总是包括在家的所有权名义之下。譬如，你问一个人，他的烟斗是属于他的还是属于他家的，他会回答是属于这两者的。说烟斗是他家的，意思是别家的人不能用这烟斗。说烟斗是他个人的东西，指的是他家里的其他成员不用这烟斗。这两种所有形式对他来说似乎并不互相排斥。个人拥有的任何东西都被承认是他家的财产的一部分。家的成员对属于这个群体内任一个成员的任何东西都有保护的义务。但这并不意味着这个群体中的不同成员对一件物的权利没有差别。家产的所有权，实际表示的是这个群体以各种不同等级共有的财产和每个成员个人所有的财产。

物还可以按其不同的用途来分类：

（1）用作生产资料的物，如土地、养蚕缫丝用的房屋、羊栏、农具、厨房等。

（2）消费品。

（a）用后未破坏或消耗尽的，如房间、衣服、家具、装饰物等。

（b）用后被破坏或消耗的，如食物等。

（3）非物质的东西，如购买力（以钱币形式出现）、信贷、服务，以及相反方面的，如债务。

二、家产

拥有财产的群体中，家是一个基本群体。它是生产和消费的基本社会单位，因此它便成为群体所有权的基础。但如前所述，家的集体所有权的部分，对这个群体的各个成员并不完全保持同等权利，所以

of objects are owned by different members and how different types of ownerhip are diffused among them.

Land is cultivated by all or some of the male adult members of the household. Boys assist occasionally and women only in irrigation. The produce is partly stored for the consumption of the household and partly sold to pay taxes, rent, and wages and to buy other goods for consumption. The right of using the land as well as the right to a share of the produce is sometimes extended to the employees by definite contract. The right of the tax and rent collectors is limited to that of deriving benefits from the land. In the village, with exceptions, the right of using and right of disposing are generally reserved by the cultivator. He may be regarded as a full owner if he does not pay rent to anyone, but pays taxes to the government. If he has lost his legal title of his holding, he must pay rent to the title holder who will pay the taxes out of the rent. In any case the cultivators are protected by law and custom from alienation of the land and from interference by the title holders. In other words, the cultivator owns the land with an attached liability to share a part of the produce with the person who holds the title (XI–4).

The right of disposing of the land is in the hands of the head of the Chia. But in daily management—such as the determining of the crop to be sown, date of sowing, etc.—the head, especially if it is a woman, does not exercise the right but leaves the decision to persons competent in the technique. But in selling or leasing the land, no one except the head can make a decision. Indeed, in practice, his action may be compelled by other members or he may act on their advice, but the responsibility is his own. In the ownership of land, we can see how the right of use, the right of enjoying the benefit and the right of disposal have been diffused among the members of the group.

The house is used for the silk industry, for threshing rice, for cooking, and for other productive work. It is also used for shelter, for sleeping and for comfort. These different functions derive from quite different types of ownership. In case of silk raising, much space is needed specially during the last two weeks of the raising period. In that period, all the rooms except the kitchen may be used for sheltering silkworms. All the members of the household will crowd in one bedroom. The individual allotment of bedrooms disappears temporarily. In threshing rice, the central hall is used in common and even sometimes shared with the newly divided siblings. The kitchen is chiefly used by women. But the food prepared is shared by all members of the household, except occasionally for special members.

必须分析不同种类的物如何为不同的成员所拥有。同时也需要分析不同类型的所有权是如何在各成员之间分配的。

土地是由农户全体成年男子或一些成年男子耕种的。男孩有时帮助耕种，女人只帮着灌溉。产品部分被贮存起来供一家人消费之用，部分出售，以纳税、交租和支付工资，并买回其他消费物品。土地使用权和产品享用权有时通过契约扩大到雇工。收税和收租人的权利只限于从土地取得的利益的范围。在村里，除了例外，耕种者一般保留使用和处理土地的权利。如果他不付给任何人地租而向政府纳税，他可被认为是一个完全的所有者。如果他失去了法定的土地所有权，他必须对持所有权者交地租，持所有权者用所收地租的一部分向政府纳税，在任何情况下，耕种者受法律和惯例的保护，使其不离开土地，不受持所有权者的干扰。换句话说，耕种者拥有土地但有一个附带的条件，即与持所有权者分享部分产品（第十一章第四节）。

处理土地的权利掌握在家长手中。但在日常管理中，例如决定播种的作物、播种日期等，家长，特别若是女人的话，不行使权利，而把决定留给一个技术熟练的人来作。但出售或出租土地的事，除家长外，没有别人能作决定。实际上他的行动可能受其他成员所驱使或者是根据其他成员的建议来作出决定，但责任由他自己来负。在土地所有权这一问题上，我们可以看到，土地的使用权、处理权和利益的享用权是如何在这一群体的各个成员中分布的。

房屋用于蚕丝工业、打谷、烹饪及其他生产性工作。房屋也是用作庇护、睡觉和休息的场所。这些不同的功能来自相当不同类型的所有权。养蚕时期，特别是最后两周需要很大的地方。在这一时期，除去厨房外，所有房间都可能用来养蚕。全家人都挤在一间卧室里，个人就暂时没有各自的房间。打谷时，中间的房屋公用，有时还需与新分家的兄弟合用。厨房主要是妇女用的场所，但做得的食品全体成员共同享用，偶尔有为特殊成员供食的情况。

Individual ownership, as meaning the exclusive use of certain objects by certain individuals, is found mostly in goods for consumption. It is clear that those goods which will be exhausted after use are necessarily owned by individuals. But those articles that can be repeatedly used may be shared by several persons successively. The clothes are shared among brothers or among sisters, and between parents and children in different periods, but during certain periods they are used more or less exclusively by one person. Valuable ornaments are exclusive to individual members. They belong mostly to women and are a part of the dowry. Dowry is considered as the "private" property of the woman and shared with her husband and children. It is the family property within the Chia. But at a financial crisis, the family property may be mortgaged for common relief of the Chia. In this case, the willingness of the woman must be secured. Selling a wife's ornaments without her consent will cause domestic disputes.

The room allotted for individual use is more or less exclusive to the family group. The furniture is partly supplied by the wife's parents. The door can be locked by the daughter-in-law although this is not considered as very polite to the mother-in-law. The keys to the boxes and drawers in the room are kept by the daughter-in-law which marks the exclusiveness of family property in the Chia.

The private use of the bedroom by the family does not undermine the final right of disposal of the house to the head of the Chia. The junior members cannot sell or exchange their rooms with anyone. As in the case of land, the head of the Chia has the final decision in any transaction concerning immovable property. It is also true for the produce of the land and the industry. Raw silk may be sold by the woman. If she is not the head, she must hand the money to the head. In this sense, the head of the Chia possesses a superior right to the property over that of anyone in the group. The rights over immaterial goods, which includes money as purchasing power, are more complicated. The main source of income derived from rice, silk, and sheep, is controlled by the head. Thus money is largely in his hand. It is he who determines the buying of implements and fertilizer, or the acquisition of new land or a new house. Theoretically, according to the ideal system, other members, whenever they get money from other sources, must hand it to the head; and when they need things must ask the head to buy them. It is a very centralized economy. But in practice the earner usually reserves the whole or a part of his or her earnings.

个人所有权，意即某些人专用某些物的权利，绝大多数是消费物品。虽然，那些用后耗尽的物品必需归个人所有。但那些能够重复使用的物件，可由几个人先后连续共用。兄弟之间和姊妹之间、双亲和孩子之间在不同时期可共用衣物，但在一定时期内，或多或少是一个人专用的。贵重的首饰等归个别成员所有，多半属于妇女，而且是嫁妆的一部分。嫁妆被认为是妇女的"私房"，但可与丈夫和儿女共享。它也是这个家的家产，遇到必要时，可以抵押出去来接济家里的困难。但在这种情况下，必须征得妇女本人的同意。未经妻子同意便出售她的首饰往往引起家庭纠纷。

分给个人住的房间，或多或少是小家庭专用的。部分家具系由妻子的父母提供。媳妇外出可以把房门锁上，虽然，一般认为这样做对婆婆是不很礼貌的。房内箱子和抽屉的钥匙由媳妇保管，这是家中的成员专有权的象征。

小家庭私用的卧室并不损害家长对房屋的最终处理权。幼辈成员不能出售或与任何人交换住房。和土地的情况一样，家长对不动产的处理有最后决定权。对土地和副业的产品也是如此。妇女可以出售生丝，如果她不是家长，她必须把钱交给家长。在这个意义上，家长对财产具有较大的权利，超过这个群体中的任何一员。对非物质的物品的权利，包括作为购买力的钱，更为复杂。种稻、养蚕、养羊是主要收入来源，由家长控制。钱主要在他手中。只有家长才能决定购买农具、肥料，添置新的土地或房屋。从理论上说，这个制度的理想做法是：每当其他成员从其他来源得到收入时，必须把钱交给家长，他们需要什么时，要求家长去买。这是一种非常集权的经济。但实际上，挣钱的人通常保留他或她的全部或部分收入。例如，在工厂做工的女孩

For instance, a girl who works in the factory usually gives her wage not to her father but to her mother to save for her own future use. A daughter-in-law will consider her wage as her own. If a daughter-in-law does not earn money directly, she will ask for more than the real cost of the daily commodities and save the surplus. In this way, she gets a little saving of her own which is called *sivon*, her "private room." It is kept in secret but always watched closely by her mother-in-law and consequently becomes a source of conflict.

The daily expenditure of the household is paid from the common source. But individual members may have a sum each month as their pocket money for free disposal. The main items such as taxes, wages, food, clothes, and other services are controlled by the head. Permission is necessary before any individual member can execute any transactions of these kinds. They are not allowed to secure loans. If a son, a bad one indeed in the eyes of the villagers, is in debt to somebody secretly, his father may refuse to repay as long as he is living. The son can only pay back the loan when he gets a share in inheritance. Therefore the interest is usually very high.

From his economic position, the head of the Chia derives the actual authority in the group. The right over objects enjoyed by a person who is not the head of a Chia is limited and incomplete.

❸ Transmission of Property

Inheritance in its wide sense is the entire process of transmission of property according to kinship affiliation. But it is limited in legal usage to referring the claim of an heir to the property of his deceased progenitor.[17] As studied by anthropologists, the problem is usually that of the disposal of the property of a deceased person.[18]

But to limit the study in this way is to leave out various facts, such as the transmission of property during the parents' lifetime and the economic obligation of the descendants towards their deceased ancestors.

Ownership is a composite concept of various rights over an object. The process of transmission usually takes place bit by bit. It is not completed even when the progenitor is dead. The fear of displeasing the spirits of the ancestors or the ethical consideration of filial piety indicate the lingering influence of the dead on the free disposal of the inheritance by the heir. Therefore for the present analysis, I shall use the term inheritance in its wider sense.

通常不把她的工资交给父亲而是交给她母亲保存，以备她将来之用。儿媳妇认为工资是她自己的钱。如果一个媳妇不直接挣钱，她向家长要的钱往往超过实际的开支，把多余的节省下来。这样，她自己有少量储蓄，称为"私房"，即她"私人的钱包"。这是媳妇秘密保存的，但总是受到婆婆严密的监视，因而往往成为冲突的缘由。

家庭的日常费用由公共财源开支。但每个人每月有一些零用钱可以自由处理。主要的项目如税金、工资、食物、衣服和其他开销由家长控制。个人在办理这类事务之前应先得到家长允许。除家长外，个人不准借贷。如果一个儿子秘密欠了某人的债，在邻居们看来就是个坏人，他父亲只要活着就可以拒付这笔债款，儿子只有在得到一份遗产后才能还债。因此，这样的贷款利息通常是很高的。

从经济地位来说，家长在这个群体中确实是有权威的。不是家长的人对物的享有权既有限也不完整。

三、财产的传递

广义地说，继承是根据亲属关系传递财产的整个过程。但它在法律上的用法限于指取得对已故祖先的财产的权利。[17] 在人类学中，通常是指一个已故者的财产处理问题。[18]

但如果把研究限制在这样一个范围内，势必把其他各种事实遗漏，例如父母活着时的财产传递、后代接受已故祖先的经济义务等。所有权是对物的各种权利的一个混合概念。传递的过程通常是一点一点进行的，甚至在祖先死后，还未必完成。惧怕惹恼祖先鬼魂的心理，或是子孙孝顺的伦理思想，都表明了死者对继承人自由处理遗产的缠绵不息的影响。因此为分析当前的问题，我将从广义方面来使用"继承"这个术语。

A child is born into the world without possessing anything. Owing to his physical incapacity to acquire objects the infant is solely dependent upon others' provision. It is the function of the family to bring up a dependent infant to become a full member of the community. The parental obligation towards the child is the basis for the universal principle of transmission of property according to the kinship affiliation.

The relation between a child and the objects that satisfy his need is through his parents. At the beginning, he cannot use anything without the consent of his parents. For instance, the basic need of nutrition is dependent on the consent of his mother. Indeed, this consent is to a certain extent guaranteed by human sentiment and social rules, but even this is not always secured. In case the child is not welcomed to the house, he may be killed by the refusal of milk. As he grows up, the objects allotted for his use increase. But he has no free access to those things. The clothes he wears are put on him or taken off according to the will of his mother. Food is put before him. He cannot take things without the permission of his mother. The gifts given by his relatives are kept by his mother. The control of the elders over the child in his relation with objects is mainly for the welfare of the child and for preventing damage to the object by the child's unskilful use. Therefore when the child knows how to take care of itself and learns the proper use of objects the control diminishes. As technical knowledge increases and he participates in productive work, the child gradually acquires the right of use over objects that belong to the Chia. But there are very few objects exclusively and freely used by him. The type and amount of goods he consumes are also always under the control of his elders.

An important step in the process of transmission of property takes place at marriage. In the marriage, the parents of both bride and bridegroom contribute to the new couple, in terms of marriage gifts and dowry, a set of objects, consisting of personal belongings, as a nucleus of family property. The new couple now have a room, more or less, for themselves. But from the point of view of the bride, she has at the same time lost at least a considerable amount of her right over the objects in her own parents' house. When she goes back after marriage, she is a guest, the more so if her parents are dead and the house is owned by her brother. She is admitted into her husband's house. But she cannot behave there freely as in her own parents' house. Her right to use objects is in practice very limited. She has no share in the personal objects of other members in the Chia except those of her husband. It is she who starts the disintegrative tendency in the collective economy of the Chia.

一个婴儿，一无所有、赤身裸体地来到这个世界。由于他的身体还不具备获得物体的能力，因此他全靠他人的供养。家庭的作用就是把一个没有独立生活能力的婴儿抚育成为社会中的一名完全的成员。父母对孩子的义务是根据亲属关系确定财产传递的一般原则的基础。

孩子通过父母同各种东西发生接触，从而满足其需要。最初时，未征得父母的同意，他不能使用任何东西。例如，对营养的基本需要依靠母亲的供应。当然，这种供应在一定程度上是受到人类感情和社会规则的保证的，但即使这一点也不一定总有保障。假如这孩子不受家庭的欢迎，他可能因为不喂奶而饿死。他长大后，归他用的东西增加了，但他不能自由取用那些东西。他的衣服，穿上或脱掉都需随他母亲的意愿。放在他面前的食品，必须经他母亲许可才能吃。亲戚送给他的礼物由母亲保管。成人控制孩子同物之间的关系，主要是为了孩子的福利或为了防止孩子由于技术不熟练而用坏物品。所以当孩子懂得照顾自己并学会正确使用物品时，这种控制便减少了。孩子的技术知识增长并参加了生产劳动，就逐步获得了那些属于家的物品的使用权。但真正专门归他用的或可由他自由使用的物品极少，他所消费的物品类型和数量也总是在他长辈的监视之下。

财产传递过程中的一个重要步骤发生在结婚的时候。男女双方的父母都要以聘礼和嫁妆的名义供给新婚夫妇一套属于个人的礼物，作为家庭财产的核心。新婚夫妇现在有了一间多少是他们自己的房间。但从新娘的角度来看，她同时失去了使用自己娘家财物的一定权利。她出嫁后回娘家，便成了客人；如果父母去世，更是如此。家屋已归她兄弟所有。她住在丈夫的家中但却不能像在自己娘家那样自由自在。实际上，她对物的使用权非常有限。除去她丈夫的东西外，家中其他成员个人的东西，她无权共有。家的集体经济的分解倾向，往往是从她开始的。

The centralized system in the domestic economy, as described in the above section, reduces the independence of the young couple. The parental control is necessary for the development of a child, but the persistence of such control over him after his marriage is a different matter. A full member of the community needs a certain amount of property under his own disposal and a normal functioning of a family requires a larger material basis; but these are precluded by the centralized system of the Chia economy. The demand for economic independence of the young then becomes one of the disorganizing forces, and finally leads to the division of the group.

The process of division is one of the most important steps in the transmission of property from the parents to the child. Through the process the young acquire a legal title over a part of the property formerly belonging to the father and enjoy a more exclusive right to it.

The division between the parents and the married son usually takes place after some accident of domestic friction. The maternal uncle acts as mediator and proposes the division on behalf of the young man. He will negotiate with the old to decide the share to be allotted to the son. But the division between married brothers is automatic when their parents are dead.

Let us take an example of a Chia, consisting of a father, a mother, two sons, and a daughter. When the first son gets married and demands a division, the land will be divided into four parts. The first part is that reserved for the parents. The second share is the extra share for the first son. The rest is equally divided between the two brothers.

The share reserved for the parents will be sufficient to provide for their daily life as well as the marriage expenses of the second son and the daughter; its size will therefore depend on the number of unmarried children and the living expenses of the parents.

The eldest son receives two shares, the extra share being a small one. The size of the extra share depends on the economic contribution that he has made to the collective unit. The first son, being older, will undoubtedly have made more contributions than his younger brother. Moreover, in the view of the villagers, he has also a greater ceremonial obligation towards the dead parents.

The share for the unmarried son is nominal. He will live with his parents and has no independent status. But he can demand the share when he is married. If one of the parents dies before his marriage,

上述集权的家庭经济体系削弱了年轻夫妇的独立性。在孩子的成长过程中，父母的控制是必要的，但婚后继续进行这种控制，就是另一回事了。社会的一个完全的成员，需要一定数量属于他自己支配的财物，同时一个家庭的正常功能需要较丰富的物质基础。但这些均受到家的集权经济体系的阻碍。年轻一代对经济独立的要求便成为家这一群体的瓦解力量，最终导致分家。

分家的过程也就是父母将财产传递给下一代的最重要的步骤之一。通过这一过程，年轻一代获得了对原属其父亲的部分财产的法定权利，对这部分财产开始享有了专有权。

父母和已婚儿子分家，通常是在某一次家庭摩擦之后发生的。那时，舅父便出来当调解人，并代表年轻一代提出分家的建议。他将同老一代协商决定分给儿子的那份财产。父母去世后，已婚的兄弟之间则自动分家。

让我们以有一父、一母、两个儿子、一个女儿的一个五口之"家"为例。长子成婚后，如果要求分家，便将土地分成不一定等量的四份。第一份留给父母，第二份是额外给长子的，剩下的一份由两个儿子平分。

父母的一份将足以供给他俩日常生活及女儿出嫁、小儿子成婚所需的费用。这一份土地的大小根据二老的生活费用及未婚子女的多少而定。

长子接受两份，额外归他的那份一般比较小，其大小将根据他对这个集体单位的经济贡献而定。长子年纪大些，肯定较其弟多作些贡献。从村里邻人的眼光看来，长子对已故双亲也具有较大的礼仪上的义务。

未婚儿子的那一份是名义上的。他与父母一起生活，没有独立地位。但成婚后，他可以要求分得这一份。如父母之一在他成婚前去世，

further division will be ruled out. The younger son who has not yet separated from his parents will support the remaining parent, who will hand over most of his or her economic authority to the married son even without division. When both parents are dead, the reserved share will go to the younger son, in consideration of the support he has given them. Thus he will also in the end inherit two shares. But if the elder brother shares in the support of their parents, he will have a claim on the reserved share. The final division will not necessarily be equal.

The house is divided in several ways. If the parents are living, the eldest son will have a house outside. In the case of Chou, the junior village head, he, being the younger son, lives with his parents in the old house. His elder brother moved, after the division of Chia, to a new house not far from the old one. If the division of Chia occurs after the death of the father, the elder son will occupy the old house and the younger son moves out with the mother. To build or to find a new house is difficult. Thus in most cases the old house is simply divided into two parts; the elder takes the east part and the younger the west. (The orientation of the house is always to the south.) The front room is occupied in common.

If there is one son only, he will demand separation from his parents only in case of serious conflict. In this case it means no more than a demand for economic independence. The amount of the son's share is not important because it is only a temporary allotment. In the end all the property will be handed over to him; when the parents are old and unable to work, they will be re-incorporated into their son's Chia. The process of re-incorporation does not undermine the rights acquired by the son, but, on the contrary, conveys to him the rights to the rest of the property.

Both the land and house are unilaterally inherited. The daughter has no share in them. When she is married her parents will give her a dowry, consisting of furniture, ornaments, clothes, and sometimes a sum of money; but never land or house. Even the poorest parents furnish the coverlet of the bed for their daughter.

The son, after the process of division, has a separate house or a part of the house. He has a separate kitchen in which his wife will cook food for the family. He has a separate piece of land. The produce of the land is at his own disposal. But, in fact, his right over these allotments is still not complete. His father, as long as he is living, can strongly influence his use of the land and house. The son cannot sell them against the will of his father. He will send food to his parents in case of need. When the parents

就不再分家。尚未与父母分家的儿子供养在世的父亲或母亲。父亲或母亲甚至不通过分家的方式就将大部分经济权交给已婚的儿子。当父母都死去时，由于小儿子曾供养他们，留给父母的那份土地便留给小儿子。这样，最终他也继承两份土地。但如长子也赡养父母，他亦可对留给父母的那份土地提出要求。长子和幼子最后分得的土地数不一定相等。

房屋有几种分法。父母在世时，长子住在外面其他房屋里。例如，该村副村长周某，他是幼子，同父母一起住在老房屋内。其兄在分家后搬到离老房屋不远的新屋内。如父亲去世后才分家，长子便占住老房子，幼子同母亲一起迁往新居。由于修建或租用新房屋有困难，因此，多数情况下将老房屋分成两部分。长子住用东屋，幼子住西屋（房屋的方向总是朝南），堂屋为公用。

如仅有一子，只有在发生严重冲突的情况下他才会要求和父母分家。在此种情况下，分家仅意味着是一种经济独立的要求。儿子分得多少，无关重要，因为这只是一种暂时的分配。最终全部财产仍将传交给儿子。父母年老不能工作时，他们又将再合并到儿子的家中去。这种再合并的过程不损害儿子已获得的权利，反而是将其余的财产权传给儿子。

不论是土地或房屋均为单系继承。女儿无继承权。女儿出嫁时，父母给她一份嫁妆，包括家具、首饰、衣服，有时有一笔现钱；但从不分土地或房屋，甚至最穷的父母也得为女儿备一份被褥。

分家以后，儿子获得单独的住房或分得一部分老房屋，其中单有一间厨房，其妻便在这厨房内为这个家煮饭。他有单独另一块土地，所得产品归他个人支配。但实际上，他对这些分配所得的权利仍是不完全的，只要他父亲在世，便可以对他使用土地和房屋施加影响。儿子不得违背父亲的意愿去出售土地。父母需要食物时，他必须送往。

are old or one of them is dead, he is obliged to support them. Therefore the process of division does not completely end the economic relation between the parents and the child.

Moreover, the property divided in this way is limited to that used for production and a part of that used for consumption. Personal belongings of the parents will be reserved for them. The son usually gets a sum of money to start his new economic unit, but debts and liabilities, except his own secret loans, will be kept back until the death of the father.

The reserved part of the immovable property will be transmitted to the son when the parents are too old to work. The final transmission occurs at the death of the parents, specially of the father. A part of the personal belongings will be buried with the dead and a part will be burnt—to be used, as it is believed, by the spirits. The remainder will be divided not only between the sons but also between other relations who have served the deceased. The daughter will have a considerable share of her mother's leavings, including clothes and ornaments. This suggests, in some degree, the matrilineal inheritance; but since the daughter-in-law also has her share, the rule is not absolute. The division of these types of property is subject more or less to the personal will of the deceased or her husband (or his wife) who has the right to decide the disposal of what is left.

❹ Effects of Inheritance on Marriage and Descent

As far as the land and house are concerned, the line of inheritance goes along the line of descent. But if a man has no son, to whom will the property be transmitted? This problem appears in two circumstances: a man may be childless; or may have a daughter but no son. Let us study the first case of the man who is childless.

Childlessness due to physiological sterility is rare. If a woman is sterile, she may be repudiated and her husband will remarry. In most cases childlessness is due to the death of the child. When a man is old and without a living child, he can adopt a boy. He is free to choose his adopted son. In adopting his son, he must invite his clansmen and before them he will sign a contract with the parents or other responsible person of the child. The contract consists of two parts. On the one hand the adopting father will give a formal promise to guarantee the full status of the adopted son, especially the right of inheritance; and on the other side the person responsible for the adopted child will promise to sever his relation with the child and also guarantee in the child's name to support the adopting parents when they are old.

父母双方年老或有一方在世时，他必须负责赡养。所以分家并非就此完全结束了父母与子女之间的经济关系。

此时所分的仅限于生产用的和一部分消费用的财产。属于父母个人的财产仍然被保留着。儿子通常分得一笔钱以开始经营他那新的经济单位。至于债务，除去儿子秘密欠的债以外，仍将留到父亲去世时才解决。

父母年老，丧失劳动能力时，保留的不动产部分将传给儿子。最后的传递在父母去世时进行，特别是在父亲去世时。部分个人用品将与死者一起埋葬，另一部分火化，被认为是给死者的灵魂使用的。其余部分不仅为儿子而且将为服侍过死者的其他亲戚所分用。女儿可分得相当一部分母亲的遗物，包括衣物和首饰。在某种程度上，这意味着母系继承，但由于儿媳也往往分得一份，这个惯例便不是绝对的了。对此类财产的分配或多或少是按照死者或其丈夫（或妻子）的意愿，他们有权决定对遗物的处理。

四、继承对婚姻和继嗣的影响

就土地和房屋而言，继承是按继嗣系统进行的。但如果一个人没有儿子，财产传给谁呢？这个问题有两种情况：一个人可能没有孩子或有女儿而没有儿子。让我们先研究一下第一种情况。

因生理原因而无子女的情况极少。如果一个妇女不能生育，就会受到遗弃，丈夫将重新结婚。多数是因为孩子死亡而无子女的。一个男人上了年纪而没有活着的孩子时，可以领养一个男孩。他可以自由选择一个养子。在领养时，他必须邀请他同族的人，在他们面前与孩子的父母或孩子的其他负责人签订契约。契约分两个部分：一方面，养父正式允诺，保证养子具有正式的地位，特别是继承权；另一方面孩子的父母或负责人保证断绝他与孩子之间的关系，同时以孩子的名义担保在养父或养母年老时赡养他们。

The endorsement of the fellow-clansmen of the contract is essential, for this action is counter to their interest. If the person dies without issue, his nearest kin in the next kinship grade will automatically become his descendant and inherit his property according to custom. But in this case, the heir will not sever social relations with his own parents. The child will live with his own parents and has done no work for his benefactors. The heir has, in fact, mainly ceremonial obligations.

From the economic point of view, it is considered preferable to adopt a child who can work for the adopted parents during their lifetime than to appoint an heir among kindred. But adopting an outsider means the loss on the side of the nearest kin of a potential claim on the property. Therefore the parents of the potential heir will do their best to prevent the action. The usual result is a compromise. Either the nearest kin will support the adopting parents or the old will adopt an outsider but promise a share to the potential heir in the inheritance. The share will not be land or house but a sum of money.

If the son dies after his marriage and leaves no grandson, his parents will find a substitute for his son as the second husband of their daughter-in-law. The substitute is called *wanipon*.[19] He will change his surname to that of his wife's former husband and live in the latter's house. His child will be regarded as a descendant of the deceased. The social status of such a substitute is low because no well-to-do person will accept this position. There are two *wanipon* in this village.

Levirate is practised in the similar condition if the deceased has a brother who has not yet been engaged. There are two cases of this type in the village. Levirate is common in case of *siaosiv* when her would-be husband dies before marriage.

We must now turn to the second case: that of the man who has only a daughter but no son. If the daughter has been married before the death of her brother, she cannot contribute anything to the continuity of her father's line. But if she has not been married, her parents, knowing that there is not hope of another son, can ask the parents of their daughter's fiancé to allow their daughter to carry on their descent. In other words, they will have the right to take one of their daughter's male children as their own grandson. This type of marriage is called *lendiugoxofen*; meaning to attach two flowery flags on the ancestral shrines of both Chia. The flowery flag is a symbol of descent used in the wedding ceremony. In this village there is one case of this type.

　　同族人在契约上签字甚为重要，因为这一行动是违背他们的利益的。如果一个人死后无子女，他的近亲层中最近的亲属便自然地成了他的嗣子，并根据惯例继承他的财产。但在此种情况下，继承人不会同他自己的父母断绝社会关系。他将与自己的父母同住，不替被继承人做事。事实上，这种继承人主要只是承担礼仪上的义务。

　　从经济观点考虑，人们认为领养一个能为养父母干活的孩子，在他们生前侍候他们，比在亲属中指定一个继承人好得多。但领养一个外人意味着在最近的亲属方面失去了对财产的潜在的继承权。因此潜在的继承人的父母往往想尽一切办法来制止这一行动。通常的结果是妥协。或者最近的亲属答应赡养领养父母，或者年老的父母领养一个外人，但是允诺把一份财产传给潜在的继承人。这份财产并非土地或房屋，而是一笔金钱。

　　假如儿子成婚后死去，未留下孩子，其父母将为死去的儿子找一个替代人作为儿媳妇的后夫。此替代人被称为"黄泥膀"。[19]他将改姓其妻子前夫的姓并住在前夫的房屋内。他的孩子将被视作死者的嗣子。这个替代人的社会地位很低，富裕的人是不会接受这种位置的。村里有两个"黄泥膀"。

　　假如死者有一个未订婚的弟弟，叔嫂婚也就在同样的情况下产生。村里有两起这样的婚姻。当"小媳妇"的未婚夫在结婚前去世，在这种情况下，叔嫂婚比较普遍。

　　现在，我们必须转入第二种情况：即一个男人仅有女无子。如果女儿在弟弟死前出嫁，她对她父系的继嗣不能作出任何贡献。但如果她尚未出嫁，父母也明白不可能再有儿子，他们便可要求女儿的未婚夫的父母允许他们的女儿为他们传嗣。换句话说，他们有权利将其女儿的一个男孩作为他们自己的孙子。这类婚姻称作"两头挂花幡"，意思是在两个家的祖宗牌位上插两面花旗。在结婚仪式上，花幡是传嗣的象征。这个村子有一起这样的婚姻。

If the daughter has not yet been engaged, her parents can adopt a son-in-law. The girl's parents will send marriage gifts to the boy's parents. The wedding ceremony will take place in the girl's house and the husband will live in his wife's house with the wife's parents. In addition to the general wedding ceremony, the girl's parents will sign a contract with the boy's parents, similar to that of adoption of a son and witnessed by their clansmen. The child of their daughter will take their surname and continue their descent. There are twelve such cases in this village. This number is significant if we take into consideration that there are relatively few cases of sonless parents and that the practice of late engagement is rare. When there is still hope for the parents to get a boy themselves, they will not arrange such a marriage. But if after the marriage, they got a boy, as seen in one case, the accomplished fact will continue to be valid. It is a generally accepted institution and has been legalized in the civil code.[20]

In the above-mentioned cases, the patrilineal principle of descent is obliterated and the marriage institution is modified. It shows that the problem of inheritance and descent should be viewed as a part of the reciprocal relation between the two generations: the transmission of property on the one hand and the obligation of supporting the old on the other. The obligation of the young to support the old is maintained not by legal force alone but by human affection. Owing to the tie of affection and economic security of the old, they prefer an adopted son from outside to an appointed heir among the kindred, and modify the patrilineal principle to adopt a son-in-law. The obligation of the young does not end when the old are dead. The care of the tomb and offering sacrifice to ancestor spirits are a part of this reciprocal relation. Furthermore, the right of free disposal of inherited property is again strongly conditioned by the religous and ethical belief of ancestor worship. Thus we must study the obligation of the young towards their parents in connection with the problem of inheritance.

❺ Obligation of the Young

To begin with, in a childless family, the adults themselves will collect grass for the sheep. But when a child is born and able to work, they are relieved of this work. In rice growing, a boy will assist first in transplanting young shoots and in irrigation. As the boy grows older, he works side by side with his father and eventually undertakes more work than his father, even before he gets married. A girl will assist her mother in the

假如女儿尚未定婚，他的父母可以领养一个女婿。女孩的父母向男孩的父母送一份结婚礼物。婚礼在女孩家中举行，丈夫将住在妻子家里与岳父母一起生活。除举行婚礼外，女孩的父母还将与男孩的父母签订一项契约，与领养一个儿子的契约类似，并有同族人联署。其女儿的孩子姓他们的姓，为他们继嗣。这类婚姻本村有 12 起。如果我们考虑到无子的父母相对来说比较少，且一般定婚比较早，12 起的数目是相当可观的了。在父母还有希望获得亲生儿子时，他们是不会安排此类婚姻的。但如女儿成婚后，父母又得一子，已办成的事仍然有效。我们见到一例。这是普遍都接受的制度，而且在民法中已有法定条文。[20]

在上述情况中，父系继嗣的原则已作修改，婚姻制度有所改变。这说明，继承和继嗣的问题应被视为两代人之间相互关系的一部分，一方面是财产的传递，另一方面是赡养老人的义务。年轻一代供养老人的义务不仅靠法律的力量来维持，而且是靠人的感情来保持的。由于感情上的联系及老人经济保证的缘故，他们宁愿从外面领养一个儿子，而不愿在亲属中指定一个继承人。他们领养女婿，改变了父系原则。老人去世后，下一代的义务并未结束。照看坟墓、祭祀祖宗便是这相互关系的一部分。此外，对继承下来的财产的自由处理权又受到崇敬祖先的宗教和伦理信念的约束。因此，我们研究年轻人赡养父母的义务必须联系继承问题。

五、赡养的义务

一开始，家庭里尚未添丁时，成人自己割羊草。家里有了孩子并能工作时，成人就摆脱了这项工作。在种稻这项工作中，男孩最初可帮着插秧，进行灌溉。男孩长大后便与父亲并肩劳动，终于，甚至在成婚前已比他父亲担任更多的工作。女孩帮助母亲料理日常

daily household work and in the silk industry. When their contribution to the family exceeds their own consumption, they begin to support their parents, although their share is not apparent owing to the collective economy.

The problem of equality between parents and children in economic contribution does not arise, but it does arise between siblings. I was acquainted with one case of a man who did not work at all on the land but was supported by his brother. He prevented his younger brother from marrying in order to continue his parasitic way of living. He was severely criticized by the community. Public opinion has forced him to arrange a marriage for his younger brother which would be followed by a division of Chia, but it had not taken place before I left the village. The accepted idea is this, that since one owes a debt to one's parents in childhood and receives property from them, it is one's duty to work for them, but not for one's brother.

However, a sense of equality between parents and children is not altogether ruled out. When a young couple undertakes the greater part of the work in the household but still is without an independent status owing to the economic power being centralized in the hands of the older generation, there will be much dissatisfaction. It will eventually force the parents to relinquish their power along with their withdrawal from work.

The obligation to support becomes apparent when the son has secured his independence. If the parents have in their old age still a share of the land, and are not able to work it themselves, the son will cultivate it for them. This means in fact that the son must set apart a share of his labour for his parents. Another form common when one of the parents is dead, is that the remaining one will re-incorporate into the son's Chia and live there. The amount of support is then not fixed. If there are two sons, they may support their parent alternately. In any case, the authority of the parents is reduced in proportion to the degree of their dependence. From the point of view of types of ownership the general line of retreat of the parents is from the right to use to the right of disposal of the produce and finally to the right of disposal of the objects itself. From the point of view of types of objects, the retreat takes place from the means of production to goods for consumption and finally to immaterial privileges and liabilities. These steps of retreat correlated with the increase of obligation of the young from entire dependence to taking a co-operative rôle and finally to bearing responsibility for the whole livelihood of

家务及养蚕缫丝。当他们对家庭的贡献超出他们自己的消费时，便已开始赡养父母。虽则由于经济收入归家庭的缘故，他们供给家庭的份额并不明显。

在父母和孩子之间并不计较经济贡献上的平等问题，但在兄弟之间确有这个问题。我知道这样一个事例，有一个人根本不在地里劳动而靠他弟弟过活。为继续他的寄生生活，他甚至阻碍弟弟结婚。他受到了社会舆论的严厉批评。公众舆论迫使他为弟弟安排了婚事，并准备婚后接着分家，但在我离开村子以前，分家尚未举行。普遍接受的观念是：既然一个人在童年时代受了父母的抚育，又接受了父母的财产，为父母劳动就是他的责任，但为兄弟劳动却不是义务。

然而，父母和子女之间平等的意识并非完全被排除了。年轻夫妇如果挑起了家中的大部分劳动重担，而由于经济权力集中在老一代手里，青年仍然没有独立的地位时，他们也会产生不满。这将最终迫使父母在逐渐退出劳动的过程中，同时放弃他们的权力。

儿子有了独立地位时，赡养父母的义务就明显了。假如父母年老时仍然掌握一份土地，但已无力耕种，儿子将代他们耕种。这意味着实际上儿子必须为父母出一份劳力。另一个普遍的形式是：当父母一方去世时，活着的一方将与儿子的家进行合并，并一起居住。供养的金额并不固定。如果有两个儿子，他们可以轮流赡养。总之，随着父母年老依赖儿子的程度的增加，他们的权威便按比例地缩小。从各类型所有权的角度看，父母退却的一般规律是从使用产品的权利退到处理产品的权利，最后到处理用具的权利。从各类物体的角度看，从生产资料退却到消费物品，最后到非物质的权利和债务。这些退却的步骤与下一代义务的增加是相互关联的。下一代从完全依赖于父母到担当合作的角色，最后到挑起赡养父母的全部责任。正如前面已经提到的，

the parents. Even the death of the parents, as mentioned, does not completely eliminate the obligation of the young towards the old. The disposal of the corpse, the mourning and the periodical offering of sacrifices are a prolongation of filial obligations. Since the privileged party cannot exert direct control over these obligations, religious belief and public opinion enter more strongly into the sanctions.

A person approaching death will be attended by the members of the Chia. All the juniors will kneel beside him with the son in the closest position. Daughters are not necessarily among the group but will come promptly after their parent's death. A package of clothes will be burnt with a paper chair before the front door. Neighbours will then gather to assist the funeral business because the members of the Chia are under heavy mourning and not able to manage the business. The son, the daughter-in-law and the daughter will put on coarse hempen cloth and their heads will be tied with a long white belt down to the ground. Shorter belts and white clothes are worn by grandchildren.

On the second or third day, the corpse will be put into the coffin. The eldest son will hold the head of the deceased and the younger son the feet. On the next day, the coffin is closed and moved to the graveyard. According to the practice of the village, which is different from the town, the coffin is not buried underground, but above the ground among the mulberry trees and covered with a shelter built in bricks and tiles. If the family cannot afford a brick-and-tile shelter, a simple straw one will do. In this way, no land is made waste for the burial.[21]

It is the duty of the descendants to repair the shelter of their ancestors' coffins up to five generations. Those decaying coffins, about which no one cares any more, will be removed by a special philanthropic institution and buried somewhere else.

The spirit of the dead, it is believed, has left the corpse and has been admitted to the world of spirits. It will come back to the house at the seventeenth or eighteenth day after death. On that day, the house will be prepared to welcome the spirit. The tablet with the name of the dead will then be put into a wooden pavilion presented by the husband of the daughter and set in the front room. Heavy mourning is observed for forty-nine days. Each meal will be prepared before the pavilion and a woman will wail beside it with dirges. This is the obligation of a wife towards her husband and a daughter-in-law towards her parents-in-law. Men never take part in such wailing.

甚至到父母死亡，尚未完全解除下一代对上一代的义务。对遗体的处理、服丧和定期祭祀，都是子女义务的延续。由于受赡养和祭祀的一方对这些义务不能施加直接的影响和控制，宗教信仰和公众舆论便成了强烈的约束力。

当一个人垂死的时候，家的成员都要聚集在身旁，小辈们跪在床前，当儿子的位置最接近死者。女儿不一定在此列，但一旦父母死亡，出嫁了的女儿便得迅速赶到。在死者大门前燃烧起一包衣服和一张纸钱。邻居们纷纷到来，协助料理丧事，因为家的成员此刻都服重孝，无心办事。儿子、儿媳和女儿都身穿麻布孝服，头缠白色长带，一直拖到地面。孙儿辈则穿白衣，头系短带。

到第二天或第三天便是遗体入殓。长子捧头，幼子扶足。再下一天，盖棺，把棺材运到坟地。村里同城镇的做法不同，棺材不埋在地下，而是放在地上桑树丛中，用砖和瓦片盖起一个遮蔽棺材的小坟屋。如果这家买不起砖和瓦，则用稻草搭成坟棚。这样，不会因为埋葬而荒废土地。[21]

后代有责任修缮祖先的坟屋，一直继续负责到五代。那些腐烂的棺材没有人再管时，有专门的慈善机关将它们运走，埋葬在别处。

人们相信死者的灵魂离开尸体，进入阴间。死后第17或18天灵魂将回到家里。那天，家中应准备就绪，迎接死者的灵魂到来，女婿将奉献木龛一个，内立有死者名字的牌位，安放在堂屋里，举哀49天。每餐都准备好食品供在灵位前，并且有一妇女在旁边哀号恸哭，如诵悼歌。这是一个妻子对丈夫的义务，也是儿媳对公婆的义务。男人从不参与这种恸哭。

During the funeral ceremony, the priest who keeps the genealogy of the Chia will be invited to recite buddhist classics before the dead. His recitation is believed to have pecuniary value in the spirit world. The name of the dead is thus put into the genealogical record by the priest and will be included on the list for worshipping.

Daily sacrifices will be ended on the forty-ninth day. The tablet pavilion will be burnt at the end of two years and two months. It concludes the mourning period. The tablet is then put in the ancestral shrine.

At ordinary time, special sacrifices are offered on the birth and death days of each particular ancestor, and collective offering for all lineal ancestors five times a year as shown in the time-table of social activities (IX–3). The mode of sacrifice is that a feast is prepared for the spirits, at the conclusion of which paper money made in tin foils is burnt. This indicates directly the prolonged economic obligation of the young towards the old even after death.

The observance of these obligations by the descendants is in one sense the legal charter of descent and the claim on inheritance. The act of holding the head of the dead when the corpse is being placed into the coffin, for instance, is regarded as justifying the extra share of inheritance of the eldest son and is a determining fact in appointing an heir from the kindred. It is true that there are no two persons who stand in exactly the same kinship order with the deceased, but if the nearest kin failed to perform this act, the second one takes up his rôle and the claim of the nearest kin is forfeited. The one who observes the obligation will be the legal heir and will inherit the property.

Furthermore, at the death of an unmarried person who possesses no property of his own, the question of inheritance does not arise and therefore no descendant is appointed.

But the obligation of mourning is not unilateral. Mourning groupings are shown in the following table.

From the table, we can see that both the period and the act of mourning are not correlated with descent but to a certain extent with the actual social relations and their standardized ties of affection. Mourning is not thought to increase the welfare of the spirit but is regarded as an expression of affection. It is different from ancestor worship, which is thought to be a definite contribution to the welfare of the spirit.

　　举行丧礼期间，邀请保管家谱的和尚在死者面前念佛经。人们相信诵经对阴间有财富的价值。从此，死者的名字便由和尚记载在家谱中，列入崇祀的名册。

　　49 天后，每天的祭祀告终。两年零两个月后烧掉牌位龛，居丧便告结束。死者的牌位便放入祖祠内。

　　在平时，每一个祖宗的生日和终日都要祭供。对所有直系祖先，每年要集休祭祀 5 次，其时间见第九章第三节社会活动时间表所列。祭祀的方式是为祖先的鬼魂准备一次宴席。席后，焚烧一些锡箔做的纸钱。这直接说明了下代对上代的经济义务，甚至延长到老人去世以后。

　　后裔遵奉这些义务，在某种意义上表明了传嗣的合法权利，以及对继承权的要求。例如，遗体被放进棺材时，捧头的行动被认为是长子继承父母那份额外的土地的合法证明，也是在亲属中指定一名继承人的决定性依据。事实上，不会有两个人与死者的亲属关系是处在完全同等的位置，但如果最近的亲属未能履行这个行动，第二个人便接过这一角色，最近的亲属便丧失了继承权。奉行这个义务的，就是合法继承人，他将继承死者的遗产。

　　此外，如果死者是一个既未结婚也没有财产的人，就不发生继承的问题，因此不指定继承人。

　　但是，服丧的义务不是单系的，参加服丧的成员如下表所列。

　　从表中，我们可以看出，服丧的时间及戴孝的轻重并不与传嗣相关，而在某种程度上与实际的社会关系及他们与死者之间的标准化的感情关系相关。人们并不认为戴孝会增加鬼魂的福利，而认为是对死者的感情的表露。这同祭祀祖宗不同，人们认为祭祀是对鬼魂福利有一定的贡献，是对阴间祖先的赡养。

Relationship to the Dead	Period	Act of Mourning
Wife	Indefinitely, until the marriage of her son.	Coarse hempen skirt and shoes, white cord on the hair at the beginning then changing to white skirt and shoes; wearing no silk.
Husband Son-in-law	Indefinite, a few months.	Blue button on the hat.
Son	2 years and 60 days.	Coarse hempen shoes, changing to white, if one parent is still living again changing to blue; white button; wearing no silk for one year.
Daughter (married or unmarried)	2 years and 60 days.	Coarse hempen skirt for 49 days; white shoes changing to blue; yellow cord.
Daughter-in-law	2 years and 60 days.	Coarse hempen skirt for 35 days, rest like the daughter.
Grandchild Brother's child Sister's child Daughter's child	1 year.	Blue button for male; blue cord for female.

Elders of the deceased observe no obligatory mourning.

The immediate control over objects and persons ceases at the time of death. But the belief in the existence of spirits even after death prolongs the influence of the deceased over property. Misfortunes and sickness are sometimes, not always, explained as the warning of ancestor spirits for some action that they do not approve, such as non-observance of the periodic sacrifice, damage to the coffin shelter, selling of land or house, etc. Pure ethical consideration is strong enough to prevent the person from selling his inheritance freely. The continuity of land holding is an expression of one's filial piety. Any act against it will be criticized by the community as bad. This is of considerable importance to the problem of land tenure.

与死者的关系	时间	服丧情况
妻子	无一定限期，直到儿子结婚	粗麻裙和鞋，开始头扎白带，然后改穿白裙和鞋；不穿丝绸
丈夫 女婿	无一定限期，数个月	帽子上带蓝顶子
儿子	两年零六十天	粗麻布鞋，然后改穿白鞋，如果父母一方未去世，又改穿蓝鞋；白顶子，一年不穿丝绸
女儿（已婚或未婚）	两年零六十天	穿粗麻裙四十九天；白鞋，后改穿蓝鞋；黄头带
儿媳妇	两年零六十天	穿粗麻裙三十五天，其余如女儿
孙子 侄子 外甥 外孙	一年	男用蓝顶子 女用蓝头带

死者的长辈无服丧的义务

人断气时，对物和对人的直接控制便停止。但人们相信鬼魂的存在，这便延长了死者对财产的影响。家中的不幸、病痛有时被解释为是祖宗的鬼魂对他们所不同意的某些行动的警告，例如，不遵奉定期祭祀、遮蔽棺材的小坟屋坏了、有人出售家中的土地或房屋等。纯粹的伦理观念考虑已足以阻止一个人随意出售他所得的遗产。继续保持土地拥有是子女孝心的表现。相反的行动就会遭到社区舆论的批评，认为是不道德的。这对土地占有问题至关重要。

❻ New Legislation on Inheritance

Having described the actual process of transmission of property in the village, now we can turn to the legal provisions. In preparation of the new civil code in China which came into force in 1929, the legislators followed the fundamental policy of the Kuomintang, the National Party in China, to promote sex equality by granting an equal right of inheritance to men and women. This has made an important departure both from the old civil code and from the traditional practice as described above.

The principle of the old and the new codes on the problem of inheritance can be summarized as follows:

"Formerly, a woman had, save a simple exception, no right to inheritance according to Chinese law. For instance, suppose a Chinese died fifteen years ago, leaving his widow, a son and a daughter, the whole of the property left by the deceased was by law to be inherited by the son only. Neither the widow nor the daughter was entitled to any share. In case the deceased had no issue except the only daughter, the daughter and the widow were still entitled to nothing if the brother of the deceased had a son. The son of the deceased's brother was the legal heir to the deceased and the whole of the property was to go to him. Again, even if the deceased had no brother, or his brother had no son, yet, so long as the deceased had a male relative descending from their common male ancestor and belonging to a younger generation than that of the deceased, surviving him, that male relative had a legal claim to inherit the whole estate left by the deceased. So the daughter could have the right of inheritance only when her deceased father had neither a son, nor a nephew, nor a male relative existing at the time of his death. The widow was in no case entitled to succession.

"But now the law has been changed very greatly. Women's right of inheritance is expressly recognized in the civil code.[22] Suppose the above-mentioned man dies now, instead of fifteen years ago, his property will be equally divided between the widow, the son and the daughter. If he has no issue other than the daughter, the daughter and the widow will inherit jointly to the estate. The patrilineal nephew and the other male relatives have been deprived of the right of succession altogether." [23]

The old legal principle prescribed strict unilateral inheritance along the line of patrilineal descent. It followed the custom so long as a person had a son of his own. His daughter after marriage would live with her husband and join the economic unit of the latter. She had no obligation to support her own parents. In the mind of the people it was fair that

六、新的继承法

在描述了村中财产的实际传递过程之后，现在我们可以看一看法律条款。在制定新的民法（于 1929 年生效）的时候，立法者是按照中国国民党的基本政策给男女以同等的继承权，以便促进男女平等的。这与旧民法和以上描述的传统做法有重要的区别。

在继承问题上，新旧民法的原则可以归纳如下：

"过去，根据中国法律，一个女人，除去个别例外，是没有继承权的。例如，假定一个中国人在 15 年以前去世，留下一个寡妇、一个儿子和一个女儿，根据法律，全部遗产只能由儿子继承，寡妇和女儿一概没有权利继承。如果死者没有子嗣，只有一个女儿，而他兄弟有一个儿子，在这种情况下，女儿和寡妇仍然没有任何继承权，死者兄弟的儿子是法定继承人，一切财产均归于他。再如，即便死者没有兄弟或他的兄弟没有儿子，但只要死者有一个男性亲属活着，他是与死者同一个男性祖先的后裔，而且是属于小辈，这个男性亲属便有继承死者全部财产的法定继承权。所以，女儿只有在她的先父去世时既没有儿子、侄子也没有活着的男性亲属的情况下，才有继承权。寡妇在任何情况下不得继承。

"但是现在，法律有了很大的改变。在民法中明确地承认女子的继承权。[22] 假定上述男人现在死去，而不是 15 年以前死去，他的财产便可平均分配给寡妇、儿子和女儿。如果他没有儿子只有女儿，母女可以共同继承遗产。父系侄子和其他男性亲属一概无权继承。" [23]

旧的立法原则规定严格沿着父系传嗣单系继承。只要一个人自己有一个儿子，就沿着这种惯例进行。他的女儿，出嫁后与丈夫住在一起并参加后者的经济单位。她没有赡养娘家父母的义务。在人们的

a woman should be deprived of the right to inherit her own parents' property. But there were cases where a person had no son. According to the old law, he had no choice but to leave his property to his nearest kin. He might adopt a son or a son-in-law but the latter had no legal right of inheritance. Under these circumstances, the custom had provided compromises. It seemed to the people unreasonable to deprive one who had supported the deceased from inheriting what the latter left. But since they also recognized the potential claim of the nearest kin, as mentioned, compensation might be demanded.

The new code has altered the unilateral principle of inheritance because it is conceived as against the principle of sex equality. But how far it has altered the principle of descent is not very clear. It recognizes the daughter, even after marriage, as being as much a descendant of her parents as were her brothers (Article 967). But as a wife, she will "prefix to her surname that of the husband" (Article 1,000), and take "the domicile of her husband as her domicile" (Article 1,002), except her parent adopt a son-in-law for her. Her children will "assume the surname of the father" (Article 1,059), except there is an agreement for another arrangement, and the domicile of her child is that of the father (Article 1,060). As a descendant, she has obligations to maintain her own parents (Article 1,115). Therefore each family has the obligation to maintain relatives of both husband and wife while husband and wife have to live together.

These legal provisions when translated into actual social practice will lead to an organization based on a bilateral principle of kinship. Professor B. Malinowski has pointed out that "unilateral descent is also intimately bound up with the nature of filiation, that is, with the handing over of status, power, office and possessions, from one generation to the other. Order and simplicity in the rule of filiation are of the greatest importance for social cohesion." [24]

It would be interesting, therefore, to investigate the social consequences of this legal system. It provides an experiment for the anthropologists to study the process of change from unilateral kinship affiliation to a bilateral one. But so far as this village is concerned, I have yet found no indication of any actual change pointing in this direction, although the new law has existed for seven years.

思想里，女人没有继承娘家父母财产的权利是公平的。但在一个人没有儿子的情况下，根据旧法律，他只能把财产留给他最近的亲属，无其他选择。他可以领养一个儿子或一个女婿，但后者没有法定的继承权。在这种情况下，习俗提供了折中的办法。在人们的眼里，剥夺一直赡养父母的人的继承权是不合理的。但正如以上所述，他们既然也承认最近亲属的潜在继承权，因此允许提出补偿的要求。

新民法改变了单系继承的原则，因为这被认为是违反男女平等原则的。但对传嗣原则，究竟作了多少改变，不很清楚。它承认女儿甚至出嫁后，仍像她兄弟一样是她父母的后嗣（第 967 条）。但同时，"妻以其本姓冠以夫姓"（第 1,000 条），"妻以夫之住所为住所"（第 1,002 条），除非她父母为她招赘。她的子女将"从父姓"（第 1,059 条），除另有安排协议外，未成年之子女以其父之住所为住所（第 1,060 条）。作为后嗣，她有义务供养娘家的父母（第 1,115 条）。因此，每个家庭，夫妻必须住在一起，他们也同时有供养双方亲属的义务。

这些法律条款付诸实际社会实施时，将形成以双系亲属关系原则为基础的组织。布·马林诺夫斯基教授曾经指出："单系继嗣是与亲子关系的性质密切联系在一起的，就是与地位、权力、官职和财产从一代传给另一代有密切的关系。亲嗣规则中的单系秩序，对社会结合来说是最重要的。"[24]

所以研究这个法律制度的社会效果是有意义的。它为人类学家研究从单系亲属关系变为双系亲属关系的过程提供了一个实验的机会。但就这个村子而论，虽然新法律已颁布七年，我尚未发现有向这一方向发生任何实际变化的迹象。

CHAPTER V   KINSHIP EXTENSIONS

Kinship is the fundamental bond uniting the members of the Chia, but it does not confine itself within this group. It extends to a much wider circle and forms the principle of association of larger social groups which will be the subject-matter of this chapter.

❶ Paternal Extension

The Chia is an undivided expanded patrilineal family, because it excludes the relatives on the mother's side and also married daughters. The larger kinship group on the father's side is the group in which members have still preserved, to a certain degree, the social relations originated in the Chia after it is divided. As we have seen, when the family nucleus in the Chia increases in size, the group becomes unstable. This leads to division. But the divided units do not entirely separate from each other. Economically they become independent, in the sense that they have each a separate property and each has its own fire place. But they are still bound together by various social obligations. At the beginning, they usually live in adjacent houses and sometimes share the big front room in common. They stand very close to each other in matters of mutual help and in daily intercourse. In the second generation, children of both units share the intimacy of the relation between their parents. The intensity of daily intercourse and mutual help varies according to the kinship proximity and also to the territorial proximity of residence. If brothers after division reside in distant houses, the opportunity for mutual help is decreased, and this is still more so among siblings of the next generation.

According to accepted principle, all the patrilineal descendants and their wives that can be traced to a common ancestor within five kinship grades consider themselves as belonging to a kinship group called Tsu, and refer to each other as *tsezomenzon*, meaning "one who comes from the same door of my Tsu." But in practice this strict genealogical accounting is not important. Firstly, there is no written document of genealogy and memory of descent is not very exact. Family trees are kept by the priests, not for the purpose of recognizing living kindred but for keeping alive the memory of lineal ancestors to whom sacrifices should be offered. Siblings do not enter into the list of spirits. Spirits of ancestors farther back than five kinship grades are removed from the list to be worshipped. Secondly, if the principle were strictly observed, theoretically

伍 亲属关系的扩展

　　使得家的各个成员联系起来的基本纽带便是亲属关系。但亲属关系并不把它自己只限制在这个群体之内。它扩展到一个较广的范围，并成为较大社会群体的联系原则。

一、父系亲属关系的扩展

　　家是一个未分家的、扩大的父系亲属群体，它不包括母亲方面的亲戚和已出嫁的女儿。父系方面的较大的亲属群体是这样一个群体：即其成员在分家后，仍然在一定程度上，保持着家的原来的社会关系。我们已看到，家中的家庭核心增大时，这个群体就变得不稳定起来。这就导致分家。但已经分开的单位，相互间又不完全分离。经济上，他们变成独立了，这就是说他们各有一份财产，各有一个炉灶。但各种社会义务仍然把他们联系在一起。开始时，他们通常住在邻近的房屋里，有时共用一间大的堂屋。他们互相帮助，在日常生活中关系比较密切。在第二代，由于他们双方父母之间的关系密切，儿辈之间也亲密相处。他们之间互相帮助和日常交往的密切程度，视亲属关系的远近和居住地区的远近而异。分家后弟兄们如果住得较远，互相帮助的机会就减少，下一代的兄弟姐妹更是如此。

　　根据已接受的原则，五代以内同一祖宗的所有父系后代及其妻，属于一个亲属关系集团称为"族"，互相间称"祖宗门中"，意思是"我同族门中的人"。但实际上，这个谱系的严格计算并不重要。第一，没有文字记载的家谱，对家系的记忆并不准确。和尚记家谱是为了记得需要定期祭祀的直系祖先，而不是为了承认活着的亲戚。兄弟并不被列入祖先鬼魂的名单。五代以前的祖先不再列入祭祀的名单。第二，如果严格遵照这一原则，从理论上说，在每一代，族都要淘汰

there would be a division of Tsu for each generation. But Tsu are seldom divided for this purpose.

The actual situation is as follows: The population in the village has been stationary for a long time. The Tsu will not be subdivided if there is no increase of members. Furthermore, if there is an increase, there must also, owing to the pressure on the land, be a migration to some other place. When people move away, they will no longer take an active part in the kinship group. After one or more generations, kinship ties cease to function. That is why I have not yet found any Tsu with members permanently in other villages.

The following note given to me by a villager may be quoted here. "The average size of a Tsu is about eight Chia. This is because when my son marries, all the Tsu will come and sit at the same table. (Each table has eight seats, for one representative from each Chia; men and women gather separately at different times.) When a table is not large enough, we do not invite our distant kindred to the celebration." Of course, this statement is not an actual rule, but indicates that the acknowledgement of membership of the unit allows individual discrimination. One can exclude those distant kin in ceremonial gatherings and they will not insist on their claim to be invited. A rich Chia is able to provide two or more tables for its clansmen, and will do so with pleasure and be praised for it. In this sense, the Tsu can be taken as no more than a ceremonial group which assembles periodically at wedding and funeral occasions, taking a common feast, offering sacrifices to the common ancestors together, and contributing a small sum barely enough to cover the food. Real social obligations of mutual aid exist between smaller groups, such as brothers with newly divided households. The people do not use the term *tzezomenzon* to describe their relation but the term *disho*, or brotherhood.

Another character of this unit is that its membership is the Chia. Therefore it is not a unilateral kinship as its individual members are concerned. A married woman entering her husband's Chia automatically becomes a member of her husband's Tsu. She takes the surname of her husband although she retains her father's surname in the second place. She kneels beside her husband in the joined offering of sacrifice to the ancestors during the ceremonial occasions of her husband's kin. When she is dead, she will receive sacrifices with her husband.

She loses her membership of her father's Tsu when she is married in the sense that she will not join the offerings of sacrifice to ancestors on the father's side and will not be offered sacrifices by them after her death.

一些远亲，但实际上族很少这样做。

实际情况是这样的：长期以来村的人口一直是变动不大。如族的成员人数不增加，就不分族。如果人数增加，对土地压力增加，就必定移民到其他地方去。人离开了，就不再积极参与这个亲属群体。一代或几代以后亲属联系就停止发生作用。这就是为什么我尚未发现任何族有成员永久居住在其他村里。

下面是一个村里人告诉我的一段话："一个族的大小平均约有八家。因为我儿子结婚的时候，全族都要围着一张桌子团坐（每张桌子有八个座位，一个座位坐一个家的代表，女人和男人在不同时候分别集会）。桌子座位不够时，我们就不请远亲来参加庆祝。"当然，这段说明并不就是实际的规则，但它表明，一个单位在承认其成员的资格时允许有区别对待。在礼节性聚会时，可以排除那些远的亲戚，他们也不会坚持要求受邀请。一个富裕的家能请两桌或更多桌的族人，他们乐于这样做，也往往受到赞扬。在这个意义上说，族也可以说是一个礼仪的群体，有婚丧大事时，聚集在一起，宴会或祭祀共同的祖先，同时也送少量礼金勉强够食物的开支。互相帮助的真正的社会义务则在更小的群体内进行，例如刚分家的兄弟。此时，人们不用"祖宗门中"这个俗语，他们用"兄弟"或用"兄弟辈"这样的字眼来描写他们之间的关系。

族这个单位的另一个特征是：它的成员是家。因此，从它的个人成员来说，族并不是单系的亲属关系。一个已婚妇女到了丈夫的家，便自动成了丈夫的族的一员。她姓丈夫的姓，把她父亲的姓放在第二位。她丈夫的亲戚遇有重大礼节性场合时，她跪在丈夫旁边，共同拜祭祖先。她死后将与丈夫一起接受祭祀。

妇女出嫁后不再是她父亲那个族的成员，她不再参加对父亲一方祖先的祭祀，死后也不受父方下辈的祭祀。

The most important function of the Tsu is in the regulation of marriage. The Tsu is an exogamous unit except in case of levirate. Persons with the same surname are not barred from marriage, provided they are not of the same Tsu. It is true that the classical rule, as well as the old legal code, prohibited marriage between two persons with the same surname, but this does not apply in the village; and so far as my informants remember, has never applied. The lack of clear distinction of Tsu does not hamper their exogamous function, because most of the marriages are inter-village and the organization of Tsu rarely goes beyond the village.

❷ Maternal Extension

In the above sections, we have already seen that the child keeps close contact with his relatives on his mother's side. His maternal grandmother comes to assist his mother in childbirth. The child will visit his maternal relatives many times a year. His maternal uncle has special obligations towards him. He is the guest of honour at the ceremony held when the child reaches one month, and is the one who selects a name for the child; he escorts him when presenting him for the first time to his schoolmaster. He will present a valuable gift, ornament, or cash, when his sister's son gets married. On the child's side his maternal uncle is a protector against harsh treatment by his father. He can run to his maternal uncle in case of need. His maternal uncle will act as mediator in conflict between father and son. When property is divided between father and son or among brothers, the maternal uncle is the formal judge. When the maternal uncle dies, his sister's children will mourn for him.

The mother's sisters, especially those married to fellow villagers of the father, also, owing to local proximity, stand in very intimate relationship.

But the kinship relation does not extend beyond the group of Chia of maternal uncle or maternal aunt. Their extended kindred is excluded from the functional grouping.

Relatives on the wife's side do not come into intimate contact before a child is born. They do not participate in the wedding ceremonial of their daughter, but pay visits in the first month after it. The bridegroom goes with the bride to visit his new parents-in-law on the third day after the wedding. After those ceremonial visitings are over, they do not visit each other except the wife herself who may go back occasionally. When a child is born the wife's mother will spend a few nights with her daughter. From that time on relatives on the wife's side become maternal relatives of the child.

族的最重要的功能在于控制婚姻规则。族是外婚制单位，叔嫂婚例外。同姓、非同族的人可以结婚。古时候的规定及旧的法律规定，禁止同姓的人结婚，但这个村并非如此，至少在向我提供情况的人所能记忆的时期内，这个村子从未这样实行过。族缺少明确的界线，这一点并不妨碍外婚制的功能，因为大多数婚姻都在各村之间进行，而族的组织很少超越村的范围。

二、母系亲属关系的扩展

从上面几节，我们已看到孩子与母亲方面的亲戚保持密切的联系。母亲生孩子时，他的外婆来帮助料理。孩子一年要看望母方亲戚数次。舅舅对孩子有特殊的义务。他是孩子满月时的贵客。给孩子取名字的是他，陪伴孩子第一次上学校去见老师的也是他。外甥结婚时，舅舅要送贵重礼物，如首饰或现金。对孩子来说，父亲若对孩子管得太严厉，舅舅是孩子的保护人，需要时，孩子也可以跑到舅舅那里去。父子有矛盾时，舅舅就出来作调解人。父子之间或兄弟之间分财产时，舅舅是正式的裁判。舅舅去世时，外甥须为他服丧。

母亲的姊妹，特别是那些嫁给父亲的同村人的，由于住得较近，关系也很亲密。但母系亲戚关系不超过舅家和姨家的群体范围。舅姨家的亲属是不属于这个功能群体之内的。

妻方的亲属，在妻子生孩子之前，并没有密切的联系。他们不参加女儿的婚礼，要到婚礼后的一个月才去探望她。婚后第三天，新郎和新娘要到岳父母家去"回门"。礼节性拜访结束后，彼此不再探望，只是妻子本人偶尔回娘家探视。生孩子时，妻子的母亲便来女儿处陪伴数夜。从这时候起，妻方的亲属便成为孩子的母系亲戚。

❸ Pseudo-Adoption

Pseudo-adoption is a system by which a person is partially included in another's kinship group without the connection of procreation or marriage. The local term for this system is *govan*, meaning "passing to another house" or *gochi*, meaning attaching. It is said to be originated from the belief in the malevolent spirits who will make trouble for those children who are specially regarded by their parents (III–4). By similar reasoning, anyone who has numerous children must possess stronger resisting power against the evil spirits. Thus by "attaching" a child to such a strong person, it will be protected. On the other hand, giving the child to others, though nominally, will be enough to show the spirits that the child is disregarded by its parents.

This belief, as shown, is related to the high infantile mortality, but the institution of pseudo-adoption means more than a spiritual protection of the child's welfare. It also provides a wider social connection for the child, if we remember that those who have numerous children, whether they really possess spiritual power or not, certainly possess wealth and social influence (III–3). By creating a pseudo-kinship relation with them, the child will acquire a better economic and social position in the community. On the other hand, the person who accepts pseudo-adopted children is pleased by the belief that this is an indication of his prestige and future prosperity.

The relation will be created by a ritual act, which consists of a sacrifice to a god called "new-official-horse" (the meaning of this term is not clear to me). The adopted child will offer a present of needles, peaches and wine, symbols of long life, to his "adopting" parents, who will in turn offer him a feast and give him a new personal name, and his "adopting" father's surname (which is in fact never used) and some ornaments and cash.

The child also acquires at the same time a new set of duties and privileges. He will address his "adopting" parents by relationship terms.

In the new year, he must greet his "adopting" parents, offer regular gifts to them. He will participate in their ceremonial occasions, and mourn for them; and he will not marry their children. He in return receives "rice of new year's eve," shoes, hats, and gowns for three years (symbolizing incorporation into the "adopting" parents' household), regular gifts and other regards.

三、名义上的收养

名义上的收养就是一个人不通过生育和婚姻，部分地被接受到另一个亲属关系群体中去的制度，当地称之为"过房"，意思是"过寄到另一家去"，过寄意思是依附。据说这来源于人们相信恶毒的鬼魂对父母娇养的孩子往往要找一些麻烦（第三章第四节）。按同样的推理，多子女的人对鬼魂的抵抗能力较强。因此，把孩子"过寄"这样一个强有力的人，孩子可以得到保护。另一方面，孩子虽然是名义上过寄别人，但也足以向鬼魂表示父母对孩子的淡漠。

这种信仰与婴儿的高死亡率有关，但这种名义上收养的制度不仅仅意味着对孩子的一种精神上的保护，这也为孩子提供了一种较新的社会联系。在前面已谈到过，那些多子女的父母，无论他们是否真正具有精神上的强大力量，他们比较富裕，社会影响大，这是肯定的（第三章第三节）。通过名义上的收养与他们建立关系，孩子将在这个社区内获得较好的经济和社会地位。另一方面，名义上收养孩子的人也感到高兴，因为他相信，这表示他的声誉和未来的兴旺。

这种收养关系将通过一次仪式来建立，那就是向一个被称为"新官马"（意思不明）的神进行祭祀。被收养的孩子向过寄的父母赠送针、桃、酒等象征长寿的礼物。收养孩子的过寄父母要给孩子办筵席，并给孩子取一个新名字，姓他过寄父的姓（实际上从不用此姓），送他一些饰物和现金。

从此，孩子便有了新的责任和权利。他须按照亲属关系来称呼他的寄父母。新年的时候，他必须向寄父母拜年，送礼物。有婚丧大事时他必须参加，为他们戴孝，他不应与他们的子女结婚。寄父母则须请寄养儿子吃年夜饭，供给他三年鞋、帽和长袍（象征孩子已被接纳到寄父母的家中来）以及定期送礼物和给予其他关怀。

This type of "adoption" is metaphorical; the child does not sever its relation with its real parents. It acquires neither the right of inheritance nor the obligation of support. It nominally changes its surname but this is, as the villagers put it, only to fool the spirits. The real meaning therefore is to create a new social relation similar to kinship by metaphorical use of relationship terms and by ritual acts.

The extension of social relations facilitates social activities but is also expensive. During the economic depression, even real kinship relations are a burden, and there is a clear sign of the shrinking of kinship organization. Pseudo-adoption becomes less popular. As my informant told me, to seek protection against the evil spirits, they "attach" their children to the god or to their father's sister's husband. Thus no new relations will be created. Since girls are much less often pseudo-adopted, the special preference for a father's sister's husband to play the part may be linked up with the idea of unlucky marriage of the "reverting" type (III–8). It does not narrow down the marriage choice when girls of father's sisters are included in the exogamous unit.

❹ Kinship Basis of the Village

In pseudo-adoption, kinship terms are used in a metaphorical sense in order to establish new social relations which are similar and derived from kinship. This type of extension of the kinship relations to persons bound neither by procreation nor by marriage is very common in the village.

All the terms for relatives on the father's side, with the exceptions of those for father, mother, grandfather, and grandmother, are used for addressing fellow villagers according to their sex and age and the consanguinity and affinity to the village. The terms for mother-side relatives, with the exception of mother's parents are used for addressing the people in the village of mother's parents in similar manner. This type of usage of kinship terms serves the function of classifying local and age groups, and defines the different types of social relation towards each of them by that derived from the existing kinship relation.

There is a definite purpose in this extended use of relationship terms. To each term there has become attached certain psychological attitudes corresponding to the intimate relationships for which they were initially devised. These emotional attitudes may, by the extended

> 这种"收养"是象征性的；孩子并不离开生父、生母。他不要继承权，也没有赡养寄父母的义务。他名义上改了姓，但正像乡亲们说的，这是骗那些鬼魂的。所以真正的意义在于通过象征性的亲属关系称谓和礼仪形式来建立一种新的与亲属关系相似的社会关系。
>
> 社会关系的扩展促使社会活动增加，但也会增加开支。在经济萧条时期，甚至真正的亲属关系也成为一种负担，那时，亲属关系的组织明显缩小，名义收养也不流行了。向我提供情况的人告诉我说，为了免于受鬼魂的侵害，他们把孩子"寄"给神或"寄"给父亲的姊妹的丈夫。这样并没有建立新的关系。由于女孩很少被"寄养"，特别喜欢让父亲的姊妹的丈夫来担当这个角色很可能与不吉利的"回乡"型婚姻观念有联系（第三章第八节）。当父亲的姊妹的女儿被包括进外婚制单位中时，并没有使婚姻的选择面变窄。

四、村庄的亲属关系基础

> 在名义收养制度中，人们象征性地使用亲属关系的称谓来建立新的社会关系，这种关系来源于亲属关系并与亲属关系相类似。亲属关系的这种扩大方式在这个村里很普遍，它既与生育无关，也不与婚姻相联系。
>
> 除了父亲、母亲、祖父、祖母的称呼外，人们根据不同的性别、年龄、血统关系和姻亲关系，用父方的所有亲属称谓来称呼同村人并用母方所有的亲戚称谓——除外祖父、外祖母以外——来称呼外祖父母村子里的人们。亲属称谓的这种延伸的用法，起到了区分不同的地方和年龄组的作用，并可由现存的亲属关系派生的这种关系来说明不同类型的社会关系。
>
> 亲属称谓的延伸使用是有一定目的的。每一个称谓，当它最初被用来称呼时就包含了与亲密的亲属相应的某种心理态度。由于称谓的

use of the term, be taken up to persons not actually standing in such an intimate relationship. For instance, a person addressing his fellow senior villagers as father's brother will tend to show the same obedience and respect to them as to his father's brother. The attitude associated with the term used for the mother's brother, is different from that with the term for the father's brother. The nephew associates the idea of his maternal uncle with indulgence and friendliness. By addressing his mother's fellow villagers as mother's brother he behaves freely among that group of persons, and enjoys their treating him as a guest.

It should be noted that the extension of such emotional attitudes to persons not actually related as the terms would imply does not necessarily involve an extension of specific privileges and obligations. It does not imply a real extension of kinship relation, but it is useful in defining a person's status in the community where the old are respected and usually possess authority.

Recently the principle of distribution of authority according to age groups has been undergoing change. The old men in the village who are not able to keep up with the rapidly changing situation cannot fulfil the rôle of leaders in the community. Thus the present village head, Chou, is from the second age grade in the community. He addresses the senior grade who either work under him or are less influential in the community, by their personal names. Formerly this manner of address was possible only between a senior and his juniors. On the other hand a new term has been introduced, *sisan* (used in towns generally as the title of a teacher, or simply as a common title such as that of mister in English), by which he is addressed by the age grade senior to him. This case illustrates very clearly how sentiment is associated with the term. When the situation has changed in such a way that a person from the senior grade has become the subordinate, the original sentiment of respect is incompatible in the context. The changed social situation thus caused a psychological difficulty, and finally a change in language.

It must be pointed out that the extended use of relationship terms should not be taken as evidence of an existence of "clan village," at present or in the past, in this part of China. A study of the distribution of the surnames in the village can demonstrate that, although kinship groups tend to concentrate in compact areas, genealogical relation does not form a basis of local groups.

延伸使用，这种感情上的态度也逐渐被用来对待实际上并不处于这样一种亲属关系的人。譬如，一个人称呼他村里的年长的人时，用父亲兄弟的称谓，这就是说，他将像对待他伯伯或叔叔那样来服从或尊敬他们。与母亲的兄弟的称谓相联系的态度，与伯伯或叔叔的称谓相关的态度不同。外甥把舅舅与友好和宠爱的观念相联系。同舅舅这个称谓来称呼他母亲村里的人便意味着，他可以在这些人之中自由自在地行动，并乐于被他们待为上客。

应当注意的是延伸地用这种感情态度来对待实际上并不是属于这种亲属地位的人，并不意味着他们之间就延伸特定的权利和义务。用这种称呼，并不等于他们之间真的建立了这样的亲属关系，但这种称呼有助于说明这个社区内不同的人的地位。在这个社区内，老年人受到尊敬，而且通常是具有威信的。

近来，按年龄组分配权力的原则有所变化。村里的老年人不能适应迅速改变着的形势的需要，因而不能胜任这个社区的领导人的角色。现任村长周某，属于村里第二个年龄组。他用个人名字来称呼在他下面工作或在社区内不太有影响的老年人。过去只有年长者能用姓名称呼年轻的人。另一方面，现在已引进一个新的名称"先生"（在城镇普遍用作教师的头衔或仅如英文中的 Mister 这个普通头衔），比周年长的人也这样称呼他。这一例子很清楚地说明了感情与称谓的关系。当情况有了变化，年纪大的人变成在他下面的人，原先的尊敬的感情与整个环境不甚相符。因此，变化了的社会环境便引起心理上的别扭，最后引起语言的改口。

必须指出的是亲属称谓的延伸使用不应被当作过去或现在在中国这部分地区有"族村"存在的证据。对这个村子的姓的分布的调查可以说明，虽然亲属关系群体倾向于集中在某地区，但家族关系并没有形成地方群体的基础。

Surname	Yu I	Yu II	Yu III	Yu IV	Total
Chou	49	23	24	2	98
T'an	7	4	17	28	56
Yao	30	4	10	—	44
Hsü	13	4	9	4	30
Shen	2	4	13	7	26
Wang	1	6	—	8	15
Lü	—	14	—	—	14
Chiu	—	10	—	—	10
Chao	7	—	—	—	7
Ni	4	3	—	—	7
Jao	—	7	—	—	7
Wu	—	4	2	—	6
Chiang	8	—	—	1	5
Lu	—	—	—	5	5
Chen	4	—	—	—	4
Fang	4	—	—	—	4
Chin	—	1	3	—	4
Ch'ien	—	—	—	4	4
Yang	3	—	—	—	3
Ch'in	1	—	—	—	1
Chia	1	—	—	—	1
Liu	1	—	—	—	1
Fêng	1	—	—	—	1
Ling	1	—	—	—	1
Huang	—	1	—	—	1
Yu	—	—	1	—	1
Li	—	—	1	—	1
Ying	—	—	1	—	1
Kuo	—	—	—	1	1
TOTAL	133	94	75	57	359*

*Excluding the priest.

姓	圩I	圩II	圩III	圩IV	总计
周	49	23	24	2	98
谈	7	4	17	28	56
姚	30	4	10	—	44
徐	13	4	9	4	30
沈	2	4	13	7	26
王	1	6	—	8	15
吕	—	14	—	—	14
邱	—	10	—	—	10
赵	7	—	—	—	7
倪	4	3	—	—	7
饶	—	7	—	—	7
吴	—	4	2	—	6
蒋	4	—	—	1	5
陆	—	—	—	5	5
陈	4	—	—	—	4
方	4	—	—	—	4
金	—	1	3	—	4
钱	—	—	—	4	4
杨	3	—	—	—	3
秦	1	—	—	—	1
贾	1	—	—	—	1
刘	1	—	—	—	1
冯	1	—	—	—	1
凌	1	—	—	—	1
黄	—	1	—	—	1
于	—	—	1	—	1
李	—	—	1	—	1
殷	—	—	1	—	1
郭	—	—	—	1	1
总计	133	85	81	60	359*

* 不包括和尚。

In the patrilineal society, the surname is handed down from father to son. But it does not imply that those who have the same surname can always trace their origin to a common ancestor. For instance, Chou told me that those who have the surname Chou in this village have two entirely separate origins. Furthermore, those with a common ancestor may not be recognized socially as kindred owing to the clan organization. But one thing is clear, those who have different surnames cannot be of the same patrilineal kinship group. Thus multiplicity of surnames in the village can be taken as an indication of their multiplicity of patrilineal kinship groups.

There are twenty-nine surnames in the village. The table above shows the number of Chia of each surname in each *yu* (II–3).

From this table, it is possible to see the distribution of the Chia of the same surname. There appears a tendency of concentration of kinship related groups. For instance, Chou and Yao are concentrated in *Yu* I; Lü in *Yu* II; and T'an in *Yu* III and IV. Some of the surnames, such as Lü and Chiu can be found only in one *yu*. These facts indicate a close relation between residence and kinship relations. In other words, there is a tendency for the Chia bearing the same surname, probably bound by kinship ties, to live in an adjacent residential area. But it is also clear that the fact of numerous surnames and their dispersion indicate the multiple kinship groups and the low correlation of consanguinial and local ties.

Similar are the affinal relations. Strictly the village is neither an exogamous nor an endogamous unit. But, as mentioned, marriage is more frequently arranged among people of different villages. There is a tendency towards local exogamy although it is not formulated. Among the villages, no special preference is made of one as against another. Therefore, affinal relation does not preserve a strong tie among the people of the same village or among the villages.

在父系社会中，姓是由父亲传给儿子的。但这并不是说，同姓的人都可溯源到同一个祖宗。例如，周某告诉我，该村姓周的人属于两个完全不同的血统。此外，有同一个祖宗的那些人，社会上不一定承认他们是宗族关系。但有一件事是明确的，不同姓的人，不可能属于同一父系的亲属群体。所以可以认为，一个村子里的居民有许多不同的姓，说明了这个村里有许多不同的父系亲属群体。

这个村共有 29 个姓，上表说明了在每个圩里（第二章第三节）每一姓的家数。同姓的家的分布情况如上表所示。

从此表可以看出同姓的家的分布情况。亲属群体有集中的倾向。例如周姓和姚姓集中在圩 I；吕姓在圩 II；谈姓在圩 III 和 IV；某些姓，如吕和邱，只分布在一个圩里。这些事实表明居住地亲属关系之间的密切联系。换句话说，有这样一种趋势，同姓的家，可能因亲属关系联系在一起并住在一个邻近的居住地区。但这个村子里的姓很多而且同姓住得也分散，这个事实也清楚地说明，村里有许多亲属群体，而亲族联系和地方联系的相互关系不大。

姻亲关系的情况也相同。严格地说，这个村既不是外婚制也不是内婚制的单位。但正如已经提到过的，不同村的人互相通婚更为经常。虽然并没有明确提出，但是有地方性外婚的趋向。各村之间，在婚姻关系上并没有特殊的偏向，因而，姻亲关系并没有在同村人之中或在各个村庄之间保持密切的纽带关系。

CHAPTER VI   THE HOUSEHOLD AND VILLAGE

Beside kinship bonds, another fundamental social tie is that of territorial bonds. Those who live near each other find it easy to co-operate in matters of common interest demanding concerted action. In this chapter, we shall review various territorial groups.

❶ Household

The Chia, held together by kinship ties, is not necessarily an efficient working unit in economic life. Members of a Chia may be temporarily absent or removed by death. The introduction of new working members, through kinship ties such as birth, marriage and adoption, is not always easy to effect and sometimes is not advisable owing to questions of inheritance. On the other hand, members of a Chia, which has broken up may wish to be temporarily in-corporated into another working unit without assuming new kinship relations. Therefore, those who live in the same house and participate in most of the economic pursuits may not be necessarily considered as members of Chia.[25] Here we may use the term household to refer to this basic territorial group.

In the village I found that in twenty-eight cases individuals have been introduced into the economic unit, living, eating, and working as members of the household but clearly distinguished from the members of the Chia. They were not connected with the Chia by the necessary kinship ties and did not permanently pool their property without discrimination into the Chia but usually joined the unit upon definite terms. The relation of such members to the group varies from that of a long-term guest to having practically no distinction from the members of the Chia except over the legal rights of property.

There are three ways in which non-Chia members may be introduced into a household. The member may be a guest of a certain family and have made a definite annual or monthly payment over a rather long period of residence. For instance, a medical doctor practising in the village had lived in the house of the owner of the medicine store for many years. He had a separate room and shared the daily life with his hosts. Another case was that of a child whose own family lived in another village, but who was brought up and nursed in a house in the village. The parents of the child made contributions each month to the family nursing it. There were five

陆 户与村

除了亲属关系的联结，另外一个基本的社会纽带就是地域性的纽带。居住在邻近的人们感到他们有共同利益并需要协同行动，因而组成各种地域性的群体。在这一章里，将加以分析。

一、户

家是由亲属纽带结合在一起的，在经济生活中，它并不必定是一个有效的劳动单位。家中的成员有时会暂时离去，有时死亡。在家中要吸收新的劳动成员，通过亲属关系，如生养、结婚、收养等办法，有时不易做到，有时则因涉及继承等问题而不宜进行。在另一方面，有些人的家破裂了，可能希望暂时参加另一劳动单位，但并不希望承认新的亲属关系。因此，那些住在一起、参加部分共同经济活动的人，不一定被看作是家的成员。[25] 我们在这里采用了"户"这个名词，来指这种基本的地域性群体。

在这个村子里，我发现 28 起个人被吸收到另外的经济单位中的情况。作为户的一员，一起居住、吃饭和劳动，但他们和家的成员有着明显的区别。他们和这家人并不存在一定的亲属纽带关系，并不把自己的财产永久地投入这一家中。通常情况是，他们在一定条件下参加这个单位。这种成员和这家的关系大有差别，有些是长期的客人，有些是除了没有财产的法定权利外，其他都和家里人是一样的。

非家成员进入一户，通常采取三种办法。其一，这个成员可能是这家庭的客人，他在一个较长时期内住在这里，按月或按年付一笔钱。例如，有一个医生在村中开业，他就在药店老板的家中住了多年。他单独有一间房，并和他的房东共同生活。另一例是一个小孩，他自己的家住在另一个村子里，但他是这个村的一家人抚养大的。这个孩子的父母每个月付给抚养孩子的家庭一笔钱。还有五例，他们都

cases of persons related to their hosts by affinity. After the breaking up of their own Chia, they join their relatives on the mother's side. They could not be in-corporated into the Chia but would remain as guests, although practically they lived in the house just as members of the Chia.

The institution of apprenticeship also provides a way of introducing a working member from outside. There were four cases of this kind. An apprentice is provided with food and shelter by the master without tuition and in return is bound to work for his master for a certain period of years without wages, except in the last year when he can demand a small amount for "renewing his shoes and stockings."

The commonest way, however, is through employment. A person may be introduced into a household as an employee under a definite contract to work on the farm or at the silk industry. The employee receives accommodation in his employer's house. He participates in the household work, is entitled to use all the implements, and is provided with food and shelter. He has also a fixed amount of wage each year.

These are all the cases in the village in which members who do not belong to the Chia were introduced into the household.

The members of a Chia may not live in the house but pursue their work in distant places. Their temporary absence from the house does not affect their kinship affiliation. But during their absence, they cannot be considered as a member of the household, although they have definite economic relations with it.

In the village the total number of individuals not living in the house of their own family was fifty-four. Of these thirty-two are females and eighteen males; they were at work in the town except four boys who lived in their master's houses in the village bound as apprentices. These numbers indicate the relatively strong movement of the population towards the town, especially among females.

❷ Neighbourhood

A number of Chia combined together to form larger territorial groups. The formation of larger groups depends on the common interests of those who live in a wider territory. For instance, there are natural menaces such as flood and drought and also the threat of invasion by an alien people, which do not affect single individuals but all those living in a locality. They must take concerted actions to defend themselves—as by

和房东有姻亲关系。他们自己的家破裂之后，跟随着母方的亲戚。虽然他们实际上和家的成员一样地生活在一起，但他们不能加入这个家，而保留着他们的客人身份。

学徒制度也是一种从外面吸收工作成员的办法。这种情况有四例。师傅为学徒提供食宿，免收学费；而学徒则必须为他的师傅做一定年限的工，没有工资，只是在最后一年，可以要少量的"鞋袜钱"。

最普遍采用的办法是雇佣。一个人可按一定契约做一名佣工进入一户，他为那家种田或养蚕缫丝，佣工在雇主的家中得到住宿。他参加该户的劳动，有权使用所有的用具，并由该户供给食宿。他每年可得到一笔事先议定的工资。

以上是村中不属于家的成员而进入户的全部情况。

家中的成员也可能不住在家里而在远处工作。他们暂时不在家，并不影响他们的亲属关系。但他们不在的时候，他们不能算作户的成员，虽然他们和这一户有着明确的经济关系。

在这个村子里，那些不住在自己家里的人，总共有54人，其中女32人，男18人。除了其中4个男孩作为学徒住在本村的师傅家里外，其他人都在城里工作，这个数字表明了人口流入城市的强烈倾向，其中尤以女性人口更为突出。

二、邻里

若干"家"联合在一起形成了较大的地域群体。大群体的形成取决于居住在一个较广区域里的人的共同利益。比如，水、旱等自然灾害以及外敌入侵的威胁，不是影响单个的人，而是影响住在这个地方的所有的人。他们必须采取协同行动来保护自己——如筑堤、救济

building dikes, relief measures, magical and religious activities. Moreover, the satisfactory exploitation of his land by an individual requires co-operation with others: similarly with the distribution of the produce and with trade and industry. The need of relaxation and amusement is another factor which will bring together individuals in games and other forms of group recreation. Thus the fact of living together and near to each other produces the need of political, economic, religious, and recreative organizations. The following sections will give a general description of territorial groupings found in the village, but those groups formed specially for economic activities will be discussed in later chapters in detail.

A neighbourhood is the group of households combined for daily intimate contact and mutual help. Conventionally people take the five households on each side of their residence as being their neighbours. For these they have a special term *shanlin*. They have towards one another special social obligations.

When a new-born baby is one month of age, his mother will carry him to visit the neighbours. They will be courteously received with tea and entertainments. When they leave, a gift, which consists of cakes, will be bestowed on the baby. This is the first visit of the baby to a house other than his own, even before he goes to his mother's father's house.

In the case of marriage, the bridegroom's family will distribute a kind of cake as an anouncement and invitation to the wedding ceremony. Neighbours are included in the list. In return they will offer a present in cash on the wedding day and participate in the feast of celebration. In case of funerals, each house in the neighbourhood will send one person to assist without payment.

In daily life when one needs extra labour in household work, such as removing heavy articles, neighbours will come to help. In case of economic stress, money can be borrowed from them in small sums without interest. Such relations of mutual help are not rigidly confined to ten households, they depend more on personal intimacy than formal prescriptions.

❸ Religious and Recreative Groups

In the village, the god, besides the ancestor spirits, who receives sacrifices most frequently is the kitchen god—his wife being sometimes included.

The kitchen god, *zončen*, is the supernatural inspector of the household, sent by the emperor of heaven. His duty is to watch the daily life of the house and to report to his superior at the end of each year.

措施、巫术及宗教等活动。此外，个人要很好地利用他的土地，需要别人的合作；同样，运送产品、进行贸易、工业生产都需要合作。休息和娱乐的需要又是一个因素，把个人集聚在各种形式的游戏和群体娱乐活动中。因此，人们住在一起或相互为邻这个事实，产生了对政治、经济、宗教及娱乐等各种组织的需要。下面几节将对这个村子的各种地域性群体作概括的描述，但有关经济活动的各种群体，将在以后几章里详细讨论。

邻里，就是一组户的联合，他们日常有着很亲密的接触并且互相帮助。这个村里习惯上把他们住宅两边各五户作为邻居。对此，他们有一个特别的名词，叫做"乡邻"。他们互相承担着特别的社会义务。

当新生的孩子满月以后，他的母亲就带他去拜访四邻。他们受到殷勤的接待，用茶点款待。离开的时候，还送点心给孩子。这是孩子第一次到别人家中去，那时他甚至尚未见过外公家。

办婚事前，新郎的家庭要分送喜糕到各家去，作为婚事的通告和参加婚礼的邀请。邻居都包括在邀请的名单里。各家在举行婚礼那天送现金作为回礼，并参加婚宴。在丧葬时，每家邻居都派一人去帮忙，不取报酬。

在日常生活中，当某人家有搬运笨重东西等类似的家务劳动、需要额外的劳力时，邻居们齐来帮忙。如果经济拮据，也可向邻居借到少数贷款，不需利息。此种互相帮助的关系，并不严格地限制在十户人家之中，它更多地取决于个人之间的密切关系，而不是按照正式规定。

三、宗教和娱乐团体

在村里，除了祭祀祖先外，最经常得到祭祀的是灶王爷，有时也包括灶王奶奶。

灶神是上天在这户人家的监察者，是由玉皇大帝派来的。他的职责是视察这一家人的日常生活并在每年年底向上天作出报告。

The god is represented by a paper inscription, bought from the shop in the town and placed in the little palace on the stove. He receives sacrifices twice a month, regularly at the first day and the fifteenth day, and on other occasions as shown in the time-table of social activities (IX–3). The first dish of each seasonal food will also be shared with the god. The sacrifice is made by laying dishes on the platform before his little palace, lighting a pair of candles and burning a bundle of incense as an invocation.

At the end of the year, the twenty-fourth day of the twelfth month, a farewell sacrifice will be made. This sacrifice consists of a big feast and takes place in the front room. After the feast the paper inscription will be burnt with the pine sticks and a paper chair. Through the fire, as indicated by the flame, the god returns back to heaven. In this annual audience with the emperor, he will make a report about his findings on the particular house in his charge. Based on the report, the fortune of the household will be decided.

The criterion for pleasing and displeasing the god, a very important daily control of human behaviour, is the observance and non-observance of certain taboos. A full list of taboos does not exist in a precise form, but a vague feeling of fear of supernatural interference in daily life due to displeasing actions is definitely found in everyday occurrence. As far as I was able to note, those taboos fall into three categories. The first is based on reverence for rice. Rice should not be trampled underfoot or wasted. Even sour rice should not be thrown away carelessly. The proper manner is to eat all the rice cooked. If this cannot be done, it must be thrown into the river in order to feed the fish. The second category of taboo is connected with the sense of dirt in sex matters. All the things and activities connected with sex must be cleared up outside the kitchen. Women during menstruation should not touch anything on the platform of the kitchen god. The third category is connected with respect for learning. Any paper with written characters of any kind, even newspapers, should be collected carefully and waste papers should be burnt, never in the kitchen, but on the open ground or in the special furnace in the temple.

The idea of a well organized supernatural kingdom complicates the connection between human actions and supernatural interference. The breaking of any taboo does not automatically provoke certain consequences directed by the supernatural powers. They must come through the supernatural administrative machinery. Therefore if anyone can

神像是刻印在纸上的，由城里店铺中买来，供在灶头上面小神龛中。灶神每月受两次供奉，通常是在初一和十五。也在其他时候受到供奉，具体时间可见社会活动的日期表（第九章第三节）。各式刚上市的时鲜食品，第一盘要供奉灶神。供奉是把一盘盘菜肴供在灶神座前，并点上一对蜡烛、一束香以示祀奉。

到了年底，农历腊月二十四祭送灶神上天。这次供奉的东西特别丰富，而且在堂屋中举行。这次供奉之后，纸的神像和松枝、纸椅一起焚化。灶王爷就由火焰的指引回到了天庭。他通过每年一次向玉帝的拜奏，对他所负责的这一家人的行为作出报告。这一户下一年的命运就根据他的报告被作出了决定。

使神道高兴或是不去触怒神道的愿望是一种对人们日常行为很重要的控制。标准就看是遵奉还是违犯传统的禁忌。我还不能列出一张表格来说明各种禁忌，但在日常生活中，却肯定地存在着一种模糊的恐惧，人们怕做出了使神道不悦的行为，而引起上天的干预。就我所知，这些禁忌可分为三类：第一类是以敬谷为基础的，有如不能踩踏或糟蹋稻米，甚至馊饭也不得随意抛弃。最规矩的方式，就是把每一粒米饭都吃下去。如果实在做不到，就把这些米饭抛到河塘中去喂鱼。第二类禁忌是和有关性的事物都是脏污的意识联系在一起的。所有与性有关的行为和东西，都必须从厨房中清除出去。妇女在月经期间，不准接触灶王爷神龛前的任何东西。第三类禁忌和尊敬知识相联系。任何字纸，甚至是新闻报纸，都应仔细地收集起来；废纸应加以焚化，但绝不在厨房里烧毁，而应送到庙宇中专门用来焚化纸帛的炉子中去加以焚化，或在露天烧掉。

有一个组织完善的天庭的观念，使得人类的行动与上天的干预这两者之间的关系复杂化了。任何违犯禁忌的行为，并不因触怒上苍而直接受到惩罚。这件事情要由天庭的管理机构来处理。因此，如果能

prevent the inspector, the kitchen god, from seeing or reporting, the taboo can be broken with impunity. The supernatural agents or the spirits are not conceived as absolutely omnipotent and omnipresent. They are actually invisible human beings with very similar human sentiments and desires. Since they are very human, they also commit all human weaknesses and follies. Thus, all the human methods, which can be used towards any human policeman such as cheating, lying, bribing, and even physical bullying, can also be used in dealing with the supernatural inspector.

In the last farewell feast before the kitchen god returns to his heavenly office, the people prepare a kind of cake made of sticky rice. This cake is a favourite of the god. It is believed that when the god eats the cake, his mouth will be stuck together; and when the heavenly emperor asks for his annual report, which is an oral one, he can only nod his head without saying anything. Therefore no unfavourable report will be possible. But it is not regarded as so certain a remedy as to be an infallible safeguard against any taboo breaking.

The police function of the kitchen god is clear from its mythology. At a certain time, when a foreign power had conquered China, every house was forced to support a foreign soldier as its inspector. This the people found intolerable and at last they made a plot each to murder his soldier at the same time. The sticky cake was prepared and offered to the soldiers, whose mouths were stuck together. They could thus make no noise when being murdered. This plot was successfully carried out at the twenty-fourth of the twelfth month. But the people at once realized the danger of revenge by the spirits of the foreign soldiers. Some sort of compromise was achieved by which from that time on the spirits of the soldiers were to be worshipped in the kitchen as the god of the household and carry on their function of inspectors.

I was told this myth by only a few informants. Most of the people do not know the origin of the god and do not care very much about it. But the myth actually reveals the attitude of the people towards the supernatural inspector. It shows their unwillingness to submit their personal freedom of action to the social restriction which is imposed on them in society. This is slightly different from ancestor worship, which reflects the sentiments of attachment to dead ancestors.

防止上天派来的监察者——灶神看到或向上天报告人们的行为，则犯了禁忌也不会受罚。人们并不认为上天的使者是无所不在和无所不能的。他们实际上只是一些肉眼所看不到的人，有着和普通人差不多的感情和愿望。既然他们和人们相像，他们也具有人们同样的弱点和愚蠢。因此，凡是人们所能使用来对付人间警察的各种方法，诸如欺骗、谎言、贿赂，甚至人身威胁等等对付天庭派下来的监察使者也都能用上。

在送灶王爷上天之前的最后一次的祭灶之时，人们准备了糯米做的团子。这是灶神非常喜欢吃的点心。大家都相信，灶王爷吃了糯米团之后，他的嘴就粘在一起了。当玉皇大帝要他作年度报告时——这是口头的报告，他只能点头而说不出话来，因此，他要说坏话也不可能了。但这也不能认为是犯了禁忌之后的一个万无一失的补救办法。

灶王爷所具有的警察职能，传说中有过清楚的阐述。有一段时间，外国人统治了中国，每家中国人都被迫供养一个外国兵。每个兵监管一家人。老百姓受不了这样的管制，终于商定了一个计谋，各家都在同一个时间把这些士兵杀掉。于是就准备了这种糯米团给士兵们吃，他们的嘴都粘到了一起。因此在他们被杀时不能发出任何声音。这个计谋在腊月二十四执行成功。但这些老百姓又立刻想起这些外国兵的鬼魂会向他们报复，于是作了这样的一种妥协：从那时起，把这些外国兵的鬼魂当作家里的神道，在厨房里受到祭拜，并继续行使监察者的职责。

这个传说只有少数人向我讲过。大部分人并不知道这个神道的根底，也不怎么关心这件事。但这个神话实际上揭示了老百姓对上天派来监管者的态度。这表明他们很不愿意把自己的行动自由驯服于社会性的限制，这种限制是社会强加于他们的。这与对祖先的祭拜是稍有不同的。祭拜祖先反映了对已故祖先的依恋之情。

Another god called *luiwan* is worshipped by a larger territorial group which consists of about thirty houses. This territorial group has a special term, *de*, meaning segment. There are eleven segments in the village:

I. Ch'eng Kioh *yu*	.	.	.	.	4
II. Liang Kioh *yu*	.	.	.	.	3
III. Hsi Chang *yu*	.	.	.	.	2
IV. T'an Chia Têng	.	.	.	.	2

Each segment has its own idol of the god. Every year households of the same segment, each represented by one member, male or female, will meet twice, in the first and eighth months. At this meeting, the god will be invited to one of the houses, and a big feast is prepared by the host in his honour.

Luiwan, lui being the personal name of the god and *wan* meaning king, is a popular god in that region. In my own childhood I was often told about this rather elaborate myth. But all my informants in this village were ignorant of this. They told me honestly that they did not know who *luiwan* was although they had worshipped him for years and years. The purpose of the meeting was said to be related to the harvest. But the link is very vague in the minds of the people. Some confessed that their real interest in the meeting was the feast. As I shall later show, the village is not a self-sufficient religious unit. In case of drought, locusts, or flood, all the religious and magical performances will take place in the district town. The town is not only the economic but also the religious centre. The god, *luiwan*, is the supernatural protector against the locust menace. His myth will be described later (X–3). But it may be interesting to point out here that the lack of independent religious activity in the village on the occasion of agricultural crises is correlated with vagueness and ignorance about the myth connected with the god.

About ten years ago, there used to be a kind of annual meeting for religious and partly for recreative functions. This would be held in the autumn after the harvest. It served as a thanksgiving to the gods responsible for the harvest and at the same time as a request for blessing for the coming year. The images of local gods would be seated among the people and an opera company would be invited to play on the stage constructed specially for the purpose. The village was divided into five groups, called *degi*, meaning "the foundation of the stage." Each group was responsible for the management and expenses of this gathering in turn.

另外有一个崇奉神道"刘皇"的较大的地域性群体，由大约 30 家住户组成。这个地域性的群体有一个专门的名称"段"，是一个地域组织的单位。在这个村中，共有 11 段。

I.	城角圩	4
II.	凉角圩	3
III.	西长圩	2
IV.	谈家墩	2

每个段都有自己的刘皇偶像，同段的每一户每年要出一名男的或女的代表，在正月和八月里各聚会一次。聚会时，把神道请到其中的一户人家，这家的主人则准备好盛宴供俸。

"刘皇"——"刘"是神道个人的姓，而"皇"则是大神的意思。这个神道在这个地区很流行。在我幼年的时候，经常听到这个精心编制的神话。但村里经常向我提供情况的人对此却一无所知。他们坦白地告诉我，虽然他们祀奉刘皇已经多少代了，但他们却不知道刘皇是谁。每年两次聚会的目的据说与收成有关。但这种联系在人们的思想上是很模糊的。有的人承认，他们的真正兴趣是在聚会时的那顿盛餐。我在后面还要讲到，这个村庄不是一个自给自足的宗教活动单位。但凡遇到干旱、蝗灾或水灾，所有宗教和巫术的活动都在该区的镇内举行。镇不仅是经济中心，也是宗教中心。刘皇是上苍派来保护免遭蝗灾的神道。以后要讲到有关他的神话（第十章第三节）。在这里指出这点也许是有意思的，在遇到农业危机的时候，村里缺少独立的宗教活动，这是与人们对有关这神道的神话模糊不清或无知有联系的。

十年以前，这里每年有一次集会，它既是宗教活动，也是当地人的娱乐消遣。一般在秋后举行，一方面对专司收获的神道感恩，同时又是祈求来年的丰收。管这地方的神像被请来入座，还有一个乐队在一个专搭的戏台上演奏。全村分成五组，叫"台基"，即戏台的基础。每个组轮流负责这种集会的管理和开支。

With the deepening of the economic depression in the village, these annual meetings have been suspended and it is difficult for the present to say whether they will be revived when the economic depression is over. The interesting fact that there is no tendency to attribute the economic depression to the suspension of the gathering, but, on the contrary, the economic depression was regarded as the cause of the suspension. This shows that the nature of the gathering was less religious or magical than recreative. The economic depression, which is due solely to the fall of silk and rice prices, is understood in its true nature, and thus the solution resorted to has been the perfectly reasonable one of introducing modern technique and new industries.

The local gods, who were invited to attend the opera in former days, are found in two temples in the village: one at the south end and the other at the west end (II–4). Each Chia sends its representative to visit the temple twice a month and make sacrifices individually. This is not obligatory and is usually neglected. But persons who continue this observance constantly direct their attentions to one of the two temples, which is determined by the location of their houses. The people living on *Yu* I, III and the north part of II, go to the west temple and the rest to the south temple. But individuals in the same area do not associate with each other in definite duties and obligations, as we found in the worship of *luiwan*. Their association is only through the temple. We must, in fact, say that there is not a religious group but a religious area.

The two temples are owned by different priests. The owner of the south temple lives in the temple, while that of the east temple is an absentee. The daily work in the temple is managed by a non-religious agent called *san-xo*, meaning "incense and fire." The priest, being himself a buddhist, lives on the income of the temple and keeps aloof from secular activities. Nevertheless, he has definite functions in the community. He entertains the visitors and participates in the funeral ceremonies of the people. These services are paid either by an amount of incense, which is kept by the priest for resale, or by cash. But these two temples do not monopolize the religious activities of the people in the village. On important occasions, such as "burning incense" for newly dead relatives and fulfilling certain promises to the god after recovery from illness, people go to the big temples in the town or at the bank of the Lake where the gods are more powerful.

　　随着村庄经济萧条的加深，这些集会已暂时停止；现在也很难说在经济不景气过去之后，这种集会是否还会恢复。有趣的是人们并没有认为由于是暂停了集会而造成了经济萧条；相反地，却认为是经济萧条造成了每年集会的中止。这表明聚会的真正意义是娱乐多于宗教或迷信。经济萧条唯一的真正原因是稻米和蚕丝价格的下降，人们对此能够正确地理解，因而最合理的解决办法就是引进新的工业和现代技术。

　　过去常被请来看戏的地方神道，现在村中的两个小庙里。一座庙在村北，另一座在村西（第二章第四节）。每家每月派代表到庙里去单独供奉祭拜两次。这不是强制性的，而且经常被人忽视。但那些继续供奉的人，经常只去其中的一个庙。去哪个庙，要由住家的位置决定。住在第一圩、第三圩及第二圩北边的人家，常去村北的庙；其余人家则去村西的庙。但同一地区的个人，在承担一定的责任和义务时并不互相联合起来，如祭拜刘皇时那样做，他们只通过庙宇而有所联系。因此，应该说这里并没有宗教团体而只有宗教区域的存在。

　　这两个庙分别为不同的和尚所有。村北的庙里住着庙主；村西的庙主则不住在内，庙内的日常工作由一位非宗教代理人代管，人们叫他"香火"。和尚信佛教，靠庙的收入为生，远离俗务。然而在社区里他有着一定的职能。他负责招待到庙里去的人，并参加村中的丧事。为人举办丧事他可以得到一笔现金或是相当数量的香，香可以留下来以后再出售。但这两个庙并不垄断村中人的所有宗教活动。到了重要时节，如为新近亡故的亲属"烧香"，因病人康复而向菩萨还愿等，人们往往改去城中的大庙宇，或到太湖边去拜佛，因为那里的神道有更大的法力。

Another important function of the priest is to keep the ancestor records for the people, and this also takes him beyond the village temples. Genealogical records of the families are kept in different temples outside. Since the record keeper is rewarded by the family whose ancestor names are kept, the record book becomes in a way the personal property of the priest. Like other kinds of personal property, it can be bought and sold. Therefore the circulation of wealth among the priests has made the allegiance of the people to the temples more complicated.

The nature of their allegiance, however, has nothing to do with belief or with sects. The priest never preaches any religious doctrine to the people, except possibly to the dead. Even then he preaches in a language alien to the local people. The stranger the accent, the more valuable, in the popular view, is the preaching.

❹ The Village Government

For various social functions, households are associated together to form larger local groups. These groups do not form a hierarchical series but superimpose on each other. The village, being an aggregate of households in a compact residential area, separated from other similar units by a considerable distance, sets a limitation on the direct extension of territorial ties for various functions. It marks a common boundary for those intimate territorial groups. It synthesizes various social functions and also takes up special functions that cannot be fulfilled by smaller units—all these are performed through the village government by the village headmen.

Village heads are always accessible, because they are known to every villager, and a stranger will be received by them immediately. The visitor will be impressed by their heavy burden of work. They help the people to read and to write letters and other documents, to make the calculations required in the local credit system, to manage marriage ceremonies, to arbitrate in social disputes and to look after public property. They are responsible for the system of self-defence, for the management of public funds, and for the transmission and execution of administrative orders from the higher government. They take an active part in introducing beneficial measures such as industrial reform into the village.

There are two village heads at the present time. The following note gives a short sketch of them.

和尚还有一种重要的职能，他们把村民祖先的记载保存在手中。这使他们所干的事超出了村中小庙的范围。各家的家谱是由外边的不同庙宇保存的。由于家谱记载了家庭祖先的姓名，这些记录的持有者得到这些家庭的酬报，所以这种记录簿在某种程度上成为和尚的个人财产。这种记录簿可以购买或出售，就像其他私人财产一样。因而，僧侣之间这种财产的流动，使得村民对哪个庙宇更为忠诚这样一个问题，变得较为复杂了。

村民们的这种忠诚与他们的信仰或教派全无关系。僧侣们从来不向百姓宣讲宗教教义，除非是为死亡者念经；甚至那些僧侣用外地口音念经。但当地普遍认为，口音越陌生，念的经就越灵。

四、村政府

为了履行多种社会职能，各户聚合在一起形成较大的地域群体。这些群体并不构成等级从属的系列，而是互相重叠的。由于村庄是各户密集在一起的聚居区，村和村之间都间隔着相当的距离，这就使它在直接扩大地域联系以实现多种功能方面受到了限制。村庄为邻近地域的群体之间标出一条共同边界。村庄综合各种社会职能，有时承担一些小的单位不能胜任的特殊职能。这一切都由村长通过村政府来执行。

一般说来，村长易于接近，村中所有人都认识他，外来的生人总能很快地得到村长的接待。来访者会对他的繁重的工作感到惊讶。他帮村里的居民写信、念信，以及代办其他文书，按照当地借贷规则算账、办婚礼、仲裁社会争议、照看公共财产。他们有责任组织自卫、管理公款，并且要传达、执行上级政府下达的行政命令。他们还积极地采取各种有利于本村的措施，村中的蚕丝改革就是一例。

目前在这个村子里有两位村长。下述的记录可以给人们一个概貌：

Mr. Chen is an old man, nearly sixty. He received his order of scholarship—Hsiu Ts'ai—under the late imperial examination system which was abolished at the end of the last dynasty. He had failed to proceed further in his scholastic career and was invited to become a family tutor in the town. At the beginning of the Republic, he came back to the village to start a private school and remained as the only schoolmaster in the village, for more than ten years. From that time on he has assumed the leadership in the village under various formal titles according to the ever-changing administrative system. In 1926, he initiated the silk reform programme with the support of the Provincial Sericultural School and started the experimental station in the village. In 1932, he was formally responsible for the establishment of the co-operative silk factory. He then gave up his job as a schoolmaster and became manager of the factory. When the new administrative system, Pao Chea, was introduced, he found work with the government was not suited to his taste and thus retired from the office, but nevertheless he has remained the *de facto* head of the village, and is still responsible for community affairs.

The other head is Mr. Chou. He is younger, being about forty years of age. He was educated by family tutors but was too late to take the imperial examination. Without scholastic interest he was content to be a simple peasant with his brother. Being literate and honest, he was picked by the reform agent of the silk industry as an assistant. He has from that time on secured the confidence both of the reformers and of the people and gradually shared with Chen leadership in public affairs in the village. When the Pao Chea system was introduced he was, on the recommendation of Chen, formally elected and actually appointed the head of the Hsiang which includes the village.

Headmanship in the village is not hereditary. Chou's father is engaged in the tile trade and his elder brother is still working on the farm. His son is in the town and is not likely to succeed him in the future. There is no kinship relation between Chen and Chou.

Although both Chen and Chou are well-to-do persons, neither is considered the richest person in the village. The richest person is, I believe, a man named Wang, who lives in obscurity and is without any outstanding prestige. It is true that a child of a poor family has less chance of attaining the position since headmanship has no direct economic reward and requires rather long and expensive preparation (to attain the necessary standard of literacy), but wealth alone does not give power or prestige.

陈先生是位老年人，近60岁。他在前清的科举制度下，曾考上了秀才。这种制度在清末已废止了。由于他在科举考试中未能进一步考中，所以被人请到城里去当家庭教师。到民国初年，他回村办私塾，自此时起十年多，他是村中唯一的教书先生。此后，他在村中担任领导工作，根据不断改变的行政系统的任命，他得到了各种正式的头衔。1926年，在省蚕桑学校的支持下，他开始实行蚕丝改良计划，在村中开办了蚕丝改进社。1932年，他正式负责合作丝厂的建厂工作。他放弃了教书的职务，担任丝厂厂长。当新的行政体制保甲推行时，他感到政府工作不合他的口味，于是退休了。然而他还是事实上的村长，并仍旧负责社区的事务。

另一位领导人是周先生。他较年轻，约40岁，他从家庭教师受业，但已不及参加科举考试。由于不再想做学问，他和他的兄弟在一起务农。他为人诚实，又有文化，被蚕丝改进社选用为助手。从这时起，他得到了改良工作者及当地人民两方面的信任，并逐渐地分担了村中公务的领导工作。当推行保甲制时，他经由陈先生推荐，正式当选并被任命为乡长，开弦弓村隶属于这个乡。

村长的职务不是世袭的。周的父亲是瓦商，他的哥哥仍在种田，他的儿子住在城里，将来不大可能接替他的工作。陈与周之间并无亲戚关系。

陈和周生活较富裕，但他们两人并不是村中最富有的人。最富的人姓王，他生活得默默无闻，在村中没有突出的威望。当一个领导人并没有直接的经济报酬，而且为达到此地位，需要经过相当长时间费钱的准备过程，才能使自己达到一定的文化水平。一个穷人家的孩子得到这种职位的机会是比较少的，但单靠财富本身也不能给人带来权力和威信。

Even legal status is not essential for the headmanship. Chen is still the senior head in the village, but he has no position in the formal administrative system. Elder persons tend to avoid the trouble of dealing with the higher government. The basis of the headmanship lies in public recognition and support in the leadership in community affairs, and in being the representative of the community against the outside world. Chen started his career as a schoolmaster and Chou as an assistant in the silk factory. Their service and ability have given them authority and prestige. In the village there are few who are literate and still less who are at the same time willing to take up the responsibility without economic reward. Young men of ambition are not satisfied with the position: it is considered by the two middle school graduates I met in the village, as sterile and hopeless. Thus the range for the selection of village heads is not very large.

Although they have no direct economic reward, they enjoy prestige and presents from the persons who have received services from them. For example, they are respected by the people, and can call the generation senior to them, except their own near kin, by their personal names without adding any relationship terms. This cannot be done by an ordinary person. Their leading position in the village also helps them to hold privileged jobs such as schoolmaster and manager of the silk factory.

Headmenship is not connected with any previleged "class." Even seniority in age is not an essential qualification, as is shown in Chou's case. But the sex disqualification has not yet been entirely overcome; women are excluded from public affairs. Only recently women have acquired the same position as men in the silk co-operative society, and a woman teacher has been appointed at the school; but the latter has very little influence in the community except among boys and girls.

❺ The Imposed Administrative System, Pao Chea

As mentioned, the village as such has no legal status because side by side with the functional territorial groups there is an administrative system imposed on the village organization. These two systems, which I have termed *de facto* and *de jure* respectively, do not coincide with each other. In this section, I shall describe the *de jure* system and compare it with the *de facto* system to show the discrepancies.

甚至法定地位对于当村长的人来说，也不是必不可少的。陈先生现在仍然是村中有资望的领导人，但他在正式行政系统中并不担任职务。年长的人都倾向于不和上级政府打交道，以避免麻烦。当村领导人的基础在于，不论他们代表社区面向外界时，或是他们在领导社区的事务中，都能得到公众的承认和支持。陈原职是教师，而周是以蚕丝厂的助理开始他的事业的。他们为公众服务的精神和能力，使他们得到了权力和威望。村中有文化的人很少，愿意在没有经济报酬的情况下承担起责任的人更少。有抱负的年轻人对这种职位并不感到满意，我在村里遇见过两位中学毕业生，他们认为这种工作枯燥无味，而且缺乏前途。因此，选择村长的范围并不很宽。

虽然他们得不到直接的经济报酬，但由于为村里人办了事，他们也乐于享有声誉，接受一些礼物。比如，他们受人尊敬，可以对长辈（除了近亲）直呼其名而不用加上辈分的尊称。普通人是不允许这样做的。他们在村里所处的领导地位也有助于他们保持有特权的工作，如当教师、当丝厂的厂长等。

当领导人并不与享有特权的"阶级"有关。从周的情况可看出，年长也不是必要的条件。但性别上的排斥却未能克服，妇女是不许参加公众事务的。只是在最近，妇女才在蚕丝合作社中获得了和男人相同的职位；学校也任命了一位女教员，但这位妇女，除了在男女学童之中之外，在当地社区中的影响很小。

五、保甲——强加的行政体制

前面已经讲到，这样的村子是没有法定地位的。因为与这种功能性的地域性群体并行存在的有一个行政体制，它是强加于村的组织之上的。我把这两种体制分别称之为事实上的体制和法定的体制。它们两者之间不重合。在本节我将描述这个法定的体制，并把与事实上的体制相比较，以观察它们的差异。

The new administrative system is called Pao Chea. The term Pao Chea is an old one. The government recently had the idea of reviving an old administrative system which had been proposed by an administrative reformer in the Sung Dynasty (960—1276). How far this old system had actually existed is another question, but for this village it is entirely new. The head of the village explained that the arrangement for the new system had only recently been completed, and it had never within living memory been in existence. He added that the villagers had been summoned by the town head and told to arrange their houses in a manner prescribed by the district government. This had been done. To study this Pao Chea system, therefore, it is necessary to go back to the statute book to see what is the intention and what principle the government followed in its organization.

On June 5th, 1929, the National Government in Nanking promulgated the Law Governing the Organization of the District, based on the principle of local self-government of the late Dr. Sun Yet-sen. According to the law, each district (Hsien) must be divided into several Chu and each Chu into twenty to fifty Hsiang (in rural areas) and Chên (in urban areas). In the rural areas, villages with more than 100 house-holds would be taken as a Hsiang and those with less than this number would be combined with other villages to form a Hsiang. In urban areas, towns with more than that number would be taken as a Chên, and those with less would combine with other villages to form a Hsiang. The Hsiang is again subdivided into Lu (twenty-five households) and Lin (five households). All these units were to be self-governing through their elected headmen and councils. The functions of these local governments are listed in the law as follows: Census taking, population registration, land survey, public works, education, self-defence, physical training, public health, water regulation, forest preservation, industrial and commercial improvement, food storage and regulation, protection and prohibition of plantation and fishery, co-operative organization, improvement of customs, public belief, public enterprise, financial control, etc.

These functions are not altogether new to the local community, most of them having been carried out by various traditional *de facto* groups. The law created new territorial groups with the purpose of facilitating the self-governing administrative functions. But, in fact, there is the danger that it will actually hamper the normal functioning of the *de facto* groups. Thus in the Second National Administrative Conference in 1931 the rigidity in the size of the units was severely criticized. Consequently, an amending bill was introduced in the Legislative Yuen.

新的行政体制叫做"保甲"。保甲是个旧词。政府最近有意要恢复一种古老的行政体制。这种体制是宋朝（公元960～1279年）的行政改革者建议的。这个古老的体制究竟实行到什么程度是另一个问题。但对这个村子来说，它完全是新的。村长解释说，新体制的实施准备最近方告完成，它从来没有在人们的记忆中存在过。他说，镇长把村民都传唤去，告诉他们要按照县政府的规定来安排他们各户在行政组织中的地位，这件事已经完成了。为了要研究保甲制，必须从法令全书中找出它的意图，以及政府在保甲组织中所遵循的原则。

1929年6月5日，根据孙中山先生地方自治的原则，南京的国民政府颁布了一个《县组织法》（以下简称《法》——编者注），按此法律每个县必须分为几个区，每区又分为20～50个乡（农村地区）或镇（城市地区）。农村地区，凡有100户以上的村子，划为一个乡；不到100户的村子，则和其他村子联合成为一个乡。城市地区，凡有100户以上的，可划为镇；如不足此数，则与附近村子合并建乡。乡则进一步分为闾（25户）及邻（5户）。这些单位都通过选出的领导人及地方自治会来实行自治。这些地方政府的职能在法律中已有规定，计有：人口普查及人口登记、土地调查、公益工作、教育、自卫、体育训练、公共卫生、水利灌溉、森林培植及保护、工商改良及保护、粮食储备及调节、垦牧渔猎保护及取缔、合作社组织、改革习俗、公众信仰、公共企业及财政控制等等。

这些职能对地方社区来说不完全是新的。其中许多项早已由传统的、事实上的群体所实施。为了促进自治政府的行政职能，法律创造了新的地域性的群体。但实际上，它会妨碍事实上的群体的正常职能。因此，在1931年举行的第二次全国行政会议上，对各种单位的大小所作的刻板规定受到了严厉的批评。结果是由立法院提出了修正案。

While the bill was still in the stage of discussion, another system was instituted which affected the local government. In August, 1932, the Headquarters of the Punitive Campaign Against the Communists in Central China issued a decree organizing the people in the area of military operation (Hopei, Honan, and Anhwei) into uniform self-defensive units under the system of Pao Chea. According to this sytem, each ten households (Hu) form a Chea and each ten Chea a Pao. The intention of this organization was stated in the decree to be "to organize the people in the devastated area in a more effective way and secure an accurate census in order to increase the power of local self-defence against the communists and to enable the army to discharge its function more efficiently." This system was introduced mainly for military purposes. Unless the population could be accurately registered, it was very difficult to prevent the communists from mixing with non-communists in the disturbed areas. To counter the active propaganda of the communists the army introduced the system of mutual responsibility of the individuals in the same Chea and Pao, so that they could act as a check one upon the other.

In 1933, the spread of communist influence drew Fukien into the military area. In Fukien the provincial government had already started the organization of the local self-governing system according to the Law in 1929. The provincial government was ordered by the Headquarters to suspend the local self-governing system and to substitute for it the Pao Chea system. In their conflict between the Law and the Decree, the provincial government submitted to the central government; and the Central Political Council decided to absorb the Pao Chea system in the self-governing system. The Law of 1929 was superseded by a series of laws of 1935. These two systems were compromised in the following six points: (1) the uniform units of Pao and Chea were substituted for the old units Lu and Lin, and the units Chu, Hsiang, and Chên were to be on the same level; in other words, the original status of Chu as an intermediary unit between district and Hsiang or Chên was abolished; (2) before the completion of the Tutelage period, the method of indirect election was to be substituted for direct election according to the Pao Chea system; (3) a census was to be taken in the process of arranging the households in the Pao Chea system; (4) military training in the Pao Chea system was to be extended into a more general civil training; (5) the system of mutual responsibility was to be applied only in cases of emergency; and (6) the Pao Chea system was to take up the function of self-government, but local modifications were to be allowed to suit particular conditions.

当此修正案尚在讨论阶段，另外一个影响到地方政府的体制却实施了。1932 年 8 月，华中的"剿共"司令部发布了一项法令，规定在军事行动区（湖北、湖南及安徽）的人民要在保甲制之下，组织起统一的自卫单位。按此制度，每十户为一甲，每十甲为一保。成立此组织的意图，在法令中有所说明，即："在遭到破坏的地区有效地组织民众，取得精确的人口统计以便增强地方自卫反共的力量，并使军队能更有效地履行其职能。"此制度主要是为军事目的而实行的。除非人口登记做得十分精确，否则，在动荡的地区，很难防止共产党人和非共产党人混合在一起。为了遏制共产党活跃的宣传活动，军队还实施了在同一个保甲之内，人与人互相担保的制度，使人们可以互相检查。

1933 年，共产党影响扩展，福建成为军事地区。福建省政府已开始根据 1929 年的《县组织法》组建地方自治体系。司令部命令省政府停止地方自治体系而代之以保甲制。面对《法》与法令的冲突，省政府选择了服从中央政府，中央政治会议决定把保甲制纳入自治体系中。1929 年的《法》被 1935 年的一系列法律所代替。这两种体系在以下六点中得到了妥协：(1) 由统一的保甲单位代替老单位闾和邻，并使区、乡、镇等单位保持同等的级别。换句话说，原来处于县和乡、镇之间的单位——区取消了；(2) 在结束训政时期前，按照保甲制度，以间接选举代替直接选举；(3) 在按保甲制编户的过程中，进行人口普查；(4) 把保甲制的军训扩大为普遍的民众训练；(5) 只在紧急情况下，才实行互相担保的制度；(6) 保甲制担负自治的职能，但允许进行地方性的修改以适应具体情况。

Obviously, the compromise has not solved the fundamental problem, that is, how far the *ad hoc* self-defensive units with their uniform size could undertake the general administrative functions listed in the Law of 1929. The real issue was not the legal conflict between the law and the decree but whether the traditional functions that have been carried out in the *de facto* territorial groups could be taken over by the arbitrarily created Pao Chea. Since the old units Lin and Lu, of a less rigid kind, had proved to be impracticable it did not seem that a more rigid system was likely to function any better. The effectiveness of the Pao Chea system in self-defence in cases of emergency also did not assure its suitability as a system for administrative self-government. It could indeed be argued that in the process of political integration in China it was desirable to substitute for the heterogenous traditional structure a rational and uniform structure. But it remains to be considered whether such a substitution was necessary and how much it will cost to enforce. Since this new system was only introduced less than a year before my visit to the village, it is too early to draw any conclusions. But an analysis of the working of the system against the background of the traditional structure will obviously throw light on the general problem, and will at least help to stress the importance of this issue in the future administrative policy.

The Pao Chea, as instituted in this village with allowance for local modifications, does not strictly accord with the numerical prescription of the law. The village with its 360 households is divided geographically into four Pao. As I have shown in the village plan, the houses in the village are built along both sides of the streams and are thus distributed in four *yu*. The houses in the same *yu* are grouped into one Pao. According to their positions, counting from east to west and from south to north, the houses are arranged in order, approximately ten in number, to form the units of Chea. These four Pao are combined with another seven Pao in neighbouring villages into one Hsiang, which is called after the name of the village Kaihsienkung Hsiang. Pao and Chea are known by numbers. The four Pao in the village are numbered from eight to eleven. A further discrepancy between practice and law is that the Chu in the old law is still preserved as an intermediary unit between the district and Hsiang, and roughly corresponds to the functional unit of the marketing area of the town (XIV–8). This village can be defined in terms of the administrative system as:

很明显，妥协并没有解决根本问题，也就是，这些特别的、有统一规模的自卫单位在多大程度上能承担 1929 年的《法》所规定的一般的行政职能。真正的问题并不在于这个法律与那个法令之间的法律性斗争，而在于事实上的地域群体早已行使的传统的职能，能否被这种专横地创造出来的保甲所接替。老的邻、闾单位并不那么严格，但已被事实证明是行不通的；那么这种更为严格的保甲制度，似乎更不大可能行得通。若发生紧急情况，保甲制的自卫效能也并不能保证它是适合于行政自治的一种制度。的确可以争辩说，在中国政治结合的过程中，用一个合理的和统一的结构来代替参差不齐的传统结构，看起来比较理想。但应当考虑到，这种替代是否必需，以及需要花多大的代价去实施它。由于我访问这个村子时，这个新制度实行了还不到一年。因此，下结论还为时过早。但以传统的结构为背景，对照这个制度的实施状况进行一些分析，显然有助于了解问题的全貌，至少会有助于在将来的行政政策中强调这个问题的重要性。

这个村所实施的并允许进行一些地方性修改的保甲制，并不严格符合法律规定的数字。村中 360 户按地理位置被分编为四个保。从前面所示的本村详图中可看出，村中的房屋沿小河的两旁建造，并分为四个圩。在同一个圩里的户被合成一个保。按照它们所处的位置，从东往西，或由南往北数，大约每十户构成一个甲。这四个保和邻村的七个保合成一个乡，这个乡按本村名而被称为"开弦弓乡"。保和甲则分别冠以数字。村中的四个保是第八保至第十一保。另一个在法律与实践之间不相符合的事，是保持了旧法律中的区，它是县和乡之间的一个中间单位，它大致上和镇的腹地相当（第十四章第八节）。按照这个行政体制，这个村可称为：

Kiangsu (province)

Wukiang (district)

Chên tsê (Chu)

Kaihsienkung (Hsiang)

No. 8–11 (Pao)

To examine the nature of the Hsiang, we must inquire into the problem of inter-village relations. Is there any special bond between the villages that are grouped into the same Hsiang? What is the functional group that corresponds to this administrative unit? Economically, villages in this region, as I shall show later (XIV–8), are independent of each other. Every village has its own agent boat which serves as the buying and selling agent of the villagers in the town market. A village, however large it may be, does not form a sub-marketing centre among its neighbouring villages. In other words, the town as the centre of the marketing area is able, owing to the ease of water transport and the institution of the agent boats, to collect from and distribute to its tributary villages without any need for intermediate stoppage of the movement of the goods. Within the area, there are several dozens of villages dependent on the town but independent of each other. These villages, which are occupied in similar work and produce similar goods, find little need for trade with one another. Thus the unit of Hsiang, standing between the marketing area and the village, has no economic basis. The same is true from the point of view of kinship relations. Although inter-village marriage is popular, there is no sign that those villages included in the same Hsiang, are preferred to those outside.

Linguistically the name Kaihsienkung in daily speech refers strictly to the village alone. It seems ridiculous to the local people to say that the neighbouring village is a part of Kaihsienkung. Their obstinacy in this is not unreasonable. The change means a great deal to the people. Some people told me, "If the neighbouring villages are part of Kaihsienkung, then the lake that belongs to Kaihsienkung people will be shared by the people of the neighbouring villages. But of course this cannot be permitted."

At present the increasing prestige and economic function of the silk reform movement, and the administrative status of the head of the Hsiang, which both have their head offices in this village, have drawn together the villages around it. I noticed that people from other

江苏（省）

吴江（县）

震泽（区）

开弦弓（乡）

第八至十一（保）

要剖析乡的本质，必须深入了解村与村之间的关系问题。在同一个乡的村子之间，是否有特殊的联系？与这个行政单位相当的职能群体是什么？我将在后面讲到（第十四章第八节），这个地区中的村子，在经济方面是相互独立的。每个村子都有自己的航船，充当村民到镇的市场上出售或购买的代理。一个村子，不论它有多大，都不成为它邻村间的一个低级销售中心。换句话说，由于水运方便，并有了航船制度，因此作为销售区域中心的镇完全有能力向所属的村庄进行商品的集散，在商品流通过程中不需任何中间的停留。在这个地区内，有数十个村庄依赖这个镇，但它们彼此之间都是独立的。这些村子做的是相同的工作，生产同样的产品，互相之间很少需要进行贸易往来。因此，乡作为销售区域与村庄之间的一个层次，是没有经济基础的。从亲属关系的观点看，情况也完全一样。虽然村与村之间的婚姻是很时行的，但并没有迹象说明，在同一个乡内的村庄，宁愿到乡外的村庄去找婚配对象的。

从语言的角度看，人们日常叫的"开弦弓"这个名字，在当地群众用语中是指这一个村庄而言。把邻村都说成是开弦弓的一部分，当地人听来可笑。他们的这种执拗并不是不合理的。这个称呼的改变对当地人来说含义很多。有人跟我说："如果邻近村庄都算开弦弓的一部分，那么，原来属于开弦弓村人的湖泊，也要被邻近村庄的人分去了。当然，这是不能允许的。"

目前，由于这个村庄的名声日增，蚕丝改良运动的经济功能及乡长的行政地位等因素，把开弦弓村周围的村子都吸引了过去。蚕丝改良运动和乡的首脑机关都在这个村里。我看到，不仅本乡各村，

villages, not limited to those of the same Hsiang, visited the village more frequently than formerly to order silkworm eggs, to supply cocoons for the factory, and to settle inter-village disputes. But in the last analysis, the head of the Hsiang, Chou, did not work in his legal capacity, but mostly through his own personal influence as the assistant manager of the silk factory, and he did not make any important steps without getting into touch with the *de facto* heads of the village concerned.

Of course, given time and increasing experience of the new administrative functions, there is no reason to say that the new unit will remain on paper for ever.

The unit of Pao, however, is different. To divide the village according to the boundary of streams is not likely to be successful. It is assumed in this case that the stream is a dividing line for social activities. This assumption is not true. As shown, boats are active on the water, and bridges are built to connect those separated pieces of land. They are means, not obstacles, of communication.

Lastly, we come to the Chea. Among the functional groupings, we have seen that there is a type of group called *shanlin*, the neighbourhood, which consists of ten households. But it does not correspond with the Chea. Chea is a fixed local segment while *shanlin* is a chain of overlapping units; each house taking its location as the centre of reference. The segmentation of Chea is very artificial and contradictory to the idea of the people.

Nevertheless, it will be interesting to study the problem in a future investigation to see how far planned social change can be started from the social structure including the form of the group, formal rules of behaviour, and formal system of thought; such attempts are evidently becoming more and more popular in a situation where state uniformity is desired.

而且外乡的人，也比过去更经常地来到这个村庄。他们前来订购蚕种，供给丝厂蚕茧，并解决村与村之间的争端。在前面的分析中所提到的姓周的乡长，并不是利用他的法定地位办事，而主要还是通过他个人的影响，即以蚕丝厂助理厂长的身份去办事的。同时，他也从不采取任何重要行动，除非他事先与各有关村庄的事实上的领导有过接触。

当然，如果给以时间，并取得新的行政职能的内容，没有理由说新的行政单位永远是停留在纸面上的一纸空文。

至于保这个单位，那就不同了。把村庄按小河为界而隔开的做法，不大可能成功。在此情况下，把小河假设为社会活动的一条分界线。但这种假设是不对的。正如已经说明的，船可以在水面上自由划动，造桥是为了把分割的土地联结起来。这些都是交通的工具而不是交通的障碍。

最后，我还要谈一谈甲。在职能性的群体中，我们已知有一种群体叫"乡邻"。它包括十户。但它与甲是不一致的。甲是一个固定的地段，而乡邻是一串相互交搭、重叠的单位。在乡邻这个结构中，每户都是以自己为中心，把左右五家组合起来。甲是一种非常人为的分段，它是同人们实际的概念相矛盾的。

然而，在将来再次调查时，来研究此问题是很有趣的，看一看有计划的社会变迁，从社会结构，包括群体形式、正式的行为准则、正统的思想体系等等开始，能进行到什么程度。在要求全国具有一致性的愿望之下，这种尝试显然会越来越普遍的。

CHAPTER VII   LIVELIHOOD

Having made a general survey of the geographical and social background of the village, we are now in a position to study the economic life of the people. I shall begin my description with the system of consumption and attempt to assess the general level of livelihood in the village. This level gives us some idea of the necessary requirements for ordinary living. To satisfy these requirements is the ultimate incentive to production and the impetus to industrial change.

From the point of view of consumption, there is no essential difference among the villagers, but in production, occupational differentiation is found. The present study is mainly limited to the farmers who form the majority. They are engaged in tilling land and in raising silkworms. These are two main sources of their income. Selling sheep and making periodic trading ventures are subsidiary sources. Before describing these activities, I will indicate through the calendar of work how these activities are arranged in a time sequence.

The legal aspect of the problem in relation to agriculture will be discussed in the chapter on land tenure. It would be sufficient to mention here that the traditional forces operating in this institution are strong enough to resist any significant changes. Even in technology, new methods and tools have not yet been successfully introduced. But in the silk industry, it is different.

The most urgent economic problem, from the point of view of the villagers, is industrial reform. The decline of the price of silk is the immediate cause of financial insolvency in the village. During the past ten years, a series of reforms have been introduced and as a result of these efforts both the technology and social organization of the silk industry have been radically changed. Therefore, we are able to analyse the process found in this village as a case study of industrial change in rural economy.

From the analysis of the systems of consumption and production we are led to the system of exchange. Through marketing, the villagers exchange their own produce for those consumed goods which they themselves do not produce. In marketing, we can see how far the village is self-sufficient and how far it is dependent on the outside world.

With the general picture of these economic activities before us, we can now examine the financial conditions in the village. As a result of the decline of domestic industry and the burden of high rent, the villagers are facing

柒 生活

对村子的地理情况和社会背景进行了综合调查之后，现在我们可以开始研究人们的经济生活了。我想先描述消费体系并且试行估计这村居民的一般生活水平。分析这一生活水平，我们可以了解普通生活的必要条件。满足生活的这些必要条件是激励人们进行生产和工业改革的根本动力。

从消费的角度看，村里的居民之间没有根本性的差别，但从生产上看，职业分化是存在的。目前的研究主要限于构成居民大多数的农民。他们从事耕种及养蚕。这是他们收入的两个主要来源。饲羊、定期出去做些贩运是次要的收入来源。在叙述这些活动之前，我将通过农历来表明这些活动是怎样按时序安排的。

有关农业法律方面的问题将在土地占有这一章中讨论。在此只略提一下，传统力量在这项制度中起着强大的作用，足以抗拒任何重大的变化发生。甚至在技术上，现在尚未成功地引进什么新方法和新工具。但在蚕丝业中，情况有所不同。

从村民的观点来看，最迫切的经济问题就是蚕丝改革。丝价下跌是农民无力偿还债务的直接原因。在过去十年中，努力进行一系列改革的结果使蚕丝业的技术以及社会组织都发生了根本性的变化。因此，我们才能够把这个村子的变化过程作为乡村经济中工业化的一个实例来分析研究。

我们将从消费系统与生产系统的分析引导到流通系统。通过市场销售，村民用他们自己的产品来换取他们自己不生产的消费品。在市场销售中我们可以看到村子自给自足的程度，以及村子对外界的依赖程度。

有了这些经济活动的概况，我们现在就可以观察一下村里的财务状况。国内工业的衰落、高额地租的负担使村民面临着空前的经济

an unprecedented economic depression. The difficulty in securing credit and the danger of becoming a victim of usury place the villagers in a dilemma. This will be the end of my descriptive account of the village economy shortly before the bursting of the great storm of the Japanese invasion.

❶ Cultural Control on Consumption

Culture provides means to procure materials for satisfying human needs but at the same time defines and delimits human wants. It recognizes a range of wants as proper and necessary and those lying outside the range as extravagant and luxurious. A standard is thus set up to control the amount and type of consumption. This standard is a measurement for plenty and deficiency by the people themselves. It enables saving when there is plenty, and causes dissatisfaction when there is a deficiency.

To be content with simple living is a part of early education. Extravagance is prevented by sanctions. A child making preferences in food or clothes will be scorned and beaten. On the table, he should not refuse what his elders put in his bowl. If a mother lets her child develop special tastes in food, she will be criticized as indulging her child. Even rich parents will not put good and costly clothes on their children, for doing so would induce the evil spirits to make trouble.

Thrift is encouraged. Throwing away anything which has not been properly used will offend heaven, whose representative is the kitchen god. For instance, no rice should be wasted. Even when the rice becomes sour, the family must try to finish it all. Clothes are used by generations, until they are worn out. Those worn-out clothes will not be thrown away but used for making the bottom of the shoes or exchanged for sweets and porcelain (XIV–7).

In a rural community where production may be threatened by natural disasters, content and thrift have practical value. If a man spends all his income, when he fails to have a good harvest, he will be forced to raise loans which may cause him to lose a part of his right over his land

(XV–3). To lose one's inherited estate is against filial obligations and thus will be condemned. Moreover, in the village there are few inducements to extravagance. Display of wealth in daily consumption does not lead to prestige. On the contrary, it may attract kidnappers as seen in the case of Wang several years ago.

不景气。村民难以取得贷款，或成为高利贷者牺牲品，他们的处境是进退维谷。我对这个村子在日本侵华战争爆发前不久的经济状况的描述将到此为止。

一、文化对于消费的控制

为满足人们的需要，文化提供了各种手段来获取消费物资，但同时也规定并限制了人们的要求。它承认在一定范围内的要求是适当和必要的，超出这个范围的要求是浪费和奢侈。因此便建立起一个标准，对消费的数量和类型进行控制。人们用这个标准来衡量自己的物质是充足还是欠缺。按照这个标准，人们可以把多余的节约起来。有欠缺时，人们会感到不满。

安于简朴的生活是人们早年教育的一部分。浪费要用惩罚来防止。孩子们饮食穿衣挑肥拣瘦就会挨骂或挨打。在饭桌上孩子不应拒绝长辈夹到他碗里的食物。母亲如果允许孩子任意挑食，人们就会批评她溺爱孩子。即使是富裕的家长也不让孩子穿着好的、价格昂贵的衣服，因为这样做会使孩子娇生惯养，鬼怪就会来找麻烦。

节俭是受到鼓励的。人们认为随意扔掉未用尽的任何东西会触犯天老爷，他的代表是灶神。例如，不许浪费米粒，甚至米饭已变质发酸时，全家人还要尽量把饭吃完。衣物可由数代人穿用，直到穿坏为止。穿坏的衣服不扔掉，用来做鞋底、换糖果或陶瓷器皿（第十四章第七节）。

在农村社区中，由于生产可能受到自然灾害的威胁，因此，知足和节俭具有实际价值。一个把收入全部用完毫无积蓄的人，如果遇到欠收年成就不得不去借债从而可能使他失去对自己土地的部分权利（第十五章第三节）。一个人失去祖传的财产是违背孝道的，他将受到责备。此外，村里也没有什么东西引诱人们去挥霍浪费。在日常生活中炫耀富有并不会给人带来好的名声，相反却可能招致歹徒的绑架，几年前发生的王某案件便是一个例子。

But the idea of thrift is absent on ceremonial occasions. Expenses in funeral and marriage ceremonies are not considered as individual consumption but as fulfilment of social obligations. A good son must provide the best possible coffin and grave for his parent. In the marriage ceremony, as mentioned, the parents on both sides will try to provide the best marriage gift and dowry, and offer the richest feasts, as their ability permits.

Thrift only sets an upper limit for the variation of livelihood. It becomes meaningless when one is not able to reach the accepted standard of proper living. It is the idea of generosity and kinship obligation in helping relatives (XV–2), that keeps individuals from sinking too much below the standard. Therefore the unequal distribution of wealth in the village is not expressed in a marked variation in the level of daily livelihood. Only a few persons have special and valuable clothes and there are no essential differences in housing and food.

❷ Housing

A house, in general, consists of three rooms. The front room is the largest. It is used for working, such as raising silkworms, manufacturing silk, threshing rice, etc.; for sitting, for dining when the weather is cold or wet, for receiving guests and for storing implements and products. It is also the place where the ancestral shrine is kept.

Behind the front room is the kitchen. It is only about one-fourth the size of the front room. One-third of it is occupied by the stove and the chimney. A small pavilion and a platform is constructed leaning upon the chimney for the kitchen god.

Next is the bedroom. It is sometimes divided by wooden partitions into two rooms if there are two family units in the Chia. Each room contains one or two beds. The married couple and their young child up to seven or eight years old share one bed. When the child grows up, he or she will have a separate bed first in the parents' room. An older but unmarried boy will sleep in the front room, as the employees do. A girl may remain until her marriage in her parents' room or may move to her grandmother's room, but never to the front room because women are not permitted to sleep in the room where the ancestral shrine is kept.

但在婚丧礼仪的场合，节俭思想就烟消云散了。人们认为婚丧礼仪中的开支并不是个人的消费，而是履行社会义务。孝子必须为父母提供最好的棺材和坟墓。如前面已经提到，父母应尽力为儿女的婚礼准备最好的彩礼与嫁妆，在可能的条件下，摆设最丰盛的宴席。

节俭仅仅为不同的生活标准提出了一个上限，当一个人未能达到公认的正常生活标准时，这个上限也就失去了意义。人们凭借慷慨相助和尽亲属义务的思想（第十五章第二节）去帮助生活困难的人，使他们的生活标准不致于同公认的标准相差太远。因此，村里财产分布的不均匀，并没有在日常生活水平方面表现出明显的不同。少数人有特殊的值钱的衣服，但住房和食物上并无根本的差别。

二、住房

一所房屋一般有三间房间。堂屋最大，用来作劳作的场所，例如养蚕、缲丝、打谷等等。天冷或下雨时，人们在这里休息、吃饭，也在这里接待客人或存放农具和农产品。它还是供置祖先牌位的地方。

堂屋后面是厨房，大小仅为堂屋的四分之一。灶头和烟囱占厨房面积的三分之一。紧靠烟囱有供灶王爷的神龛和小平台。

再往后是卧室，家中如有两个家庭单位时，就把卧室用木板隔成两间。每间房里放一两张床。已婚夫妇和七八岁以下的孩子合睡一张床。孩子长大以后，他或她先在父母屋里单独睡一张床，再大一些的未婚男孩就搬到堂屋里睡，像那些雇工一样。女孩出嫁前一直睡在父母屋里，也可以搬到祖母屋里去，但决不睡在堂屋里，因为妇女是不允许睡在供祖先牌位的房屋里的。

In its broad sense, a house includes an open field in front or behind the building. This open field is, at the same time, used as a public road as well as private ground for work and storage. All the threshed straw is heaped on this ground; it can also be used as a little garden where gourds or cucumbers are planted. Adjacent to the main building, there are little huts for the sheep and sometimes also for storage.

Human manure, being the most important fertilizer in the farm, is preserved in the pits made of earthenware, half buried in the ground at the back of the building. Along the southern bank of the Stream A, the public road is lined up with these manure pits. The government have ordered the villagers to remove these pits for hygienic reasons but nothing has been done about it.

Stream 河

Public road 路

Front room 堂屋	
Kitchen 厨房	Open yard 庭院
Bedroom 卧室	Bedroom 卧室
Back door 后门	
Sheep hut 羊圈	Garden 后院 / Manure pit 粪缸 / O O

Houses are built by special craftsmen from the town. During the period of raising silkworms, building is suspended, otherwise, according to the local belief, the industry of the whole village will be ruined. Breaking soil is considered as a dangerous action which might provoke supernatural interference. Thus it is necessary to perform certain magical rites which are done by Taoist priests. An ordinary house costs at least five hundred dollars for the total expenses. The length of life of the house is difficult to estimate. It depends on constant mending and oiling. Every two or three years the wooden parts of the house must be oiled once again and the tiles of the roof partially rearranged; this costs on the average ten dollars a year.

❸ Transportation

Boats are extensively used for heavy and long-distance traffic. But the villages do not build their boats. They buy them from outside. Each boat costs, on the average, about eighty to a hundred dollars. Nearly every household possesses one or more boats except those who are not

广义地说，一所房屋包括房前或房后的一块空地。这块空地既作为大家走路的通道，也用作一家人干活、堆放稻草或其他东西的地方。在这块地里种上葫芦或黄瓜就是小菜园。房屋附近还有养羊或堆放东西的小屋。

人的粪尿是农家最重要的肥料，在房后有些存放粪尿的陶缸，半埋在土地里面。沿着 A 河南岸，路边有一排粪缸，由于有碍卫生，政府命令村民搬走，但没有实行。

房屋是由城镇里的专门工匠来修建的。养蚕期间，停止房屋施工，否则当地人相信全村的蚕丝业会毁掉。他们认为破土是一种危险的行为，会招致上天的干预。于是就要请道士来做法事。修建一所普通的房屋，总开支至少 500 元。房屋的使用寿命根据修缮情况而异，难以作出肯定的估计。每隔两三年必须把房屋的木结构部分重新油漆一遍，部分瓦片要重新铺盖，诸如此类的修缮费用每年平均为 10 元。

三、运输

人们广泛使用木船进行长途和载重运输，但村庄自己并不造船，而是从外面购买。每条船平均价格约 80～100 元。除那些不从事农业、渔业劳动的人家以外，几乎每户都有一条或几条船。男人、妇女

engaged in agricultural or fishing work. Both men and women can handle the boat. The art of rowing is acquired in childhood. Once having acquired this skill, one can row for hours without rest. The energy spent on rowing is not in proportion to the weight of the load but to the conditions of the water current and the direction of the wind. Therefore, the cost of this type of transport is reduced as the weight of the load is increased. If the boatman is able to use the wind, distance is a problem of time, not of energy; cost is thus further reduced. This is an important character of water transport. It makes possible the concentration of houses in one area and determines the position of the house near the stream. It also makes possible the system of scattered farm holding and influences the system of exchange by the part it plays in marketing. All these related aspects will be treated in other appropriate connections.

No animal labour is used in transport. On land, the men have to carry the load themselves.

❹ Clothing

The domestic industry of weaving in the village has been practically ruined. Although nearly every house has a wooden weaving machine, at the time when I was there, there were only two of them still working. The material for clothing thus largely comes from the outside, mainly linen and cotton. The silk industry works not for self-consumption but mainly for export. Only a few people wear silk dresses on formal occasions.

Owing to the wide variations of climate during the year, the villagers keep at least three sets of clothes: for the hot summer, for the mild spring and autumn, and for the cold winter. In the summer, men wear only shorts, but they will put on a skirt when meeting visitors or when going to town. Village headmen keep their silk gowns at least on their arms, when they leave the village even under the hot sun. Women wear sleeveless jackets and long skirts. Wearing a skirt is a characteristic of the region where women do not work on the farm. In colder weather, distinguished men wear the long gown when they do not work. The ordinary people only wear short jackets.

Clothing is not only for protecting the body but also for making social distinctions. Sex differentiation is clear. Age difference is also expressed; for instance, girls before maturity will not put on the skirt. Social status is directly indicated in the style. The long gown, for instance, is indispensable for persons of distinction. Two middle school students had changed their style of clothing when they came back from their school. They wore trousers and shirts in the European style but without coats.

都会划船。人们在小时候就学会了划船。只要一学会这门技术，一个人就可以不停地划几个小时。划船所耗的力量并不与船的载重量成正比，而是与水流、风向等情况密切有关。所以，载重增加时，此类运输的费用就降低。如果船夫能够利用风向，距离只是一个时间问题，而不是花力气的问题，这样，费用就可进一步减少。这是水运的一个重要特点。这就有可能使一个地区的住房集中在靠河边的位置。它也使分散的农田占有制成为可能。此外，水运在市场贸易中的作用也影响了流通系统。所有这些有关的方面将适当结合其他有关内容进一步论述。

畜力不用于运输。在陆地上，人得靠自己的力量来搬运货物。

四、衣着

村里的家庭纺织业实际上已经破产。我在村里的时候，虽然几乎每一家都有一台木制纺织机，但仍在运转的只有两台。因此，衣料大部分来自外面，主要是亚麻布和棉布。村里的缫丝工业主要为商品出口，并非为本村的消费。只有少数人在正式场合穿着丝绸衣服。

由于一年四季气候变化很大，村民至少有夏季、春秋和冬季穿用的三类衣服。夏天，男人只穿一条短裤，会客或进城时便穿上一条作裙。村长要离开村子外出时，即使是炎日当头，至少手臂上要搭上一件绸子长袍。妇女穿不带袖的上衣和长裙。这里的妇女不下农田干活，穿裙子是这个地区妇女的特点。天气较冷时，有身份的男子不干活时就穿长袍，普通人只穿短上衣。

衣服并不仅仅为了保护身体，同时也为了便于进行社会区别。性别区分是明显的。衣着还表现出年龄的区别，譬如，未成年的女孩不穿裙子。社会地位直接在服装的款式上表现出来，例如，长袍是有身份的人不可缺少的衣服。村里两个中学生上学以后服装式样有了变化，他们穿西式长裤和衬衫，但不穿外衣。

Sewing is women's work, except for tailors. Most of the women have skill enough to make ordinary clothes for their husbands and children, because this is a necessary qualification for a bride. At the end of the first month of her wedding, the bride will send an article of her own sewing to each near relative of her husband, whose approval is her pride and a support of her position in the new social group. But for preparing dowries, marriage gifts, and dresses of higher quality for formal use, professional tailors are as a rule called in.

The total expenses for buying clothing materials for an average Chia is estimated as about thirty dollars a year, excluding ceremonial dresses.

❺ Nutrition

Food is the main item of household expenditure. It amounts to 40 per cent. of the total annual current expenses. Furthermore, it is different from the above-mentioned items. Housing does not involve expense every day, and clothing usually is not so urgent as food. The amount of food that is necessary in order to maintain a normal living is more or less constant and consequently represents a relatively constant item in the domestic livelihood.

The staple food is rice. According to my informants' estimate the quantities needed for the annual consumption of different individuals are as follows:

Old man above 50	9 bushels.
Old woman above 40	$7\frac{1}{2}$ "
Adult man	12 "
Adult woman	9 "
Child above ten	$4\frac{1}{2}$ "

For an average household, including an old woman, two adults, and a child, the total amount will be thirty-two bushels. This estimate is fairly exact because the people must know the amount they need before they store the rice. Rice is produced by the people themselves; the surplus is sold in the market to get money for other expenses. The estimate given above is the amount which the people consider to be necessary to reserve in store.

In vegetables, including cabbages, fruits, mushrooms, nuts, potatoes, turnips, etc., the village is only partially self-supporting. The people have only very small gardens adjacent to the houses and limited space under

除裁缝以外，缝纫是妇女的工作。多数妇女的手艺足以为她们的丈夫和孩子做普通衣服，因为这是做新娘必备的资格。新娘结婚满一个月以后会送给她丈夫的每一位近亲一件她自己缝制的东西，亲属的称赞是她的荣誉，同时也是对她在这新社会群体中的地位的一种支持。但是在置办嫁妆、彩礼或缝制正式场合穿的高质量服装时，照例是要请专门的裁缝来做的。

一个普通的家，每年买衣料的费用估计为 30 元，礼服除外。

五、营养

食品是家庭开支的一个主要项目，占每年货币支出总额的 40%。而且它与上述几项支出不同。住房费用无需每天支付，衣服也不像饭食那样迫切。为了维持正常生活所必需的一定数量的食物，或多或少是恒定的，因此它在家庭生活中成为一个相对恒定的项目。

主食是稻米，为我提供情况的人估计，不同年龄或性别的人每年消费所需稻米数量如下：

50 岁以上的老年男子	9	蒲式耳
40 岁以上的老年妇女	7.5	蒲式耳
成年男子	12	蒲式耳
成年妇女	9	蒲式耳
10 岁以上的儿童	4.5	蒲式耳

对一个有一名老年妇女、两个成人和一个儿童的普通家庭而言，所需米的总量为 33 蒲式耳。这一估计是相当准确的，因为农民在储存稻米以前必须知道他们自己的需要量。稻米是农民自己生产的，剩余的米拿到市场上去出售，换得钱来用于其他开支。上面的估计是人们认为必须贮存的数量。

蔬菜方面有各种青菜、水果、蘑菇、干果、薯类以及萝卜等，这个村子只能部分自给。人们只能在房前屋后的小菜园里或桑树下有限

the mulberry trees for growing vegetables. They are largely dependent on the supply of the neighbouring villages along the Lake Tai where vegetable cultivation has become a specialization; and the produce has become one of the important sources of supply for the people in this region.

Oil is produced by villagers themselves from the rapeseeds which are planted in spring before the rice. But owing to the low level of the farms in this part, the crop is very limited and the produce is enough only for domestic use. Fish is supplied by the fishing households in the village. The only kind of meat eaten is pork, which is supplied by the town through retailers in the village. Sugar, salt, and other necessities for cooking are bought daily from the town chiefly through the agent boat (XIV–5).

There are three meals a day: morning, noon, and evening. They are cooked separately. But during the period when men are busy on the farm they will prepare their lunch in the morning with the breakfast. The woman is the first to get up. She cleans the stove and warms the water and then prepares the meals. Breakfast consists of rice porridge and some preserved salty cabbage. Porridge is made by boiling the dried rice crust in the water. Lunch is the big meal of the day, but during the time when men have to work on the farm, they carry with them their prepared lunch. They do not come back until evening. Women and children who are left in the house also take the prepared lunch which is rather light.

In the evening when the men come back, the whole household take dinner together, in the front room. But in the hot weather the table is arranged in the front of the house; it is very impressive to walk in the street on a summer evening. The street is lined by a row of tables. Neighbours talk with each other while they are eating at their own table. All the members of the household sit around the same table, except the woman who is busy in the kitchen and serves the table.

At the table they have definite positions, following the kinship order of the family. The head of the family sits at the "upper side," facing south.

The left side, facing west, comes next and then the right side. The women, especially the daughter-in-law, take the lower side, or they do not appear at the table but take their food in the kitchen.

The commensalism of the evening meal is important in domestic life, especially for the father and child to see each other. The father is absent the whole day and the child may not be able to see him until that time. At the table they are together. The disciplinary function of the father operates at this time. Relevant to this context is the manner of eating.

的土地上种菜。农民主要依靠太湖沿岸一带的村庄供给蔬菜。种菜已经成为这一带的专业，他们的产品已是这一地区人们蔬菜供应的重要来源之一。

食油是村民自己用油菜籽榨的，春天种稻之前种油菜。但这个地区农田水平面较低，油菜收成有限，产量仅够家用。鱼类由本村的渔业户供给。人们吃的肉类仅有猪肉，由村里卖肉的人从镇里贩来零售。食糖、盐和其他烹调必需品主要通过航船每天上镇购买（第十四章第五节）。

一天三餐：早饭、午饭、晚饭，分别准备。但农忙期间，早上就把午饭和早饭一起煮好。妇女第一个起床，先清除炉灰、烧水，然后煮饭。早饭是米粥和腌菜，粥系用干米饭锅巴放在水中煮开而成。午饭是一天之中主要的一餐。但农忙季节，男人们把午饭带往农田，直到傍晚收工以后才回家。留在家中的妇女和儿童也吃早上煮好的饭，但吃得较少。

晚上男人们回家以后，全家在堂屋里一起吃晚饭。但天气热的时候，就把桌子搬出来摆在房屋前面场地上；夏天傍晚，到街上走一走，印象非常深刻。沿街摆着一排桌子，邻居们各自在桌边吃饭，边吃边谈。全家人都围着桌子坐着，只有主妇在厨房里忙着给大家端饭。

家中每一个人在桌旁都有一定的位置。按家庭的亲缘顺序，家长面南，坐在"上首"，第二位面向西，在家长的左侧，第三位在右侧。主妇，特别是媳妇，坐在下首，或者不上桌，在厨房里吃饭。

同进晚餐，在家庭生活中是很重要的，父亲和孩子这时有机会互相见面。父亲整天外出，孩子直到晚饭时才能见到他。他们一起在桌旁吃饭。父亲常利用这机会对孩子进行管教。吃饭要讲吃饭的规矩。

The child must not complain about the food or show special preference for certain dishes. If he does so, he will be at once scorned and sometimes beaten by his father. At the table the child is usually silent and obedient.

During the period of agricultural work, the dinner is comparatively rich. They have meat and fish. But in ordinary times meat is not very often served. Pure vegetarianism is rare except for a few widows. Ordinary women take vegetarian meals twice a month, the first and the fifteenth day; this is because of the religious teaching that heavenly gods do not like killing animate creatures. Thus vegetarian practice will help one to have a better after-life.

Food prepared in the kitchen should not be set aside for individual members. But occasionally the family unit may have some special dish for themselves out of their own expenses and eat in their own room. This is considered to be bad behaviour and offensive to the other members. Cakes and sweets bought with one's own pocket money are private.

❻ Recreation

Relaxation from muscular and nervous stress after hard work is a physiological necessity. In so far as recreation needs collective action, social institutions develop for this function. The collective action in recreation reinforces the social ties among the participants. Thus its function goes beyond pure physiological relaxation.

In the household the period for domestic gatherings is in the evening when the daily work is over. In this gathering the family bonds are strengthened and an intimate feeling develops.

Work in agriculture and in the silk industry affords periodical intervals. The people after having been busy for a week or ten days may have a pause. The period of recreation is inserted into the time-table of work. During the intervals, rich dinners are prepared and visits among relatives take place.

Men will use this pause to enjoy themselves in the teashops. Teashops are in the town. They bring together the people from different villages. Business bargainings, marital negotiations and arbitration of disputes take place. But they are, primarily, men's clubs. Only occasionally some women will appear with their men in the shop. Women spend their intervals of work in visiting relatives, especially their own parents and brothers. Most of the children go with their mothers.

孩子不准抱怨食物不可口，也不准挑食。他如这样做，就立刻会受到父亲的责备，有时还要挨打。通常在吃饭时孩子都默不作声地顺从长辈的意见。

在农忙期间，饭食较为丰富。他们吃鱼、吃肉。但平时不经常吃肉食。除去几个寡妇以外，很少有素食主义者。普通妇女每月素斋两次，初一和十五各一次，这是由于宗教告诫人们，天上的神仙不愿意伤害生灵。吃素被视为有利于人死后升天过好日子。

在厨房里做的东西不应该留藏给家里个别人独自吃。但是偶尔，小家庭可以自己花钱买些特别的菜在自己房间里吃。这种做法被认为是不好的，会惹得家里其他成员生气。一个人用自己的零花钱去买点心、糖果吃是私事，不一定告诉别人。

六、娱乐

辛勤劳动之后，放松肌肉和神经的紧张是一种生理需要。娱乐需要集体活动，于是社会制度发展了这种功能。娱乐中的集体活动加强了参加者之间的社会纽带，因此它的作用超出了单纯的生理休息。

在家中全家团聚的时间是在晚上，全天劳动完毕以后。大家聚集起来，家庭间的联系得到了加强，感情也更加融洽。

农业劳动和蚕丝业劳动有周期性的间歇，人们连续忙了一个星期或十天之后，可以停下来稍事休息。娱乐时间就插入工作时间表中。在间歇的时候，大家煮丰盛的饭菜，还要走亲访友。

男人们利用这段时间在茶馆里消遣。茶馆在镇里。它聚集了从各村来的人在茶馆里谈生意，商议婚姻大事，调解纠纷等等。但茶馆基本上是男人的俱乐部。偶尔有少数妇女和她们的男人一起在茶馆露面。妇女们在休息时期一般是走亲戚，特别是要回娘家看望自己的父母和兄弟。孩子们大多数是要跟随母亲一起去的。

The evening gathering of the domestic group, the gatherings in the teashops and frequent visiting among relatives during the rest periods are informal and not obligatory. In this respect, they are different from the festivals and formal communal gatherings. The time-table for social activities, given in Chapter IX, summarizes all the occasions of festivals in relation to other chronological activities.

It is fairly clear that festivals come always in between periods of industrial activity. The "New Year," celebrated in February by fifteen days for rejoicing and obligatory visiting of relatives, comes at a time of few agricultural activities. Wedding ceremonies also come in that period, which is regarded as a proper time for marriage. Shortly before the active period in the silk industry, is the festival of Ch'ing Ming for ancestral worship and visiting tombs. At the third exuviæ of silkworms, a rejoicing feast is prepared at Li Hsia. After the silk reeling work and before the transplantation of young shoots of the rice to the main field, the festival of Tuan Yang comes in. Full moon in the eighth month, Chung Ch'iu, is celebrated at the time when the rice bears fruit and in the middle of the first long interval of agricultural work. At the end of that interval another festival of Ch'ung Yang is on the schedule. When the agricultural work is completed it is the festival of Tung Chih. All these festivals are obligatory and usually connected with religious worship of ancestors and of the kitchen god. Celebration of such festivals is limited to domestic groups and intimate relatives.

Occasions for periodical obligatory gatherings of larger local groups, such as *luiwanwe* of the *de*, the annual meeting of the village (VI–3), and the inter-village parade every ten years along Lake Tai, *sanyanwe*, are also connected with religious ideas. For more than ten years all these occasions, except *luiwanwe*, have been suspended. The immediate reason for the suspension is the disapproval of the government. According to the government these activities are superstitious and luxurious, and it is one of the duties of the magistrate to prohibit them.[26] But the ultimate and more effective cause is the economic depression of the rural district. When immediate needs such as food and clothes have become a burden to the people, there is no surplus money to finance such less urgent social activities.

How far the suspension of community gatherings has weakened the local ties among the people is difficult to ascertain from my present material. But when I sat among the people and listened to their narrations of the past exciting events of the inter-village parade, their feeling of loss

家人在晚间的聚会，朋友们在茶馆相会，以及农闲时看望亲戚，都是非正式的，不是必须履行的。从这一点来讲，这些活动与节日期间的聚会以及正式的社区聚会有所不同。第九章所列的社会活动时间表总结了一年中的所有节日，与其他活动一起按年月顺序排列。

很明显，各个节日总是出现在生产活动间歇之际。阳历二月份，农闲时节，庆祝"新年"十五天，人们欢欢喜喜地过年，并尽亲戚之谊，前去拜年。婚礼也往往在这时候举行，人们认为这是结婚的好时节。在蚕丝业繁忙阶段之前不久的是清明，进行祭祖和扫墓。蚕第三次蜕皮时，就到了立夏，有一次欢庆的盛宴。在缫丝工作之后，插秧之前，有端阳节。阴历八月满月的日子是中秋。此时正值稻子孕穗，也是在农活第一次较长间歇期的中间。在此间歇的末尾是重阳节。农活完毕之后就是冬至了。每逢这些节日都要有一定的庆祝活动，通常是同祭祖和祭灶联系在一起。庆祝这样一些节日只限于在家人和近亲中进行。

较大的地方群体的定期集会有每年一次的"段"的"刘皇会"（第六章第三节），和每十年一次在太湖边举行的村际的庆祝游行"双阳会"，俗称"出会"，它们也与宗教思想有关。十多年来，除"刘皇会"以外，所有这些集会都已停止。停止的直接原因就是政府不赞同。政府认为，这些活动是迷信而且奢侈。地方行政官的职责之一就是禁止这些集会。[26] 但是更实际的根本的原因是乡村地区的经济萧条。当食品、衣服之类的必需品都成为人们的负担时，他们就不会有多余的钱去进行不太急需的社会活动。

根据我目前的材料，难以确定社区停止聚会在多大程度上削弱了当地人民之间的联系。但当我坐在人们中间，听着他们叙述村际"出会"那些令人兴奋的往事时，我明白地觉察到他们对于目前处境的

and disappointment at the present situation was very clear to me. I am not going to try to reconstruct the grand occasion and estimate the social value involved in it, but the memory of the past forms an important element in the present attitude towards the existing situation. The suspension of these festivities is a direct indication, in the mind of the people, of deterioration of social life. In so far as they are looking forward for a return of the happy days, they will not reject any possible measure which they are convinced as making for improvement. This psychology has its significance in the lack of strong resistance to social change, as I shall show later (XII–2).

❼ Ceremonial Expenses

Ceremonial expenses connected with the crises of life—birth, marriage, and death—looked at from the economic point of view are indispensable items of liability to the domestic economy. Marriage gifts and dowries are the necessary provisions of the new family unit. Funeral arrangements are necessary measures of disposing of the dead. The sentiments arising from these crises of the individual life and of the related social groups cause the ceremonies to be more elaborate and to involve considerable cost. When the ceremonial procedure has been generally accepted, one cannot pass these crises except through this costly channel.

The economic depression has, however, affected the ceremonies. For instance, the institution of *siaosiv* has been adopted to modify the expensive marriage procedure (III–8). It is adopted for economic expedience but has far-reaching consequences in kinship organization. The total or partial reduction of affinal relationships has influenced the social position of women and children. The cancelling of marriage gifts and dowry prolongs the economic dependence of the young. All these illustrate the fact that the ceremonial expenses are not altogether waste or luxury. They perform essential functions in social life.

Again, the marriage feast provides an opportunity for the gathering of relatives for recognizing newly established kinship ties and reinforcing the old. The kinship tie is not a matter of sentimental relation only. It regulates various types of social relation. From the economic point of view, it prescribes the mutual obligation to join the financial aid society (XV–2), and the periodical offering of gifts. In the modified marriage ceremony, the list of guests invited is usually shortened. This loosens the wider kinship ties and thus closes, in the long run,

沮丧和失望之情。我并不想再恢复那些盛大的场面，并对其社会价值进行估计，然而对往事的回忆是形成人们目前对现状的态度的一个重要因素。在人们心目中，停止这些庆祝活动，直接说明了社会生活的下降。由于他们盼望着过去的欢乐日子复而再来，所以他们不会拒绝任何可能采取的确信会改善社会生活的措施。在对社会变革没有强大抵触的情况下，上述这种心理至关重要，我以后还要说明（第十二章第二节）。

七、礼仪开支

礼仪开支与一生中的重大事件——出生、结婚、死亡——有着密切联系。从经济观点来看，这种开支是一家不可缺少的负担。彩礼和嫁妆是新家庭必要的准备。丧葬安排是处理死者所必须的措施。个人生活及其相关的社会群体所发生的这些红白大事里产生出来的感情，使得这些礼仪得到更加精心的安排而且花费相当的钱财。当一种礼仪程序被普遍接受之后，人们就不得不付出这笔开销，否则他就不能通过这些人生的关口。

然而，经济萧条使礼仪受到了影响。例如采取了"小媳妇"的制度来改变昂贵的婚礼（第三章第八节）。它是由于经济便利才被采用的，但对亲属组织却发生了深远的影响。姻亲关系的完全或部分退化已使妇女和儿童的社会地位受到影响。彩礼和嫁妆的取消延长了青年在经济上依赖父母的时间。所有这些说明了这样一个事实，礼仪开支不全然是浪费和奢侈的。这些开支在社会生活中起着重要的作用。

再者，结婚时的宴会为亲戚们提供了一个相聚的机会，对新建立的亲属纽带予以承认，对旧有的关系加以巩固。亲属纽带不仅仅是感情上的关系，它还调节各种类型的社会关系。从经济观点来看，它规定了参加这种互助会的相互义务（第十五章第二节），以及定期互赠礼物。在已经改变了的婚姻礼仪中，所请客人的名单通常已经缩减。这使原来较广的亲属纽带变得松散。从长远看，就可能封闭了一些

a possible channel of financial help. These consequences may not be immediate and apparent but will be felt eventually. This is why the people reject the institution of *siaosiv* and revert to the normal course as soon as economic conditions allow. Many even, in order to maintain the traditional procedure, delay marriage or borrow money to stage the ceremony in an unimpaired form.

In view of the importance of ceremonial occasions in the life of the people, it is not surprising to find the high percentage of ceremonial expenses in the domestic budget. For an average family of four members, assuming the average length of life to be fifty years, there will be one ceremonial occasion every five years. The minimum expenses for these ceremonies are estimated as follows: birth 30 dollars, marriage 500 dollars, and funeral 250 dollars. The average annual expense will be 50 dollars. It amounts to one-seventh of the whole annual expenditure.

To this sum we must also add the gift presented by the house to their relatives who are passing through these life crises. Their presents vary according to the nearness of kinship and of friendship, from 5 dollars to 20 cents. The average amount per year per Chia is about 10 dollars at least.

These estimates seem to be rather high as compared with other rural communities in China. According to J. L. Buck's study, the average amount for a wedding per family is 114.83 dollars and for a funeral 62.07 dollars, in East Central China.[27] The difference may be due to local characters or to the number of items of expenditure included in this heading. The expenses on the wedding day in Kaihsienkung lie between 250 to 100 dollars. There was a notorious case, quoted by my informants as exceptional, of a ceremonial manager who could conduct a wedding for less than 100 dollars. The estimate here given includes also the marriage gifts. So it is reasonable that it should be higher.

The funeral expenses vary greatly according to the social status of the deceased. As observed in Peiping, for children "the funerals cost a little more than one-eighth of the family's monthly income. The funerals of older people are naturally more expensive. The total varies from 1.25 to 1.3 months' income. None of these included a funeral feast. Funerals for husbands, wives, older brothers, mothers, cost their families from 2.5, 3.5, and 5.5 months' income." **28** Buck's average is derived from 2.8 per cent. of all the families that had funeral expenses to pay during the year. It may be a little lower than the amount regarded as proper expenditure for the funeral of an adult member of the family, as given by my informants.

经济援助的渠道，这种结果可能不会很快或明显地表现出来，但最终会感觉到的。这就是人们拒绝"小媳妇"制度的原因。一俟经济条件许可，就要恢复正常的程序。为了维持传统的礼仪，甚至有许多人宁可推迟婚期或借钱也要把婚礼办得像个样子。

从礼仪事务在人们生活中的重要性来看，就不难理解礼仪开支在家庭预算中占有很高的百分比。在一个普通的四口之家，假设平均寿命为 50 岁，那么每隔 5 年将有一次礼仪事务。对于礼仪事务的最低开支估计如下：出生 30 元，结婚 500 元，丧葬 250 元，平均每年开支 50 元，这个数字为每年全部开支的七分之一。

亲戚家有这些婚丧娶嫁等大事时，他们还须送礼，所以我们也必须把这笔开支计入总和。根据亲友关系亲疏的不同，礼品的价值从 0.2 至 5 元不等。每家每年的平均数量至少约为 10 元。

同中国的其他乡村相比，这些估值似乎相当高。根据巴克的研究，在华东每家用于一次结婚的平均费用为 114.83 元，丧葬费平均为 62.07 元。**27** 差别可能由于地方的特点不同，或者由于列入礼仪开支的项数不同。在开弦弓，结婚当天的开销在 100 至 250 元之间。为我提供资料的人引述一个众所周知的例外情况：一家仅花了不到 100 元办了一次婚礼。此处所作对婚礼开支的估计还包括了结婚礼物的费用，所以总数理应高一些。

丧葬开支，根据死者社会地位的高低而大不相同。如在北平所观察到的，孩子的"丧葬费用比家庭每月收入的八分之一略多一点。年长者的丧葬费自然要贵一些，总共要花费月收入的 1.25 至 1.3 倍不等。但这些数字都不包括丧宴费用。丈夫、妻子、哥哥、母亲的丧葬，其费用为月收入的 2.5、3.5、5.5 倍。"**28** 巴克的平均数是从有丧事的人家的 2.8% 中推算出来的。该数字可能略低于本地人提供给我的有关该村一个成年人死后所需的适当的丧葬费用。

These periodical expenses demand saving during the interval. It may take the form of payment of loans, but usually, of subscriptions to a financial aid society, which is a local institution of saving (XV–2). Thus we can check the estimate of ceremonial expenses with the average annual amount of subscription per Chia. In general, as I found, each Chia joins two societies at the same time with a total annual subscription of 40 dollars. It tends to support the reliability of these estimates.

❽ Minimum Expenditure

All the quantitative assessments given in the above sections represent only the recognized minimum requirement of a proper living in the village. To secure these estimates, I consulted a number of informants. Differences between individual estimates were very small. It shows a high comformity of such estimates. The average Chia under consideration consists of four individuals: an old woman, an adult man, an adult woman, and a child, who are full owners of a holding of nine *mow* of land.

These estimates are useful for several reasons: (1) A single-handed field investigator finds it practically impossible to adopt the account-book method, especially in a village where keeping accounts is not a habit of the people, unless he devotes his whole time to investigating this problem. (2) These estimates can give a certain general idea of the livelihood of the villagers because they represent the minimum requirement of a normal living which cannot be very far from the actual average. (3) The lack of striking differentiation in the standard of living in the village allows such a simple approach. (4) As mentioned, these estimates form a standard in the minds of the people as a measurement of sufficiency of material well-being in the community, and consequently an actual social force in controlling consumption.

Moreover, in studying the problem of the standard of living in a rural community, the account-book method has its limitations. The rural community is partially self-supporting. The livelihood will not be comprehended in full in the daily accounts which are usually limited to money transactions. The account-book only reveals the extent to which the villagers depend on outside supplies of goods. The degree of dependence does not always indicate the standard of living. For instance, under normal conditions, the villagers will not buy rice because they have their own reserves. Only when the reserves have been sold

这些定期的开销需要在平时积蓄起来。积蓄可能采取贷款的形式，但通常采取向互助会交纳储金的形式。互助会是本地的一种储蓄制度（第十五章第二节）。这样，我们可以把估计的礼仪开支费用同每家每年交纳储金的平均数作一比较。我发现，一般每家同时加入两个互助会，每年总共交纳储金 40 元。这一数字有助于证实以上估计的可靠性。

八、正常生活的最低开支

前几节中所作的全部定量估计仅仅代表村里公认的正常生活的最低需要。为了取得这些估计，我曾请教了不少知情人。个人估计之间的差别非常小，这说明了这样的估计具有较高的一致性。我们所考虑的普通的家是由四个人组成：一位老年妇女、一位成年男子、一位成年妇女和一个小孩。这四个人是九亩土地的完全所有者。

这些估计之所以有用，有以下几条理由：（1）单独的实地调查者几乎不可能采用簿记研究法，特别是在村里，人们没有记账的习惯，除非调查者把他的全部时间用于研究记账问题。（2）这些估计可以使人们对本村人的生活得到一个一般的概念，它代表正常生活的最低需要，与实际平均数不会相差太远。（3）村里的生活标准没有显著的差别，因而可以使用这种简便的方法。（4）如上所述，这些估计在人们心目中形成了一个度量社区中物质福利充足的标准，其结果是产生了一种控制消费的实际社会力量。

此外，在研究乡村社区生活水准问题方面，簿记研究法有一定的局限性。乡村社区是部分自给经济，生活上的各项费用并不完全包括在日常账目之中，因为账目通常限于记录货币交易。账簿只能说明村民依赖外界商品供应的程度，而这种依赖程度并不一定能够表明生活水准。例如，在正常情况下，村民不会去买米，因为他们自己有储备。只有在家庭经济困难、储存的大米已被卖光时，村民才去买米来吃。

under financial distress, will they buy rice to feed themselves. In this case the increased amount of money transactions is related to the decline of livelihood and not the reverse, as might appear from the accounts only.

It is clear that in a study of the standard of living of a rural community it will not be enough simply to give a summary of the family budget in terms of money income and expenditure. The investigator must prepare a double entry for the goods consumed to assess those bought from the market and those produced by the consumers themselves. The former should be expressed in terms of money value. The sum of this category represents the amount of money needed to finance the life of the people. It determines the amount of produce sold by them in order to get that amout of money. Those goods produced by the consumers do not enter into the market. Their money value is unknown because the price would be affected if they entered the market. To express them in terms of market price is theoretically unsound. Indeed, without reducing them to a money value, it would not be possible to give a general index of the standard of living of the people. But such a general index is unreal and has little value in an empirical analysis. To keep these two categories apart will help us to investigate the relation between them, and this relation is very important in the study of rural economy. For instance, one of the important problems in the present Chinese rural economy is the decline of the price of the rural produce. For a given necessary requirement of living, the villagers are forced to sell more of their produce to the market. It thus reduces the degree of self-sufficiency of the villagers. On the other hand, the process of de-industrialization in the rural districts has reduced the amount and type of rural produce and increased the need of money for buying manufactured goods. To approach these problems, it is important to analyse the relation of these two categories of consumers' goods.

This "double-entry" method demands much more work from the field investigator. It may be impractical for him to make statistical observations. Thus I suggest the method of consulting estimates. If possible, it could be supplemented by sampling observation—selecting a few representative cases and systematically assessing the amount of consumption for a period. But the present work is not able to provide this type of data. The following table gives only the money value of those items that the villagers have to buy from the market, and the obligatory payment of tax and rent. It is useful as an estimate of the minimum amount of money needed for the livelihood of the villagers.

在这种情况下，现金交易量的增加与生活下降有关而不是与生活改善有关。只有这种情况才会在账目中有所反映。

很明显，在研究乡村社区生活水准时，简单地以货币的收支来总计家庭预算，是不足以说明问题的。调查者必须从两方面入手来对消费品进行估价：一方面是那些从市场买来的消费品；另一方面是消费者自己生产的物品。前者应以货币值来表示，其总和代表着人们生活所需的货币量。这个数额确定了人们为得到此数额的货币而出售的产品量。消费者自产自用的物品不进入市场。这些物品的货币值无人知晓。因为如果它们进入了市场，价格就会受到影响。如以市场价格表示这些物品，从理论上讲是不正确的。的确，若不把它们折合为货币价值，就不可能得出人们生活水准的总指数。但是，这样的一个总指数是不真实的。把这两类物品分开研究，有助于我们调查其间的关系，而这种关系在农业经济研究中是非常重要的。例如，目前中国农业经济中最重要的问题之一是农产品的价格下跌。为了满足必需的生活条件，村民被迫向市场多出售他们的产品。这样就降低了村民的自给程度。另一方面，农村地区的辅助工业的萧条，减少了农产品的品种和数量，增加了对货币的需要，以购买所需的工业品。为了探讨这些问题，分析这两类消费品之间的关系是很重要的。

这种"从两方面入手的方法"需要实地调查者付出更多的劳动。收集统计资料可能是不实际的，所以，我建议采用咨询估算的方法。如果可能的话，再用抽样观察来补充。选定几个有代表性的实例，在一个时期中，系统地记录消费项目和数量。但本文尚不能提供这一类的数据。下表仅仅列出了村民必须到市场上购买的物品之货币价值，以及强制支付的租金和税款。该表可以用来估计村民生活所需的最低货币量。

Those goods produced by the consumers themselves include the foodstuffs, such as rice, oil, wheat, and vegetable, and a part of the clothing materials. The most important part of the self-sufficient economy is labour and service. As mentioned, only a few households employ labourers on the farm. Further analysis of this category will be given in connection with the process of production.

I. Things bought from the market:

Foodstuffs	. . . . . .		47
Vegetables and miscellaneous	. .	30	
Sugar		5	
Salt		12	
Clothing materials	. . . . .		30
Presents			10
Fuel, light, etc.			36
House and boat oiling			20
Tools and fertilizer			10
Expenses in silk industry		50	203
II. Land tax	.		10
III. Periodic expenses (expressed in saving)	. .	.	50
			———
TOTAL			$263

消费者自己生产的物品包括食物，例如米、油、麦子、蔬菜及部分衣料。自给经济最重要的部分是劳动和服务。如上所述，只有少数农户雇工种田。关于这方面的分析，将进一步结合生产过程来进行。

1. 从市场购买的物品

食品	47	
蔬菜和杂项	30	
糖	5	
盐	12	
衣料	30	
礼品	10	
燃料、灯火等	36	
房屋及船上用油	20	
农具及肥料	10	
蚕丝业开销	50	203
2. 土地税		10
3. 定期费用（以积蓄的形式表示）		‥50
总　计		263 元

CHAPTER VIII   OCCUPATIONAL DIFFERENTIATION

❶ Agriculture as the Basic Occupation

In the process of consumption there are no essential classifications into which the villagers must be divided, but in the process of production occupational differentiation is found. According to the census, occupations are classified under four headings: (1) agriculture, (2) special occupations, (3) fishing, and (4) non-occupied.

These classes are not mutually exclusive. Persons not classified as agricultural may nevertheless be partly engaged in agricultural activities. Agriculture is the fundamental occupation common to nearly all the villagers except among the landless outsiders. The difference is only a matter of emphasis. Those who are classified under the heading of agriculture do not depend on land exclusively but are also engaged in raising silkworms and sheep, and in trade ventures. The fourth category includes households whose adult male members have died and where the widows or the children are living on the rent of the leased land but not through their own productive effort.

The occupation of a Chia is recorded in the census according to the occupation of its head. Members of the Chia may be engaged in different occupations—for example, the children of the store-keeper may be engaged in agriculture and the farmer's daughter engaged in industrial work in the town. This, however, is not indicated. The number of Chia in each category is given in the following table:

I. Agricultural	274
II. Special occupations	59
III. Fishing	14
IV. Non-occupied	13
TOTAL	360

The above table shows clearly that more than two-thirds, or 76 per cent., of the total population are mainly engaged in agriculture. Owing to the limited time of my field work, my investigations were chiefly concerned with this group. A fuller analysis of the productive activities of the group will be given in the following chapters. Other occupational groups I can only describe briefly.

捌 职业分化

一、农业——基本职业

在消费过程中，没有必要把该村的居民进行分类，但在生产过程中，则有职业的区别。根据人口普查，有四种职业：（1）农业；（2）专门职业；（3）渔业；（4）无业。

这些职业类别并不是互相排斥的。没有被划入农业的人也可能参与部分的农业活动。除去无地的外来人以外，对几乎所有居民来说，农业是共同的基本职业，区别仅仅在于侧重面不同而已。被划归农业的人并不是只依赖于土地，他们还从事养蚕、养羊和经商。第四类人包含这样一些农户：成年男子业已死亡，寡妇和儿童靠出租的土地生活，而不是靠他们自己的生产劳动过日子。

在人口普查记录里，家庭的职业是根据一家之长的职业而定的。家庭的成员可以从事不同的职业，例如，店主的孩子可能从事农业，农民的女儿可以到城里的工厂工作。这些情况都没有表示出来。该村各类职业的家庭数字如下：

I.	农业	274
II.	专门职业	59
III.	渔业	14
IV.	无业	13
总 数		360

上表清楚地说明，占人口总数三分之二以上即 76% 的人主要从事农业。由于实地调查的时间有限，我的调查工作主要是有关这个职业组的。下章再详细分析这个职业组的生产活动。其他职业组，我只能简单地描述一下。

❷ Special Occupations

A further analysis of the second category is given in the following table:

I. Engaged in special occupations in town . . .	14
II. Silk spinners	6
III. Retail traders	10
IV. Agent boats	4
V. Crafts and professional services . . .	25

Carpenters	4
Tailors	3
Staff members of the co-operative factory	3
Basket makers	2
Barbers	2
Millers	2
Operators of modern pumping machines	2
Mason	1
Midwife	1
Priest	1
Shoemaker	1
Silversmith	1
Weaver	1
TOTAL	59

The first heading includes only those Chia whose heads are living in the town engaged in trade or in other occupations. The girls working in the silk factories outside are not included.

Silk spinners represent a special occupation. They work for the silk houses in the town, which collect the native raw silk from the villagers. The quality of the silk is irregular, and it must be sorted out by means of spinning before it can be exported or sold to the weaving factories. This sorting work is done by the villagers. The collectors distribute the raw material to the spinner and collect the silk again. Wages are paid according to the amount of work done.

A description of the retail traders and of the agent boats is given in the chapter on marketing (XIV–4–6).

二、专门职业

第二类的进一步分析，见下表：

I.	在城镇从事专门职业的	14
II.	纺丝工人	6
III.	零售商	10
IV.	航船	4
V.	手工业与服务行业	24
	木匠	4
	裁缝	3
	合作丝厂职工	3
	篾匠	2
	理发匠	2
	磨工	2
	抽水机操作者	2
	泥水匠	1
	接生婆	1
	和尚	1
	鞋匠	1
	银匠	1
	织工	1
总 计		58

表中第一项，只包含那些家长在城里经商的家庭或家长从事其他职业，住在城里。不包括那些在村外丝厂工作的女工。

纺丝工人代表一种专门职业。他们为镇上的丝行工作，丝行从村民手里搜集土法缫制的生丝，质量不整齐，在出口或卖给丝织厂以前，必须通过反摇整理。这种整理工作由村民来做。丝行把原料分配给纺丝人，然后再收集起来，按照工作量给予工资。

零售商人和航船，在讨论贸易的一章中另作描述（第十四章第四节至第六节）。

The whole group of craftsmen and professional men includes only 7 per cent. of the total households in the village. This low percentage is striking. It is due firstly to the fact that such work is not exclusively specialized. Tailoring, shoemaking, and milling are common work in all households. Wood, bamboo, and mason's work of a crude type requires very little knowledge and skill and the necessary tools are found in most houses. The modern pumping machines are not in wide use, and are used mainly in time of emergency. Childbirth does not always need expert help. In the above list, besides the work of the operators of the modern pumping machines, perhaps only the work of the barbers, the temple keeper, the priest, and the staff members of the co-operative factory is so specialized as not to be more usually undertaken by the farmers themselves.

Moreover, when the people need goods or services, they do not necessarily depend on the supply available in the village. Wood, bamboo, and metal articles of better quality can be bought from the town. Even the barber once complained to me that the villagers were gradually tending to have their heads shaved in the town. In the case of funeral ceremonies priests are sent for from distant temples. Serious cases of childbirth cannot be trusted to the village midwife.

All the outsiders living in the village are traders and craftsmen and form, in fact, one-third of the total number of that group (II–5). I have no information showing whether the trades and crafts were originally novel occupations introduced from outside, but there is good reason to suspect that new crafts are often introduced by their agents from outside. Since technical knowledge is usually transmitted through the kinship line, it is often not easily assimilated by the indigenous population. Moreover, even when the crafts are open for apprenticeship, parents who are able to provide their children with the opportunity of tilling land like to keep them on the farm. Land in the village is insufficient to support an increase of population. It is, therefore, difficult for an outsider to acquire land, and land in any case seldom comes into the market. Thus, as mentioned above, at present all the outsiders are landless and the only means for them to find a living is to engage in certain new crafts or in trades.

整个手工业和服务行业人员占这个村庄总户数的7%。这样低的百分比是惊人的。首先，这是由于这些行业还不完全是专业化的。缝纫、做鞋、碾磨等工作，是各户自己劳动的普通工作。比较粗糙的木工、竹工和泥水匠的工作不需非常专门的知识和技巧，所用工具在大多数住家中都自备。现代抽水机尚未被广泛使用，主要在紧急时用。生孩子也不一定需要专家的帮助。在上表中，除了现代抽水机操作者外，也许只有理发匠、和尚、庙宇看守人和合作丝厂的职工的工作比较专业化，农民自己不能兼任。

此外，人们不一定都要村里供应他们所需的物品或依赖这个村里的人来解决他们生活服务的问题。质量较好的木器、竹器或铁器可以在城镇里买到。甚至有一次理发匠对我抱怨说，村民逐渐倾向于到镇里去剃头了。有丧事时，人们往往到远处庙宇去请和尚。妇女难产时不能信托村里的接生婆来接生。

所有住在村里的外来人都是商人和手艺人，他们实际上占这个群体（第二章第五节）总人数的三分之一。关于商业和手艺是否原来就是从外面传来的一种新的职业，我手头没有资料可以说明这一点，但我们有理由猜想一些新的手工艺往往是通过某些渠道从外边引进的。由于技术知识通常是通过亲属关系传授，本地人不易很快地吸收这种知识。即使师傅可以公开传授手艺，但那些有条件让孩子们种地的父母仍愿意让他们种地。村子里的土地不足以提供额外人口谋生，因此，外来人很难获得土地，而且土地也很少在市场出售。所以，正如上面已提到的，目前，所有外来人都没有地，其谋生的唯一手段是从事某种新手艺或经商。

❸ Fishing

There are two groups of fishing households, differing in methods of fishing and in their residential areas. The first group, living at the west end of the village on *Yu* I and II, only follow fishing as a supplementary occupation. Their method is by nets and hooks. Their heavy work is in the winter. At that time, when agricultural work is at a pause, they start their large scale "circle fishing." Several boats co-operate together to form a team. Small hooks are hung close to each other on a strong and long rope, to which are added several heavy weights. The fishing team distribute themselves in a circle, letting the hooks sink into the bottom of the lake. In cold weather, especially when snow has fallen, the lake does not freeze, but the fish are all half-hibernated in the mud, and, as the hooks drag through the mud, the fish are easily gathered. This "circle fishing" is sometimes continued for several weeks and yields a large return. On ordinary days the fishermen spread their large nets in the water and collect fish from them several times a day. This kind of fishing can be done only by those whose houses are near the lake. That is the reason for the localization of this group in the area at the west end.

Shrimps are collected from the lake by a kind of trap, made of basketry. Shrimp trapping is a common occupation of those households which live near the lake. According to reports I gathered in the summer of 1935, there were forty-three boats engaged in this work. The traps are connected by cords to a long line and put into the water. Every four hours they are cleared, because the shrimps will die if they are allowed to remain too long in the traps, and dead shrimps are of less value on the market. The average income is one dollar per boat per day worked by two persons.

The other group of fishing households are found along the middle course of Stream B, on *Yu* II. These raise fishing birds, which will dive into water to catch fish. Raising and training these birds requires special knowledge which is transmitted in the family, and thus this occupation is hereditary. These families form a special group and co-operate with their fellow professional men even in other villages. Since they may need to go very far from the home village and the birds must be carefully sheltered at night, they form a super-residential group based on their common professional interest. All the fishermen engaged in the same profession are obliged to extend their hospitality to their fellows.

三、渔业

有两类渔业户，他们的捕鱼方法不同，居住地区也不同。第一类渔户，住在村的西头，圩Ⅰ、圩Ⅱ，仅以捕鱼为副业。他们的捕鱼方法是用网和鱼钩。冬季工作较忙。那时，农活告一段落，他们便开始进行大规模的"围鱼"作业。几只船合作组成捕鱼队，在又粗又长的绳子上密挂小鱼钩，然后再加上一些重量，捕鱼队队员围成一个圈，把鱼钩沉入湖底。寒冷天气，特别是下雪以后，湖面不结冰，但鱼都在泥里冬眠，鱼钩在泥里拉过，很容易把鱼钩住。这样的"围鱼"作业有时持续数周，收获量颇大。平时，渔民撒大网捕鱼，一日数次。这种捕鱼方式只有那些住在湖边的居民才能采用。这也就是这群渔户局限在村西地区的原因。

虾是用一种竹编的捕虾篓从湖里捕捉。捕虾也是住在湖边的渔户的普遍职业。根据1935年夏我所收集的情况，共有43条船从事这项工作。捕虾篓用一条长长的绳索连结起来，放入水中。每四小时清一次篓子，因为时间过久，虾在篓里容易死去，死虾在市场上的价格低于活虾。两个渔民一条船，平均收入每天一元。

另一种渔户在B河中游沿岸圩Ⅱ居住。这种渔民喂养会潜入水中捕鱼的鱼鹰。喂养和训练此种鸟需要专门知识，是由家庭传授的，因此是一种世袭的职业。这些家庭形成一个特殊群体，甚至与其他村里的同行渔民合作。由于他们需要到离本村较远的地方去，夜间鱼鹰需要细心保护，因此，这些渔民在共同的专业利益基础上形成了一个超村庄的群体。从事同一专业的渔民，对他们的同行都有友善招待的义务。

CHAPTER IX   CALENDAR OF WORK

❶ Systems of Time-Reckoning

To study the productive system of a community, it is necessary to investigate how their activities are regulated in time sequence. It is especially so in analysing a rural economy because crops are usually directly dependent on climatic conditions.

The knowledge of the seasonal cycle of the organic world is of practical importance to the people. Their activities in production are not individualistic and spontaneous. They need collective actions and preparations. They must know when the seeds can be germinated in order to determine the date of sowing. They must know how long it will take for the bud to develop into the young shoot, so that they can determine when they should prepare the soil and transplant the shoot into the main field. The knowledge of the right time for certain actions cannot be secured without a system of time-reckoning.

Recognition of time is not a result of philosophical contemplation or of astronomical curiosity. As Professor B. Malinowski has clearly pointed out, "a system of reckoning time is a practical, as well as sentimental, necessity in every culture, however simple. Members of every human group have the need of co-ordinating various activities of fixing dates for the future, of placing reminiscences in the past, of gauging the length of bygone periods and of those to come." [29]

The functional approach to the problem of time-reckoning leads us to examine the calendar in detail in order to see how the system regulates and is defined by the social activities.

The traditional calendar used in the village is based on the lunar system. The principle of the lunar system is as follows: the full moon is taken as the night of the fifteenth day of a month. Thus the number of days in each month is either twenty-nine or thirty. (The synodic lunar month consists of 29.53 days.) Twelve months will be counted as a year which contains 354.36 days. The total number of days fails to make the required total of 365.14 days a year for the solar system. An intercalary month is added every two or three years to make good the annual deficiency. But the seasonal cycle of the organic world is due more to the relation between the earth and the sun than to the relation between the earth and the moon. Although the two systems are adjusted in the long run by the intercalary month, the date of one system can never regularly correspond with that of the other.

玖 劳作日程

一、计时系统

为研究一个社区的生产体系必须要调查他们的各种活动在时间上是如何安排的。在分析农村经济时更需如此，因为庄稼通常直接依赖于气候条件。

有机世界的季节循环的知识，对人们有重要的现实意义。农民的生产活动不是个人自发的活动，他们需要集体的配合和准备。他们必须知道种子何时发芽以便确定播种日期，必须知道秧苗需要多长时间才能长成以便把土地准备好进行移植。如果没有农时的计算，就不能保证在正确的时间里采取某种行动。

辨认时间不是出于哲学考虑或对天文学好奇的结果。正如布·马林诺夫斯基教授已明确指出的："计时法不论如何简单，它是每一种文化的实际的需要，也是感情上的需要。人类每一群体的成员都需要对各种活动进行协调，例如为未来的活动选定日期，对过去的事进行追忆，对过去和未来时期的长短进行测量。"[29]

从功能上来研究计时问题，我们就必须仔细地观察一下历法，以便了解计时系统如何安排社会活动，这一系统又是如何由社会活动来表示的。

中国农村中使用的传统历法是以纪月系统为基础的阴历。它的原理如下：望日被视作一个月的第十五天的夜晚。因此，每一个月的天数是 29 或 30 天（实际上一个月历时为 29.53 天）。12 个月为一年，共 354.36 天，其总数与纪日系统的阳历 365.14 天为一年的数字不合。每隔两年或三年有一个闰月以补足每年缺少的天数。但是有机世界的季节循环更多地是遵循地球和太阳之间的关系，与地球和月亮之间的关系较小。虽然两种系统最后有闰月来调整，但这两种系统的日期永远不能有规律地一致起来。

The date in the lunar system does not indicate consistently the position of the earth with reference to the sun and consequently the seasonal climatic changes. For example, supposing the people catch the right time for sowing at the seventeenth day of the fourth month this year, they will, owing to the intercalary month, be too late if they sow at the same date next year. The discrepancy between the lunar system and the seasonal cycle renders the former ineffective as a guide in time-reckoning in agricultural activities. This theoretical consideration leads to a further examination of the traditional calendar.

In the traditional calendar, in fact, there is an underlying solar system. It indicates the exact position of the earth in its solar orbit at various periods. The unit in this system is Chieh, meaning section or joint. The whole solar year is divided into twenty-four Chieh. The total number of days of the twenty-four Chieh in 1936 was 364.75. It shows that there is still a slight difference of 0.59 day with the synodic solar year. The principle in determining the Chieh system is not known to me. But in the old-type calendar book, one can always find that the exact time for the commencement of each Chieh is defined in terms of Shih (two-hour), K'ê (quarter-hour) and Fen (minute). The intercalation takes place in the slight variation between the lengths of different Chieh in different years. It therefore needs no special indication for it. The following table gives the name and the time of commencement of each Chieh in the year 1936.

Name of the Chieh	Traditional Calendar and Time	Western Calendar and Time
Li Ch'un (Beginning of Spring)[30]	13th of 1st month Ch'en Ch'u 3 K'ê	Feb. 5—7.45 a.m.
Yü Shui (Rain Water)	28th of 1st month Yin Ch'u 2 K'ê 10 Fen	Feb. 20—3.30 a.m.
Ching Che (Waking of Insects)	13th of 2nd month Ch'ou Ch'u 3 K'ê 12 Fen	March 6—1.57 a.m.
Ch'un Fen (Spring Equinox)	28th of 2nd month Yin Ch'u 3 Fen	March 21—3.3 a.m.

Name of the Chieh	Traditional Calendar and Time	Western Calendar and Time
Ch'ing Ming (Pure Brightness)	14th of 3rd month Ch'en Ch'u 1 K'ê 2 Fen	April 5—7.17 a.m.
Ku Yü (Corn Rain)	29th of 3rd month Wei Chêng 1 K'ê 14 Fen	April 20—2.44 p.m.
Li Hsia (Beginning of Summer)	16th of 3rd (intercalary) month Ch'ou Ch'u 14 Fen	May 6—1.14 p.m.

阴历的日期不能始终如一地说明地球对太阳的相对位置，因而也不能表明季节性气候的变化。譬如说，假定今年人们抓住了正确的播种时间——四月十七，但由于闰月的关系，他们明年如果在同一天播种，就为时太晚了。阴历和季节循环两者之间的不一致性，使得阴历在农事活动中不能作为一种有效的推算农作物生长期的指南。这种理论上的考虑必然引导人们进一步来考察传统的历法。

实际上，在传统历法中，有一种潜在的纪日系统。它表明各个时期地球在其太阳轨道中的确切位置。这一系统中的单位是"节"，意思是"段"或"接头"。整个太阳历年分成 24 个节。1936 年 24 个节的总天数为 364.75 天。这说明实际上一个年度的时间仍有微弱的 0.59 天之差。我不知道定节气的原理，但在旧历本中可以找到每个节气开始的准确时间，它是用时辰（两小时）、刻（四分之一小时）和分（分钟）为单位来表示的。在不同年份里不同节气的长短上，闰期的变化微小，因此不需要特殊的说明。下表为 1936 年每个节气开始的时间和节气的名称。

节气名称	传统历及时间	西历及时间
立春	正月十三 辰初三刻	2月5日晨7点45分
雨水	正月二十八 寅初二刻十分	2月20日晨3点40分
惊蛰	二月十三 丑初三刻十二分	3月6日晨1点57分
春分	二月二十八 寅初三分	3月21日晨3点3分
清明	三月十四 辰初一刻二分	4月5日晨7点17分
谷雨	三月二十九 未正一刻十四分	4月20日下午2点29分
立夏	三月（闰月）十六 丑初十四分	5月6日下午1点14分

Name of the Chieh	Traditional Calendar and Time	Western Calendar and Time
Hsiao Man (Grain Full)	1st of 4th month Wei Chêng 1 K'ê 13 Fen	May 21—2.28 p.m.
Mang Chung (Grain in the Ear)	17th of 4th month Mao Ch'u 3 K'ê 10 Fen	June 6—5.55 a.m.
Hsia Chih (Summer Solstice)	3rd of 5th month Hai Chêng 3 K'ê 4 Fen	June 21—10.49 p.m.
Hsiao Shu (Slight Heat)	19th of 5th month Shen Chêng 1 K'ê 11 Fen	July 7—4.26 p.m.
Ta Shu (Great Heat)	6th of 6th month Ssŭ Ch'u 3 K'ê 9 Fen	July 23—9.54 a.m.
Li Ch'iu (Beginning of Autumn)	22nd of 6th month Ch'ou Chêng 1 K'ê 5 Fen	Aug. 8—2.20 a.m.
Ch'u Shu (Stopping of Heat)	7th of 7th month Yu Ch'u	Aug. 23—5.0 p.m.
Pai Lu (White Dew)	23th of 7th month Mao Ch'u 13 Fen	Sept. 8—5.13 a.m.
Ch'iu Fen (Autumn Equinox)	8th of 8th month Wei Chêng 2 K'ê	Sept. 23—2.30 p.m.
Han Lu (Cold Dew)	23rd of 8th month Hsü Chêng 2 K'ê 8 Fen	Oct. 8—8.38 p.m.
Shuang Chiang (Frost's Descent)	9th of 9th month Tzŭ Ch'u 2 K'ê	Oct. 23—11.30 p.m.
Li Tung (Beginning of Winter)	24th of 9th month Tzŭ Ch'u 1 K'ê 4 Fen	Nov. 7—11.19 p.m.
Hsiao Hsüeh (Slight Snow)	9th of 10th month Hsü Chêng 2 K'ê	Nov. 22—8.30 p.m.
Ta Hsüeh (Great Snow)	24th of 10th month Shen Ch'u 2 K'ê 3 Fen	Dec. 7—3.33 p.m.
Tung Chih (Winter Solstice)	9th of 11th month Ssŭ Ch'u 11 Fen	Dec.22—9.11 a.m.
Hsiao Han (Slight Cold)	24th of 11th month Ch'ou Chêng 10 Fen	Jan. 6—2.10 a.m.
Ta Han (Great Cold)	8th of 12th month Hsü Ch'u 1 K'ê 7 Fen	Jan. 20—7.22 p.m.
Li Ch'un (Beginning of Spring)	23rd of 12th month Wei Ch'u 2 K'ê 4 Fen	Feb. 4—1.34 p.m.

节气名称	传统历及时间	西历及时间
小满	四月初一 未正一刻十三分	5月21日下午2点28分
芒种	四月十七 卯初三刻十分	6月6日晨5点55分
夏至	五月初三 亥正三刻四分	6月21日晚10点49分
小暑	五月十九 申正一刻十一分	7月7日下午4点26分
大暑	六月初六 巳初三刻九分	7月23日上午9点54分
立秋	六月二十二 丑正一刻五分	8月8日晨2点20分
处暑	七月初七 酉初	8月23日下午5点
白露	七月二十三 卯初十三分	9月8日晨5点15分
秋分	八月初八 未正二刻	9月23日下午2点30分
寒露	八月二十三 戌正二刻八分	10月8日上午8点38分
霜降	九月初九 子初二刻	10月23日晚11点30分
立冬	九月二十四 子初一刻四分	11月7日晚11点19分
小雪	十月初九 戌正二刻	11月22日晚8点30分
大雪	十月二十四 申初二刻三分	12月7日下午3点33分
冬至	十一月初九 巳初十一分	12月22日上午9时11分
小寒	十一月二十四 丑正十分	1月6日晨2点10分
大寒	十二月初八 戌初一刻七分	1月20日下午7点22分
立春	十二月二十三 未初二刻四分	2月4日下午1点34分

The Western solar calendar has been also introduced into the village since it has been adopted as the legal system. It differs again from the traditional solar system because it takes a round day as a unit and consequently has a regular intercalary system. Thus they cannot have exact corresponding dates in different years.

❷ Three Calendars

These three calendars are all used by the villagers. But each has its own function and is used in its own particular context. The Western system is used in connection with those newly introduced institutions such as the school, the co-operative factory, and the administrative office. These institutions have to adjust their work with the outside world where the Western system is employed.

The traditional lunar system has its widest use in such situations as remembering sentimental events and making practical engagements. It serves as a system of names for the dates in the traditional social activities. In the sphere of religious activities, the lunar system is largely used. Regular sacrifices are offered to the kitchen god on the first and fifteenth day of each month. The people visit temples and observe vegetarian ritual also on these dates. Ceremonies of ancestral worship are carried out on the dates of birth and death of the ancestors and on regular festivals; though among the festivals some of them are regulated according to the traditional solar system.

The traditional solar system is used not as a system of dates but of climatic changes. With this general system, each locality can adjust its calendar of work according to its local conditions.

This system is used chiefly in reference to productive work. Beside daily conversations, the following folk song will document this statement:

Balou ba mimi	.	.	.	.	Pai Lu white indistinctly (referring to the blossoms of the rice).
Tchiu fen da shiou tchi		.	.	.	Ch'iu Fen rice bears fruit completely.
Tson gian gjien tzao da		.	.	.	Shuang Chiang reap early rice.
Li dong i tchi dao		.	.	.	Li Tung all completely fall.

A part of a letter from my informant can also be quoted:

"People in the village have two periods of leisure every year. The first period is in the autumn from Ch'u Shu to Han Lu and lasts about two months.... The second period is in the winter from Ta Hsüeh to the end of the year, also covering two months. During this leisure time, we go out for trade ventures."

既然西方的阳历是法定通行的，自然也传入乡村，它又与传统的纪日系统的节气有区别，因为它以一个整天作为单位，所以有一个规则的闰日方法。这两种历法不同年份相应的日期不同。

二、三种历法

这三种历法均被村里的人们采用。但各有各的作用，西历通常在新建的机构如学校、合作工厂和行政办公室里使用。这些机构必须与使用西历的外界协调工作。

传统的阴历最广泛使用在记忆动感情的事件以及接洽实际事务等场合。它被用作传统社会活动日的一套名称。在宗教活动上，人们也广泛使用阴历。每月初一及十五要定期祭祀灶神。人们还在这两个日子里去庙宇拜佛或吃素斋。在祖先的生日、忌日和固定的节日要祭祖，但有些节日是根据传统的节气来安排的。

传统的节气并不是用作记日子的，而是用来记气候变化的。有了这一总的系统，每个地方可根据当地情况来安排农活日程。

这个系统主要用于生产劳动。除日常谈话外，下列歌谣说明了它的作用：

白露白迷迷（指稻花开）
秋分稻秀齐
霜降剪早稻
立冬一齐倒

向我提供情况的人曾来一信，也可引述其中一段：

"村里的人，每年有两个清闲的时期，第一个阶段是在秋天，从处暑到寒露，为时约两个月。　第二阶段是在冬天，从大雪到年底，也是两个月，在这农闲季节，我们出去经商。"

The villagers remember and predict their sequence of work in terms of the traditional solar system. But this system cannot stand alone because it is very difficult to understand without a system of dating. The system of date in the village is the lunar calendar. The people have to learn what is the corresponding date for each section in different years. For instance in the above table, the first Li Ch'un is on the 13th of the 1st month and the second is on the 23rd of the 12th month. Therefore it is also correct to say that the lunar calendar regulates the sequence of work of the people through the Chieh system.

The villagers do not arrange their calendar themselves. They simply follow the published calendar in the form of a little red booklet bought from the town. The principle of these systems is not understood by them. They even do not know where the calendar is issued and who is the authority. Since the government prohibited the traditional calendar, publication of these booklets has been illegal. I was not able to find out who was the publisher responsible.

The government's action had not in any sense affected the popularity and prestige of the booklet. It is to be found in any house and in most cases it is the only book in the house. It is usually put on the stove before the kitchen god, and regarded as a kind of amulet. It is consulted not only for arranging work but also for various social activities and personal affairs. In the booklet, each day has a column indicating those things which are lucky or unlucky. For illustration I give a few columns below:

March 1st (1936), Sunday; 8th of 2nd month.

Birthday of Chang Ta Ti (God of flood).

Good for: Offering sacrifice, praying, asking for posterity, making petitions, visiting relatives, trading, accepting office, arranging marriage, offering marriage gifts, weddings, entering new houses, changing lodging, tailoring, mending buildings, laying foundations, fixing beams, mending

storerooms, opening market, making contracts, opening
storerooms, planting, breaking soil, burying dead.

Bad for: Thatching roof, introducing water to the field, hunting.

March 2nd, Monday; 9th of 2nd month.

Good for: Visiting relatives and friends, catching animals.

Bad for: Making accusations in court, curing diseases, taking medicine.

(Plants begin to bud.)

农民用传统的节气来记忆、预计和安排他们的农活。但节气不能单独使用，因为没有推算日期的办法，在使用上有困难。农村用阴历来算日子。人们必须学习每年各个节气的相应日期。例如上表所示，第一个立春是在正月十三日，而第二个立春则在十二月二十三日。因此，也可以这样说，阴历通过节气系统来安排人们的工作顺序。

历本并非村民自己编排，他们只是从城镇买来一红色小册子，根据出版的历本来进行活动。他们也不懂其历法的原理，他们甚至不知道历本是哪里发行或经谁批准的。因政府禁止传统历，出版这些小册子是非法的。我未能找到谁是负责的出版者。

然而政府的行动丝毫没有影响小册子的普及和声誉。在任何一家人的房屋中都可以找到这本册子，而且在绝大多数情况下，这往往是家中唯一的一本书。人们通常将它放在灶神爷前面，把它当作一种护身符。不仅在安排工作时，而且在进行各种社会活动和私人事务的时候，农民都要查询这本历书。在历书中，每一天有一栏专门说明哪些事在这一天做吉利，哪些事不吉利。我列举数栏说明如下：

三月一日（1936 年），星期日；阴历二月初八

张大帝（洪水之神）生日。

宜祭祀，祈福求嗣，还愿，会亲友，经商，上官赴任，结婚姻，行聘，嫁娶，迁入新宅，移徙，裁衣，修造，竖柱上梁，修店铺，开市，立券，开仓库，栽种，破土，安葬。

不宜用茅草铺盖房顶，灌田，行猎。

三月二日，星期一；阴历二月初九

宜会亲友，捕捉畋猎。

不宜诉讼，求医疗病。

（植物发芽）

March 16th, Monday; 23rd of 2nd month.

    Good for nothing.

    Bad for everything.

March 27th, Friday; 5th of 3rd month.

    Good for: Taking a bath, fishing, catching animals,

        clearing houses.

    Bad for: Fixing a bed, buying land and other properties.

                      (Beginning of thunder.)

It is not true that people always follow the advice of the column. But they actually consult the booklet in such activities as building houses, arranging marriages, starting long trips, etc. They generally distinguish "good day" and "bad day" according to the length of the column of "good for." They avoid taking any important and adventurous activities on these bad days, especially those which are explicitly stated as "good for nothing." At the end of the column every few days, there is an item, given in parentheses, indicating certain recurrent natural phenomena such as "Plants begin to bud" and "Beginning of thunder," etc. It is an additional system of reckoning time by recurrent natural phenomena.

❸ Time-Table of Economic and Other Social Activities

With these systems of time reckoning, we are now able to tabulate the time-table of various economic and social activities in the village. It will serve as a system of reference for the further analysis. Explanations for specific items will be given elsewhere in their appropriate connections.

三月十六日，星期一；阴历二月二十三
　　诸事不宜。

三月二十七日，星期五；阴历三月初五
　　宜沐浴，畋猎取鱼，扫舍宇。
　　不宜安床，买地纳财。

（开始雷鸣）

　　农民并非完全按照栏内所列的忠告行事。但盖房、安排婚事、开始长途旅行等事，他们确实要查询此种历本。他们根据栏内所列吉利的事情多少，笼统地区别"宜"或"不宜"的日子。他们避免在"不宜"的日子——特别是那些表明"诸事不宜"的日子——进行重要的冒风险的活动。每隔数天，在这一栏的末尾有一项括号内的说明，如"植物发芽"和"开始雷鸣"等。这是用周期性的自然现象来推算时间的一种附加系统。

三、经济活动和其他社会活动时间表

　　有了以上的这些计时系统，我们便能列出村庄各种经济和社会活动的时间表。它可供进一步分析作参考。对某些具体项目，将在其他恰当的有关之处再作一些解释。

Other Social and Religious Activities According to Lunar System	Lunar System	Western Solar System	Temp. (F.)	Rain (mm.)	Section System	Silk Industry	Agriculture	Other Social and Religious Activities According to Section System
1st: New Year, Sacrifice to Buddha, Reception of new kitchen god, Visiting temples. 1st–8th: Men visiting relatives. 8th–15th: Women visiting relatives.	I	Feb.	39°	57	Li Ch'un		Wheat / Rapeseed	Sacrifice to kitchen god
					Yü Shui			
5th: Sacrifice to god of wealth 10th–30th: Good for wedding.	II	March	46°	70	Ching Che			
					Ch'un Fen			Sacrifice to kitchen god
	III	April	56°	90	Ch'ing Ming	Hatching eggs ⎫		Sacrifice to ancestors and god of silkworms / Visiting tombs / Sacrifice to kitchen god ⎫ Prohibition of house building
					Ku Yü	Third exuviæ ⎬ Main crop		Rejoicing feast / Visiting relatives' silkworms ⎭
Funeral preparation for old people in the intercalary month.	III (Intercalary)	May	65°	90	Li Hsia	Cocoons ⎭		
					Hsiao Man		Sowing seeds / Young shoot in nursery farm / Preparation in main farm ⎫	
	IV	June	73°	166	Mang Chung	Domestic reeling	Transplantation ⎬ 1st busy agricultural period	
					Hsia Chih		Weeding and irrigation ⎭	
5th: Tuan Yang, rejoicing feast, sacrifice to kitchen god.	V	July	80°	127	Hsiao Shu	Second crop		

按节气进行的其他社会活动与宗教活动	农业	丝业	节气	气候（上海）		西方的阳历	阴历月份	按阴历历进行的其他社会活动和宗教活动
				温度（华氏）	雨量（毫米）			
祭灶神	麦 〔油菜籽〕		立春	39	57	2月	一	初一：新年、祭菩萨、迎灶神；初一上庙拜佛；初一至初八：男人探亲戚
			雨水					
祭灶神		〔孵化蚕种〕主要的二批	惊蛰	46	70	3月	二	初八至十五：女人探亲戚；初五：祭财神
		〔第二次蚕蜕〕〔一蚕茧〕	春分					初十至三十：吉利的婚日
祭祖宗和蚕神／扫墓／祭灶神			清明	56	90	4月	三	
欢宴／探亲戚的蚕	〔播种／育秧苗 主要农田准备／插秧〕第一农忙时节	家庭抽丝	谷雨					
		第二批	立夏	65	90	5月	三（闰）	在闰月为老人准备葬礼
禁止造房屋			小满					
	除草和灌溉		芒种	73	166	6月	四	
			夏至					
			小暑	80	127	7月	五	初五：端阳、欢宴、祭灶神

Other Social and Religious Activities According to Lunar System	Lunar System	Western Solar System	Climate (in Shanghai) Temp. (F.)	Climate (in Shanghai) Rain (mm.)	Section System	Silk Industry	Agriculture	Other Social and Religious Activities According to Section System
3rd, 15th, and 23rd: Sacrifice to kitchen god.	VI				Ta Shu			
	VII	August	80°	148	Li Ch'iu		Rice in blossom	First trading venture
	VII				Ch'u Shu			
3rd: Birthday of kitchen god, sacrifice.	VIII	Sept.	73°	118	Pai Lu		Rice bears fruit	
15th: Chung Ch'iu, full moon, rejoicing feast. 24th: Birthday of kitchen goddess, sacrifice.	VIII				Ch'iu Fen		(Agricultural interval)	
9th: Ch'ung Yang, rejoicing feast, sacrifice to kitchen god.	IX	Oct.	63°	73	Han Lu			
	IX				Shuang Chiang			
1st: Sacrifice to ancestors' new rice.	X	Nov.	52°	46	Li Tung		Reaping Husking	Second trading venture / Sacrifice to ancestors
	X				Hsiao Hsüeh		Storing Selling	
	XI	Dec.	42°	29	Ta Hsüeh		Wheat (Second period of busy work in agriculture)	
	XI				Tung Chih			
24th: Farewell sacrifice to kitchen god. 30th: Sacrifice to ancestors.	XII	Jan.	38°	54	Hsiao Han			
	XII				Ta Han			

按阴历进行的其他社会活动和宗教活动	阴历月份	西方的阳历	气候（上海）雨量（毫米）	气候（上海）温度（华氏）	节气	丝业	农业	按节气进行的其他社会活动与宗教活动
初三、十五及二十三：祭祀灶神	六	7月	127	80	大暑			
					立秋		稻开花	第一次外出经商
初三：祭祀灶神，十五：中秋，满月，二十四：灶神娘生日祭祀	七	8月	148	80	处暑		稻秀穗	
					白露		农闲	
	八	9月	118	73	秋分			
初九：重阳，欢宴，祭祀灶神	九	10月	73	63	寒露		收割 碾米 储藏 出售（第二个农忙时节）	第二次外出经商 祭祀祖宗
					霜降			
初一：新稻登场，先祭祀祖宗	十	11月	46	52	立冬			
					小雪		麦	
	十一	12月	29	42	大雪			
					冬至			
二十四：送灶神爷 三十：祭祖宗	十二	1月	54	28	小寒			
					大寒			

CHAPTER X AGRICULTURE

The importance of agriculture in the village economy has been shown in the above pages. More than two-thirds of the households are engaged mainly in this occupation. Nearly eight months are spent in work on the land. And for foodstuffs the people are entirely dependent on the produce of their own farms. Thus in a study of the problem of production, agriculture must come first in view.

The term agriculture is used here only in a narrow sense, and refers to the use of the land for cultivating desirable crops. The study of how the land is used must start with an analysis of the land itself. The chemical composition of the soil, the topography of the land and the climate—all these are conditions governing agriculture. It is also necessary to know the biological nature of the crop. But these analyses, essential as they are, demand special knowledge which an anthropologist does not usually possess. However, the land that enters into agriculture is more than a natural entity. It has been transformed by culture into farms. Moreover, what immediately directs human labour in agriculture is the knowledge about the land and the crop possessed by the people themselves as expressed in their technology and beliefs.

To start our analysis from the material substratum we will first attempt a description of the farm. The lay-out of the farm, based on technical considerations, has far-reaching effects on the organization of labour, on land tenure, and on the kinship organization. The study of it will be the best introduction to these more intricate aspects of the relation between man and land.

❶ Lay-out of the Farm

The lay-out of the farm depends on what kind of crop the people select for cultivation. In this village the chief crops cultivated are rice, rapeseeds and wheat. Rice starts in June and ends at the beginning of December. It is the main crop. After this crop a part of the higher land can be used for cultivating wheat and rapeseeds. But these two crops are only supplementary. The produce is only enough for domestic consumption.

More than 90 per cent. of the land is used for these crops. Along the margin of each *yu*, ten to thirty metres of land is left for plantation of mulberry trees and a wider space for house building. This land on the margin is higher. It also serves as a dyke for the farm.

拾 农业

农业在这个村子经济中的重要性，已经在以上章节中显示出来。这村有三分之二以上的农户主要从事农业。一年中有八个月用来种地。农民的食物完全依赖自己田地的产品。因此，要研究生产问题，首先必须研究农业问题。

本章所使用的农业一词，只是从它的狭义说的，指的是使用土地来种植人们想要种的作物。要研究如何使用土地，必须先分析土地本身。土壤的化学成分、地形和气候都是影响农业的条件。我们也需要了解谷物的生物性质。这些分析尽管比较重要，所需要的专门知识却往往是人类学者所不具备的。然而，农业占用的土地不只是自然实体，文化把土地变成了农田。此外，在农业中，直接指导人类劳动的是人们自身掌握的关于土地和谷物的知识，通过技术和信仰表现出来。

从分析物质基础开始，我们首先来描述一下这个村子的农田。根据技术需要出发的农田安排，对劳力组织、土地所有权和亲属组织都有深远的影响。研究这个问题对进一步研究人与土地关系问题的各个复杂的方面将是最好的开始。

一、农田安排

农田的安排取决于农民选择种植哪一种作物。这个村农业的主要作物是水稻、油菜籽和小麦。水稻的种植期从 6 月开始，12 月初结束，这是主要农作物。收稻以后，部分高地可用来种小麦和油菜籽。但后两种仅是补充性的农作物，其产量仅够家庭食用。

村里 90% 以上的土地种植上述这些农作物。沿着每一圩的边缘，留有 10～30 米的土地种桑树，有三个圩再留一块大一些的空地盖房屋。在边缘的土地较高，也用作农田的堤堰。

The land used for the growing of crops is divided into farms. Rice cultivation requires a regular supply of water. Thus the lay-out of the farm depends on the measures for water regulation.

My informant said: "Water is the most important thing in the farm. The rice will die if the soil begins to break due to dryness and it will also die if water covers its 'eye'." The "eye" of the rice is the upper joint of the leaf with the stalk. When this point is covered by water, according to local opinion, the rice will wither within six or seven days. It may not perhaps be strictly true that this point in the rice plant is so vulnerable; nevertheless the "eye" is used as a mark for the proper level of water in the farm. This level must be adjusted to the growth of the rice and effort must be made to irrigate the farm when the level is too low and to drain it when the level is too high. Water regulation is one of the main tasks in agriculture and dictates the topography of the farm.

The land is divided up by streams into tiny pieces which are called *yu*. Each *yu* is surrounded by water. The accessibility to water of each particular farm depends on its location in the *yu*. The farther one goes into the centre of the *yu*, the more difficult is it to get supplies of water from the stream. In order to make it possible for the centre part to obtain water, the levels of the *yu* must be graded like a dish. But this dish-shaped surface creates a difficulty in the storage of water. The water tends to find its level and, instead of there being an equal distribution of water over the farm, there will be a pool in the centre with the marginal land left dry. Dykes, therefore, have to be constructed, parallel to the margin. Another difficulty is that water must be brought in from the lower level of the stream. Pumps must be used to carry the water up to the higher level. To fix the pump, a spot must be selected along the bank and a ditch is dug out leading to the interior parts. Each strip of land, depending on water supplies from the same pumping spot, is marked out by dykes perpendicular to the margin. These two kinds of dykes, crossing each other, divide the farm into small pieces which are called *be* or plots.

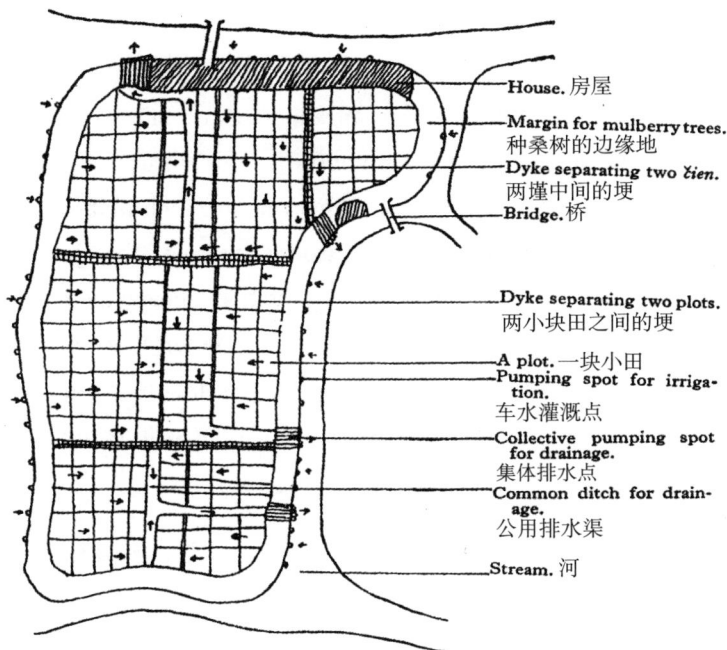

House. 房屋	
Margin for mulberry trees. 种桑树的边缘地	
Dyke separating two *žien*. 两墂中间的埂	
Bridge. 桥	
Dyke separating two plots. 两小块田之间的埂	
A plot. 一块小田	
Pumping spot for irrigation. 车水灌溉点	
Collective pumping spot for drainage. 集体排水点	
Common ditch for drainage. 公用排水渠	
Stream. 河	

MAP IV Lay-out of the Farms in Hsi Chang Yu

地图 IV 西长圩农田的安排

　　种庄稼的土地被分成若干农田。由于种水稻需要定期供水，因此农田安排还取决于水利管理措施。

　　向我提供情况的人说："水是农田中最重要的东西。如果土壤干裂，稻就会枯死，如果水太多，淹过稻'眼'时，稻又会淹死。"稻"眼"即上方叶和茎的接节点。当地人认为，这部分被淹了，六七天之内，稻就枯萎。把稻的这一部位说得如此脆弱，未必那么真实。但稻"眼"确实被用作标志稻田中水多水少的一个基准。必须按照稻的长势调节水面，水位太低时进行灌溉，太高时则及时排水。水的管理是农业中的一件主要任务，它决定农田的地形。

　　土地被河流分割成小块，称作"圩"。每一圩周围是水。每一块农田得水机会的多少视这块农田在圩中的位置而异。圩正中间的一块田离河最远，被灌溉的机会也最少。为使中间的农田得到足够的水，人们必须把圩的土地平整得犹如一个碟子。但碟状土地表面又为储水带来困难。水总是趋向水平面，因此农田不能得到水的平均分配，反而中间形成水塘，边缘土地干旱。所以必须筑起与土地边缘平行的田埂。另一个困难是必须从较低的河流中将水引到较高的田地中来。这样，便必须用水车。人们在河岸上选择一个地点，安装好水车，同时还要挖一道水渠以便将水引到里面的稻田。靠这一车水点供水的每一大片田地，还要有与边缘相垂直的田埂。两种田埂相互交叉，把农田分成小块，称作小块田或"爿"。

209

Within each plot, the level must be even in order that there should be an equal distribution of water. This is a frequent cause of dispute among cultivators of the same plot when it is not owned by the same Chia. There is a common ditch running through each strip, and each plot in a strip has an outlet to it. When the farmers introduce water to the plots, they start from the marginal plot. They close the ditch just below the outlet of the particular plot so that the water runs onto it. When it is sufficiently irrigated, they close the outlet and open the ditch to irrigate the next plot in the same way. They go on until the last. Thus the strip is the unit of irrigation (Map V).

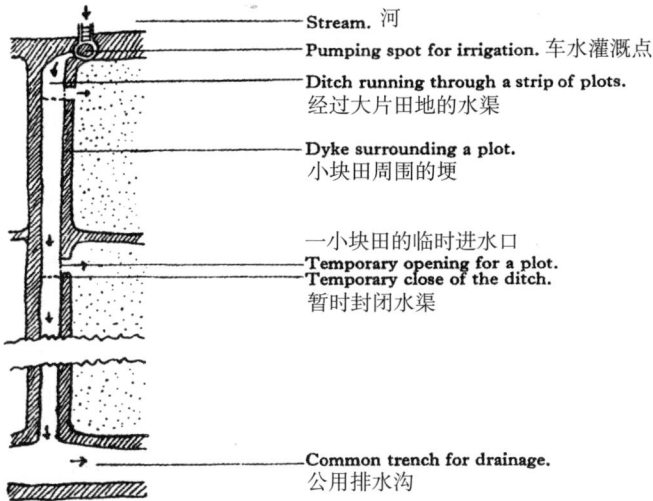

Stream. 河
Pumping spot for irrigation. 车水灌溉点
Ditch running through a strip of plots.
经过大片田地的水渠

Dyke surrounding a plot.
小块田周围的埂

一小块田的临时进水口
Temporary opening for a plot.
Temporary close of the ditch.
暂时封闭水渠

Common trench for drainage.
公用排水沟

MAP V Sytem of Dykes and Ditches in the Farm

地图 V 田埂和水渠系统

When there is too much water on the farm, due to over-abundance of rainfall, the system used for irrigation cannot be used for drainage because the water does not flow from the lower centre to the higher margin. A big trench has therefore to be constructed in the lowest part of the whole dish-shaped *yu*. This collects the surplus water from all the strips and pumps are fixed at the end of the trench for draining it away. The different system in irrigation and drainage calls for different organization of work, as we shall show presently.

The difficulty involved in the problem of drainage, purely from the technical point of view, is the size of the *yu*. The size is determined by the natural distribution of streams. It varies enormously. For instance, in the village we are describing there are eleven *yu* which vary from eight *mow* to more than nine hundred *mow* (II–2). The bigger the size, the more difficult it becomes to fit it into the process of collective drainage. To meet the need of urgent and efficient work, the big *yu* must be divided into smaller drainage units, which are called *čien*. Larger dykes are constructed to separate *čien* from one another. These dykes are also used as the main roads in the farm.

The plan of the lay-out of the farm is illustrated in Map IV. It is much simplified but sufficient to show the principles just described.

　　每小块田的高低必须相同，以便能得到平均的灌溉。小块田的所有权如果不属同一个家，那么耕种者之间常常因灌水发生争执。每一片田地有一条共同的水渠通过，在每片田地的小块田间有一个通水口。农民引水进田时，先从边缘的小块田开始。在一小块田的进水口处下面把水渠堵住，这样水便流入这小块田地。水灌足后便堵住这一进水口，打开水渠再灌溉下一块田地。这样继续下去直到最后一块田浇灌完毕。一片田地为一个灌溉单位（见地图 V）。

　　雨水多的时候，这一灌溉系统不能把田里多余的水排出，因为水不能从较低的田中央往较高的田边缘流出。所以必须在整个碟形圩地的最低部分挖一水沟。它汇集了各大片田里多余的水，水沟终端装部水车把水排出。接着，我们将看到灌溉和排水需要不同的社会组织工作。

　　单纯从技术观点来看，排水问题的困难主要是各圩面积大小不等的问题。圩的大小取决于河流天然分布的情况，大小相差极大。例如，这个村里有 11 个圩，大小从 8 亩至 900 余亩不等（第二章第二节）。圩的面积越大，将它纳入集体排水系统的困难越多。为适应紧急需要并提高工作效率，大圩必须分成较小的排水单位，称"瑾"，各"瑾"之间筑了较大的埂。也是农田里的主要道路。

　　农田安排平面图，如地图 IV 所示。图比实际情况简单得多，但足以说明刚才描述的情况。

❷ Rice Cultivation

The land is mainly, not exclusively, used for the cultivation of rice. The present study will be restricted to this aspect.

Rice cultivation starts in June. A small piece of ground is prepared as a nursery for the young shoots. Seeds are sown in the nursery. In about one month the rice has grown to about thirty centimetres in length. During this period the young shoots do not need much space but require more care in water regulation. It is thus convenient and economical to keep them in a small space while the main field is under preparation.

Before the young shoots can be transplanted into the main field, the soil must be prepared. Preparation consists of breaking, refining and levelling the soil, and then of irrigation. All the work is done by human labour. One characteristic of the agricultural work in this region is the absence of animal labour. As we shall see later, the size of the farm is small and the holding of each household is scattered in such widely separated places, that animal labour cannot be used. The farmers use only the implement called *tid'a*, which is an iron hoe with four teeth, fixed on a wooden stick about a man's height. These form a slight acute angle. Holding the implement by the end of the stick, the workman swings the hoe behind his back and over his head. The teeth strike with a considerable momentum and penetrate into the soil at a sharp angle. By pulling the hoe backwards, he is able to break the soil pressing on the teeth. Ploughs are not used in the village.

The surface of the soil, after having been broken, is rough and uneven. The second step is to refine the soil and to level the surface. The same implement is used in these processes. It takes about four days for the preliminary preparation of each *mow* of land by one man.

At this stage water is introduced onto the land. Dykes and ditches must be first examined and repaired if necessary. The water is introduced from the stream by a pump. A pump consists of a long, rectangular, box-like three-sided wooden tube in which there is a series of valves, made of small wooden plates connected by a chain of movable sections and forming a circle. The small valves touch the three sides of the tube and thus form a series of small empty squares in the tube. The chain is connected by a pivot to the wheel. When the farmer tramps on the projections of the wheel, the chain of valves revolve in a circle. The lower end of the tube is fixed in the water and the upper end opens towards a little pool leading to the ditches. The small squares, formed by the valves and the sides of the tube, will be filled with water at the lower end. The revolving of the chain of valves in the tube

二、种稻

田地主要用来种稻，但不完全是种稻。目前只限于研究种稻这一方面。

6 月开始种稻。先准备好一小块田地育秧，把种子撒在秧田里。约一个月以后，稻子长出 30 厘米长的嫩秧。这一时期稻秧不需要大的间隔，只是在浇灌方面需要细心调节。在小块田地上育秧，同时在大块田地上做准备工作，这样比较方便、经济。

移秧之前必须作好以下准备：翻地、耙地、平地，然后是灌溉。一切工作都是人力做的。这个地区农业劳动的一个特点就是不用畜力。下面我们将看到，农田较小，每户的土地又是如此分散，以致不能使用畜力。农民只用一种叫做"铁镗"的工具，它的木把有一人高，铁耙上有四个齿，形成一个小锐角。农民手握木把的一端，把耙举过头先往后，再往前甩，铁齿由于甩劲插入泥土，呈一锐角，然后向后拉耙，把土翻松。这个村子不用犁。

翻地以后，土块粗，地面不平。第二步就是耙细和平地，使用同一工具。一个人翻耙平整一亩地需要四天。

这一阶段要引水灌溉，必要时需检修田埂和水渠。用水车从河流车水。水车有一个长方盒形的、三面用木板做成的管道，木管内有一系列用小木片做成的阀，由活动的链条连在一起形成一个环。小阀接触三面木头的管道便在管内形成一系列方形空间，链条通过枢轴与一个轮子相连。农民踏动轮旁的踏脚板时阀链便按圆环形转动。木管的下部置入水中，上部打开，对着一个通向水渠的小水塘。由阀和木管三面形成的小方空间在下端充满了水，阀链转动时便将

carries the water contained in the small squares up to the upper end. As soon as a valve reaches the upper end, the direction of its movements turn upwards and the water falls into the pool. The water is brought up to the pool not through the differential air pressure but through the movement of the valves.

The implement is not very efficient in carrying water to the upper level. The squares formed by the valves and the sides of the tube can never be very tight and the friction is high. It takes about one day to fill one *mow* with ten or more centimetres above the land surface. The inefficiency of irrigation creates a difference in the value of the successive plots in each strip. As I have shown above, the water flows from the margin to the centre passing through successive plots. When water is needed, the central plot must wait until the marginal plot has been irrigated; and when there is too much water, the central plot must remain longer under water while the margin is drained. The length of time spent in waiting for irrigation and for drainage depends on the efficiency of the pump. The unsatisfactory system of irrigation and drainage is certainly a factor in reducing the amount of produce. It is also responsible for a difference in land value. The difference between the marginal plot and the central plot sometimes amounts to ten dollars or one-fifth of the average value of the land.

In the past two years, two air pumps, run by motor engines, have been introduced into the village. One is owned by an individual and the other by the co-operative factory. A fee is charged per *mow* for the regulation of water during the whole year. This collectivizes the irrigation process and specializes the work. However, these machines have not yet been widely used, mainly because the labour saved by the machine has not yet found any productive use. From the point of view of the villagers, they still prefer working on the old pump to paying a fee and being themselves idle for months. Some told me that someone who was lazy and relied on the air pump had ruined himself in the gambling house in the town because he had nothing to do. It is still too early to see the effect of this labour-saving machine, and the process of collectivization in irrigation, on the social organization as well as the lay-out of the farm.

After water has been brought on to the land, it takes another day for each *mow* of land to be levelled. The total amount of time spent on the land for preparation can thus now be estimated. If there are seven *mow* for one person to work, it will take about thirty-five days, approximately equal to the amount of time needed for the growth of the rice in the nursery.

水带上来，流入水塘。水并非通过空气压力的差别带入塘内，而是由于阀的转动把水带到水塘。

用这种工具把水车至高处，效率不很高。由木阀形成的方形空间结构不严密，阻力较大。为一亩地车水高出地面十余厘米约需用一天的时间。灌溉上的低效率使每一大片田地中相连的小块田地产生了不同的价值。我在前面已经提到，水从边缘的田地依次流到中间，中间的田地必须等边缘的田地灌溉结束后，才能得到它所需要的水。雨水太多时，中间的田地又必须等待边缘的田地排完水后，多余的水才能排除。而等待排灌时间的长短则有赖于水车效率的高低。排水系统的不能令人满意的效率，当然是产量降低的一个因素。因此也就产生了土地价值的差别。边缘田地与中间田地价值的差别有时可达十元或相当于土地平均价值的五分之一。

前两年，村里有了两台动力抽水泵：一台为私人所有，另一台为合作工厂所有。承包全年的灌溉，按每亩收费。这使整个灌溉过程逐步转入集体化和专业化。然而，这种机器尚未被普遍采用，主要是因为使用机械而节约下来的劳力尚未找到生产性的出路。从村民的观点来看，他们宁愿使用旧水车，不愿缴纳动力泵费而自己闲搁数月。有些人告诉我，有个人依赖动力泵灌溉，自己没有事，便到城镇的赌场去赌博，害了自己。现在尚未看到节约劳力的机器和水利集体化过程对社会组织和农田安排的影响。

引水到田以后，每亩田还需要用一天的时间加以平整。现在就可以估计在准备土地过程中总共需要多少时间。一个劳力如果种7亩地，大约需要35天，相当于稻秧在秧田里生长所需的时间。

There is no ritual ceremony at the beginning of the agricultural work and every household is free to determine its own time for starting. The difference in time covers a range of two weeks.

Transplantation of the young shoots from the nursery farm to the main field is a major part of rice cultivation. The people describe this period as "busy in farm." The farmers start in the early morning for the nursery, which sometimes is far from the main field; they must transport the young shoots by boat. Children are brought to help in the work, but not women. The young shoots are planted in the main field in bunches of six or seven stalks. Children make themselves useful by handing the young shoots to the leaders while they are planting. One person will plant six or seven bunches in one row within his reach without stepping sideways. Finishing one row he will take one step backwards and start another row. Finishing one strip he will start another from the beginning. If there are several persons at work on the same farm, they will form a row and move backwards at the same time. The rhythmatic movement of the workers is very impressive. To maintain the rhythm, which is helpful in this monotonous work, they often sing rhythmic songs. Special songs have grown up under the name of *yengo*—"Young shoot song." But since in this region women do not participate in the work, the development of such songs is less than in the neighbouring areas.

Each person can plant about half a *mow* a day. To plant seven *mow* well thus takes about two weeks.

In July it is already summer. In hot weather (80°F.) rice grows very fast. During this period rain is plentiful (5.5 inches); heaven helps people to supply water to the young rice shoot. But nature cannot always be relied on. If there are two or three days without rain, the delicate young shoots will need to be watered by pumping, which calls for human labour. If it rains for three or four days continuously, the people will, on the other hand, be busy in pumping out the surplus water.

The wild grass mixed in the rice grows sometimes still faster. Only one week after the people have finished their work of transplantation, they must again be busy in weeding. A special instrument is used. This is a plate which has many nails on one side and is fixed to a long bamboo pole. The workman handles the pole by drawing the nails through the mud to uproot the wild grass.

When the field is weeded, the next task is to supply fertilizer for the soil. Fertilizer consists of human and animal manures and bean cakes. Bean cakes are made of the sediment of the soya beans after the oil has been pressed out. The cake is minced into small pieces and is evenly distributed over the farm.

　　农活开始的时候没有什么仪式，每个农户自己掌握农活开始的时间。时间先后的差别约为两个星期。

　　把稻秧从育秧田里移植到大田里，是种稻的重要部分。人们把这段时间描述为"农忙"时节。农民一早出发到秧田去，秧田有时离稻田很远。农民必须用船来往运送秧苗，孩子们那时也被动员起来帮忙干活，但不用妇女。插秧时六七棵秧为一撮插在一起，孩子们的工作是把秧递给插秧人，一个人不旁移脚步，在他所能达到的范围内，一行可插六七撮，这一行插完后，向后移动一步，开始插另一行。插完一片地以后，再从头开始插另一片。在同一块田地，如果同时有几个人工作，他们便站成一行同时向后移动。插秧人那有节奏的动作给人留下深刻的印象。对这种单调枯燥的工作加点节奏是有益的，为保持这种节奏，农民常常唱着有节奏的歌曲。这随之发展而成专门的秧歌。但这一地区的女子不参加插秧，秧歌流传不如邻区广泛。

　　每人一天大约可插半亩，插七亩约共需两周。

　　7月已经是夏天了，在华氏80度的气温下，稻的长势很快。这时期雨水很多（5.5英寸），老天帮忙，为幼秧提供水源。但自然界不总是那么可靠的。如果两三天没有雨，秧就需要车水灌溉，这就需要人力。如果连续下三四天雨，人们又要忙着车出多余的水。

　　和稻混杂在一起的野草有时长得更快。插秧工作刚刚结束一个星期，农民便需忙于除草。专用于除草的工具是一片装在竹竿柄上的木板，上面有很多钉子，农民手握耙柄，把钉耙向后拉过泥土，便把野草拔除。

　　除草后，下一件工作便是给土地施肥。肥料有人粪肥、畜粪肥和豆饼。黄豆榨油以后剩下的渣压成豆饼。豆饼被碾成碎片，均匀地撒在田地里。

Human manure is preserved in special pits behind the house. Sheep manure is collected from the hut. After long exposure in the air, and after being mixed with grasses, it is distributed over the field. Fresh manure is not used.

When the rice has reached a considerable height, and before it blossoms, the farmer must weed it thoroughly. This time the nailed plate cannot be used, because it might damage the root of the rice. The farmer has therefore to use his hands. To avoid damaging the rice, a saddle-like bamboo basket is attached to the upper leg. This brushes the rice away as the farmer walks in the mud.

Weeding and watering take all the farmer's time from July to September with several short intervals. The amount of work varies according to the amount of rain. In the early part of September the rice blossoms, and at the end of that month it bears fruit. No special work is necessary during that period. This is the long interval in agricultural work. During the latter part of October some of the early rice can be reaped. The instrument for reaping is a long curved sickle. The rice is cut near the root of the stalk, and is carried in bundles to the open space in front of the house. Threshing is done in the open space or in the front room, by striking the ears of the grain against the side of a big box. Grains are thus separated from the stalk and collected at the bottom of the box. Threshed stalks are heaped on the ground beside the public road.

Grains are hulled in a wooden mill. Husks are separated from the seeds by a whirling machine. The hulled seeds of rice can be sold but cannot be cooked without another process of refined husking. The last process has been entirely taken over by the modern machines. The old instruments of mortar and pestle are not used any more.

❸ Science and Magic

The knowledge embodied in the lay-out of the farm, in irrigation, in drainage, in breaking the soil, in transplantation, in weeding, etc., is accumulated from the long experience of the population, transmitted from generation to generation and learned by practical demonstration. It is an empirical knowledge that enables the people to control the natural forces in order to attain human ends. A detailed investigation would show how highly developed is the science of agriculture in this region. The above account has already indicated that the people understood definite general principles of biology concerning the process of growth of the rice, the quantity of water needed during different periods, the function of leaves and roots in plant physiology, and of physics concerning the level of surface and the movement of water.

　　人粪肥保存在房屋后面的专用的粪坑里。羊粪从羊栏里收集，曝露、晾晒并与草混合以后，撒在田里。不用新鲜粪肥。

　　当稻长到相当高度，开花以前，还需彻底除一遍草。这时便只能用手来拔草，因钉耙容易伤害作物的根部。为避免伤害稻，农民在大腿部系一马鞍形竹筐，他们在泥里行走时，它可先把稻撇开。

　　从7月到9月农民几乎都在除草和灌溉，中间有数次短的间歇。工作量的大小依据雨量的多少。9月上旬，稻子开花，月底结谷。这一时期没有特殊的工作可做，是最长的农闲时节。到10月下旬，某些早稻可以收割。长长的弯形镰刀便是收割的工具。割稻时把稻秆近根部割断，扎成一捆捆放在屋前空地上。打谷在露天空地或堂屋中进行，用谷穗打击着一个大打谷桶的一边，谷子便从秆上落下，留在桶底，然后收集起来。打过的稻秆便堆放在路边。

　　稻谷被放在一个木制磨里去壳，碾磨转动，壳便与米分开。粗磨的米可以出售，再经过一次精磨，才能食用。最后一次碾磨过程完全用现代机器进行。旧式工具杵臼已不再使用。

三、科学与巫术

　　在上述农田安排、灌溉与排水、翻土与平地、插秧与除草等农活中所用的知识，是通过农民的实践经验的长期积累一代一代传授下来的。这是一种经验性的知识，使人们能控制自然力量，以达到人们的目的。详细的调查研究会表明这个地区的农业科学发展到如何高的程度。上述情况已经说明，人们懂得稻的生长过程中的普通生物原理、不同时期所需的水量、植物生理中叶子和根部的作用以及有关水的运动、水平面等物理常识。

Their empirical approach to their enterprise is again seen in the way in which they adopt new technique and implements. The selection of implements is solely based on the principle of efficiency and economy. For instance, the air pump is used when there is urgent need of water regulation, but not when it proves to be expensive.

Science, however, only rules in so far that the natural factors can be successfully controlled by human effort. There are uncontrollable factors in nature. For instance, the primary need of a water supply can only be partially controlled by human means through irrigation, drainage, and the construction of dykes and ditches. It still largely depends on the rainfall. If there is too much or too little rainfall, rice will die regardless of how hard the people work on their pumps. Locusts may come unexpectedly. In this fateful sphere, and in this only, we find magical beliefs and practices.

It does not mean that the people conceive rain and locusts as supernatural manifestations. They have scientific meteorological knowledge. "When it is too hot, the lake will evaporate too much and when the temperature changes there will be rain." But these natural phenomena are beyond human control. They might be a great menace in practical life and turn all effort to nothing. At this vital point, the people say, "We depend on heaven." The recognition of human limitations gives birth to magic. But magic is not a substitute for science. It is only one means for combatting natural disasters. It does not rule out other means. Science and magic go hand-in-hand to attain a practical end.[31]

Magic is not a spontaneous and individual action. It is an organized institution. There is a definite person who is charged with the function and possesses magical powers. Secondly, there is a traditional ritual to call in the supernatural intervention. Lastly, there are myths to justify the ritual and the ability of the magician.

The occasions for magical performances are threats of flood, drought and locust plagues. Whenever the occasion arises, the people go to the district government and appeal for magical help. By ancient tradition the district magistrate was the magician of the people. In case of flood, he would go to the river or lake to demand the receding of the water by throwing his official belongings into the water. In case of drought he would issue an order to stop killing pigs and would organize a parade with all the paraphernalia suggesting rain, such as umbrellas and long boots. In case of locust plagues he would parade with the idol of *luiwan*.

通过他们采用新技术和工具的方式，也可以看到他们对所经营的事业采取了一种经验式的方法。对工具的选择完全是从经济和效率原则出发的。例如，需要紧急排灌时就用水泵，但作为平时灌溉，花费太大时就不用它。

然而，科学只在人力可有效控制的自然因素方面才具有决定作用。自然界中尚有不能控制的因素方面才具有决定作用。譬如对水的基本需要只能通过排水、灌溉、筑堤、挖沟等人为的手段进行部分的控制，大部分还是要靠雨水。如果雨水太多或太少时，不管人们如何努力使用水泵，稻还是会枯死或淹死。蝗虫可能出乎意料地突然到来。在这种性命攸关的领域，也仅仅在这一范围内，我们发现人们有非科学的信仰和行动。

这并非意味着人们把雨和蝗虫当作是超自然的表现。他们有气象知识："天气太热时，湖水蒸发太多，气温一有改变，就会下雨。"但这些自然现象，人不能控制。它们对实际生活可能是巨大的威胁，可能顿时把一切努力化为乌有。在这个关键时刻，人们说："我们靠天吃饭。"承认人的力量有限，转而产生了种种巫术，但巫术并不代替科学，它只是用来对付自然灾害的一种手段。它不排除其他手段。科学和巫术同时被用来达到一个现实的目的。[31]

巫术不是一个自发的个人的行动，而是一种有组织的制度。有一个固定的人，这个人拥有魔力并负责施展巫术。其次，有一套传统的礼仪来唤起超自然的干预。最后还有一些神话来维护这种礼仪和巫术师的能力。

当遭到水灾、旱灾和蝗灾的威胁时，便要施行巫术。过去每逢这种时机出现，人们纷纷到县政府去要求巫术的帮助。按照古老的传统，县行政官就是百姓的巫术师。有水灾时，他就到河边或湖边把供物扔进水里，祈求洪水退去。干旱时，他就发布命令禁止宰猪，并组织游行，游行者带着一切象征雨的用具如伞、长统靴等。有蝗灾时，他就带着刘皇的偶像游行。

The obligation of the magistrate to act as the district magician and his efficiency in this rôle, is explained by the following myth. About a mile outside the north gate of the city of Wukiang, the headquarters of the district, there is a temple worshipping the god called Chang Ta Ti (Chang the Big Emperor), whose birthday is on the 8th of the 2nd month (IX–2). According to the belief of the people he was a magistrate of the district at a remote historical period. During his term of office there was a threat of flood from continuous heavy rain and the overflow of the water in the lake. Going to the lake, he commanded the water to recede at once, and threw his shoes, his clothes, and his official jade girdle one after another into the water. But the water still overflowed, and rain continued to fall. At last, he threw himself into the water. The menace was conquered. At the present time, it is said that whenever there is a threat of flood in the district the gown of the idol will be always very wet because he still performs his function invisibly.

The myth connected with *luiwan* and his function in locust magic is not known in this village, so far as I could find out. But it is very popular in the neighbouring city of Wukiang. *Luiwan* was a historical person. He had been maltreated by his step-mother throughout his life. He was a very mischievous boy and possessed magical power. One night he invited all his friends to a big feast and killed all the cows of his family. In the morning he arranged the heads and tails of the cows in such a way that they looked half buried underground. But before he had finished the arrangement the day began to break. He ordered the sun to wait a minute. The sun went down under the horizon. Even at the present time, it is said, the sun will recede for a minute in the morning. When his step-mother found the cows half buried underground, the cows, owing to the magical power of the boy, lowed towards their master and moved their tails. As the result of his tormenting his step-mother, she treated him outrageously and he at last died. After his death his spirit has been believed to be continuously powerful in magic and able to drive away locusts. This myth testifies to the magical ability of the mischief-making boy and is the charter for the present belief and practice in locust magic of the people.

The magical function of the magistrate runs counter to the modern concept of civil office. Furthermore, the present government regards superstitious beliefs among the people as a great obstacle to social improvement. Various orders have been issued for the prohibition of magical performances of any sort. The present magistrate, therefore, not only denies his traditional function to be the people's magician,

以下神话解释了地方行政官担任巫术师的义务以及他担任这一角色的效果。在县政府所在地，吴江城北门大约一英里开外的地方，有一个拜祭张大帝的庙宇，他的生日是阴历二月初八（第九章第二节）。按照人们的信仰，他是很久以前历史上的一个县行政官。在他任职期间，有一次大雨连绵不断，湖水泛滥，造成了水灾的威胁。他便到湖边下令退水，把他的鞋、衣服和标志官衔的玉带，一件件扔进水里。但是水仍然上涨，雨继续不停地下着。最后，他自己纵身投入水中。水灾被征服了。直到现在，据说每当县里发生水灾时，张大帝偶像的长袍总是非常潮湿，因为他仍旧在暗暗地履行他的职责。

就我所知，村里不知道有关刘皇和他的灭蝗的神话。但在吴江附近的城镇里，刘皇是人人皆知的。刘皇是一个历史人物。他一生受后母的虐待。小时候是一个淘气的男孩，还能施展巫术。一夜，他邀请了所有的朋友来赴宴，还把他家中的牛全部杀死了。清早，他把牛的头和尾巴安放得犹如把牛半埋在地下一般。但天快破晓，他尚未安放完毕。他命令太阳慢些升起，太阳便又落到地平线下。据说，甚至到如今，早上太阳还推迟片刻升起。当他后母发现牛被半埋在地下时，由于刘皇的巫术，牛都哞哞地向主人呼叫，摇着尾巴。后母十分恼怒，后来便更加残暴地虐待刘皇，直至他死去。他死后，人们仍然相信他的阴魂有能力赶走蝗虫。这一神话证明了这个淘气男孩的魔力，也是目前人们信仰和施行驱蝗巫术的依据。

地方行政官的这种巫术师的职能是与现代行政公务的概念相违背的。而且，现在的政府认为人民中间的迷信是社会进步的障碍。因此政府发布了各种命令禁止任何巫术。所以现今的地方行政官不仅拒绝履行人民的巫术师的传统职能，而且还应该执行反对巫术的法律。

but is supposed to enforce the law against magic. But the natural menaces of flood, drought, and locusts continue to threaten the people. Their scientific knowledge and equipment are still not sufficient to control many of the disasters of nature, and the need for magic remains unchanged.

An ex-magistrate told me how the problem was solved. "Under the pressure of popular demand to do something against the drought, I had to issue an order to stop killing pigs. I considered it to be very useful since epidemics always go together with drought, and vegetable food helps to check an epidemic. This is the real function of the belief. The parade was organized in my absence. It was no good to force the people to do nothing against the drought."

Magic exists in spite of government orders and various justifications, so long as it plays a useful part in the life of the people. A change in theory from conceiving magic as a kind of pseudo-science, and obstacle to technological development to recognizing its practical function will throw light on practical measures for dealing with this problem. It is not a thing to be prohibited by order, but to be eliminated by providing more effective human control over nature. Since complete control is inconceivable at present, it is difficult to rule out magic in human culture.

❹ Organization of Labour

Who are working on the land? On what occasions do the farmers need to co-operate? Who will co-operate? What kind of organization has resulted? Let us examine these questions—still from the technical point of view and leaving the legal problem to the next chapter.

I have said that the household is the basic economic unit. But the members of a household do not all participate in agricultural work; children go to the farm only occasionally and women are entirely free from it. Agriculture is chiefly men's occupation. This division of labour between men and women is a characteristic of the silk-producing area. It suggests that the development of the silk industry is a factor responsible for the practice. During the period when domestic reeling was prosperous, women were busy in reeling while men were busy in preparing the soil. On the other hand, the income secured from the silk industry was comparable to the income secured from agriculture. It enabled the people to live on small farms. The size of farms therefore remains limited and the amount of labour required in agriculture is correspondingly restricted.

但水灾、旱灾、蝗虫的自然威胁仍然危害着人民。他们的科学知识和装备仍然不足以控制许多自然灾害，对巫术的需要依然保留不变。

一个前地方行政官告诉我这个问题是如何得到解决的："在人们普遍要求对旱灾有所举动的压力下，我不得不发出命令禁止宰猪。我认为这是很有用的，因为流行病往往与旱灾俱来，素食能防止传染病流行。这是这种信仰的真正的作用。在我缺席的情况下组织了游行。强迫人们对旱灾不作为是不利的。"

只要巫术对人们的生活起着一些有用的作用，不管政府发出多少命令，阐述多少理由，它仍然会存在。在理论上，从把巫术当作一种假科学，并认为它对科学发展是一种障碍，转变到承认它的实际作用，对于处理这个问题采取实际态度方面，能给以一些启示。这种事情不是命令所能禁止的，只有提供更有效的人为控制自然的办法才能消灭巫术。既然目前不可能有完全的科学控制办法，那么在人类文化中也难以完全消除巫术。

四、劳动组织

谁在田里劳动？在什么情况下农民需要合作？谁和谁合作？形成了何种组织？让我们仍然从技术的角度来考察这些问题。把法律上的问题留到下一章去探讨。

我已经讲过，户是基本经济单位。但一户中并不是全体成员都参加农业劳动；孩子只是有时候到田地里去，女人完全不参加农业劳动。农业主要是男人的职业。男人和女人的这种劳动分工是产丝地区的一个特点。它说明了蚕丝工业的发展是产生这种特点的主要因素。在家庭缫丝业兴旺时期，女人忙于缫丝时，男人正忙着准备稻田。另一方面，从丝业得到的收入可与农业收入比拟。这也使人们有可能靠小块农地生活下去。因此农田的大小一直保持在有限的范围内，农业所需的劳动量也相应地有所限制。

To show how well adjusted are labour and land in the village, some statistics may be cited. The total number of adult men, the real or potential workers on the land, between 15 to 55, is 450. The total area of land, including a small percentage of non-cultivated land, is 3,065 *mow*. If the land is equally distributed among the workers, each will get 6.6 *mow*. In the above section, I showed the rate of work and the length of time needed for the growth of the rice, and came to the conclusion that the amount of land that can be cultivated by a single man is about seven *mow*. From the point of view of technology, I have also shown that the use of the hoe in cultivation has made most of the work very individualistic. Group work yields no more than the sum total of individual efforts. It also does not increase the efficiency very much. Present technology has fixed the amount of labour required by the size of the land. Thus we have approximately identical figures for the amount of land which can be cultivated by each worker. This fact has far-reaching influence on land tenure, on the scattered system of farms, on the frequency of family division, and on the small size of the household.

The present decline of the silk industry has dislocated the traditional adjustment of economic activties. The size of farms has remained the same while the silk industry has been taken over by modern factories. The small farm cannot absorb the female labour that has been set free by the industrial change. The maladjustment is seen in the leisure enjoyed by the women in the village and the higher mobility of female population from the village to the town. In the neighbouring villages where farms are comparatively large, in the process of adaptation to the new situation female labour has been introduced into agriculture. This shows that the traditional division of labour, orginating as a part of economic adjustment, is a practical arrangement and is not due to any non-empirical cause. So far as men work by themselves and so long as the farm cannot be extended, female labour is not needed in agriculture. The only occasion for female labour is during the urgent period of irri-gation and drainage. Water regulation sometimes requires prompt action.

Women will not hesitate to work on the pump when they are needed.

The male members of a household work together on the same farm. But they have no special division of work. Everybody does the same work, except that in transplantation the children do not take part in actual planting but supply the young shoots to the adults. Thus the work is largely individualistic.

The need of co-operative work is in water regulation. In the process of irrigation, the members of the household, including women and children, always work on the same pump. In the process of drainage, the water is

为说明村里的劳力和土地是如何恰当安排的，可引用几个统计数字。成年男子是实际的或潜在的农业劳动者，年龄在 15 至 55 岁之间，总数共 450 人。如果将 2,758.5 亩耕地平均分配给劳动者，每人将得 6.1 亩。上文我已经说明了工作速度、稻的生长所需时间，以及得出一个人可耕种约 7 亩地的结论。从技术上来说，我已经表明了使用铁耙耕作使得大部分劳动成为非常个体性的。集体工作不比个体劳动增加多少收成，效率也不会提高很多。目前的技术已决定了这样大小的一片土地需要多少劳动量。因此，我们也有了每个农业劳动者能种多少亩地的近似数字。这一事实对土地占有、对农田分散的制度、对分家的频率以及对小型的户都有深远的影响。

目前，丝业的衰落打乱了传统协调的经济活动。缫丝工业被现代工厂接收后，农田的大小仍然同过去一样。由工业变化而剩下的妇女劳动力不能为这种小块农田所吸收。这种失调的情况可以从妇女在村里闲暇时间较多这一情形中观察到，也可以见于妇女人口从农村到城镇的高度流动性中。在邻近的村庄里农田较大，在适应工业变化的新情况过程中，妇女劳力被农业所吸收。这说明传统的劳动分工是出于实践的安排，而不是由于非经验的原因。它是经济调节的一个部分。在男子只靠自己劳动，而农田不能再扩大的情况下，农业是不需要女劳力的。唯一需要女劳力的场合是紧急灌溉或排水的时期。控制水有时候需要立即行动，女人便毫不犹豫地去车水。

一户里的男子在同一农田里工作。他们之间没有特殊的分工。每个人做同样的工作，除在插秧时，孩子不插秧而是给成人递秧苗。所以大部分劳动是个体性的。

水的调节是需要合作进行的。在灌溉过程中一户的成员，包括女人和孩子都在同一水车上劳动。在排水时必须把一埂地里的水

pumped out from the common trench of a *čien*. The people who work in the same *čien* share a common fate. Hence develops a well organized system of collective drainage. To describe this system, I will take a concrete example of the North *čien* of the Hsi Chang *Yu*.

This *čien* consists of 336 *mow* of land. The common trench opens on to the Stream A at the north margin. At the opening there are fifteen pumping spots. This means that there can be fifteen pumps working at the same time. Each pump requires three workers. The amount of labour contributed by each member of the *čien*, taking the household as a unit, is proportional to the size of his holding. The system of apportionment is calculated in terms of labour units. A unit is 1/3366 of the total amount of labour in four days. Each of the fifteen pumps shares 22.4 units. Each person working for four days counts as 6 units and the contributor of the pump and manager of the team counts as 4.4 units. This system of counting is called "six *mow* starting." It means that each holder of six *mow* in the *čien* should contribute a person to work every day, each holder of three *mow* should contribute a person every alternate day, and so on. Every *čien*, owing to varying size, has its particular system of calculation.

The members of the *čien* are organized into fifteen teams corresponding to fifteen pumps. Each year one of a group will be charged with contributing the pump and managing the team. This position is taken in turn by the members of the group. Among the fifteen groups, there is a chief manager. This position is also taken in turn. At the beginning of the year, the chief manager calls the fourteen other managers to a meeting. A feast is prepared as a formal inauguration. The chief manager has authority to determine when the drainage should begin and stop.

Whenever drainage is needed, the chief manager will give orders to the managers. Early in the morning these managers will inform the workers on duty by beating a bronze brace. If anyone on duty does not show himself at the pump half an hour after the signal, the other two charged to work on the same pump will stop their work, take the pivot of the pump to the nearest grocery and bring back to the spot fifty-three pounds of wine and some fruit and cakes, the cost of which will be charged to the absentee as a fine. But if the manager has not informed the absentee he himself must bear the responsibility.

The collective responsibility of drainage has made the introduction of the modern pumping machine difficult, because it requires the unanimous consent of the whole *čien*. It still remains to be seen how this type of organization will adjust itself to the technological change.

从公共水沟里排出去。在同一塍地里劳动的人是共命运的。因此便出现了一个很好地组织起来的集体排水系统。为描述这种系统，我试举两长圩北塍为具体例子，加以说明。

这一塍地有 336 亩地。在北面边缘有一条通向河 A 的共同的水沟。在出口处有 15 个车水点。这就是说，可以有 15 架水车同时工作。每一水车需要 3 名劳动者。塍的每个成员所提供的劳动量，以户为单位，是同他所有的土地大小成比例的。派工是以劳动单位来计算的。一个单位是在 4 天内总劳动量的 1/3366。15 架水车，每车分 22.4 单位。每个人工作 4 天算作 6 个单位，提供水车的人和小队管理人算作 4.4 单位。这种计算方法叫做"6 亩算起"。这就是说这塍地里每 6 亩地的土地所有者应每天派一个人参加劳动，3 亩地的拥有者每隔一天派一个人参加工作等等。每塍田，由于大小不同，各有其计算方法。

塍的成员按照 15 架水车组织成 15 个小队。每年由队里一个人负责提供水车并管理队的工作。这一职务由队里的成员轮流担任。15 个队，有一个总管理人。这个职务也是轮流担任的。年初，总管理人召集其他 14 个管理人开会，准备筵席，作为正式开始的仪式。总管理人有权决定何时开始或停止排水。

每逢需要排水时，总管理人向其他管理人发布命令。清晨，这些管理人敲着铜锣通知值班人员。半小时以后，如果任一值班人员没到水车前来，在同一水车前工作的另两个人就停止工作，拿着水车的枢轴到最近的杂货铺去带回 40 斤酒和一些水果、点心等，这些东西的费用作为对缺席者的罚款。但如果是管理人没有通知那个缺席者，管理人自己必须承担责任。

排水的集体负责制使得引进现代水泵发生了困难，因为用新式水泵需要获得全塍的一致赞同。这种组织将如何适应技术改革的需要，还有待于进一步的观察。

CHAPTER XI LAND TENURE

Land tenure is commonly conceived as the customary or legal system of titles over land. "But," as Professor Malinowski has pointed out, "this system grows out of the uses to which the soil is put, out of the economic values which surround it. Therefore land tenure is an economic fact as well as a legal system.

"We could lay down at once the rule that any attempt to study land tenure merely from the legal point of view must lead to unsatisfactory results. Land tenure cannot be defined or described without an exhaustive knowledge of the economic life of the natives."[32]

"The maxim that you cannot understand the rules of the game without a knowledge of the game itself describes the essence of this method. You must know first how man uses his soil, how he waves round it his traditional legends, his beliefs and mystical values, how he fights for it and defends it; then and then only will you be able to grasp the system of legal and customary rights which define the relationship between man and soil."[33]

We have, in the last chapter, studied how the villagers use their land and water. We are now prepared to go into the problem of land tenure.

❶ Lakes, Streams, and Roads

In so far as the water is used for communications, it is not exclusively for anybody. But when one enters the village, one sees rails constructed at the entrance of the stream. These are closed during the night. In this way the use of the stream as a means of communication is restricted. The reason is to prevent the communication route being used in such a way as to threaten the life or property of the villagers.

On the other hand, since the communication route is not the exclusive right of anyone, nobody is allowed to interfere with the general convenience by stopping boats in the middle of the stream. The same restriction is found in the use of water for drinking and cleaning. The silk factory had to be built at the lower course of the stream, otherwise the sewage would have dirtied the water and prevented others from using it for drinking purposes.

拾壹 土地的占有

　　土地的占有通常被看作习惯上和法律上承认的土地所有权。马林诺夫斯基教授指出:"但是,这种体系产生于土壤的用途,产生于与其关联的经济价值。因此,土地的占有不仅是一种法律体系,也是一个经济事实。

　　"我们能够立刻提出这样一条原则,任何仅从法律的观点来研究土地占有的尝试,必然导致不能令人满意的结果。如果对于当地人的经济生活不具有完备的知识,就不能对土地的占有进行定义和描述。"[32]

　　"对游戏本身一无所知,就不能理解游戏的规则——这句格言说明了这种方法的本质。你必须首先知道人类怎样使用他的土地;怎样使得民间传说、信仰和神秘的价值围绕着土地问题起伏变化;怎样为土地而斗争,并保卫它。懂得了这一切之后,你才能领悟那规定人与土地关系的法律权利和习惯权利体系。"[33]

　　在前一章中,我们已经研究过村民是如何利用土地和水的。现在我们准备讨论土地占有问题。

一、湖泊、河流及道路

　　就水用于交通来说,它并不为任何人所专有。但是当你进村的时候,可以看到在河的入口处装着栅栏,夜间栅栏关闭。作为交通手段,河流的使用在这方面受到了限制。这是为了防止坏人利用此交通路线对村民的生命和财产进行威胁。

　　另一方面,由于交通航道不是任何人专有的权利,所以,不允许任何人将船只停在河道中央,干涉公众的便利。在饮用水及洗涤用水管理方面也有同样的限制。丝厂不得不建在河的下游,否则脏水就会污染河水,使得他人无法饮用。

Regulation of water for irrigation is much more complicated. People are not allowed to build dykes in the stream in order to monopolize the water supply. This is a common issue of dispute between villagers especially during drought. The water introduced on to the farm by human effort belongs exclusively to the person who has effected this by labour. The dykes are not allowed to be opened in order to "steal" water from the higher plot. But a single plot may be owned by several persons. Each has a part in it. Since there is no dyke to separate the parts owned by different persons, the water is shared by all. In such a case, the labour spent in irrigation is equally distributed between the owners according to the size of the land in the plot. Most important of all, the level of the plot is maintained evenly in order that there should be a fair distribution of water. This is another cause of dispute, because, as I witnessed on several occasions, each farmer tries to lower his own part in order to receive a favourable reserve of water.

The natural products of water—consisting of fish, shrimps, and weeds which are used for fertilizing the farm—are the common property of the village. This means that the inhabitants of the village have equal rights to these products, and that people from other villages are excluded. To illustrate the implication the following case can be cited.

The fishing right in a lake west of the village, was in 1925 leased by the village head, Chou, to people who came from Hunan Province. This was because at that time the village needed money to repair the rails on the stream for self-defence. When the contract was made, Chou announced to the villagers that henceforth no one would go to fish in the lake. The villagers kept this agreement. When I was in the village, there was a dispute. The Hunanese arrested a boat engaged in shrimp trapping and took the fishermen to the police office in the town, accusing them of theft. Chou protested that it was not the lake that had been leased to the Hunanese but the fishing rights which did not include the right of shrimp trapping. Eventually the arrested persons were released.

The villagers also prevent outsiders from gathering weeds in the streams.

The right of collecting natural products in the water surrounding and inside the village is shared by the villagers, but those fish and weeds that have been collected are the exclusive property of the collectors.

The public road and dykes on the farm, so far as they are used for communications, are not the exclusive property of anyone, like the water route. No one can stop any other person walking on the public roads or dykes.

灌溉用水的管理要复杂得多。人们不允许为垄断水源而在河中筑堤。这是村民之间经常发生争执的问题，在旱期尤为如此。人力引入农田的水属于参加这项劳动的人所专有。为了从较高的地块"偷"水而掘开田埂是不允许的。但一块地可能属几个人共有，每人各占其中一部分。由于各人占有的各部分之间没有田埂隔开，所以水是大家分享的。在这种情况下，根据这块田地上各人地片大小不同来公平分配每个人在灌溉中应付出的劳动量。最重要的一点是，这块田的地平面要保持平坦，为的是使水的分配公平。这是产生争论的又一个起因。我目睹了几起这样的争执。因为每个人都想降低他那部分的地面，以有利于水的蓄留。

水中的自然产品包括鱼、虾和水藻。水藻可用来肥田。所有水产是村子的共同财产。这就是说，村里的居民对于这些水产享有平等的权利，其他村庄的人们则排除在外。为了说明其涵义，可以引用以下的例证。

1925年，周村长把村西的湖中捕鱼的权利租给了湖南省来的人。这是由于那时村庄需要钱来修理河上自卫用的栅栏。签订合同以后，周向村民宣布，今后不得有人去该湖捕鱼。村民遵守了这个协定。我在村里的时候，发生了一起争端。那些湖南人抓获了一条捞虾的船，把渔民押送到城里警察署，控告他们偷窃。周抗议说，租给湖南人的不是那个湖，而是在湖中捕鱼的权利，这个权利不包括捞虾的权利。最后，被抓的人获释。

村民还要阻止外来者在河里采集水藻。

在村内和村周围水中采集自然产品的权利由村民共享。但捞获的鱼和水藻是属于捞获者专有的财产。

田埂和公共道路，就交通用途而言，像水路一样，不是任何人的特有财产。任何人不得拦阻公共道路或田埂上行走的任何其他人。

But the roads and dykes are also used for growing vegetables. The right to use them for this purpose is exclusive to a group which have special claims—the Chia. The problem is complicated because the public road passes across the open space in front of houses, which is used for heaping straws, for fixing silk machines and manure pits, for arranging dining-tables, and for drying laundries. Each house has the exclusive right to the use of the road for these purposes.

❷ Ownership of Farm-Land

All the farms are divided between Chia for cultivation. Before we come to the owners, the idea of ownership of the farm-land must be clearly defined.

According to the native theory of land tenure, land is divided into two layers: namely, the surface and the subsoil. The possessor of the subsoil is the title holder of the land. His name will be registered with the government because he pays the taxes on the land. But he may possess only the subsoil without the surface, that is, he has no right to use the land directly for cultivation. Such a person is called an absentee landlord. The person possessing both the surface and the subsoil is termed the full owner. The one possessing only the surface without the subsoil is termed tenant. I shall use these terms only in the meanings defined above.

The owners of the surface, whether full owners or tenants, can cultivate the land themselves; this distinguishes them from absentee landlords. They also can lease the land to others, or employ labourers to work for them. The lessee who possesses the right of using the land temporarily can also employ labourers. In these cases, the person who owns the surface rights, may not be the actual cultivator of the land. Thus we must distinguish between the actual cultivator, the surface owners, and the owner of the subsoil. They may be the same persons and they may be different persons with reference to the same piece of land.

All of them have definite claims on the produce of the land. The owner of the subsoil can demand rent from the tenant. The surface owner can demand rent from the lessee. The employee can, in return for labour, obtain wage from the employer. The absentee landlord, the lessor, the employee receive fixed shares in terms of rent and wage irrespective of the actual return from the land. Therefore the risk involved is born by

但是道路和田埂也用来种菜。这种道路和田埂的使用权，是对此有特殊权利的家所专有的。因为公共道路要通过各家门前的空地，这空地是用来堆放稻草、安放缫丝机和粪缸、安排饭桌、晾衣服的地方，所以这个问题比较复杂。每一家都有把道路作这些用途的专有权。

二、农田的所有权

所有农田都划分归各家耕种。在我们讨论农田所有者之前，必须为农田所有制的概念下一个明确的定义。

根据当地对土地的占有的理论，土地被划分为两层，即田面及田底。田底占有者是持土地所有权的人。因为他支付土地税，所以他的名字将由政府登记。但他可能仅占有田底，不占有田面，也就是说他无权直接使用土地，进行耕种。这种人被称为不在地主。既占有田面又占有田底的人被称为完全所有者。仅占有田面，不占有田底的人被称为佃户。我将只按照以上定义使用这些词语。

无论是完全所有者还是佃户，只要是田面的所有者，就能自行耕种土地；据此可以把这种人与不在地主区别开来。这种人也能够把土地租给他人，或雇工为自己种地。承租人有暂时使用土地的权利，他也能雇工。根据以上情况，拥有田面权利的人可以不是土地的实际耕作者。因此我们必须把实际耕作者、田面所有者以及田底所有者区别开来。对于同一块土地，他们可以是同一个人，也可以是不同的人。

所有这些人都对土地的产品有一定的权利。田底所有者可以要求佃户交地租。田面所有者可以要求承租人交租。雇工可以从雇主那里取得工钱作为劳动的报酬。无论土地的实际收成如何，不在地主、出租者以及雇工分别取得固定的地租和工钱。所以，完全所有者、

the full-owner, the tenant, and the lessee. The latter, except sometimes the employees, are also the owners of the implements used in cultivation. The following table summarizes these points.

Title	Legal Right	Reward	Obligation	Owner of Implements
Employee (a) Short-term.		Daily wage	Cultivation	No or yes.
(b) Long-term.		Yearly wage, food and shelter	Cultivation	No or yes.
Lessee	Temporary use of the land surface	Produce	Cultivation, rent to lessor	Yes.
Tenant	Permanent ownership of the land surface	Produce	Rent to absentee landlord, cultivation	Yes.
Absentee landlord	Ownership of subsoil	Rent From tenant	Taxes to government	No.
Full-owner	Ownership of land surface and subsoil	Produce	Taxes to government	Yes.

❸ Farm Labourers and Land Leasing

Ownership of the land surface is always held by the Chia group, which supplies male members to work on the farm. But sometimes the group may not be able to supply enough labour and the institution of farm labourers comes into being. The persons thus introduced are long-term employees. They live in the house and are provided with food and shelter. They are paid a yearly wage of eighty dollars with two months' holidays at the new year when agricultural activities are suspended. Short-term employees are taken on when there is a short-period need for labour. They live in their own houses and provide their own food. They usually have their own land and are employed only when they have completed their own work.

The long-term employees sell their labour and do not possess means of production except sometimes the hoe. They come from those Chia whose land holding is too small to absorb their labour. Especially those in need of money to enable them to obtain a wife will seek employment for a few years. I did not meet anyone who had been landless all his life. The total number of employees in this village is only seventeen (VI–1). This shows that this institution does not play an important part

佃户和承租者都要承担风险。后者（有时雇工除外）也是农具的所有者。下表对以上几点进行了归纳。

名称	合法权利	报酬	责任	农具的所有者
雇工 （a）短工 （b）长工		日工资、 年工资、食宿	耕种 耕种	不是或是 不是或是
承租者	暂时使用田面	产品	耕种、付给 出租者地租	是
佃　户	永久地拥有田面	产品	付给不在地主 地租、耕种	是
不在地主	拥有田底	向佃户收租	向政府交税	不是
完全所有者	拥有田面及田底	产品	向政府交税	是

三、雇农及小土地出租

田面所有权通常属于家这个群体。家提供男子到田里劳动，但有时它也许不能提供足够的劳力，这就产生了雇农制度。从事这种劳动的人是长工。长工住在雇主家里，得到食宿供应。每年付给长工80元的工钱，在新年农闲期间有两个月的假期。在需要短期劳动力的时候就雇用短工。短工住在自己家中，自供膳食。短工通常有自己的土地，只有当他们完成了自己的工作后才受雇。

长工出卖自己的劳动力，不拥有生产工具，偶有锄头。长工来自那些土地太少，以致劳力有余的家庭。尤其是那些需要钱娶妻的人，他们愿意为别人做几年长工。我没有遇到过一辈子都没有土地的人。这个村庄中的雇工总共只有17人（第六章第一节）。这说明，在这个

in the village economy, and if we examine the population statistics this phenomenon can be explained. As mentioned (III–3), any Chia which has a land holding above the average is likely to raise more children. When the children grow up, the estate is divided. In other words, the chance of labour in the Chia proving insufficient is considerably reduced by the population pressure and the ideology of kinship. Moreover, there is no sign of people leaving their land in search of other occupations and meanwhile employing labourers to cultivate the land. This is due, first to the low degree of occupational differentiation (VIII–1), secondly to the special value attached to land (next section), and lastly to the under-development of industry in the town.

The institution of land leasing is also very limited. It occurs in most cases when the male members of a Chia are dead and the widows and children are unable to work on the land. Leasing of land is quite different from tenancy. The lessor preserves the right of ownership. There is a definite period for the contract. He is free to choose his lessee and to make changes when the contract expires.

It is interesting to compare this with the situation in South China, where both the hired labourers and landless peasants are numerous and the system of land leasing is far more elaborate.[34] This seems to be chiefly due to the presence of the system of "permanent tenancy" as a character of the absentee landlordship in Eastern China, while it has died out in South China. This leads us to an examination of the system of absentee landlordship.

❹ Absentee Landlordship

To study the institution of absentee landlordship, it is necessary to examine first the values attached to land. The primary function of land is to yield a food supply. But land is not only a means for producing food.

The productivity of land fluctuates according to the amount of attention and labour devoted to it. Furthermore, it is only partially controllable. There are unexpected risks. Thus land acquires its individuality through its variability in reacting to human expectation. Fear, anxiety, expectation, comfort, and love complicate the relation between man and land. People can never be certain what will come from the land. Land provides the means for self-assertion, for conquering the unknown and for the pleasures of accomplishment.

村子的经济生活中，雇工制度不起重要作用。如果我们考察一下人口统计数字，这个现象就能得到解释。前面已经提到（第三章第三节），任何一家只要其占有的土地在平均数以上，这家就很可能有较多的孩子。孩子长大之后就要分家产。换句话说，家中原来就不多的劳动机会，在人口压力和亲属关系的意识之下，更加减少了。况且也没有迹象表明人们要离开自己的土地去寻求其他职业而同时又雇工来耕种土地。首先，这是由于职业分化的程度很低（第八章第一节）；其次，是由于土地附有特殊价值（下一节）；最后一点是，由于城里的工业不发达。

小土地出租制度也是非常有限的。出租土地大多是因为家里的男人死亡，孤儿寡母无力耕种土地。小土地出租与佃租是大不相同的。出租者保留土地的所有权。合同有一定的期限。出租者可以自由选择承租人，在合同期满时，可以更换承租人。

将这里的情况与华南的情况相比较是很有意思的。华南的雇工与无地的贫农为数较多，土地出租制要复杂得多。[34] 这似乎主要是由于华东不在地主制的特点——"永久性佃权"制的存在；而在华南，不在地主制已经消失了。接着让我们来考察一下不在地主制。

四、不在地主制

为了研究不在地主制度，必须首先考察土地所附有的价值。土地的基本作用是生产粮食。但土地不仅仅是生产粮食的资料。

土地的生产率随着人们对农田的照料和投入的劳动量而波动。而且人只能部分地控制土地，有时会遭遇出乎意料的灾情。因此，对人们的期望来说，土地具有其捉摸不定的特性。恐惧、忧虑、期待、安慰以及爱护等感情，使人们和土地间的关系复杂起来了。人们总是不能肯定土地将给人带来些什么。人们利用土地来坚持自己的主张，征服未知世界，并表达成功的喜悦。

Although the productivity of the land can be only partially controlled, this partial control supplies an empirical measurement of workmanship. Honour, ambition, devotion, social approval are all thus linked up with the land. The villagers judge a person as good or bad according to his industry in working on the land. A badly weeded farm, for instance, will give a bad reputation to the owner. The incentive to work is thus deeper than the fear of hunger.

The relative inexhaustibility of the land gives the people a relative security. Although there are bad years, the land never disillusions the people completely, since hope for plenty in the future always remains and is not infrequently realized. If we take the other kinds of productive work, we shall see that the risks involved in them are much greater. The sense of security is expressed in the following statement made to me by one of the villagers:

"Land is there. You can see it every day. Robbers cannot take it away. Thieves cannot steal it. Men die but land remains."

The incentive to hold land is directly related to the sense of security. The farmer says, "The best thing to give to one's son is land. It is living property. Money will be used up but land never."

It is true that there are many ways of getting food. But the people will not exchange their land for other means, even if more productive. They do take up other occupations, such as the silk industry and fishing, but agriculture remains the principal occupation in the village.

The deeper we analyse the situation, the more it appears, not only that land in general has a particular value to the people, but that the property inherited by a Chia has for it a particular value. Land is transmitted according to fixed rules (IV–3). People inherit their land from their fathers. The sentiment originating in the kinship relation and reinforced by ancestor worship is manifested also in this personal attachment to the particular plots of land. Religious belief in the importance of the continuity of descendants finds its concrete expression in the continuous holding of land. To sell a piece of land inherited from one's father offends the ethical sense. "No good son will do that. It is against filial piety." This comment sums up the traditional outlook.

Personal familiarity with a particular piece of land as the result of continuous work on it is also a cause of personal attachment to the land.

　　尽管土地的生产率只能部分地受人控制，但是这部分控制作用提供了衡量人们手艺高低的实际标准。名誉、抱负、热忱、社会认可，就这样全都和土地联系了起来。村民根据个人是否在土地上辛勤劳动来判断他的好坏。例如，一块杂草多的田地会给它的主人带来不好的名声。因此，这种激励劳动的因素比害怕挨饿还要深。

　　土地那相对的用之不尽的性质使人们的生活有相对的保障。虽然有坏年景，但土地从不使人们的幻想彻底破灭，因为将来丰收的希望总是存在，并且这种希望是常常能实现的。如果我们拿其他种类的生产劳动来看，就会发现那些工作的风险要大得多。一个村民用下面的语言向我表述了他的安全感：

　　"地就在那里摆着。你可以天天见到它。强盗不能把它抢走，窃贼不能把它偷走。人死了地还在。"

　　占有土地的动机与这种安全感有直接关系。那个农民说："传给儿子最好的东西就是地，地是活的家产，钱是会用光的，可地是用不完的。"

　　的确，获取食物的方法很多。可是人们不愿意拿自己的土地去和其他资料交换，即使其他的生产率更高，他们也不愿意。他们确实也从事其他职业，例如丝业和渔业，但农业始终是村里的主要职业。

　　对于情况的分析越深入，这个问题就越明显，土地不仅在一般意义上对人们有特殊的价值，并且在一家所继承的财产中有其特殊价值。土地是按照一定的规则传递的（第四章第三节）。人们从父亲那里继承土地。起源于亲属关系又在对祖先的祭祀中加深的那种情感，也表现在对某块土地的个人依恋上。关于绵续后代的重要性的宗教信仰，在土地占有的延续上得到了具体表现。把从父亲那里继承来的土地卖掉，就是触犯道德观念。"好儿子不做这种事。这样做就是不孝。"这种评论总结了这一传统观念。

　　一直在某一块土地上劳动，一个人就会熟悉这块土地，这也是对土地产生个人感情的原因。人们从刚刚长大成人起，就在那同一块

It is very common for people to work on the same piece of land from early adulthood to death. To say that their land is an integral part of their personality is scarcely an exaggeration.

The non-economic value of the land complicates the transactions in land. Although land has its non-economic value, it does not in any sense lose its economic value. The sentimental and ethical reactions to the selling of land do not rule out completely the possibility of land transactions. People sometimes need money urgently. Economic strain compels them to treat the land as an economic commodity. But I found no case of alienation except under real pressure. Even then the process usually takes a roundabout form.

A person needing money urgently, either for taxes or rent payment, is forced to borrow from the money-lender. After a definite period, if the borrower cannot pay back the capital as well as the interest, he is forced to transfer his title over the land, limited to the subsoil, to the lender.[35] This transaction in practice means very little to the borrower, since the borrower under the ever-increasing burden of interest can hardly hope to repay his debt. To pay high interest is more unbearable than to pay a definite rent.

In fact the conversion from annual payment of interest to rent does not make a great difference to the debtor. I found one case where the person concerned did not even understand the meaning of the change. "I borrow his money, and he takes my land. I have no hope of redeeming my pledge. What does it matter whether the money I pay is rent or interest?"

The difference is again obscured by the existence of the native theory of land tenure. The tenant preserves his title to the land surface. This right cannot be interfered with by the owner of the subsoil. By this custom the tenant is protected from any direct intervention by the owner of the subsoil.[36] His only obligation is to pay the rent. According to law, if the tenant is unable to pay his rent for two years, the landlord can give him notice to quit, but the law does not apply to those places where custom is paramount.[37] The practical difficulty of ejecting a tenant is to find a substitute. Absentee landlords do not cultivate the land themselves. Outsiders from the villages will not be welcomed into the community if they come at the expense of old members. Villagers are not willing to cut the throat of their fellow members who for any good reason cannot pay their rent. In these circumstances it is in the interest of the landlord to

土地上一直干到死，这种现象是很普通的。如果说人们的土地就是他们人格整体的一部分，并不是什么夸张。

土地的非经济价值使土地的交易复杂化。虽然土地具有非经济价值，但从任何意义上讲，它都没有失去其经济价值。在感情和道德上对于出卖土地的反应，并不完全排除土地交易的可能性。人们有时急需用钱，经济紧张迫使人们把土地当作商品对待。除了在真正压力很大的情况下，我没有发现其他转让土地的事例。即使在那时，出卖土地也要通过迂回的形式来完成。

一个急需用钱的人，不管是纳税还是交租，都是被迫向放债者借钱。在一定时期之后，如果借款者无力偿还本金及利息，他就被迫把土地所有权（限于田底所有权）转交给放债者。[35] 实际上，这种交易对于借款者没有什么意义，因为在日益加重的利息负担下，借款者很难有希望偿还债务。偿还高利比交付定租还要难以承受。

事实上，从每年偿付利息变为每年交付租金，对负债者而言并无很大差别。我遇到一例情况，有关的人甚至还不理解这种改变的意义。"我借了他的钱，他占了我的地。我没有希望赎回我抵押出去的地。我付给他的钱到底是租还是利，这又有什么关系呢？"

当地的土地占有理论进一步掩盖了这种差别。佃户保留着他的田面所有权。这个权利不受田底占有者的干涉。按这种惯例，佃户的权利得到了保护，不受田底所有者任何直接的干涉。[36] 佃户的唯一责任是交租。根据法律，如果佃户连续两年交不起租，地主即可退佃。但该法律并不适用于惯例至上的地方。[37] 逐出佃户的实际困难在于寻找一个合适的替换者。不在地主自己不耕种土地。如果由外村人来挤掉本村人的位置，那么这些外村人也不会受到本社区的欢迎。只要是有正当的理由交不起租，村民们是不愿意卡同村人的脖子的。在这种情况下，抱着将来收回租子的希望，宽容拖欠是

tolerate the default in the hope of getting rent in the future. This situation does not really challenge the status of the landlord, since there are positive sanctions to enforce payment of rent whenever this is possible.

By this analysis several important points in the problem of land tenure are cleared up. The actual cultivators of the land in the village— except labourers—continue unchanged even in the event of a change of ownership of the subsoil. Since the practice of usury is regarded as morally wrong, it is not possible for neighbours to squeeze each other. The institution of absentee landlord arises only in the relation between village and town. The ownership of the land surface remains in the hands of the villagers; even the outsiders who live in the village do not find it easy to become owners of land surface, *i.e.* cultivators of the soil (II–5).

The institution of absentee landlord, thus described, has acquired a new significance as the result of the close financial relation between the town and the village. Professor R. H. Tawney has rightly put it, "What appears to be occurring, in some regions at least, is the emergence... of a class of absentee owners whose connection with agriculture is purely financial."[38] Again he said, "Nor must it be forgotten that the nominal owner is often little more than the tenant of a money-lender."[39]

The change in ownership of the subsoil actually means the investment of town capital in the village. Thus the value of the land in the town market is quite different from the real value of the land. From the point of view of the landlords the value of the land resides in the ability of the tenant to pay rent. The price of land fluctuates according to the amount of capital available for investment in land and the security of rent collection. Thus the market price of land does not include the price of the land surface. As my informant told me, if his landlord likes to cultivate his land, he must buy the land surface from him. Since such a case has never been known, the price of the land surface cannot be calculated.

The ownership of the subsoil implies only a claim to rent and can be sold on the market in the same way as bonds and stocks. It may belong to any legal person, whether an individual, a clan, or the government. It can be private or public. But we cannot here go into details, since this would require an investigation beyond our present scope.[40]

The security for rent payment, an important condition for the development of the instituion of absentee landlordship, leads to an examination of the method of rent collection and the attitude of tenants

符合地主利益的。这种情况并不会对地主的地位造成真正的威胁，因为，只要有可能交租时，就有规定的制裁办法迫使佃户还租。

按以上分析，在土地占有问题中的几个重点已经明确了。村里土地的实际耕种者（雇工除外）保持不变，甚至在田底所有者变更后仍然如此。因为放高利贷被认为是不道德的，所以邻居不可能互相压榨。不在地主制度仅仅出现在农村和城市的关系之中。田面所有权一直保留在村民的手中；即使是住在村里的外来户也难以成为田面所有者，即土地的耕种者（第二章第五节）。

城镇和村庄之间发生密切的金融关系的结果，使上述不在地主制度获得了新的意义。R. H. 托尼教授正确地说道："看来，在某些地区正在出现……不在地主阶级。这个阶级与农业的关系纯属金融关系。"[38] 他又说道："也不应忘记，土地的名义占有者常常和放债人的佃户差不多。"[39]

田底所有权的这一变化实际上意味着城镇资本对乡村进行投资。这样，城镇市场中的土地价值与土地的真实价值相差甚大。从地主的观点来看，土地的价值寓于佃户交租的能力之中。土地的价格随着可供土地投资的资本量以及收租的可靠性而波动。于是，土地的市场价格不包含田面的价格。正如我的情况提供者所说，如果他的地主想要种地，地主就得向他购买田面。因为从来没有听说过这种事，所以无法计算田面的价格。

田底所有权仅仅表明对地租的一种权利，这种所有权可以像买卖债券和股票那样在市场上出售。田底所有权可以属于任何法人，不论是个人、家族或政府。这个所有权可能是私人的，也可能是公共的。但在这里我们不能详加探讨，因为这需要进行超出我们目前范围的调查。[40]

交租的可靠性是不在地主制度发展的一个重要条件。由此引入了对收租方法和佃户对交租责任所抱态度的考察。由于城里土地

245

towards this obligation. Owing to the free market for land (*i.e.* the subsoil) in the town, the personal relation between the owners and the land they own has been reduced to the minimum. Most of the absentee landlords know nothing about the location of the land, the crop raised upon it, and even the men who pay the rent. Their sole interest is the rent itself.

Rent is collected in various ways. The simplest system is the direct one; the landlord comes in person to the village. But this is not a very efficient way. It takes time and pains for the landlord to visit each tenant in different villages. Most of the landlords are unwilling to burden themselves with this. Moreover, direct and personal contact sometimes handicaps the process of collecting. The tenants may be poor and always ready to ask for exemptions or reductions. The landlord, on the other hand, is not infrequently inspired by humanitarian teachings, especially if he belongs to the old literati. On several occasions I knew that they were reluctant to squeeze their tenants. The conflict between traditional ethics and the practice of living as parasites sometimes leads these gentlemen landlords to derive only moral satisfaction from their trip but not enough money to pay the tax. But this direct system is limited to a small group of petty landlords. The majority collect their rent through agents.

Landlords of big estates establish their own rent-collecting bureaux and petty landlords pool their claims with them. The bureau is called Chü. The tenants do not know and do not care who is their landlord, and know only to which bureau they belong.

Names of the tenants and the amount of land held by each are kept in the bureau records. At the end of October, the bureau will inform each tenant of the amount of rent that should be paid that year. The information is forwarded by special agents. These agents are employed by the bureau and have been entrusted with police power by the district government. The bureau is thus in fact a semi-political organ.

Before deciding the amount of rent to be collected the landlords will hold a meeting in their union to decide what exemptions are to be made on account of flood or drought and also to decide the rate of exchange for converting rice rent to money. (The rent is regulated in terms of quantity of rice but payment is made in money.) The rate of exchange is not the market one, but is arbitrarily determined by the union of landlords. The peasants must sell their rice in order to get money for the payment of rent, and at the time when this is due the market price is usually low. Thus the combination of rent in kind and rent in money considerably increases the burden of the rent payer.

（即田底）市场的交易自由，地主和他们占有的土地之间的个人关系弱化到最小的程度。大多数不在地主对于土地的位置、土地上种的庄稼、甚至对于交租的人都一无所知。他们的唯一兴趣就是租金本身。

收租可以有各种各样的方式。最简单的一种是直接收租，地主亲自到村子里来收租，但是这种方式的效率不很高。地主跑到各村去找佃户要花时间和力气，大多数地主不愿意自找麻烦，加之，地主与佃农的直接接触有时反而阻碍了收租的进程。佃户可能很穷，一开口就要求免租或减租。另一方面，若是这个地主属于老的文人阶层，他有时会受人道主义教育的影响。我知道几件地主不愿逼迫佃农的事。传统道德与寄生虫生活之间的冲突，有时使这些地主绅士们的乡下之行只能得到精神上的满足，而得不到足够的钱来纳税。但这种直接收租的方式限于少量的小地主，大多数地主通过他们的代理人收租。

家产大的地主建立自己的收租局，而小地主则与大地主联合经营，租款分成。收租所被称作"局"。佃户不知道，也不关心谁是地主，只知道自己属于哪个局。

佃户的名字和每个佃户耕地的数量，收租局均有记录。在阳历10月底，收租局就会通知每个佃户，当年该交多少租。通知由专门的代理人传达。这些代理人是租局雇用的，并且县政府把警察的权力交给他们使用。这样，收租局事实上是一种半政治机构。

在确定收租数量之前，地主联合会举行一次会议，根据旱、涝情况，商定该作何项减免，并决定米租折合成现金的兑换率（地租是以稻米数量为标准来表示的，但以现金交付）。这个兑换率并不是市场上的兑换率，而是由地主联合会专断制定的。贫农必须卖米换钱交租，并且往往正值通常市场上米价较低的时候。租米和租款的双重作用更加加重了交租者的负担。

Nine grades are made in rent for different qualities of land. The average is about eight pints (2.4 bushels) of rice per *mow*. This amounts to 40 per cent. of the total rice produce of the land.

In the village, rent is paid into the hands of agents of the bureau. This is a peculiar practice different from that of other parts of the same district. The actual amount of payment is not necessarily equal to the amount written on the demand notice. As an old agent told me, "The villagers are illiterate. They don't know how to calculate from rice to money. There is no receipt or anything like that." If the tenant refuses to pay, the agent has power to arrest him and put him into the prison of the district government. But if the tenant is really unable to pay, he will be released at the end of the year. It is no use keeping him in prison and leaving the farms uncultivated.

A more detailed description of the system of rent collecting would be beyond the scope of the present study. But it is interesting to notice the different attitudes of the tenants towards their obligations.

By the old people, rent payment is regarded as a moral duty. As some of them said: "We are good people. We never refuse to pay our rent. We cannot steal even when we are poor. How then can we refuse to pay rent?"—"Why do you pay your rent?"—"The landlord owns the land. We cultivate his land. We only have the land surface. The surface cannot exist without the subsoil." These positive sanctions are adequate to maintain the institution. It is not only the fear of imprisonment that makes the tenants discharge their obligation. Where the tenant does not pay the rent, it is on account of distress for which he has no responsibility such as famine, illness, etc. A good landlord will then allow exemptions and reductions.

Recently the situation has been changing. The economic depression in the rural district has made rent a heavy burden on the peasant, and the income derived from the rent much more vulnerable for the landlord. The peasants are more susceptible to new ideas offered to the institution. "Those who till the land should have the land" is a principle laid down by the late Dr. Sun Yat-sen and accepted, at least theoretically, by the present government.[41] A more extreme view is spreading among the communists and other left groups. All these ideas have affected the sanctions described above. Peasants unable to pay rent now feel justified in neglecting to do so, and those who are able to pay will wait and see if they are compelled to do so. On the side of the landlords, strong measures must be taken to

　　对于不同品质的土地，地租被分为九等。平均每亩地约交 2.4 蒲式耳租米。这等于土地全部产米量的 40%。

　　在村里，租金交付到租局代理人的手中。这是本村独特的做法，与本县中其他地方不同。交租的实际数量并不一定与收租通知上写明的数量相等。正如一个老代理人告诉我的："村里的人不识字。他们不知道怎样把米折算为钱。没有收据之类的东西。"如果佃户拒不交租，代理人有权力把他抓起来关到县政府的监狱里去。但如果佃户真的没有能力交租的话，就会在年底得到释放，把他关在狱里无济于事，反而荒了田地，无人耕种。

　　更加详细地叙述收租方法，就会超出目前的研究范围，但注意佃户对于自己责任的不同态度，是非常有趣的。

　　按老年人的看法，交租被认为是一种道义上的责任。正如有些老人说的："我们是好人，我们从不拒绝交租。我们就是穷，也不会去偷东西，我们怎么会拒绝交租呢？"——"你为什么要交租呢？"——"地是地主的，我们种他的地，我们只有田面。没有田底，就不会有田面。"这些习惯规定的约束力是有利于维护这个制度的，不仅是对于监禁的恐惧心理才使得佃户履行职责。佃户不交租是由于遇到了饥荒、疾病等灾难，佃户对这些是没有责任的。一个好心的地主，这时就会同意减免地租。

　　最近局势正在发生变化。乡村地区的经济萧条已使得地租成为贫农的沉重负担；对地主来说，地租收入很难得到保障。农民对有关土地制度的一些新思想比较容易接受。"耕者有其田"是已故孙中山先生提出的原则，至少在理论上已被现政府接受。[41]在共产党人和其他左派团体中，正传播着一种更加激进的观点。所有这些思想都已对上述的制裁措施发生了影响。交不起租的贫农现在感到不交租是正当的，那些交得起租的人则先观望是否要强迫他们交租。在地主方面，他们必须采取强硬措施来维护自己的特权，他们也不再

maintain their privileges, and their available capital tends to be no longer in agricultural land. The result is an intensification of conflict between tenants and landlords, and a financial crisis in rural economy. The district jail has been repeatedly crowded with default cases. Organized action of the peasants in refusing rent payment has provoked serious conflict with the landlords who are backed by government force. In this part of China, a peasant revolt took place in 1935 and led to the death of many peasants in villages near Soochow. The value of land has depreciated rapidly, and the whole financial organization of the village is at stake. This situation is general in China. The gravest part is found in central China, where the issue has taken the form of a political struggle between Chinese Soviets and the Central Government. But in the village which we are now describing the problem is less acute. The better natural endowment and the partial success of reforming rural industry have been effective palliatives. The positive sanction in favour of rent payment is still functioning.

❺ Full-Ownership

Absentee landlordship is only found when there is close financial relation between village and town. Corresponding to the investment of town capital in the countryside, the ownership of the subsoil of the farm land passes into the hands of the townspeople. At the present time, about two-thirds of the subsoil of the village is owned by absentee landlords. The other third is still in the hands of the villagers. (I am not able to give accurate statistics on this point. The estimate was given to me by my informants.) The villagers themselves may lease their land, may employ labourers, but never acquire the title to the subsoil only.

The full-owners, lessees and tenants do not form clear-cut or water-tight classes. The same Chia may possess all rights to some part of its land, may lease another part from or to others, and a part may belong to absentee landlords. The amount of land actually cultivated by each Chia is determined by the amount of labour available. Since the number of male adult members of each Chia does not vary much, the amount of land cultivated by each is much the same. But if we inquire how far a Chia is cultivating its own land, or how much land is fully owned by each Chia we find a considerable variation. The administration office of the village gave me the following estimate:

把可用的资本放在农田上了。结果是佃户与地主间的冲突加剧，乡村经济发生金融危机。县监狱中不断挤满了欠租者。贫农组织起来采取行动，拒绝交租，与政府支持的地主发生了严重冲突。在华东，1935年发生了农民起义，导致了苏州附近农村中的许多农民死亡。土地迅速贬值，村子里全部财务组织濒临险境。这个局势在中国具有普遍性。局势最严重的地方是华中，以上问题已表现为中国的苏维埃政权与中央政府间政治斗争的形式。但在我们所述的开弦弓村，问题尚未如此尖锐。较好的天然条件以及乡村工业改造的部分成功，起了缓冲作用。有利于交租的那种约束力仍然在起作用。

五、完全所有制

只有当城乡金融关系密切的时候才出现不在地主制。与城镇资本在乡下的投资相应，农田的田底所有权落到了城里人的手中。目前，该村约有三分之二的田底被不在地主占有，余下的三分之一仍在村民手中（对于这点，我不能提出精确的统计数。此估计数是我的情况提供者提供的）。村民自己也可以出租土地，也可以雇工，但绝对不会只拥有田底所有权。

完全所有者、承租者以及佃户并没有形成界限清楚、区分严格的不同阶级。同一个家可能拥有家里一部分土地的全部权利，可能承租或出租土地的另一部分，也可能还有一部分土地属于不在地主。每家实际耕种的土地量取决于可用的劳动量。因为每家的成年男性人数差别不大，所以每家耕种的土地量也相差无几。但如果我们来了解一下每家耕种自己土地的程度，或者说每家有多少土地是完全属于自己的，我们就会发现这个差别是相当大的。村公所向我提供了下列估计数：

Amount of land (*mow*)	Percentage of Chia
50–70	0.6
30–49	0.7
15–29	0.9
10–14	4.0
5–9	18.0
0–4	75.8

According to this estimate, about 90 per cent. of the population in the village have less than ten *mow* or 1.5 acres of their own land. They have surplus labour but not enough land. Therefore they become lessees and tenants.

Theoretically the tenants are free from the obligation to pay taxes. Land tax falls on the owner of the subsoil. But the practice is somewhat different. The system of tax collecting in the region is a peculiar one, and differs from that of other parts of the same district.

From the ex-magistrate, I received the following explanation. At the end of the last imperial dynasty, the government tried to register the tax payers. But this was never completed. The tax in the region has been divided yearly between the cultivators of each *yu*; a definite amount is assigned to them. One of the cultivators who owns more than twenty *mow* in the *yu* will be responsible for collecting the sum. This job is taken in turn by all the qualified persons in the *yu*. The government will not interfere with the way in which the collector distributes the tax.

The amount of tax to be paid by each *yu* is determined by its size. But since the land was only recently surveyed, and the land register has not yet been completed, the size is determined according to the estimate of the local collectors. The estimate is thus made not strictly according to the actual size of the land but according to the ability of the people to pay taxes. The collector is obliged to hand over the assessed amount to the government regardless of how much he has actually collected. To avoid the danger of having to pay a deficiency himself, he will submit a low estimate on the pretext that land has been deserted. In case of flood or drought, he will request the government to make reductions. (This request was formerly made in connection with petitions for magical help.)

Thus the actual distribution of the burden of tax is not rigid. The collector is able to use common sense in distributing the burden according to the ability of the people. Honesty and the sense of equality checks the abuses possible under such an informal practice.

土地的数量（亩）	家的百分比
50—70	0.6
30—49	0.7
15—29	0.9
10—14	4.0
5—9	18.0
0—4	75.8

根据这个估计，村中自己有地不到 10 亩（1.5 英亩）的人口约为 90%。他们有剩余的劳动力，但没有足够的土地。这样，他们就成了承租者或佃户。

理论上讲，佃户无交税的责任。土地税由田底所有者承担。但实际不然，此地的税收制有些特殊，与本县其他地方不同。

我从前地方行政官那里得到了以下解释。在清朝末年，政府试图对纳税者进行登记，但没有完成。这个地方的税款每年一次分派给每一圩的耕种者，指定他们缴纳一定的数额。每圩中有地 20 亩以上的一个耕种者负责征收此款额。此工作由每圩中的各位合格者轮流担任。政府对收税人分派税款的方式不加干涉。

每一圩交税的数额取决于该圩的面积。但由于土地最近才得到测量，土地的登记尚未完成，所以现在还是根据当地收税者的估计来决定其面积。这个估计不是严格地根据土地的实际大小作出的，而是根据交税人的能力作出的。无论收税人实际收到多少税，他必须向政府上交估定的数额。为了避免他自己必须补足缺额的危险，收税人便以土地荒芜为借口，提出较低的估计。遇到水旱灾情，他就会请求政府减税（这种请求以前是与祈祷神明相助联系在一起的）。

于是，税款负担的实际分派并不严格。收税者可根据人们的能力，通情达理地分配负担。诚实与平等的观念可以防止这种非正规工作中可能发生的弊端。

Under the present system, tenants are not actually exempted from the obligation to pay taxes. I have no definite material on this point to show how the actual allocation is made.

The government will try to collect taxes according to the actual size of the land of each individual owner when the land survey and registration are completed. By this action the traditional system is likely to be changed. It may relieve the burden of the tenants but it will certainly increase the total sum of taxes if the rate is not reduced because the reported size is always smaller than the surveyed size. The villagers realize the possibility and frequently try to sabotage the government action. At present, the problem is far from settled.

❻ Inheritance and Agriculture

In Chapter III, I postponed the problem of how the land is actually divided in the process of transmission of property, because it required a prior knowledge of the system of land tenure. On the other hand, some points of land tenure and of agricultural technology still remain obscure unless the factor of kinship is taken into account. In this section, I intend to link the land tenure and agriculture with kinship.

Let us take the example, given in the previous chapter, of the division of a Chia among a father and two sons. The land is divided in this case into three unequal parts. Let us suppose that before division the Chia possesses a strip of farms consisting of four successive plots: A, B, C, and D. These four plots are different in value because their distances from the streams are different. In principle the father can choose his own share. Suppose he takes plot A and half plot B, which may be divided parallel to the margin. The rest of plot B is assigned to the first son as his extra portion. The remaining two plots are equally divided among the two brothers. To ensure equality of division, they must be divided perpendicularly to the margin. Each son takes one belt. If, on the death of the father, the share reserved to him is divided again, it would be divided in the same way. This is illustrated in the following diagram.

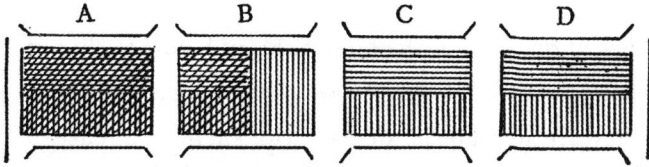

	For the first son when the Chia is divided.
	分家时给大儿子的。
	For the second son when the Chia is divided.
	分家时给二儿子的。
	For the first son after the further division of their father's reserve.
	再次分配父亲的地时给大儿子的。
	For the second son after the further division of their father's reserve.
	再次分配父亲的地时给二儿子的。

按目前实行的办法，佃户实际上没有免除交税的责任。关于这一点，我没有确定的资料来表明实际的分派是怎样进行的。

在土地的测量和登记工作完成之后，政府将根据每一个土地所有者拥有土地的实际面积征收税款。通过这一措施，传统税制很可能发生变化。佃户的纳税负担可能解除，但在税率不降低的情况下，肯定要使总税额增加，这是因为以前上报的土地面积总是小于测量面积的。村民意识到了这个可能性，经常想方设法破坏政府的行动。目前，这个问题还远远得不到解决。

六、继承与农业

在第三章中，我推迟了对这个问题的论述，即在家产的传递过程中，土地实际上是如何划分的。这是由于谈这个问题需要预先了解土地的占有制。另一方面，如不考虑亲属关系这一因素，在土地占有及农业技术方面仍有些问题尚不明了。在这一节，我想把土地占有和农业与亲属关系联系起来。

让我们仍以前面章节中一父两子的分"家"为例。此例中土地被划分为三个不相等的部分。让我们假设：在分家前，这家有一片农田，包括相连的 A、B、C、D 共四块。因为这四块地距河流的远近不同，所以它们的价值亦各不相同。按照规矩，父亲可以挑选自己那一份。假设他选中了田块 A 和田块 B 的一半，这半块可以沿着地头平行划分。田块 B 的其余一半分配给大儿子，作为额外部分。剩下的两块田两兄弟均分。为了保证分配平均，必须使分界线垂直于地头，每个儿子取一条。如果父亲死了，他那一份地还要再分配，划分方式同上。上图说明了比例土地划分情况。

These lines of division, or the boundaries of holdings, do not necessarily coincide with the dykes constructed for the regulation of water. They are immaterial demarcations, and are marked by planting two trees at each end of the plot on the dykes. The boundaries of individual holdings become very complex as the result of successive divisions upon inheritance. The farms are divided into narrow belts, with a width of a few tens of metres.

Non-contiguity of farms is widely observed in China. It is found in the village. Although the frequency of land division cannot be taken as the origin of this, it definitely intensifies the scattering of holdings. Each Chia possesses several belts of lands widely apart. It sometimes takes twenty minutes for the boat to go from one belt to another. According to the estimate of my informants, few belts are above six *mow* in size. Most of them are not more than one or two *mow*. Each Chia, at the present time, has three to seven belts.

The narrow belt and the scattered holdings hamper the use of animal labour or other collective methods of farming. They are the chief causes of the technical backwardness of farming in China.

Moreover, in a single plot there may be several owners, each of whom is responsible for his own belt. We have seen how this gives rise frequently to disputes on water regulations.

The small size of holding of the Chia limits the number of children who can be raised. On the other hand, the relatively large landholders will raise more children and consequently the size of their holding will be reduced within a few generations. Under these conditions, the ratio between land and population is adjusted.

这些划分线，或土地分界线，并不一定要同调节水的田埂一致。这些分界线是非实体的，在田块两端的田埂上栽两棵树，用来作为分界标志。遗产的各次相继划分，结果使个人占有土地的界线变得非常复杂。农田被分为许多窄长的地带，宽度为几米。

在中国广大地区都可见到农田的分散性。这个村子亦不例外。虽然不能认为频繁的土地划分就是农田不相邻的起源，但这种划分确实加大了土地的分散程度。每"家"占有相隔甚远的几条带状田地。从一条地带到另一条地带，有时要乘船20分钟。根据情况提供者的估计，极少有面积在六亩以上的地带。大多数地带不超过一两亩。目前，每一家有三至七条地带。

狭窄的地带和分散的地块妨碍了畜力的使用，也妨碍了采用其他集体耕作方式。这是中国农业技术落后的首要原因。

再者，一块田地可能有好几个所有者，而每人只对自己那一条地带负责。我们已经看到过这种情况怎样引起了用水方面的频繁争执。

每家土地面积窄小，限制了抚育孩子的数量。另一方面，土地相对较多的农户生养较多的孩子，从而在几代人之后，他们占有土地的面积就将缩小。在这些条件之下，人口与土地之间的比例得到了调整。

CHAPTER XII   THE SILK INDUSTRY

The silk industry is the second main source of income of the villagers. This is characteristic of the villagers around Lake Tai. The domestic silk industry has been carried on by the people for more than a thousand years. But during the last decade, for the reasons mentioned above (II–3), it has been declining. A new factory system of silk manufacturing has been introduced. The industrial change has deeply affected the life of the people in the villages. It has also called forth various attempts on the part of the government and other institutions to control the change in order to reduce or eliminate its disastrous consequences. The village we are studying, being one of the centres of the industry, provides a typical case for analysing the process; and also, owing to the fact that an experiment has been made by the Sericultural School to reform the industry, it is specially interesting to see the possibilities and difficulties involved in such a deliberate effort of economic change.

❶ Scheme of the Process of Change

The present analysis will take into view the different forces effecting the situation. They are classified into outside forces working for the change and traditional forces bearing on the change. The interplay of these forces results in a changing situation. Thus the process can be schematically represented by three columns as follows.[42] The items listed in the scheme will be discussed in the following sections.

❷ Conditions Working for Industrial Change

Several facts already mentioned in the above chapters must be noticed once more in order that a proper estimate may be made of the relative importance of agriculture in the domestic economy. The average holding of land is about $8\frac{1}{2}$ *mow* (III–3). Under normal conditions each *mow* can produce six bushels of rice every year. The total produce will then be 51 bushels for that average holding of land. The amount of rice needed for direct consumption by members of the household is 42 bushels (VII–5). Therefore there is a surplus of 9 bushels. At the time when the new rice comes to market the price of rice is about $2\frac{1}{2}$ dollars per bushel. If the surplus is sold the return will be about 22 dollars. But for current expenses alone a Chia needs at least 200 dollars (VII–8).

拾 贰 蚕丝业

蚕丝业是这个村里的居民的第二主要收入来源，这是太湖一带农民的特点。农民从事家庭蚕丝业已有几千年的历史。但近十年来，由于上面已讲过的原因（第二章第三节），蚕丝业有所衰退，并引进了蚕丝业的新改革。蚕丝业的衰落深深地影响了农村人民的生活。政府和其他机构已经作了各种尝试来控制这个变化，以减轻或消灭其灾难性的后果。我们所研究的村庄是蚕丝业中心之一，它为我们分析这一过程提供了典型的例子；同时，江苏女子蚕业学校已经开展了改革蚕丝业的实验。因此对于这样一个有意识地进行经济改革过程中所遇到的各种可能性和困难进行观察更具有特殊的意义。

一、变迁过程图解

目前所作的分析将把影响情况的各种不同力量考虑进去。力量可分成两类：促使变化的外界力量和承受变化的传统力量，这两种力量的互相作用导致了情况的变化。因此变迁过程，可以三栏图解表示如下，[42] 图表中所列的项目将在以下各节讨论。

二、促进工业变迁的条件

为了对农业在家庭经济中的相对重要性作恰当的估价，我们必须再注意一下在上述章节中已经提到过的一些事实。平均一户拥有土地约 10 亩（第三章第三节）。在正常年景每亩每年可生产 6 蒲式耳的稻米。对拥有平均土地量的农户来说，总生产量是 51 蒲式耳。平均一家四口，需直接消费米 33 蒲式耳（第七章第五节），所以有 27.36 蒲式耳余粮。新米上市后，每蒲式耳米价约 2.5 元，如把余粮出卖约可得 68.4 元。但一个家目前的开支需要至少 200 元（第七章第八节）。

A. Outside Forces Making for a Change	B. Changing Situation	C. Traditional Forces Bearing on Change
I. World economic depression; and worldwide development of silk industry on scientific lines and by factory methods.	I. Decline of the price of raw silk. Decay of domestic silk industry. Resulting economic poverty in the Chinese village as seen in: (A) Deficiency in family budget and shortage of food. (B) Suspension of recreative meetings and postponement of marriage. (C) Usury.	I. Minimum standard of living. Domestic silk industry as an indispensable supplement to farming in a Chinese village. On which rest: (A) Daily necessities. (B) Ceremonial expenses. (C) Capital for productive work.
II. The Sericulture School as an active agent for industrial changes.	II. Readiness of the people for change. Support of the local leaders: (A) Assuming leadership in the reform. Increase of personal influence through participating in the reform. New leader created by the reform. (B) Economic benefit of the reform to the leaders.	II. Lack of sufficient knowledge for industrial change on the part of the villagers. Social position and function of local leaders. (A) Source of influence not hereditary, not by wealth but by strategic position in cultural contacts. (B) No direct economic reward for the position of the village head as such.

A. 促使变革的外界力量	B. 变化的情况	C. 承受变化的传统力量
I. 世界经济的衰退；及蚕丝业在世界性范围内向科学方法工厂企业的发展。	I. 生丝价格的下跌。家庭蚕丝业的衰退。中国农村经济贫困有以下三点表现：	I. 最低生活水平。家庭蚕丝业是中国农村中对农业不可缺少的补充。 靠它来支付：
	(A) 家庭收入不足，食物短缺。	(A) 日常所需。
	(B) 文娱性活动停止，婚期推迟。	(B) 礼节性费用。
	(C) 高利贷。	(C) 生产的资本。
II. 江苏省女子蚕业学校是工业变革的积极力量。	II. 居民有变革的准备。当地领导人的支持：	II. 农民缺乏工业改革方面的知识。当地领导人的社会地位和作用。
	(A) 在改革中担任领导。通过参加改革扩大个人影响。在改革中产生新的领导人。	(A) 声望的来源不是世袭，不是通过财富而是通过文化接触中的战略地位。
	(B) 改革对领导人的经济利益。	(B) 对这种村长职位没有直接经济报酬。

A. Outside Forces Making for a Change	B. Changing Situation	C. Traditional Forces Bearing on Change
III. Intentions of the agent of change:	III. Programme of Reform:	III. Traditional method subject to change:
(A) To apply scientific knowledge of the silk industry in order to:	(A) Initiating, organizing, and directing the reform programme by the staff and students of the School in:	(A) Technical defects of the traditional method:
(1) Prevent disease germs carried by the egg of the worm.	(1) Dependence on the specialists for egg supply.	(1) Infected eggs produced by individual families or by local hatcheries caused widespread disease.
(2) Increase the quantity and improve the quality of the cocoons.	(2) Raising worms under the supervision of the teaching centre.	(2) Customary method leaves the process of growth of the worm unregulated, causing high reduction in production and poor quality of the cocoons.
(3) Produce raw silk up to the export standard.	(3) Establishment of factory equipped with modern machines.	(3) Irregular fineness and frequency of break of the silk fibre reeled by the old type of machine.
(B) To organize the industry on the principle of co-operation.	(B) In the reform programme. (1) Co-operative aspects: (*a*) Common house for raising young worms. (*b*) Co-operative factory. (i) Ownership belonging to members. (ii) Raw material supplied by members. (iii) Profit distributed among members.	(B) Individualistic nature of the domestic industry. (1) Confirmation of the new idea from the tradition: In classical teaching, and In practice in collective drainage and credit system.

A. 促使变革的外界力量	B. 变化的情况	C. 承受变化的传统力量
III. 变革力量的意图：	III. 改革的计划：	III. 被改革的传统技术。
(A) 应用蚕丝业的科学知识以便：	(A) 蚕业学校师生发起、组织和指导改革计划：	(A) 传统技术的缺点：
(1) 防止蚕种带有病毒细菌。	(1) 依靠专家供应蚕种。	(1) 个体家庭或当地育种者生产的受过感染的蚕种，使传染病毒广泛传播。
(2) 增加蚕茧产量和改善质量。	(2) 在教学中心的监督下养蚕。	(2) 习惯的方法不能使蚕的生长过程得到控制，因而大大降低蚕茧的产量和质量。
(3) 生产合格的出口生丝。	(3) 开设有现代机器的工厂。	(3) 旧型机器缫丝粗细不一，断率高。
(B) 以合作原则组织企业。	(B) 在改革计划中。	(B) 家庭副业的个体性质。
	(1) 合作方面： (a) 稚蚕公育。 (b) 合作工厂。 (i) 所有权属于社员。 (ii) 社员供应原料。 (iii) 利润分给社员。	(1) 传统观念认可的新思想：在经典思想中，在集体排水实践和信贷系统中。

A. Outside Forces Making for a Change	B. Changing Situation	C. Traditional Forces Bearing on Change
	(2) Non-co-operative aspects:	(2) Lack of education in practising the system of popular control and in exercising the new right.
	(*a*) Labour is paid by wage system.	
	(*b*) Management is in the hand of reformers and local leaders.	
	(*c*) Members have no practical control over the management.	
	(*d*) Lack of initiation of the members and of auditing.	
	(3) Counter-co-operative aspects:	(3) Interested only in practical benefits.
	(*a*) Members refuse to subscribe their shares in full after the factory has failed to distribute annual profit.	
	(*b*) Members reluctant to fulfil their obligation in supplying raw material.	
(C) To improve the economic condition of the village.	(C) Improved economic condition in the village.	(C) Expectation of economic recovery.
	(1) Success:	(1)
	(*a*) Reduction of cost in the process of raising worms. Production of cocoons increased.	(*a*) High cost of production of the traditional method.
	(*b*) Wage as a new source of family income.	(*b*) Labour did not form a commodity.

A. 促使变革的外界力量	B. 变化的情况	C. 承受变化的传统力量
	(2) 非合作方面: (a) 劳动由工资制付酬。 (b) 改革者及当地领导人进行管理。 (c) 社员没有参加实际管理。 (d) 社员缺乏创议力；缺乏账目审查。	(2) 对实施大众管理和行使新权利缺乏教育。
	(3) 反对合作方面: (a) 工厂不分年利后，社员拒绝续交全部股金。 (b) 社员不愿完成供应原料的义务。	(3) 仅对实际利益有兴趣。
(C) 改善村庄的经济情况。	(C) 改善村庄的经济情况。 (1) 成功: (a) 养蚕成本降低。蚕茧生产增加。 (b) 工资是家庭收入的新来源。	(C) 希望经济恢复。 (1) (a) 传统技术生产成本高。 (b) 劳动没有形成商品。

A. Outside Forces Making for a Change	B. Changing Situation	C. Traditional Forces Bearing on Change
	(2) Failure: (*a*)Profits have not reached the expected amount. (*b*) Waste of female labour in the household owing to the labour-saving of machine work. (*c*) Delayed payment of the full value of raw material supplied to the factory.	(2) Survival of traditional reeling. (*a*) Small profit in domestic industry. (*b*) Division of labour between sexes, small size of farm and no other work to absorb female labour. (*c*) Need of raw material for domestic reeling which is still partially preserved in the village.
IV. Government as change agent with the intentions: (A) Balance of international trade. (B) Rural reconstruction policies concerning rural industry. (1) Encouraging technical improvement. (2) Encouraging the co-operative movement.	IV. Government supports the reform programme. (A) Subsidizing silk export and giving high price for the production of the factory in 1935. (B) Governmental participation in the reform. (1) Inspection of egg production and taking over the work in supervising the raising of worms. (2) Dependence on governmental loans of the factory.	IV. Local autonomy and suspicion of the government by the people. (A) Importance of raw silk in Chinese export. (B) Economic obligation towards the government. (1) Inferior production affecting export. (2) Lack of financial ability of the people to maintain the new enterprise.

A. 促使变革的外界力量	B. 变化的情况	C. 承受变化的传统力量
	(2) 失败：	(2) 传统缫丝的残存。
	(a) 盈利没有达到预期的数量。	(a) 家庭企业利益微少。
	(b) 由于使用机器，剩余女劳力在家庭中浪费掉。	(b) 男女劳动分工，农田面积小，没有其他工作吸收女劳力。
	(c) 延迟支付供给工厂的原料的全部价值。	(c) 村里保留的部分家庭缫丝业需要原料。
IV. 政府作为变革力量所持的意图：	IV. 政府支持改革计划。	IV. 地方自治及人民怀疑政府
(A) 平衡国际贸易。	(A) 1935 年对工厂产品付高价补助生丝出口。	(A) 中国生丝出口的重要性。
(B) 有关农村企业的乡村建设政策。	(B) 政府参加改革。	(B) 对政府的经济义务。
(1) 鼓励技术改进。	(1) 检查蚕种生产，接办养蚕监督工作。	(1) 产品质量低劣，影响出口。
(2) 鼓励合作运动。	(2) 工厂依赖政府贷款。	(2) 人民没有财力来维持新企业。

It is thus evident that life cannot be supported by agriculture alone. The deficiency amounts to 175 dollars a year. The situation is much worse with the tenants, and these are the majority of the villagers (XI–4). Tenant farmers with an average holding have to pay 20 bushels of rice as rent to the landlord. This amounts to 40 per cent. of the total produce. The remaining 30 bushels are barely enough for the consumption of the household.

Thus it becomes clear that a supplementary industry is indispensable for maintaining a normal livelihood, which must be sufficient to cover daily necessities, ceremonial expenses, tax and rent and capital for future production. (Col. C. I) When the silk industry was prosperous the production of raw silk could yield an average household about 300 dollars with a surplus (profit and wages) of 250 dollars. (The highest price of native silk exceeded 1 dollar per Liang, 1/14 lbs. and the total production for an average household is 280 Liang. The cost of production, excluding wages, is about 50 dollars.) Under these conditions the standard of living was much higher than the minimum expected standard given above (VII–8). The villagers had then sufficient money to finance the various recreative and ceremonial activities which have been suspended for more than ten years.

The price of native silk has fallen. In 1935 the price was 1 dollar for 3 Liang. Without any decrease in the amount of production, an average household could then only obtain a profit of 45 dollars. In such conditions and with the traditional system of production, it is difficult to balance the domestic budget. In the next chapter, I shall show how a new industry has been introduced and how the villagers have also attempted to increase their income by expanding their trading activities. But in many cases they have sold their rice reserves in the winter and borrowed rice from the shop in the summer (XV–3). In case of urgent need they have appealed to usurers (XV–4). On the other side they have tried to cut down expenses which are not immediately necessary, such as those for recreative meetings and marriage. (Col. B. I)

The fall of income of the villagers is not due to a deterioration of quality or decrease of quantity of their production. Villagers produce the same type and the same amount of silk but it does not command the same amount of money from the market. The factors affecting price lie, of course, outside the village, and here I will only note two of the most important of them, namely, the post-war depression of world economy and the uneven quality of the domestic silk which renders it unsuitable to the highly mechanized weaving industry. (Col. A. I)

显然，单靠农业，不能维持生活。每年家庭亏空约为 131.6 元。佃农情况更为悲惨，而村民中大多数是佃农（第十一章第四节）。佃农按平均土地拥有量，必须向地主交付相当于总生产量的 40%，即 24 蒲式耳米作为地租。剩余 36 蒲式耳仅仅够一户食用。

因此，很明显，为维持正常生活所需，包括日常必须品、礼节性费用、税和地租以及再生产所需的资金等，从事辅助产业是必不可少的。（C 栏 I 项）缫丝工业兴旺时，生产生丝可使一般农户收入约 300 元，除去生产费用可盈余 250 元（当地生丝最高价格每两超过 1 元，一般农户总生产量为 280 两。生产成本约 50 元。工资在外）。在这种情况下，生活水平要比上述预期最低水平高得多（第七章第八节）。这样，农民便有了一些钱可以开展各种文娱和礼节性活动。这种活动已停止了约十余年。

当地生丝价格下跌。1935 年 3 两丝约值 1 元。生产量没有任何降低，但一般的户仅能获利 45 元。在这种情况下，用传统生产技术所获利益便难以平衡家庭预算。下一章我将叙述如何引进新的工业，村民如何尝试扩大商业活动来增加收入。很多人不得不在冬天出售存粮来维持生活，夏天到粮店借粮（第十五章第三节）。遇紧急需要时，他们不得不向高利贷者求援（第十五章第四节）。另一方面，他们试着削减非必需的开支，例如娱乐性聚会、婚事开支等。（B 栏 I 项）

农民收入的减少不是由于他们的产品质量下降或数量减少的缘故。村民生产同样品种、同等数量的生丝，但从市场上不能赚回同等金额的钱。当然，影响生丝价格的因素来自外界，我在此仅举两个最重要的因素，即战后世界经济萧条以及质量不匀的家庭缫丝不适合高度机械化的丝织工业的需要。（A 栏 I 项）

❸ Agents of Change and Their Intentions

The relation between the decline of silk prices and the increase of poverty was clear to the people. At first they tried to discover what changes in the industry were necessary in order to restore the former conditions. But with their limited knowledge they were by themselves not able to take any definite action. Initiative and direction in the process of change come from outside.

The initiating party in this case was the Sericulture School for Girls, in Houshukuan, near Soochow. This has had a profound influence on subsequent development but has of course been a factor outside the village.

A technical school in China is one of the centres for spreading modern technique in industry. Modern technique has been chiefly introduced from foreign countries, in the case of the silk industry chiefly from Japan. It is the result of the meeting of Chinese and Western civilizations—a typical contact situation. The difficulty of the technical school in fulfilling its function is that unless the new technique is accepted by the people, it cannot by itself serve progress. A failure in this respect is reflected in unemployment of the trained students. The situation there is most acute in the silk industry. The silk industry, especially the process of raising silkworms, is a kind of domestic work in the villages. In order to make the improved technique acceptable to the people and to find jobs for the students, industrial reform in villages has become an urgent problem for the technical schools. They cannot remain as purely educational institutions. Therefore, the Sericulture School has established a special department responsible for spreading in rural districts a knowledge of the new methods.

The nature of the change agent is important because it determines the change programme. The measure introduced to cope with the situation is formulated and actions are organized by the agent whose understanding of the situation is the premise. But the definition of situation influenced by the social setting of the agents is usually a partial representation of the reality.[43] To come back to our village, the causes of the fall in silk prices are multiple. The capitalistic structure of world economy, the struggle among imperialistic countries, the control of world finance by a special "racial group," the political status of oppressed nations as well as the modern girls' newly acquired æsthetic valuation of bare feet—all these might directly or indirectly be responsible for the decline of the price of the silk produced in Chinese rural districts, but not all of them came under the consideration of the change agent. Since the change

三、变革的力量及其意图

生丝价格低落及贫困加剧两者之间的关系，人们已经清楚。开始为了恢复原有的经济水平，他们试图发现技术上需要什么样的变革。但他们的知识有限，靠他们自己并不能采取任何有效的行动，发起和指导变革过程的力量来自外界。

在这种情况下，发起单位便是苏州附近浒墅关的女子蚕业学校。它对后来的发展起着深远的影响，当然这是来自村外的一种因素。

中国的技术学校是传播现代工业技术的中心。现代技术主要来自国外，至于缫丝工业则主要来自日本。这是中国和西方文明接触的结果，一种典型的接触情境。技术学校在执行任务过程中的困难是：除非新技术为人民所接受，否则单靠它本身，事业并不能开展。从这方面来说，受过训练的学生找不到职业便反映了这种失败。蚕丝业的情况最尖锐。蚕丝业——特别是养蚕的过程——是村里的一种家庭副业。为了使进步的技术为人们所接受，并为学生找到职业，村庄的工业改革便成为技术学校迫切需要解决的问题。技术学校不能停留在纯教育机构的性质。因此，蚕业学校建立了一个推广部门，负责在农村地区传播新的技术知识。

变革力量的性质如何是重要的，因为它决定变革的计划。它制定应付形势的措施并组织行动。它对形势的理解是行动的前提。但变革力量受其社会环境影响，对形势所作的阐述往往不能代表现实的全貌。[43]再回头来说这个村庄，生丝价格下跌的原因是多方面的。世界经济的资本主义结构、帝国主义国家之间的斗争、被压迫国家的政治地位以及摩登女郎新近接受的赤脚审美观等等，这一切都可能直接或间接成为中国农村生产的生丝价格下跌的原因，但变革力量不会把这些全部都考虑进去。由于当前的变革力量是蚕业学校，

agent in this case is the technical school, the situation is defined in terms of technical factors. The person responsible for initiating the reform programme in the village gave me the following account.

In the worst years, by means of the traditional method only about 30 per cent. of the total silkworms reached the final stage and produced cocoons. The amount of silk given by the worms was small. This unsatisfactory state of affairs was due to the lack of preventive measures against the spread of disease among the worms. The micro-organism responsible for the disease was carried by the mother moth to the eggs through physical contact between them. Thus disease was handed down from generation to generation, and there was no way of stopping it. The house and the implements were not disinfected before they were used for raising new worms. Once a house was infected by disease, it would suffer for years and years. The diseased or dead worms were cast under the mulberry trees. People thought that these dead worms were fertilizer for the trees. But actually they spread the germs, which were brought back with the mulberry leaves to the house. (Col. C. III. A. 1.)

The temperature and humidity, which are very important conditions in the process of the growth of the worms, were left unregulated. According to custom, after the third exuviæ, fire was put out regardless of the actual fluctuation of the climate. In the village there were not enough mulberry trees. The people had to buy mulberry leaves from neighbouring villages. Owing to the difficulties of transport they usually fed the worm with leaves already withered. The quantity and frequency of feeding were irregular. Even those worms unaffected by disease were unhealthy and not able to produce good cocoons. (Col. C. III. A. 2.)

The fundamental principle in silk reeling is to draw the silk fibre from the cocoon and to combine several fibres into one thread that can be used in weaving. The old type machine used for reeling consisted of three parts, namely, a furnace to boil water, a wheel to collect the thread after the fibre had been combined into one thread, and a rotating axle connected to a plate for treading by foot. Warmed water was used for dissolving the sticky matter of the cocoon. But the temperature was not constant. Thus the degree of dissolution was uneven. This affected not only the lustre of the silk thread but the frequency with which the fibre broke.

Several cocoons are drawn at the same time by the movement of the wheel. The fineness of the thread depends on the number of fibres combined. The fibres from different layers of the cocoon are not of the same fineness. To maintain regular fineness of the thread, it is essential to keep a constant number of fibres and adjust the fibres from different

对情况的阐述是从技术因素来考虑的。村里负责改革计划的人对我讲了以下情况。

用传统方法养蚕，在最坏的年景里，只有30%的蚕能成活到最后阶段并结茧。蚕的吐丝量少。这种不能令人满意的情况是由于对蚕的病毒传播没有预防措施。蚕蛾通过接触把致病的微生物带给蚕卵。这样，病毒便一代代传下去，无法控制。喂养新蚕前，房屋和器具未经消毒。一旦房屋被病菌污染，蚕便连年闹病。病蚕或死蚕被扔在桑树下。人们以为死蚕可用作桑树的肥料，但实际上它们传播细菌，桑叶又把细菌带回到养蚕的房子里。（C栏，III项，A.1）

蚕生长过程中的重要条件——温度和湿度——得不到调节。按照习惯，不管气候有何变化，蚕第三次蜕皮后就停止烧火。村里桑树不足，人们必须从邻村购买桑叶。由于运输困难，他们往往用干萎的桑叶喂蚕。喂食的质量和次数都没有规则。即使那些没有感染病毒的蚕也不健康，不能结出好的茧子。（C栏，III项，A.2）

缫丝的基本原则是把蚕茧的丝纤维抽出来，把数条纤维合成一根丝线供纺织用。旧式缫丝机器分成三部分：煮水的炉子、绕丝线的轮子和连着踏脚板的旋转轴。当纤维合成一股丝线后，用脚踏板使轮子转动，抽缫丝线。用热水可以把蚕茧的粘性物溶解。但水温不稳定，因此溶解的程度不匀。这不仅影响丝的光泽而且影响纤维的折断率。

轮子转动，同时从几个蚕茧抽丝。丝线的粗细取决于合成的纤维数目。从蚕茧的不同层次抽出来的丝，粗细不同。为保持丝线粗细的匀称，必须保持抽取固定数目的纤维，并不断地调整从不同

layers of the cocoon. This was not easy to attain by hand reeling, because firstly, the frequency of breakage was high, secondly the movement of the wheel was not even, and thirdly the workers were not specially trained. (Col. C. III. A. 3.)

Silk is the raw material for the weaving industry. Since the silk produced in the village is mostly exported, it must be adjusted to the technical development in the weaving industry in Western countries. The highly mechanized weaving industry has imposed a new standard on the raw silk. The degree of fineness should be uniform and accurately defined. Breaks should be reduced to a minimum. Such requirements cannot possibly be fulfilled by traditional hand reeling. The result is that the silk produced by the villagers is unsuitable for the improved weaving industry. The decline of demand for such crude silk leads to a decline of price. That is the reason why we must introduce the scientific method to the village. (Col. A. III. A.)

But technical change cannot be produced without corresponding changes in social organization. For instance, the smooth movement of the wheel can be attained only through the regular mechanical movement of a central power. Introduction of the steam engine for technical purposes leads to a change from individual domestic work to collective factory work. The use of electric power, which might again decentralize the productive process, requires a much more complicated coordination among industries. Under a system of collective enterprise, the relation between the means of production and labour also becomes more complicated. To introduce new social organizations for production, the agent must also teach new social principles. The selection of the social principle in organizing the new industry is also related to the interest of the agent. The technical school is not interested in making a profit for itself because it is not an economic institution. Who would therefore gain from industrial reform? The agent's answer is the people. The organization of the new industry is on the principle of "co-operation." (Col. A. III. B.) The agent justified this change as follows:

Machines should be used to increase human happiness. Unfortunately, they have been used for the contrary purpose. But I still believe that it is the duty of the reformer who is trying to introduce these types of tool into China to find a way of using them properly. To me, the most important thing is that

层次里抽出来的纤维。手工缫丝不易达到这一目的，因为首先，纤维折断率高；第二，轮子转动不均匀；第三，工人没有受过专门训练。（C栏，III项，A.3）

生丝是纺织工业的原料。既然农村生产的生丝大部分出口，它就必须与西方国家的纺织工业技术发展相适应。高度机械化了的纺织工业为生丝规定了一个新的标准。粗细程度必须一致，而且有精确的规定。断头现象必须减到最少程度。这样的要求，用传统手工缫丝是不能满足的。结果是，村民生产的生丝不适用于改进了的纺织工业。西方纺织工业对这种生丝需求下降，因而价格下跌。这也就是为什么我们必须把科学方法引进村里的原因。（A栏，III项，A.）

但如果没有社会组织的相应变革，技术变革是不可能的。例如，轮子平稳的转动只有通过中心动力有规则的机械运动才能达到。为了改进技术，引进蒸汽引擎，必然引起一种从家庭个体劳动到工厂集体劳动的变革。电力的使用，又可能使生产过程分散，从而需要各产业之间复杂得多的协作。在一个集体企业系统下，生产资料和劳动之间的关系也变得更加复杂。为了生产，引进新的社会组织，变革力量也必须传授新的社会原则。在组织新工业中选择社会原则也与变革力量的利益相关。蚕业学校本身对盈利不感兴趣，因为它不是一个企业机构。那么工业改革使谁得益呢？变革者的回答是人民。新工业组织的原则是"合作"。（A栏，IV项，B.）变革者对变革的正确解说如下：

机器用来增添人类的幸福。不幸的是，它被用来为相反的目的服务。但我仍然相信，试图把这些工具引进中国的改革者的责任，是寻找一种正当的办法使用机器。对我来说，最重要的是，

men should not be the slaves of machines. In other words, machines should be owned by those who use them as a means of production. That is why I insist on the principle of co-operation. It would be much easier to organize the new factory on capitalistic lines, but why should I do it? Should I work for the interests of the capitalists and intensify the sufferings of the people? The profit secured from the improved technique should go to the people who share in the production.

My other conviction is that the silk industry has been, and should remain, a rural industry. My reason is that if we attract the industry away from the village, as has been done by many industrialists and is so easy to accomplish, the villagers will in fact starve. On the other hand, I know very well how the workers are living in the cities. Village girls have been attracted by the opportunity to work in the city factories for a small wage, on which they can hardly support themselves. They have left their own homes. This process has ruined both the city workers and the village families. If Chinese industry can only develop at the expense of the poor villagers, I personally think we have paid too much for it.

The aim of my work is to rehabilitate the rural economy through the introduction of scientific methods of production and the organization of the new industry on the principle of co-operation.

The socialistic ideas of the reformers represent a part of the current ideology of the present literate class in China. In their new version they are introduced from the West, side by side with the modern technology and capitalistic system of industry. The position of the Chinese people in the world economy and the repeated struggle with the Western powers have created a situation favourable for the spreading of socialist ideas. A reaction against capitalism, as understood by the Chinese people, prevails among the general public. Even those who stand for capitalism do not dare openly to justify its principles. This attitude was explicitly stated in the "Three people's principles" of the late Dr. Sun Yat-sen, which have been accepted, theoretically, by the present government as the guiding principle of its national policies.

On the other hand, socialist ideas are nothing new in China. The basic political idea of Dr. Sun Yat-sen was to realize the traditional teaching such as, "Under the heaven every thing is public," or "Those who till the land should have the land." (Col. C. III. B. 1.)

> 人不应该成为机器的奴隶。换句话说，把机器当作一种生产资料的人应该拥有机器。这就是为什么我坚持合作的原则。要按照资本主义的方式来组织新的工厂容易得多，但我为什么要这样做呢？我应该为资本家的利益工作而使人民更加痛苦吗？技术改革所得到的利益应该归于参加生产的人们。
>
> 我的另一个信念是，蚕丝工业曾经是而且应该继续是一种乡村工业。我的理由是：如果我们把工业从农村引向别的地方，像很多工业家所做的那样，也是非常容易做到的，农民实际上就会挨饿。另一方面，我也很了解，工人们在城市里是如何生活的。农村姑娘被吸引到城市工厂去工作，挣微薄的工资，几乎不能养活自己，她们离开了自己的家。这种过程既损害了城市工人，又破坏了农村的家庭。如果中国工业只能以牺牲穷苦农民为代价而发展的话，我个人认为这个代价未免太大了。
>
> 我工作的目的是，通过引进科学的生产技术和组织以合作为原则的新工业，来复兴乡村经济。

变革者趋向社会主义的思想代表了当前中国知识阶级的部分思想状况。这是同西方的现代技术和资本主义工业系统一起引进的新看法。中国人民在世界经济中的地位以及同西方列强的不断斗争，为传播社会主义思想创造了有利条件。正如中国人民所了解的，公众普遍反对资本主义，甚至于那些代表资本主义的人也不敢公开为资本主义的原则辩护。这种态度在已故孙中山先生的"三民主义"里阐述得很清楚，从理论上说，它被现今政府所接受并作为国家政策的指导原则。

另一方面，社会主义思想在中国并非新的东西。孙中山先生的基本政治思想是实现传统的教导，诸如"天下为公"和"耕者有其田"。(C栏，III项，B.1)

❹ Local Support for Change

As we have seen, the Sericulture School, being outside the village, was only a potential agent. To turn the potential agent into an active one there was needed another factor. There was no direct social relationship between the School and the villagers. The group which possessed the new knowledge had no direct use for it and the group which needed the knowledge had no opportunity of acquiring it. A bridge by which the agent of change could be made to function in the village was essential. It was found in the local leaders.

According to the published report of the co-operative factory the initiative was due to the local leaders. The following passage written by Chen may be quoted.

> Kiangsu is known as a silk-producing area. But the industry depended more on natural factors than upon human effort. The result was the failure of the villagers in the industry. This had frequently ruined the people. In view of such conditions I (Chen) and Mr. Sen (a local leader in the town, Chên Tsê), proposed to the town council, in the regular summer meeting in 1923, that a teaching centre should be established to reform the method of raising silkworms. The proposal was passed and 600 dollars were allotted for the purpose.

> It happened that the president of the Sericulture School had, also as a result of the fall of silk prices, started a department for extension work for reforming the traditional methods of the silk industry. In the winter of that year, he came to Kaihsienkung, accompanied by Misses Fei and Hu and gave a series of public lectures. The people were greatly interested. Then the chairman of the town council, in accordance with the resolution, authorized the president to organize the proposed teaching centre. The president consented to co-operate with the town council and subsidize the plan, and it was decided to start the work also in Kaihsienkung.

In addition to my own family, I called together twenty other families which had suffered very much in the past from continuous failure in the industry. The reform work was started in the spring of 1924.**44**

I have mentioned that the village headmanship is not a hereditary office. He has no other ground for his authority than the usefulness of his services to the community (VI–4). One of his most important functions is to interpret local needs and to assume leadership in taking necessary

四、当地对变革的支持

我们已经看到，蚕业学校由于在村外，因此仅仅是一种潜在的力量。为把潜在力量转变成现实力量，还需要另一个因素，学校和村民之间没有直接的社会关系。占有新知识的群体没有直接使用知识，而需要这种知识的群体又没有机会获得知识，要使变革力量在村中起作用，中间必须有一座桥梁，这是重要的。当地领导人是充当这个桥梁的角色。

根据合作工厂已公布的报告，主动在于当地领导人一边。可以引陈写的一席话来说明：

江苏以产丝著称，但这一工业更多地依赖自然因素而不是人的力量，结果是农民在丝业中失败了。这经常损害人民。鉴于这种情况，我（陈）和沈先生（震泽镇的一个领导人）在1923年的夏季例会中向镇改进社建议，应设立一个教学中心以便改革养蚕方法。建议获得批准后，拨款600元来筹办此事。

恰巧蚕业学校的校长也因生丝价格下跌正想为改革缫丝工业传统技术开办一个附设的推广部门。当年冬天，他由费女士和胡女士陪同来到开弦弓，并讲了一些课。人们都非常感兴趣。然后，镇改进社的主席根据决议，授权校长组织拟议的教学中心。校长同意与镇改进社合作，资助这一计划并决定就地在开弦弓开始工作。

除了我自己的家庭以外，我还把过去由于丝业的不断失败而受苦的20家召集在一起。改革工作于1924年春开始了。[44]

我已提过，村长的职务不是世袭的。除了他的服务对社区有用以外，他的权威没有其他的凭借（第六章第四节）。他的一项最重要的职能是了解当地的需要，采取必要的措施来实行领导。村长的职务

measures. The village head receives no economic reward for his position. But through introducing special work in the village, he can derive economic benefit from it. These were the intentions of Chen in supporting the programme of industrial reform. (Col. B. II. A. and B.)

The strengthening of the social position of the local leaders by industrial reform appears still clearer in the case of Chou. Chou had had no social influence before the industrial reform was introduced. Owing to his literacy and ability, he became an assistant in the work and gained prestige from it. Finally he was appointed by the higher administration to be the head of the Hsiang (VI–5). His social position has been acquired wholly through his participating in the reform programme.

This analysis is important in explaining why the village heads did not prove, on the contrary, a force resisting social change. Active resistance against the reform was not experienced at the initial stage. There was promise of improved condition on the side of the Sericulture School, and hope on the side of the people.

The rapid fall in prices had forced the people to accept certain changes in the traditional industry. But they lacked sufficient knowledge to define the situation or to formulate a definite programme of change. (Col. C. II.) They were also not properly equipped to judge the desirability of the proposed programme. The suspicion of novelty went hand-in-hand with the readiness to accept reforms when, by demonstration, the new technique could be proved useful. That is why at the beginning there were only twenty-one households in the programme, and, as the report specifically stated, these had suffered from hopeless failure when working by traditional methods. But it took only two years to draw the whole village under the supervision of the teaching centre.

❺ Programme of Change in Raising Silkworms

The primary aim of the reformers, as I have explained, is the technical improvement of rural industry, but change in one aspect of culture automatically calls forth a series of changes in other aspects. Such a process once started tends to go on until a complete re-organization of the whole system has been affected. The sequence of change is of special interest for studying the functional relations between social institutions.

没有经济报酬，但通过为村里做一些特殊的工作，他可以得到经济上的收益。这就是陈支持蚕业改革计划的意愿。（B 栏，II 项，A. 及 B.）

当地领导人的地位通过丝业改革加强了，这从周的情况来看更为明显。在丝业改革以前周没有什么社会影响。由于他识字，有能力，他成为这项工作的助手并提高了声望。最后，他被高一级的行政管理机构任命为乡长（第六章第五节）。他的社会地位是通过参加这项改革计划而获得的。

在解释村长在社会变革中为什么不是一股反对改革的力量时，上述分析有重要参考价值。在最初阶段没有人积极反对改革。蚕业学校作了情况会得到改善的允诺，在人民一方面则抱着希望。

蚕丝价格的急剧下跌迫使人民接受对传统丝业的某些改革。但他们缺乏足够的知识来判明情况或制定变革计划。（C 栏，II 项）他们对已经提出的计划所要达到的要求也缺乏判断能力。新的技术虽然已被证明有用时，人们一方面准备接受改革，一方面还在怀疑新鲜事物。这就是为什么一开始参加这项计划的仅有 21 户，正如该报告具体说明的那样，这些户用传统技术操作时遭受了惨痛的失败。但总起来说，只用了两年工夫便把整个村子纳入蚕业教学中心的指导。

五、养蚕的改革计划

如同我已经解释过的，改革者的主要目的是从技术上改进农村企业，但是对文化的某一方面进行变革，自然会引起其他诸方面的变化。这样的过程一旦开始，便会继续下去，直到整个系统完全重新改组为止。在研究社会制度之间的功能关系时，研究变迁的顺序是特别有意义的。

The reform programme has proceeded along the line of the natural process of the silk industry. This starts from the production of eggs through the breeding of moths and continues with the hatching of the eggs and raising of the silkworms, and collection of cocoons; it ends, as far as the village is concerned, with the reeling of the silk thread. The problem of marketing I shall deal with in the chapter after next.

Scientific knowledge in egg production consists of two parts, namely, the breeding of superior species through experimental crossing, and the separation of infected eggs through microscopic examination. Formerly the people produced eggs through pure line breeding of their own worms. They would also allow the germs to be handed down to the second generation. To reform the system of egg production, it was not practical to teach each villager the principles of genetics and the use of the microscope. It is much cheaper to employ a specialist to produce the eggs for the use of the villagers. The School therefore took over this work at first and supplied the villagers. It is interesting to note that in this respect the reformers were inconsistent in their aims. They decided to keep industry in the village, but egg production has been removed from the village into the hands of specialists. But egg production is economically unimportant, because the cost of the eggs is only 3 per cent. of the total cost of the production of raw silk.

The demand for disinfected eggs increased rapidly as the silk reform gradually spread over the whole region of the lower Yangtze valley. The School could not meet the demand and thus many private egg producers seized the chance to make a profit. The quality of eggs could not be maintained and the bad effects on the reform programme became evident. This situation led to government interference. A bureau for censoring the eggs was established by the provincial government with authority over the private producers and prices were also controlled. (Col. B. IV. B. 1.)

The people receive their eggs only a short time before the period for hatching. Eggs are treated by the producers with special care. From hatching up to the collection of cocoons, the whole process of work is comprised in the term "raising silkworms." This process is carried out in the village under a special organization. At the beginning of the reform, directors were sent from the teaching centre to teach the villagers how to make use of scientific knowledge, especially in the prevention of disease of the worm and in the regulation of temperature and humidity. To facilitate management and supervision, the young worms of different owners are concentrated in a common house, on the principle of co-operation.

改革计划是沿着蚕丝业的自然过程向前推进的。这是从蚕蛾产卵生产蚕种开始，接着是孵化、养蚕、收集蚕茧，从农村来说，到缫丝作为结束。关于市场销售问题，将在以后章节中讨论。

生产蚕种的科学知识可分成两个部分，即通过实验杂交培育良种，以及通过显微镜检查分离受感染的蚕种。过去，人们是通过他们自己喂养的蚕的纯系繁育生产蚕种的。这也会使病菌传给第二代。为了改革蚕种生产系统，把遗传学的原理和使用显微镜的方法教给每一个农民是不实际的，聘请一个专家为农民生产蚕种要便宜得多。因此，蚕业学校首先接过了此项工作，供应村民蚕种。有趣的是我们发现在这一点上，改革者的行动与他们的目的不那么一致。他们决定把工业留在农村里，却把蚕种的生产从农村转移到专家手里。但蚕种的生产从经济上来说是不重要的，因为蚕种的价格仅为生丝生产总费用的 3%。

当蚕丝改革工作逐步普及到整个长江下游地区时，对于灭菌蚕种的需求量迅速增加。蚕业学校已不能满足需要，很多私人便来生产蚕种，乘此机会牟取利益。蚕种的质量不能保证，对改革计划的坏影响明显起来，这引起了政府的干预。省政府成立了蚕种检查局，对私人生产的蚕种有权检查，并进行价格控制。(B 栏，IV 项，B.1)

人们只在孵化前不久收到蚕种。蚕种在生产者手里是得到特殊照料的。从孵化到收茧子，这整个工作过程都包括在"养蚕"这个词中。这个过程是在一个特殊组织之下在村里开展起来的。改革开始阶段，学校派出指导人员教村民如何利用科学知识，特别是在防止蚕病、控制温度和湿度方面。为了便于管理和指导，各家的幼蚕，按照合作的原则，集中到公共房屋里，称作"稚蚕公育"。

Expense and labour are shared by the owners in proportion to the amount of worms put in the common house. At present there are eight common houses in the village, containing practically all the young worms raised in the village. A special building with eight big rooms was built for this purpose. The money for the building was collected by adding 20 cents to each sheet of eggs during the years 1923 to 1925. (Col. B. III. B. 1. *a.*)

The collective process of raising silkworms can be effective only when the worms are young and small. Within six weeks they grow from a tiny size to two and a half inches at the time of maturity. After the third exuviæ the present common houses are not large enough to accommodate the worms. The collective system has then to be discontinued unless big buildings are available. The construction of such buildings is economically not worth while, because the period during which a large space is required is short, and it is much more convenient to use private houses. For the last two weeks all the rooms in the house, except the kitchen and half of the bedrooms, are occupied by the worms. This fact alone means that, unless the material substratum of the village is radically changed, silkworm raising must remam mainly a domestic industry.

After the third exuviæ, the worms are removed to the private houses and each household raises its own worms separately. Before the removal, the private houses are disinfected under instructions given by the teaching centre. Constant supervision is maintained during this process. Diseased worms are removed at once to prevent the disease spreading. Temperature and humidity are regulated according to the need of the worms. (Col. B. III. A. 2.) The result of these measures is that the loss of worms due to disease has been kept under 20 per cent., and the total production of cocoons has increased at least 40 per cent. as compared with that under the traditional method.

When the teaching centre had proved its success in the village, the provincial government extended its work to the whole silk-producing area. We will describe this more fully in another section.

Before we go into the process of reeling, an estimate of the production and cost in this part of the process may be attempted. The total amount of silkworms that can be raised by a Chia depends on the size of the house and the labour available. Silkworms are raised in rectangular and shallow containers about $1\frac{1}{2}$ by 1 metre in size. They are put on the shelves of a stand. Each stand has eight containers. Each house has enough room for five stands. The silkworms hatched from a sheet of eggs (which is of

费用和劳动根据蚕主放在公用蚕室内的蚕种按比例分摊。目前村里共有八间公用蚕室，基本上包括了村里养的全部幼蚕。为了这一目的，专门造了这所有八间房屋的建筑物。从 1923 年至 1925 年对每张蚕种增收两角作为建筑费。（B 栏，III 项，B.1.a）

集体养蚕的方法只有在幼蚕时期有效。六个星期之内，它们从极为细小的"蚕蚁"长到两英寸半长蚕身。第三次蜕皮以后，目前公用的房间便不足以容纳这些蚕了。如果没有更大的房屋，集体喂养的方法便只得中断。建造能容纳全部的蚕的一所房屋从经济上来说并不值得，因为需要大地方喂养的这一段时间较短，用私人的房子方便得多。最后两个星期，家里的全部房间，除去厨房和一半卧室以外，都用来养蚕。仅这一事实就意味着除非村里的物质基础有根本的改变，否则养蚕基本上只能依旧是家庭副业。

第三次蜕皮以后，蚕被搬到各户。每户分别喂养自己的蚕。在搬蚕以前，个人养蚕的房子要经过消毒，学校的指导员要告诉他们注意事项。在这一阶段经常要去检查。有病的蚕立即消灭以防传染。根据蚕的需要控制室内温度和湿度。（B 栏，III 项，A.2）采取这些措施的结果是，因病而损失的蚕，其数量控制在 20% 以下，蚕茧的总生产量同用传统方法喂养时相比至少增加 40%。

当学校指导工作在村里被公认取得成功时，省政府便把它的工作向整个产丝区推广。在以后章节中我们再进一步描述这一情况。

在讨论缫丝程序以前，可尝试估计一下这一部分的生产及其成本。一家养蚕的总数取决于房屋大小和劳力多少。蚕是养在约 1.5×1 米大小的长方形匾里。匾放在支架的搁杆上。每一个支架可放 8 个匾。每间房间可放 5 个支架。一张蚕种（标准大小）孵出来

standard size), require in the final stage of development a whole stand for accommodation. One person can manage two or three stands. Each stand will yield 34 pounds of cocoons which can be reeled into 48 Liang (or 3.4 pounds) of raw silk. Under reformed conditions, the total amount of cocoons produced by an average Chia is about 200 pounds, which can be sold at a price of 60 to 70 dollars per 100 pounds (according to the reports mentioned above).

Each stand of silkworms needs about 400 pounds of mulberry leaves. The price of mulberry leaves fluctuated very much during the period of silkworm raising. The highest price for a 100 pounds sometimes exceeds $3\frac{1}{2}$ dollars, and at the lowest is under $1\frac{1}{2}$ dollars. The total expense for feeding worms lies between 30 to 40 dollars. In addition to other expenses, the cost of cocoon production, excluding labour, is about 50 dollars per Chia. If the cocoons are sold, this will give an income of 70 to 90 dollars for an average Chia.

The reform programme has also included the introduction of multiple crops. In this region three crops can be grown. But owing to the climate, more equipment and precautions are needed in summer and autumn crops. At present, these two crops are still very limited.

❻ The Co-operative Factory

We now come to the process of reeling, that is, the transformation of cocoons into the final stage of raw silk. Reform in this process is directed to producing a better quality of raw silk. Quality is judged by uniformity in fineness and reduction of frequency of breaks in the thread. According to the expert of the Sericulture School, the weakness of the traditional method lies in (1) the irregular temperature of water used in dissolving the sticky matter of the cocoon, (2) the indefinite number of fibres forming a thread, (3) lack of regard for the different fineness of the fibres from different layers of the cocoon, and (4) the irregular movement of the wheel. To improve the quality of the silk, the reformers have tried several methods. The following statement made by the agent will explain the situation.

At the beginning, we had no idea of introducing the factory system. We tried to keep the work in the household. As a substitute for the old type of machine, we introduced a better wooden machine which is only a modification of the old. The wheel was turned by foot and everyone could work separately in her own house. Chemicals were used in dissolving the sticky matter, but the temperature of the solution could not be strictly controlled. Skill in maintaining a constant number of fibres and in adjusting

的蚕，到最后阶段需占一个支架的地方。一个人可管理 2 或 3 架。每架可收蚕茧 34 磅，可缫生丝 48 两（或 3.4 磅）。在改革条件下，一户一般可生产蚕茧约 200 磅，每 100 磅可卖 60 至 70 元（根据上述报告）。

每养一架蚕约需 400 磅桑叶。在养蚕期间，桑叶价格升降幅度很大。每 100 磅的最高价格有时超过 3.5 元，最低价格不到 1.5 元。养蚕所需总的开支约 30 至 40 元。除其他费用以外，蚕茧生产费用不包括劳动，每户约需 50 元。如果出售蚕茧，一般的户可收入 70 至 90 元。

改革计划还包括引进秋种。这个地区一年可育三次蚕。但因气候关系，夏季和秋季养蚕需要更多的设备和注意的地方。目前，养夏季和秋季蚕的仍然非常有限。

六、合作工厂

现在我们就要说到缫丝过程，这就是把蚕茧缫成生丝的最后阶段。对这一过程的改革主要目的是生产质量较好的生丝。根据丝的粗细划一、断头减少来评定生丝的质量。据蚕业学校的专家说，传统方法的缺点在于：（1）用于溶解蚕茧上胶质的水温不恒定；（2）一股丝线中所含纤维数不固定；（3）从蚕茧不同的层次抽出来的丝粗细不同，未予重视；（4）缫丝机轮子的运动不规则。为了改进生丝质量，改革者试了数种方法。他们的下述谈话将说明这个情况。

一开始，我们并没有想要引进工厂。我们想的是继续在家里进行这种劳动。我们只不过采用一种改良的木制机器来代替旧式机器。用脚踏转动轮子，每个人可分别在自己家中工作。用化学品来溶解胶质，但溶液温度无法达到严格的控制。蚕业学校在镇里组织

the combination of different layers of the cocoons was taught in training classes lasting three months, organized by the School in the town. In 1924, there were only ten machines of this type in the village. But in 1927, the total number had increased to more than one hundred. More than seventy young women were trained in the special class. But owing to the irregular movement of the wheel, the quality of the produce was still below the requisite standard for export. On the other hand, the depression of the market was more acute. In 1928, the price for this type of "reformed silk" had dropped to sixty dollars per hundred Liang. Although it was better than the native silk, we were not satisfied with its condition. We knew very well from the experiment that unless we could have a central power equipped with a steam engine, the quality could not be raised to the export standard. But the introduction of the steam engine must go hand-in-hand with the collective factory system. In other words the domestic system of production could not be retained if we were to improve the quality of the produce. We decided therefore to test out what is the smallest size of silk factory in which all the advantages of applying modern technique of production can be realized but which at the same time is not too large to be maintained in the village and to use local labour and local supplies of raw material. This experiment has a wider significance. If we can produce, with lower labour costs, silk equal in quality to that of the larger scale factories, we can extend this system without fearing competition from factories in the cities. Through this small scale factory, rural industry can get a firm basis and the rural economy can be rehabilitated. We started the experiment in 1929. Our experiment proved to be successful only after the re-equipment in 1935, with the new machine which is a modified form of the latest Japanese type. With this we are able to produce the best silk in China. In 1935 the produce of this factory was ranked by the export bureau as of the highest grade.

From this account it is very clear that the substitution of the collective factory for the domestic system was dictated by technical considerations. The steam engine which makes possible a controlled and smooth movement of the wheel, and consequently speed and evenness in drawing the fibres from the cocoons, leads inevitably to a centralized system. Whether the introduction of electric power might again change the centralized system is a matter for future experiment. (Col. B. III. A. 3.)

了训练班，为时 3 个月，教授调整蚕茧各层的丝以及保持固定数量纤维的技术。1924 年的时候，村里只有 10 台这样的机器。到了 1927 年，机器总数增加到 100 多台。在训练班里有 70 多名年青妇女。但由于轮子的运动不规则，产品质量仍然达不到出口标准的要求。另一方面，市场萧条更加严重。1928 年，这种"改良丝"的价格跌到每 100 两 60 元。虽然它比土产丝好些，但我们不满意这种情况。我们从实验中了解到，除非能有一个用蒸汽引擎的中心动力，质量就不易达到出口水平。但引进蒸汽引擎必须同时有集体工厂系统。换句话说，如果我们要提高产品质量，就不能保持家庭手工业的生产方式。所以我们决定试验设计一个要能实现应用现代生产技术的一切有利条件的工厂。这个工厂同时又不宜太大，要能办在农村里，用当地的劳力和由当地供应的原料。这个试验具有比较广泛的意义。如果我们能用较便宜的劳动力生产与大工厂同等质量的生丝，我们就能扩大这种缫丝工厂而不必惧怕城里工厂的竞争。通过开办这种小规模的工厂，乡村工业能打下一个坚实的基础，乡村经济从而可以复兴。1929 年我们开始试验。我们的试验直到 1935 年重新装备了新机器之后才证明是成功的。这种机器是由日本最新型机器修改而成。我们用它生产出中国最好的生丝。1935 年，这个工厂的产品被出口局列为最佳产品。

从上述情况可以明显地看到合作工厂代替家庭手工业是由技术考虑决定的。蒸汽引擎使轮子转动可以控制，并且平稳，从而使抽丝均匀，速度加快，因而不可避免地产生了一种集中的系统。至于引进电力是否会再改变集中的系统，则是将来试验的问题了。（B 栏，III 项，A.3）

A factory system of production requires a building suitable for equipment with machinery. To construct the factory needs technical knowledge and money. Technical knowledge was supplied by the School, but where did the money come from? This question led to the problem of ownership and the problem of distribution. According to the intentions of the reformers, the basic principles on which these were regulated had been laid down before the factory was established. The principle was that the factory should be owned by the people. But how can the people own it and who are the people?

Ownership is vested in the group of people who are members of the co-operative society. Their liability towards the factory is limited to the share they contribute. Membership is voluntary and is not limited to the people of this village. Anyone who observes the obligations of membership can be admitted as a member of the society. The obligation of a member is to hold a share in the factory and to supply a definite amount of raw material, cocoons, every year. There are 429 members of the society, including practically all the households in the village, and more than fifty members from neighbouring villages.

Final control of the factory is, according to the regulation, vested in the general meeting of the members. At the general meeting an executive council is elected, which is in theory responsible to the general meeting. In practice, it works the other way round. The people work according to the instructions of the local leaders, the executive council, and the local leaders work according to the instruction of the reformers, the School. The members have nothing to say, since the whole work is under the direction of the reformers, and the people have not sufficient knowledge to run the factory by themselves. A high percentage of illiteracy and the lack of educational opportunity on the part of the villagers have made it very difficult for the reformers to carry out their plan of training the villagers, the real masters of the factory. (Col. C. III. B. 2.) There has been no attempt by the members to exercise their right of vote to control the factory, since the ballot system is entirely new to them. The members do not understand more of the factory than that its practical benefit in terms of profit are distributed among them. (Col. C. III. B. 3.) They do not know on what basis they have a claim to the profit, just as they do not know on what basis they should pay rent to the landlord. Ownership then actually means to them only a grant for the distribution of profit. This will be still clearer when we examine the financial side of the factory.

　　一个从事生产的工厂需要有适合安装机器的房子。建造工厂又需要技术知识和经费。技术知识由蚕业学校提供，但经费从哪儿来呢？这个问题就关系到所有制和分配问题。根据改革者的意图，在工厂开办以前，制定这些规章所依据的基本原则都已经确定了。原则是工厂应属于农民。但农民如何拥有它，谁是农民？

　　所有权属于这个合作社的社员。他们对工厂的责任限于他们所贡献的股份。入社以自愿为原则，并不限于本村的人。凡愿遵守社员义务者便可被吸收为社员。社员的义务是在工厂里有一份股金，每年供给工厂一定数量的蚕茧作原料。这一合作社共有 429 名社员，基本上包括了村里所有的住户及邻村的 50 多户。

　　根据规章，工厂的最高权力机构是社员全体大会。大会选出一个执行委员会，理论上它对大会负责。实际上恰恰相反，人们按照当地领导人和执行委员会的意见工作，当地领导人遵照改革者和蚕业学校的意见行事。由于整个工作是在改革者的指导下进行，人们对开办工厂也没有足够的知识，社员没有什么可以说的。由于农民缺乏受教育的机会，文盲率高，这使改革者在实施训练计划中发生很大困难，这些需要受训练的农民才是工厂的真正的主人。(C 栏，III 项，B.2）社员对投票制度完全不熟悉，他们也未想过行使投票的权利来管理工厂。他们只关心以利润形式分给他们的实际利益，对工厂的其他工作很不了解。(C 栏，III 项，B.3）他们不知道根据什么他们可以要求利润，正如他们不知道根据什么他们应该给地主交租。对他们来说，所有权只意味着他们可以分得一份利润。当我们讨论工厂的财务问题时，这个问题将表现得更加清楚。

There was of course no surplus capital in the village to finance the factory (Section 2). The total expense of its establishment was 49,848 dollars (about £3,000). This amounted to 114 dollars, or £27, from each member. In fact, of the total amount, the share contributed by the members in the first year, was only 2,848 dollars, about £180, *i.e.* 5.7 per cent. of the total.

Nominally, the "capital," or the contribution of the owners of the factory or the limits of the liability of the owners, is fixed at 10,000 dollars (£625). This is divided into a thousand shares of 10 dollars each. Each member subscribes at least one share. In the first year, 700 shares were taken up. These shares were payable over five years. At present only half of the amount has been collected. (Col. B. III. B. 3. *a.*) It is clear, therefore, that the finance of the factory depends on other sources than the owners.

The steam engine and the machines (of older type) were borrowed from the School. Their value was assessed as 4,000 dollars or £250. It was agreed that the factory would pay back that amount, out of profits, to the School within five years. But, owing to financial conditions, the factory has not yet fulfilled the promise. For the building and other expenses the factory had secured a long-term loan from the Provincial Peasant Bank of 15,000 dollars (or £800). This loan was not granted by the bank for strictly commercial reasons. It is clear that the liability is limited by the "capital," 10,000 dollars, and in case of bankruptcy the buildings and other immobile property could not be put up to auction since it is located in the village. But it was the government's policy to finance rural industry and this made it possible to raise the loan. (Col. B. IV. B. 2.) Another short-term loan of 3,000 dollars, or £190 (with land and building as mortgage) was secured from a local bank in Chên Tsê, the nearest town. From this examination of the financial basis of the factory, it is clear that the factory is actually based on government credit, not on the investment of the people.

The raw material is supplied by the members. Fresh cocoons are collected every year. Members receive a payment of 70 per cent. of the value of the cocoon supply at delivery. The money for this is borrowed yearly from the Provincial Bank, cocoons being accepted as mortgage.

As 30 per cent. of the payment is delayed, the members do not take much interest in supplying more than the lowest limit, especially since 1930, which was the last year that profit was distributed among the members. The following statistics supplied by the factory can be quoted.

当然，村里没有多余的资金来资助工厂（本章第二节）。开办工厂所需的经费总共为 49,848 元。每个社员约需分担 114 元，第一年，社员入股金额实际上仅 2,848 元，约为总额的 5.7%。

名义上，"资本"，或工厂所有者的贡献，或工厂主的有限责任固定在 10,000 元。这一数目被分成 1,000 股，每股 10 元。社员每人至少购买一股。第一年，认购了 700 股，可在五年期间交款。目前，只收到一半的股金。（B 栏，III 项，B.3.a.）显然，工厂的资金还需靠其他来源。

蒸汽机和机器（旧式）是从蚕业学校借来的，估计价值 4,000 元。有协议规定，五年以后工厂从利润中抽出钱来还给学校。但由于经济困难，工厂尚未履行这一诺言。为建造厂房和其他开支，工厂向省农民银行借了 15,000 元的一笔长期贷款。农民银行并不是由于商业上的原因才批准这笔贷款的。显然，负债是受"资本"10,000 元的限制的，由于工厂在农村，一旦工厂破产，厂房和其他不动产无法拍卖。但政府的政策是要为乡村工业提供资金，这才有可能向银行借贷。（B 栏，IV 项，B.2）另外，工厂向最近的镇——震泽的一个地方银行借了一笔 3,000 元的短期贷款（用土地和厂房作抵押）。从上述情况可以看到，工厂资金的基础实际上主要是政府的信贷，并不是靠人民的投资。

原料由社员供应。每年收集新鲜蚕茧。社员交蚕茧时，工厂交付蚕茧价值的 70%。这笔钱是每年从省银行借来的，蚕茧作为抵押。

由于 30% 是延期付款，社员多交蚕茧也得不到多少好处，因此他们只交最低限额的蚕茧，尤其是 1930 年以后。1930 年是把利润分给社员的最后一年。以下是工厂提供的统计数字。

Year	Members' Supply	Bought from Outside	Silk Reeled	Silk Reeled for Others	Days of Working
1929	527.07	—	41.31	—	175
1930	591.55	—	43.18	—	204
1931	415.73	—	32.21	—	145
1932	202.92	92.10	22.21	25.63	107
1933	307.87	45.37	40.46	5.00	186
1934	255.35	330.00	57.84	—	187
1935	375.80	301.08	64.21	—	199
1936	424.80	—	—	—	—
(incompleted)			(units in piculs)		

The above table shows the gradual decline of the supply of cocoons by members from 1930 to 1935. (Col. B. 111. 3. *b*.) In 1932, the total supply was too small to keep the factory working more than a hundred days. For the machines to stand idle is not economical. Thus cocoons had to be bought from the market. In 1934, the amount bought from outside was more than the amount supplied by members. On the other hand, the factory received orders from other factories to reel for them, using the latter's supply of raw material. This system is called *teza*, reeling for others. In 1932, the amount of silk reeled for other factories exceeded twenty-five piculs, which was practically equal to the amount of silk reeled from the raw material supplied by the village. After the factory had been re-equipped in 1935, the total production of silk was increased one-third over the average of preceding years. But the supply of cocoons from members did not keep step although it increased a little in 1935. For raw material the factory was half dependent on outside supply.

Labour is recruited from members. By introducing the factory system, the labour needed in production is much reduced as compared with that needed under the domestic system. In the reeling process thirty labourers are sufficient. These are all young women varying from sixteen to thirty years of age. Ten to fifteen unskilled labourers are enough for the selecting and cleaning of the cocoons. After the silk has been reeled it must be re-wheeled and wrapped in a standard form for export. Six to eight skilled labourers are employed in this. The total number of labourers is about fifty. In addition there are two managers, one technical director, one treasurer, one engine keeper, and two servants.

年	社员供应	从外面购买	缫丝	为其他单位缫丝	工作日
1929	527.07	—	41.31	—	175
1930	591.55	—	43.18	—	204
1931	415.73	—	32.21	—	145
1932	202.92	92.10	22.21	25.63	107
1933	307.87	45.37	40.46	5.00	186
1934	255.35	330.00	57.84	—	187
1935	375.80	301.08	64.21	—	199
1936	424.80	—	—	—	—
	（不完全）		（以担为单位）		

上表说明从 1930 年到 1935 年社员供应蚕茧的数量逐渐下降。（B 栏，III 项，3.b）1932 年总供应量还不足以供工厂开工一百余天之用。机器闲着不转是不经济的，因此，还需从市场购买一些蚕茧。1934 年从市场购买的蚕茧量比社员供应的多。在另一方面，工厂还接受其他工厂供给的原料代为缫丝的订货。这种方法被称为"代缫"，即为其他人缫丝。1932 年为别厂缫丝超过 25 担，实际上相当于从村里供应原料的缫丝量。1935 年工厂重新装备以后，丝的总产量超过前几年平均量的三分之一。但社员的蚕茧供应没有跟上来，虽然 1935 年稍有增加。在原料供应方面，工厂是半依赖于外界的。

劳力来自社员。由于引进工厂，生产中所需的劳力比在家庭手工业中所需的劳力少得多。这个工厂的缫丝部分 30 个工人已足够。她们都是年轻妇女，年龄从 16 至 30 岁不等。选茧和清洗蚕茧需要非技术工人 10 名。丝抽出来以后必须重新整理并按出口标准包扎，这一部分工作需要 6 至 8 名技术工人。工人总数约 50 人。此外，尚有两名经理、一名技师、一名司库、一名机器维修保养工、两名杂工。

In reeling and re-wheeling special training is needed. Thus employment and membership must be differentiated. Those who work in reeling and re-wheeling are paid in terms of a daily wage, forty to sixty cents a day. Those who work in selecting and cleaning cocoons are paid by piece-work. They receive about twenty to thirty cents a day. (Col. B. III. B. 2. *a.*)

The technical director is recommended by the School and the treasurer is recommended by the local bank. General business management is in the hands of local leaders, Chen and Chou. But the final authority is the Extension Department of the School. The staff are all paid fixed salaries. The total amount of wages and salaries, in 1929, was 7,557 dollars, or 57 per cent. of the total current expenses. Each common labourer can get roughly 70 dollars a year from 150 days of work.

From the above analysis, we can see that the factory is (1) owned by the members, (2) financed largely by the Provincial Peasant Bank, (3) managed by the School through the local leaders, and (4) worked by a part of the members. The so-called co-operative principle is significant chiefly in the problem of distribution.

The profit made by the factory in 1929, the first year, was 10,807.934 dollars. It was distributed according to the following principle:

"To encourage the members and to expand the organization, we decided to fix a high percentage for dividends. It should amount to seventy per cent. of our total profit. We will ask the members to lend half of their dividend to the factory to clear the loans. Fifteen per cent. of the profit will be our reserve fund. The rest will be divided into (1) reserve for improvement, (2) allowance for next year's current expenses, and (3) bonus for the staff, in the proportion of 4 : 3 : 3."[45]

In that year the amount of dividend actually received by the members was double the share they had contributed. But since that year, the price of silk had dropped to such a degree that no profit was made. The balance sheets since 1931 have not been published. I can only give the figures of the first three years.

Year	Net Profit	Net Loss
1929	$10,807.934	—
1930	—	$3,010.330
1931	—	$4,183.655

From 1931, the factory has tried to pay back the loan. For instance, in 1929, as shown in the balance sheet, the loan amounted to 135,663.763 but in 1931 it was reduced to 77,271.544. The interest of the large loan

在缫丝和整理丝时需要特殊训练。因此，工种不同，待遇也不同。缫丝和整理工按日工资计算，每天 4 至 6 角。挑选和清洗蚕茧工按计件工资计算，一天可得约 2 至 3 角。(B 栏，III 项，B.2.a)

技师由蚕业学校推荐，司库由当地银行推荐。总的管理业务由当地领导人陈和周负责。但最高职权在蚕业学校推广部。职员均是固定工资。1929 年总工资为 7,557 元，占当时总开支的 57%。每一个普通工人一年工作 150 天约可得 70 元。

从以上分析，我们能看到工厂：(1) 属于社员所有；(2) 主要由农民银行给予资金；(3) 由蚕业学校通过当地领导人管理；(4) 部分社员参加劳动，担任工作。所谓合作原则其意义主要在于分配上。

1929 年即第一年，工厂的利润为 10,807.934 元，按下列原则进行分配：

"为鼓励社员并扩大组织，我们决定提高红利，约为总利润的 70%。我们要求社员借一半红利给工厂以便工厂还债。利润的 15% 将作为我们的储备基金。其余金额将被分成：(1) 改良储备金；(2) 明年开支津贴；(3) 职员奖金。比例为 4:3:3。"[45]

那一年，社员所分到的红利确实相当于他们所购股份的两倍。但自从那年以后，丝价跌落到如此程度，以致毫无利润可得。1931 年以来一直没有公布资产负债表。我只能提供头三年的数字。

年	纯利润	纯损失
1929	10,807.934 元	
1930	—	3,010.330 元
1931	—	4,183.655 元

1931 年起，工厂想开始还债。如 1929 年资产负债表上所示，负债达 135,663.763，但 1931 年减为 77,271.544 元。大笔借款的利息

was also a cause for the loss. In 1929 it was 5,060, in 1930, 5,500, and in 1931, 4,121. In 1935, the factory was reequipped with modern machinery. It is expected to gain some profit after 1936. They want to revise the principle of distribution. Both the change agent and the local leaders told me that to give a high dividend in the beginning was a mistake. The members took it as a matter of course. But when the factory failed to distribute profit, they complained and were disillusioned. They realized that it would be better in the future to distribute a constant but small dividend every year instead of high dividends periodically.

❼ Government Support

I have indicated above how the government had entered into the change situation. In the very beginning, the local government in the town, the town council, co-operated with the School to start the reform programme. But at that time, 1923, the Provincial government was in the hands of a war lord who had no interest in any measure of that kind. Only after the establishment of the Nationalist Government in Nan-king in 1927 had rural reconstruction gradually become one of the main policies of the government. Special attention has been paid to the rural silk industry as well as to the co-operative movement. The co-operative factory in this village was therefore able to secure its financial support from the government. Moreover, the experiment in the village was the forerunner of the big programme of change in this rural industry in China; it will be interesting to review how the government took up the trend and spread the programme to many silk-producing areas in China.

The following quotations from *The Chinese Year Book* are selected to represent the governmental programme in this connection.

(1) *Sericulture Reform*

"One of the most important of China's rural industries is sericulture, but of recent years it has been hard to stand up against Japanese competition, largely because of the superiority of the silkworms bred in that country.

"In all the provinces where the production of silk is extensive, the local authorities are either acting in co-operation with the National Government, or taking special measures to improve the condition of those engaged in sericultures. What is being done in Kiangsu and Chekiang may be cited as typical of the measures being taken all over the country to revive the silk industry. The raising of the silkworms was

也是亏损的一个原因。1929 年利息为 5,060 元，1930 年为 5,500 元，1931 为 4,121 元。1935 年工厂重新装备现代机器。预期在 1936 年之后可有一些盈利。他们想要修改分配原则。改革者和当地领导人都认为一开始分配这样高的股息是错误的。一般社员把这看成是理所当然。但当工厂不能分配利润时，他们便抱怨和失望。他们认识到以后如能每年分到少一些但固定的红利比在一个时期分到一大笔红利要好。

七、政府的支持

上面我已说明政府是如何进入改革事业的。一开始，镇地方政府，即镇公所与蚕业学校合作草拟改革计划。但 1923 年那时候，省政府在一个军阀手里，他对那种措施没有任何兴趣。南京国民党政府在 1927 年成立以后，农村建设才逐渐成为政府的主要政策，对乡村丝业和合作运动给予特殊关切。所以，这个村子的合作工厂才能得到政府提供的资金。此外，村里的试验是中国农村工业中大的改革方案的先驱。回顾一下政府是如何接受这个趋势并把这种改革计划传到中国产丝的其他许多区域，是颇有意思的。

下面摘引的几段文章是选自《中国年鉴》中有关这个问题的、有代表性的官方计划。

（1）蚕丝业改革

"中国农村工业中最重要的一项是蚕丝业。但近年来甚难与日本竞争，主要是因为在该国培育了最好的蚕。

"在所有大量生产蚕丝的省份中，地方当局或与国民政府合作，或采取特殊措施，都努力改善蚕丝生产的条件。江苏、浙江两省之所为，可作为全国各地为振兴蚕丝业而采取的措施的典型。过去，

formerly left in the hands of the farmers, whose conservative attitude and lack of resources precluded the possibility of introducing reforms to improve the industry.... The Kiangsu and Chekiang officials, as a preliminary step towards improvement, organized a Commission for controlling the silk industry. At the outset the Commission contented itself with preventing competition among cocoon merchants by suggesting an official price for fresh cocoons. In the autumn season the Commission's attention was directed to stock improvement, which it tried to accomplish by replacing inferior indigenous varieties of silkworms with improved breeds. The egg-cards used by the Chekiang farmers were issued by the government sericultural experimental stations, the production of egg-cards by private hatcheries being prohibited. In Kiangsu similar control was exercised during 1934, though the measure, being tentative, was not so thorough-going as in Chekiang.... In addition to stock improvement, the Commission also fixed an official price for fresh cocoons and limited the number of collecting agencies in each locality.

"A three-year plan for the improvement of the silk industry in the provinces of Kiangsu, Chekiang, Shantung, Szechwan, and Kwangtung has also been drawn up by the Sericulture Improvement Commission of the National Economic Council. The scheme calls for the expenditure of $1,500,000 for the realization of the first year's plan in 1935.

"For the financial year, July 1934, to June 1935, the National Economic Council has allotted $400,000 for the use of the Sericulture Improvement Committee."[46]

(2) *Co-operative Movement*

"Since the introduction of the Co-operative Movement in China in 1919 it had enjoyed only a slow development; but with the success of the Northern Expedition and the unification of the country, the Co-operative Movement began to occupy an important place in the programme of the Kuomintang, which was dedicated to developing China on a basis of equality with foreign nations. Since then, the Co-operative Movement has enjoyed a very rapid growth. The Kuomintang began to be interested in the Co-operative Movement as early as 1919. In his lecture on local government, Dr. Sun Yat-sen once suggested the promotion of co-operative enterprises among workers and farmers.... At the second National Congress of the Kuomintang, it was resolved to organize farmers' banks and to promote co-operative enterprises among the Chinese peasants. During the Plenary Session of the Central Executive Council of the Kuomintang in August 1936, it was resolved that the government should push the organization of co-operative societies among farmers....

蚕都由农民饲养，他们的保守态度以及缺少资金的条件，阻碍了引进改良办法来改进工业的可能性。　　江苏、浙江的官员组织了一个蚕丝业委员会，作为改良工作的第一步。一开始，委员会为避免与茧商竞争，提出了收购鲜茧的官价。在秋季，委员会倾注全力于改进蚕种，用改良的品种来代替当地的蚕种。浙江农民用的蚕种由政府的蚕丝实验站颁发，私人培育的蚕种禁止使用。1934 年江苏实行了同样的控制，措施是试验性的，不像浙江那样彻底。　　除改良品种外，委员会还对新鲜蚕茧规定一个官价以及对每一地区的收购代理处限定了数目。

"江苏、浙江、山东、四川、广东等省改进蚕丝工业的三年计划也由国家经济委员会的蚕丝改良委员会制定。为实现 1935 年的第一年计划，所需经费为 1,500,000 元。

"1934 年 7 月至 1935 年 6 月的财政年度，国家经济委员会为蚕丝改良委员会拨款 400,000 元。"[46]

（2）合作运动

"自从 1919 年中国开始了合作运动以来进展很慢；但随着北伐胜利和国家统一，合作运动在国民党计划中开始有了重要的地位，这个计划旨在同外国平等的基础上发展中国。从那时起，合作运动迅速发展。国民党早在 1919 年便对合作运动有了兴趣。孙中山先生在地方政府的演说中曾建议，在工人、农民中促进合作企业。　　国民党第二次全国代表大会决定组织农民银行，在中国农民中间推广合作企业。1936 年 8 月国民党中央执行局全体会议决议中指出政府应在农民中推进合作社的组织。

"With the establishment of the Nationalist Government in Nanking many provinces began seriously to push the Co-operative Movement. At the fourth Plenary Session of the Central Executive Council of the Kuomintang in February 1928, General Chiang Kai-shek and Chen Ko-fu jointly proposed the organization of a special Committee on Co-operation. In October of that year, the Central Executive Council of the Kuomintang issued an order to all the branches in the country, asking them to include co-operative work as a part of their political activities.

"In addition, the Kiangsu Provincial Government promulgated a set of Provisional Regulations regarding Co-operative Societies and organized the Kiangsu Agricultural Bank on July 16, 1928, with a view to developing rural economy, and to offering credit facilities to the farmers at low costs."[47]

❸ Difficulties in Change

The intention of the people to accept the reform is due to its practical benefit as expressed in increase of family income. Now we can examine how far the reform programme has met this expectation.

The disinfection of silkworm eggs, the organization of a common room for raising young worms and the supervision given by visiting instructors in the later stages have reduced the cost and increased the production of cocoons. This part of the reform has enabled the people to get an income roughly twice as much as they had before. (Col. B. III. C. 1. *a*.) The result of the reform in reeling is not so promising. In 1929, the members had received as dividend about ten dollars per share. But ever since that year, they have got nothing of that sort from the factory. On the other hand, they were under obligation to supply raw materials with a delayed payment of 30 per cent. Up to the present, those whose income has actually been increased by the introduction of this factory are the labourers and the staff in the form of wages and salaries. They are the minority of the community. (Col. B. III. C. 1. *b*.)

The inability of the factory to distribute yearly profit among the members is due to two fundamental factors. First of all the reformers are not able to control the price level. They have succeeded in producing silk of high quality, but between the quality and the price the ratio is hardly proportionate. It is true that better silk can be sold at a higher price, but the price of silk in general fluctuates at different times. So long as the reformers cannot control the market, mere improvement in the quality of production cannot necessarily bring back higher returns and is not able to increase the income of the villagers.

> "南京国民党政府成立以后，很多省开始认真推动合作运动。1928 年 2 月国民党中央执行理事会第四次全体会议上，蒋介石将军和陈果夫联合提议组织专门的合作委员会。当年 10 月，国民党中央执行局向所有分支发布命令，要求它们把合作事业作为其政治活动的一个组成部分。
>
> "此外，江苏省政府颁发了一系列有关合作社的暂行规章制度，并于 1928 年 7 月 16 日组织了江苏农民银行以便发展农村经济，并为农民提供方便的低息贷款。"[47]

八、改革中的困难

人民愿意接受改革，主要在于实际利益，例如增加了家庭收入。现在我们可以看一看改革计划在多大程度上满足这种期望。

蚕种的消毒、稚蚕公育、教员的定期指导使成本有所降低，蚕茧增产。这一部分改革使得农民的收入大约比以前增加了一倍。（B 栏，III 项，C.1.a）缫丝改革的成果并不理想。1929 年每股分得红利约 10 元。但自从那年起，他们再也没有从工厂拿到什么。相反，他们还有义务供应原料，而且是延期付款 30%。至目前为止，由于有了工厂而收入真正有所增加的是工厂的工人和职员，以工资的形式增加了收入。他们是这一社区的少数。（B 栏，III 项，C.1.b）

工厂未能分给社员年利是由于两个基本因素。首先，改革者不能控制价格水平。他们成功地生产了高质量的丝，但质量和价格之间比率不相称。确实，好丝应该能卖好价，但丝的总的价格在不同时期波动较大。只要改革者不能控制市场，单是改进产品质量未必能获取高的报酬，因此，村民的收入未见提高。

A more immediate factor responsible for the present state of affairs is the financial problem. It is not true that the factory has not made profit during the years 1930 to 1936, because the total amount of loans has been reduced every year. In other words, the factory saved from its own profit in production so as to buy over the means of production which was so far borrowed. The people do not account for this. They only know the concrete income of the family. As soon as their expectations could not be realized they began to be disillusioned. The direct reaction was discontinuance of further payments of their subscriptions. Up to the present time, only about one-half of the amount subscribed has been paid in.

Of course, according to the regulation, the members have the right to audit the account themselves and demand explanations from the manager. But the people are satisfied on the level of suspicion and occasional gossip without taking any definite steps to investigate. They are mostly illiterate. They do not understand what is written on the balance sheet. Their rôle given in the regulation is new to them. The reformers have only taught the girls how to reel silk but not the members how to be the masters of the factory. They have no knowledge of their own responsibility. As long as the educational work cannot keep pace with the industrial reform, the co-operative factory can be only run for the people and can partially belong to the people but can never be really controlled by them.

Introduction of modern machinery into the village economy, as we have seen in the case of water pumping in agriculture, has created a new labour problem under the domestic system where every household had its own reeling machine. In other words, there were at least three hundred and fifty women in this village engaged in the work of reeling silk. Now under the factory system, the same amount of work can be done easily by less than seventy persons. The amount of labour needed in production has been reduced. For instance, by the present reeling machines, each worker can look after twenty spindles at the same time while with the older machines one could only handle four or five. From the technical point of view it is a great improvement. But what does this improvement mean to the rural economy? Nearly three hundred women have lost their opportunities to work. (Col. B. III. C. 2. *b*.) The problem of "unemployment" has its wider repercussions—the traditional division of work according to sex remains unchanged, but the size of the farm is so small that introduction of female labour to the land is impossible; and no new industry has been introduced to absorb the surplus of female labour. (Col.C. III. C. 2. *b*.)

　　造成目前这种状况的更直接的因素是资金问题。在 1930 年至 1936 年间工厂并不是没有盈利，因为贷款的数目每年有所降低。换句话说，工厂节约下自己生产的盈利，买回了借来的生产资料。人们不算这笔账，他们只知道家庭的具体收入。一旦他们的愿望没有实现，他们就会感到希望破灭，其直接反应就是不再继续向工厂交纳股金，至目前为止，只缴纳了认购股金的半数。

　　当然，根据规章，社员自己有权查账，并可要求经理解释。但人们只停留于怀疑和偶尔的议论上，而不采取切实的措施进行调查。他们大多数是文盲。他们不明白写在资产负债表上的数字。规章赋予他们的角色，对他们来说是新的。改革者只教授女孩子如何缫丝，而没有教社员如何当工厂的主人。他们对自己的责任没有认识。只要教育工作跟不上工业改革的步伐，合作工厂可以只为人民而开设，部分属于人民，但决不可能真正由人民管理。

　　现代机械被引进农村经济，正如我们已经看到在农业中引进了水泵，使有缫丝机的家家户户发生了一个新的劳动力的问题。换句话说，这个村庄过去至少有 350 名妇女从事缫丝工作。现在开办了工厂，同等量的工作，不到 70 个人就能轻易地担负起来。生产所需的劳动量减少了。例如，现代的缫丝机，每个工人同能照看 20 个锭子，而旧缫丝机一个人只能掌握 4 至 5 个。从技术观点来看，这是一个很大的改进。但这一改进对农村经济意味着什么呢？将近 300 名妇女失去了她们的劳动机会。（B 栏，III 项，C. 2. b）"失业"的问题引起了比较广泛的反响——根据男女性别不同的传统分工仍然不变，但农田面积如此之小，要把妇女劳力引向田地是不可能的。然而也没有引进新的工业来吸收多余的妇女劳力。（C 栏，III 项，C. 2. b）

The reformers have tried to solve the problem by the system of distribution of profit. But it has not been successful, as we have shown above. The results are (1) for those who cannot go to town for various reasons, survival, or, to a certain extent, revival of the traditional domestic industry which becomes a kind of resistence of the reform programme through competition in securing raw material, (2) movement of the female population to the towns, which is contradictory to the original intention of the reformers, and (3) creation of a special wage-earning class in the village.

The survival of the traditional domestic industry can be quantitatively estimated. The total amount of cocoons produced in this village is about 72,000 lbs. The decrease of members' supply to the factory indicated the increase of domestic reserve, taking the total production as constant and the amount of cocoons directly sold to the town as insignificant. In 1929 the reserve was about one-sixth of the total production but in 1932 it increased to two-thirds. In 1936, before I left the village, the reserve was about one-third. How much more one can get by selling native silk instead of selling cocoons, it is difficult to say, because the prices of cocoon and that of silk fluctuate and villagers do not know how to forecast them. As we can see under the lowest price of native silk, one dollar for three Liang, the producer can get little more than the value of the raw material, if the price of the latter is about fifty dollars per picul. But the price of native silk is not known when the market for cocoon is open. It is not the real calculation of the prices of silk and cocoon that makes the people reserve their raw material for domestic reeling but the belief that they can get more money if they reel silk instead of selling the raw material.

The substitution of the factory for the domestic system in the silk industry is a general process which is not limited to the village. The development of silk filature in the nearby cities in the last twenty years has been rapid.[48] The urban industry attracts rural labour. This movement of population undoubtedly is a disruptive force in the traditional social structure of the rural community. To counter this process was one of the original intentions of the reformers. But the small-scale factory in the village, as limited by its local supply of raw material, cannot fully utilize the available labour in the village. On the contrary, it has not been able to check the outflow of rural population. I have shown above that in 1935 there were thirty-two girls between the ages of sixteen to twenty-five who lived outside the village (VI–1). They were engaged in silk factories in Wuhsi. At the time when I was in the village another silk factory was

改革者曾经想用分红的办法来解决问题。但如我们在上面表明的，这并未获得成功。结果是：（1）为那些由于多种原因不能到城镇去的人保存了或在某种程度上恢复了传统的家庭工业，原料的竞争使其成为改革计划的一种阻力；（2）妇女向城镇移动，这是与改革者原来的意图相矛盾的；（3）农村中产生了一种特殊的挣工资的阶层。

对残存的传统家庭工业，可以作量的估计，这个村庄蚕茧的总生产量约为 72,000 磅。假定这一生产量是稳定的，直接卖给城镇的茧子为数极少，那么对工厂的供应减少表明了家庭的储存增加。1929 年，留给家庭的蚕茧约为总生产量的六分之一，但 1932 年增加到三分之二。1936 年我离开村庄以前，留给家庭的约为三分之一。卖生丝能比卖蚕茧多得多少，很难说，因为蚕茧和生丝价格都有波动，农民不知如何预测。如果我们按生丝最低价格看，一元钱三两，生产者仅能比原料的价值多拿少许，如果后者的价格约为每担 50 元。但蚕茧市场开放时生丝的价格还是未知数。农民保留原料从事家庭缫丝的原因，并不在于实际考虑丝和茧的价格，而是因为他们相信缫丝能比卖原料多挣钱。

在蚕丝工业中工厂取代家庭工业是一个普遍过程，并不限于这个村庄。近二十年来附近城市缫丝业的发展极快。[48] 城市工业吸引农村劳力，无疑这种人口流动对农村社区的传统社会结构是一种破坏性的力量。改革者的原意之一就是要阻止这一过程。但村庄里的小型工厂为当地原料供应所限，未能充分利用村里现有的劳力。相反，它也不能阻止农村人口的外流，我已经在上面表明，1935 年有 32 名 16 ～ 25 岁的女青年住在村外（第六章第一节），她们在无锡丝厂工作。我在村里的时候，震泽又开了一家蚕丝工厂。村中更多

established in Chên Tsê. More girls were recruited from the village. The total number of girls between the age of sixteen to twenty-five is one hundred and six in this village. More than 80 per cent. of them are now engaged in factories outside of the village or in the co-operative factory. They are new wage-earners.

A wage-earning class is not traditional in the village. The employees in agriculture are few. Labour enters into the realm of commodity in a very limited sense. Only by the decline of domestic industry, female labour has created a labour market in the village. To this problem we shall devote our discussion in the next section.

❾ Effects on Kinship Relations

Wage-earning is now regarded as a privilege, because it makes an immediate contribution to the domestic budget. Those who have no adult daughters begin to regret it. The woman's position in society has undergone a gradual change. For instance, a girl who was working in the village factory actually cursed her husband because he forgot to send her an umbrella when it rained. It is interesting because this little incident indicates changes in the relation between husband and wife. According to the traditional conception, the husband is not supposed to serve his wife, at least he cannot do so in public. Moreover, the husband cannot accept his wife's curse without any protest or counter-curse.

The traditional economic status of a girl is subordinate to her father or to her husband. She has no opportunity to possess any large amount of money (IV–2). The financial power of the Chia is in the hands of the head. It is correlated with the traditional system of collective production. The men who work on the farm are dependent upon their women for the supply of their food. The mulberry leaves needed in feeding the silkworms are carried from a distance by the man. The private sense of the production is overshadowed by the collective aspect. But the wage-earning is essentially individualistic. The earner feels that the wage is the result of her own effort. This sense is shared by both parties, the owner herself and the head of the Chia. Furthermore, the wage is paid by the factory to the earner herself. At least during that moment, she is able to spend a part of her earnings in accordance with her own wishes. Therefore, the economic relation in the Chia is gradually modified. For instance, if the girl spends her wage within reasonable limits and for proper purposes such as buying clothes, it will be accepted without

的女青年被吸收到工厂里。本村 16 ～ 25 岁的女青年共有 106 名，80% 以上现在村外的工厂或在合作工厂工作。她们就是新的挣工资的人。

挣工资的阶层并不是村里传统的结构。农业雇工非常少。劳动在非常有限的意义上进入商品领域。只有在家庭手工业衰落的情况下，妇女劳动力才在村里形成了一个市场。我们将在下一节再讨论这个问题。

九、对亲属关系的影响

现在挣工资被看作是一种特殊的优惠，因为它对家庭预算有直接的贡献。那些没有成年女儿的人家开始懊悔了。妇女在社会中的地位逐渐起了变化。例如，一个在村中工厂工作的女工因为下雨时丈夫忘记给她送伞，竟会公开责骂她的丈夫。这是很有意思的，因为这件小事反映了夫妻之间关系的变化。根据传统的观念，丈夫是不侍候妻子的，至少在大庭广众之下，他不能这样做。另外，丈夫不能毫无抗议或反击，便接受妻子的责备。

一个女孩的传统经济地位是依附于她的父亲或丈夫的。她没有机会拥有大宗的钱财（第四章第二节）。家的财权在一家之长的手里。这与传统的集体生产相互关联。在地里工作的男人靠他们的女人送饭，饲养蚕所需的桑叶由男人从远处运来。个人不容易意识到在一家的集体生产中的贡献。但挣工资基本上是个人的事。挣钱的人能感觉到她的工资收入是她自己劳动的结果。这是收入者本人和家长都会感觉到的。此外，工资由工厂直接付给她本人。至少在这个时候，她可以将她的一部分工资按她自己的愿望去花费。因此，家中的经济关系就逐步地得到改变。比如，女孩子在合理范围内，为了正当的目的，如买一些衣服，那是可以允许而不受干涉的。

interference. But she is not allowed to spend all her wage; a large portion of it must be handed over to the head to go into the common budget. To maintain the collective and centralized system of economy under the new situation, the head of the Chia, even at the expense of his authority, will be forced to be considerate towards fellow members of the Chia. Complications come again in the problem of to whom she will hand over her earnings. When the girl is not married and has a mother, but when the head of the Chia is her grandfather, her mother may hold up a part of her earning for future use in her marriage. If the economic condition is not favourable for saving, the amount will be absorbed in the general budget. A married woman will keep a part of her earnings as her own savings. These facts show the increasing differentiation of the individual family from the compound group Chia.

The physical separation of the wage-earner from the members of her family may also produce essential changes in the kinship relations. The separation of a daughter-in-law from her mother-in-law will reduce the possibility of daily conflict. But the separation of wife from husband will loosen the marital tie. One extreme case can be cited for illustration. A girl left her husband about one year after she had married. She stayed in a factory in Wuhsi and fell in love with a workman in the same factory. They were both discharged by the factory when the illegal union was discovered. Having lived together for two months, but being pressed for money, they separated. The girl returned to the village and was greatly disgraced. Her parents-in-law refused to admit her, but afterwards accepted her because they planned to arrange a remarriage for her in order that they could get a sum of money for compensation. Later, in view of her earning capacity in the silk factory in the village, her parents-in-law cancelled their plan and treated her as usual. Her husband took a passive attitude towards the entire affair.

The separation of the child from its mother rearranges the intimate relation in the Chia. The suckling period is shortened. The grandmother will take up the mother's obligation in further nursing and care of the child. This also establishes new relations between the daughter-in-law and mother-in-law. Similarly, with those women who work in the village factory and cannot bring their children with them, the same situation is found.

All these facts point to the re-organization of the kinship relations in a new pattern which will find adjustment with the industrial changes. My present material is only sufficient to suggest the problem for further investigations.

　　但不允许她把所有的工资都花掉，工资的大部分要交给家长，归入一家的共同预算。在这个新的形势下，为了保持集体和集中的经济体系，即使牺牲他的权威，家长也必须对家中的成员作出考虑。女孩子挣的钱交给谁，是一个复杂的问题。女孩子未婚时，如果她有母亲，而家长是她的祖父，她的母亲会将她的钱收下一部分以供她将来结婚时所用。如果经济状况不允许存钱，全部金额归入家的总预算之中。一个已婚的妇女则将她收入的一部分留作她自己的积蓄。这种情况说明了单个家庭不断从家的复合群体中分化出来。

　　挣钱的人同其他家人分开，对亲属关系也产生了实质的变化。儿媳从婆母处分离出来可以减少日常的争吵。但妻子同丈夫分开会使婚姻的关系松散。可以举出一个极端的例子来说明。有一个妇女，在结婚一年后离开了他的丈夫。她在无锡的一家工厂里工作，并和这个厂里的一个工人发生了恋爱。他们这种不合法的结合被发现之后，他们被厂方开除。他们同居了两个月，由于经济所迫不得不分离。这妇女回到村中，受到很大的羞辱。她的公婆拒绝再要她，但后来又收留了她，因为她的公婆准备将她另嫁他人，以便可以收到一笔钱作为补偿。最后，考虑到她在本村丝厂里能工作的本领，她的公婆取消了原来的打算，待她一如既往。她的丈夫对这件事则完全采取被动的态度。

　　孩子从母亲处分开，就会使家中的亲密关系发生新的安排。母亲喂奶的时间缩短了。当祖母的接过母亲的责任，继续照看、抚养孩子。这也使婆媳之间产生了新的关系。那些在本村工厂里工作而不能带孩子的女人，也有类似的状况。

　　以上事实说明了亲属关系以新的形式进行着重新组合，并将随着工业的变迁得到调整。我现有的材料只能为进一步的调查提出一些问题。

CHAPTER XIII   SHEEP RAISING AND TRADE VENTURES

The reform of the silk industry is only one of the attempts being made in the village to increase income and thus to counteract the decline in silk prices. But my present material does not allow me to give such a detailed analysis of the other measures which are being taken.

The most important of the new enterprises is sheep raising. This was introduced about ten years ago, but only recently became an important industry. Its development was not due to the initiative of any one agent. People in the village learned from their neighbours that in the town there was a new shop collecting sheep foetus, or newly born sheep. The demand in the market called forth the new industry in the village. Even now the people have no exact knowledge of what is the use of the sheep foetus, and they often asked me about this. Some supposed that the mother sheep was killed in order to get the foetus, the skin of which is valuable. This idea does not accord very well with traditional ethics, although the people themselves practise infanticide.

The main difficulty in sheep raising is the problem of feeding. 90 per cent. of the land is used for farming (X–2). Except for a few plots of ground occupied by tombs belonging to the people of the town, there is practically no pasture land available for sheep. The farms are open; there are no fences to prevent possible damage by wandering animals. In such circumstances it is impossible to raise sheep in the open. Therefore special huts have been built, and the sheep are kept enclosed. As I mentioned above, the sheep hut has become a common appendage of a house.

To feed the sheep, grass must be collected; in winter dried mulberry leaves are used. A new division of labour in the household has been developed in this connection. Collecting grass is left to the children. Walking through the village you will see children even below ten scattered everywhere in small groups, collecting grass under the mulberry trees, along the streams, and on the open tomb ground. The children's labour is thus incorporated into the domestic economy. This has created a new problem for the public school. Literary education seems to the people less valuable than the immediate contribution which children can make to the family income. The list of absentees in the classes is correlated with the number of sheep raised in the village. Chen remarked with regret that the school curriculum is too rigid to be adjusted to present economic conditions (III–5).

拾叄 养羊与贩卖

　　进行蚕丝业的改革仅仅是为增加居民的收入、抵制丝价下跌所做的各种努力之一。但根据我现有的资料不可能对目前采取的其他措施进行详尽的分析。

　　新兴事业中最重要的一项是养羊。大约十年前就有人开始养羊。但到最近才变得重要起来。养羊业的发展并不是由于某个人的倡议。村里的人从邻居那里听说，镇里新开了一家店铺，收购羊胎和新生的羊羔。市场的需要使这个村子里兴起了这项新事业。但甚至到现在，人们还不甚了解羊胎究竟有何用处，他们经常向我提出这个问题。有些人想要杀掉母羊好取羊胎，羊胎皮是值钱的。这个主意与传统的伦理观念很不相符，尽管人们自己还要溺杀婴儿。

　　养羊所遇到的主要困难是饲养问题。土地的90%是农田（第十章第二节）。除几块属于城里人的坟地外，几乎没有适于放羊的场地。农田是敞开的，没有篱笆，牲畜乱走，可能损害庄稼。在这种情况下无法在田野中放羊。所以，就盖起了专用的羊圈，把羊关在里面。正如我上面提到的，羊圈已变成了住家普遍都有的附属建筑了。

　　为了喂羊，就必须割草，冬天用干桑叶喂羊。就这一点而言，家庭劳务中就产生了一种新的劳动分工。割草的事由孩子们担任。如果你在村里走一走，就可以看见到处有三五成群割草的孩子，有些还不到十岁，他们有的在桑树下，有的沿着河边，还有些在坟地里。这样，孩子们的劳动与家庭经济结合了起来。对于小学校来说，这就产生了一个新问题，文化教育的价值在人们眼里，还不如孩子们割草为家庭收入作出的直接贡献有价值。缺课人数与村里养羊的头数相关。陈曾遗憾地表示，学校的课程过于死板，难以与

This leads to interesting questions on the relation between economics and education, but this I cannot deal with at present.

Another advantage of keeping the sheep enclosed in the hut, is that the sheep manure can easily be collected. This is a valuable fertilizer. There are more than three hundred small huts in the village. The number of sheep in each hut varies from one to five. A rough estimate of the total number of sheep raised in the village is about five hundred.

For starting sheep raising, a certain amount of capital is necessary, at least enough to buy the ewe. Rams can be borrowed from relatives or hired for breeding. Payment for this service is not fixed and is made mostly by means of gifts. If a farmer cannot himself raise the money to buy an ewe, he can raise sheep belonging to other people. A special system is thus developed, which the villagers call *fenyan*, literally "dividing sheep." The person raising the sheep is responsible for their feeding and gets half the young sheep as well as the manure in the hut. Chou's father is the biggest owner of sheep. He owns forty sheep, of which only four are kept in his own hut.

The ewe can be sold shortly before the foetuses are fully developed. The price for each foetus is three to five dollars. The owner can also sell new-born sheep and keep the mother. In this case the price is lower. But a mother sheep may bear young ones once or twice a year, while to raise a young sheep to maturity takes more than a year. People therefore prefer to sell young sheep instead of the foetus. The tradition against killing pregnant animals reinforces this preference. On the average a mother sheep produce two to four young ones every year, which will yield the owner an income of twenty to thirty dollars.

Another source of income to the people is trade ventures, which are embarked on in the lengthy intervals in the agricultural activities (IX–3).

The people go to the neighbouring province, Chekiang, to transport goods—not those produced by themselves—by their own boats, and from there to some towns along the coast. This is a kind of interlocality trade. But from the point of view of the villagers, it is really selling their services as trading agents or as transport hands.

目前的经济状况相适应（第三章第五节）。这使人们注意到关于经济与教育的关系的令人感兴趣的问题，但目前我不能讨论这个问题。

把羊关在羊圈里饲养的另一个好处是便于收集羊粪。羊粪是一种有价值的肥料。村里有 300 多个小羊栏。每个羊圈养 1 ～ 5 只羊。粗略估计，村里养羊的总数约为 500 头。

为了开展养羊业，需要一定数额的资金，至少要有足够购买母羊的钱。公羊可以从亲戚那里借来或者租来为繁殖之用。对于这项服务所付的报酬没有固定的数目，多数是采取送礼的形式。如果一个农民自己筹不起款子来买母羊，他可以养别人的羊。这样就产生了一种特有的方式，村民称之为"分羊"，从字面上讲就是"把羊分开"。养羊的人的责任是饲养，到时便能分得半数小羊羔和羊栏里的一半粪肥。周的父亲是最大的羊主，他有 40 只羊，其中只有 4 只养在他自己的羊圈里。

当羊胎即将长成前不久，就可以把母羊卖掉。每只羊胎的价格为 3 ～ 5 元。羊主也可以把刚生下的羊羔卖掉，把母羊留下。这时，羊羔的价格略低，但一只母羊一年能生一两次羊羔，而把羊羔饲养成熟却需要一年多的时间。所以人们喜欢卖羊羔，而不卖羊胎。反对屠杀孕期动物的传统也使得人们更加愿意这样做。一只母羊平均每年生产 2 ～ 4 只羊羔，能为羊主增加 20 ～ 30 元的收入。

农民收入的另一个来源是贩卖。在较长的农闲季节里，人们从事这种买卖（第九章第三节）。货物并非自己生产，而是用自己的船从邻省浙江运至沿岸的一些城镇贩卖。这是一种地区之间的流通。但从村民的观点看来，这实际是像贩卖或搬运工一样出卖自己的劳务。

My informants stated that each boat engaged in this venture can yield forty dollars a year. Of course, this depends on the type of goods transported and sold and the fluctuation of their price. I had no chance of following their route because their activity in this line takes place from the end of August to the middle of October, and from the middle of December to the end of January, when I had already left the village. These ventures are regulated by the solar calendar. I cannot go into details here, except to mention that this is an important source of income. According to my informants, the number of boats thus engaged has increased in recent years.

为我提供情况的当地人说，每条贩运船一年可赚 40 元。当然，收入取决于贩运货物的种类及其价格的波动情况。我没有机会跟着他们一起去，因为他们这行的活动时间是 8 月底至 10 月中，然后又从 12 月中至 1 月底，那时我已经离开这个村庄。这些商业活动都是按阳历时间安排的。我不能在此作很深入的分析，只是想说明，这是农民收入的一个重要来源。根据提供情况的人说，从事该项行业的船只数目近几年来有所增加。

CHAPTER XIV   MARKETING

❶ Types of Exchange

Exchange is a process of reciprocal transfer of goods or services between individuals or groups of individuals on the basis of some sort of equivalence. Exchange is necessary wherever there is specialization of production. Specialization of production takes place even between the members of a family. But the process of exchange within a family takes a form different from that found in the market. For in the first place the processes of distribution and exchange in a collective economy are not easily differentiated. The husband who works on the farm depends on his wife for the cooking of his food. In so far as the wife has contributed to the process of production, her claim on the farm produce comes under the head of distribution of the product. But when she consumes more than her share, exchange actually takes place. Secondly, the element of exchange is obscure where property is held in common by the members of a group. Where there is division of labour, the members contribute by their different occupations to the common source from which each derives his living. What exchange actually takes place between the members is thus not apparent.

This does not mean that the ideas of reciprocity in privilege and obligation, and of equivalence in contribution and share do not exist in the intimate social groups. On the contrary, they are among the most frequent causes of disputes and dissatisfactions in domestic life and are jealously upheld. Quantitative assessment of these economic relations in the domestic group requires a very refined field technique, but is not impossible.

The less apparent and less immediate forms of exchange are made possible by positive sanctions inherent in the institutions of the group.

For example, parental obligation towards the child is balanced by the support given later by the young to the old, by the obligation to the next generation, or both. The longer the time involved and the more roundabout the transfer of goods and services, the stronger are the social ties in the group. The exchange of goods or services is a concrete expression of social ties. Where obligations can be fulfilled only

拾 肆 贸易

一、交换方式

交换产生于个人之间或一些人之间，是物品或劳务在某种等价的基础上相互转换的过程。哪里有专业化的生产，哪里便需要交换。生产专业化甚至发生在家庭的不同成员间，但在家庭中，交换方式同在市场中所见到的不同。因为首先在集体经济中，分配和交换的过程不易区别。在田里劳动的丈夫靠妻子为他煮饭。从妻子对生产过程的贡献来说，她对农产品的权利，应该列在产品分配的项目下。但如果她消耗的要比她分配所得的那一份多，实际上便产生了交换。其次，当财产为一个群体的成员共同所有时，交换的要素是模糊不清的。有了劳动分工，成员通过不同的职业向共同生活的来源作出自己的贡献，同时从这一来源获取各自生活所需的资料。各成员之间究竟作了些什么交换因而是不明显的。

这并不意味着权利和义务的相互关系的概念、贡献和享受对等的概念不存在于亲近的社会群体中。相反，它们是家庭生活中发生争吵和不满的最常见的原因，并且往往发生一种出于妒忌而坚持不下的局面。对这种家庭群体的经济关系作出定量分析，需要精确的实地调查技术，但并不是不可能的。

比较不明显的、不直接的交换形式通过群体固有的制度的约束，已经成为可能了。例如，父母对孩子的义务可以通过年轻一代以后对父母的赡养，或者年轻一代对下一代的义务来取得平衡。时间越长，物品和劳务的转换范围越大，群体中社会纽带亦越强。物品或劳务的交换是社会纽带的具体表现。只有在一些需要很长

over a long period of time the individuals involved tend to feel more strongly their social relationship. This is in consequence one of the cohesive forces of the group. From this angle generosity can be viewed as the advance from one person to another of services or goods, bringing in consequence the persons closer to one another.

A similar type of exchange is found in larger social groups such as extended kinship groups and neighbourhood groups. Neighbours in the village are often allowed to take things from each other for consumption or other use in case of need. Within certain limits a man is glad to be useful to his neighbour. If the borrower makes repayment immediately and states the equation of exchange explicitly, the lender will be offended. "We are not outsiders to each other," they will say. In case extra labour is needed on the farm, relatives living nearby will come to help without payment; so will neighbours on ceremonial occasions (VI–2). Mutual accommodation and services between relatives and neighbours are balanced out in the long run. Exchange on the basis of definite and calculated equivalence tends to diminish in proportion to the intimacy of social relationships.

The making of gifts may be considered as another type of exchange. This is not a result of specialization of production. Even relatives who are engaged in different occupations do not present their special produce as gifts. The type of objects used for formal gifts is prescribed by customs and consists mostly of food, besides offerings of cash on ceremonial occasions. The food offered as gifts is either bought from the market, such as ham and sweets sent at the end of the year, or produced by the people themselves such as special kinds of triangular-shaped rice pudding sent at the festival of Tuan Yang (IX–3). The receiver makes the same type of pudding and buys similar objects to offer to his relatives in return. This type of transfer of goods is significant not in making up mutual deficiency but in strengthening social ties.

From the foregoing analysis, it will be seen that social obligations, mutual accommodations and gift-making are not sufficient to enable a household in the village to secure all the daily necessities which it does not itself produce. Of goods consumed, those produced by the consumers are less than one-third of the total (VII–8). On the other hand, of the goods produced in the household, many are not consumed by the producers. The actual use of the young sheep and sheep foetus does not even seem to be known to the people who raise the sheep (XIII). In the silk-producing area, silk clothes are rare.

时期才能相互完成的义务，有关的个人才会更强烈地感受到他们之间的社会关系，其结果是形成了群体的一种内聚力量。从这一角度考虑，慷慨可以被看作是一个人向另一个人预付的劳务或物品，这种行为使两个人之间的关系更加密切。

在大一些的社会群体中有同类的交换。例如扩大的亲属关系群体和邻里群体。在村里邻居之间，需要时可以互相挪拿东西用于消费或其他用途。在一定的限度内，一个人对他的邻居有用，他会感到高兴。如果借用者立刻要付酬并说明同等交换，出借者便会很不高兴地说："我们不是外人。"田里如果需要额外劳力，住在附近的亲戚便来帮忙，不要报酬；有重大婚丧喜事时，邻居也这样来帮忙（第六章第二节）。从长远看，亲戚和邻居之间的互相接待、留宿和服务都是取得平衡的。社会关系越亲密，经过计算的绝对的对等交换也越少。

送礼亦可被看作是另一种交换。这不是专业化生产的结果。不同职业的亲戚，也不把他们的专业产品作为一种礼物。用来作为正式礼品的一些东西是根据习俗而来的，主要是食品。在重要礼仪场合则送一些现金。人们送礼的食品，或是从市场买来的，如年底送的火腿和糖果；或是自己制作的，如端阳节（第九章第三节）送的三角形的糯米粽子。接受礼物的人，也做同样的粽子，买相同的东西回送亲戚。这种类型的物品转让意义不在于弥补相互间的欠缺，而是加强社会联系。

从上述分析可以看出，社会义务、互相接待、留宿和互赠礼物是不够的，它不足以使村里的一个农户获得他自己不生产的日常必需品。在消费品中，消费者生产的只占总数的三分之一（第七章第八节）。另一方面，农民生产的东西，很多不是生产者消费的。羊羔和羊胎的真正用处，看来养羊人本身也不知道（第十三章）。在产丝区，

Even the rice is only partly consumed by the people themselves. Thus it is clear that there must be an extensive exchange system. The predominant type of exchange in the village is marketing.

❷ Internal and External Marketing

By marketing is meant the type of exchange in which equivalence in value is explicitly expressed in the transaction and immediately given or promised. In simple language, it is the process of buying and selling. In the village it is carried out, with a few exceptions, through money.

We can distinguish two types of marketing: internal and external. Internal marketing is the exchange of goods and services within the village community, and external marketing is that between the village and the outside world. They are interdependent.

The internal market of the village is bound up with the occupational differentiation in the community (VIII–1). As we have seen, more than two-thirds of the total population in the village are engaged in producing rice, silk, and sheep. These do not sell their produce in the village but to the town. Those engaged in fishing sell only a small portion of their produce to their fellow villagers. Those who produce special goods and render special services to the villagers are limited to a small group which is only 7 per cent. of the total population (VIII–2). Most of their work is not exclusively specialized but is supplementary to common household work. Carpenters, basket makers, and masons are engaged mostly in repair work. They keep a working place in their own house but they also work in the houses of their clients. Tailors work mostly in clients' houses.

The small degree of occupational differentiation in the community has made the internal market very narrow. People depend on the outside world for the supply of goods and services. This raises a general problem: how do the goods flow into the village? Goods may be bought by the villagers directly in the outside market and brought back to the village.

Or they may be carried to the village by different kinds of middlemen. Among these three general types can be distinguished:

(1) Pedlars who visit the village periodically and sell goods at the house of the buyer.

(2) Retail stores which keep a permanent place in the village to store imported goods and attract buyers to their places.

(3) Agent boats which buy goods from the town on behalf of the consumers and transport the goods to the village.

丝绸衣服很少。甚至于米，也只是部分地供人们自己消费。所以非常明显，必须有广泛的交换系统。村里最主要的交换类型就是购销。

二、内外购销

购销是一种交换方式，在交易中对等的价值被明白地表达出来，立即付给或许诺偿付。简单地说，这就是购买和销售的过程。在农村里，除少数例外，交换一般是通过货币来进行的。

我们可以把购销分成内部和外部两种：内部购销是在村庄社区范围内交换货物和劳务，外部购销是村和外界进行的交换，它们是互相依赖的。

村的内部市场是同这个社区的职业分化有密切联系的（第八章第一节）。我们已经看到，村里三分之二以上的人口从事生产稻米、生丝和养殖羊羔的工作。他们不在村里出售这些产品，而要到城镇里去出卖。从事渔业的也只能出售一小部分产品给同村的人。生产专门货物和给村民提供专门服务的限于少数，只占总人口的7%（第八章第二节）。大部分工作并非完全专业化而是普通农户所需工作的一种补充。木匠、篾匠、泥水匠主要是从事修理工作，他们在自己家里干活，也到顾客家中去做活。

职业分化程度小，这使社区内部市场非常狭窄，人们靠外界供应货物和劳务。因而，产生了一个问题：货物如何运到村里来？农民可以直接在外部市场购买货物并带回村来，或者货物可由不同的中间人带到村里来。中间人主要可分三类：

（1）定期到村里来的小贩，在买主家门口卖东西。

（2）零售店，在村里有固定的地点，店铺里存放着从外界买来的货物，吸引顾客去购买。

（3）航船从城镇代消费者购买货物并运到村里。

❸ Pedlars

Pedlars may be regular or irregular. This depends on the type of goods they sell. Goods may be produced by the pedlars themselves or may be retailed from the market. Most of the irregular pedlars sell their own produce and do not come from the town but from other villages. This is a type of decentralized inter-village marketing outside the town. The extent of such markets is limited by the fact that the local differentiation of production within the nearby villages is not very far developed. The only differentiation, as mentioned (VII–5), is in vegetable cultivation. In the village gardens are too small to grow an amount sufficient for the consumption of the villagers. But the villagers near Lake Tai can produce large quantities of vegetables, and find their market among the nearby villages. Similarly seasonal fruits which are not grown in the village are supplied by neighbouring districts. The sellers carry their produce by boat and visit the surrounding villages.

These pedlars start with only a general expectation of a gross return and do not insist on a fixed price for each particular transaction. The seller offers a price, for instance, two coppers for three sweet potatoes. The buyer will not negotiate on the money value, but after the money has been given to the seller she will take several extra pieces. The seller may resist or pretend to resist, but I have never seen the transaction repudiated because the buyer takes too much. Such a kind of bargaining is made possible by various factors: the seller has no rigid conception of price, and the buyer no rigid idea of his demand. Moreover, there is no immediate competition on the side of either the seller or the buyer. The amount of extra goods taken will not exceed what seems reasonable to the buyer, and also varies according to many factors. For instance, men will not ask for extra pieces since, as they put it, this would hurt their self-respect; but their wives are free to do so. Conversation and joking, especially between different sexes, will increase the number of extra pieces. In such cases, the seller will voluntarily offer the extras without persuasion. Of course, the taking of extras cannot go too far, except the extras approximate to presents. In the long run it appears that the prices determined by this kind of bargaining are not higher than the market price in the town; for if it is discovered that this is in fact the case, the seller will not find it easy to sell his goods

三、小贩

　　小贩可以是固定的或不固定的，根据他们出售的货物种类而定。小贩卖的货可以是他们自己制作的，也可能是从市场上零买来的。大多数不固定的小贩出售他们自己的产品，他们来自其他村，不是来自城镇。这是一种城镇外的分散性的村际贸易活动。这种市场的范围受到这种情况的限制，即附近村子的地方生产方面分化程度不大。如已经提到过的（第七章第五节），唯一的分化是蔬菜的种植。在村里，菜园太小，不能种足量的蔬菜供村民消费。但太湖附近的农民可以种植大量蔬菜，并把附近的村子作为他们的市场。同样，时令水果，村里没有种植，是邻县供应的。卖者用船载着他们的产品到周围的村子来兜售。

　　这些小贩只盼望回去时赚到一些钱，对每一笔交易并不坚持一个固定的价格。譬如卖者报一个价，三个甜薯卖两个铜板，买者并不和他讨价还价，而是给了钱以后，再拿几块甜薯。卖者可能拒绝不给或装着拒绝，但我从未见到过因为买者拿得太多而取消交易的。这种讨价还价之所以可能是由各种因素造成的：卖者对价格没有严格的概念，买者对他自己的要价也没有严格的想法。卖者和买者都没有直接竞争者。付钱以后买者拿取额外货物的量不会超出买者看来是合理的范围，同时还有其他不同的情况。譬如说，男人就不拿额外的货物，因为他们认为，这有损于他们的自尊心；但他们的妻子可以随便这样做。对话和开玩笑，特别是异性之间开玩笑，将增加拿取额外货物的数量。在这种情况下，卖者将不经要求自愿多给一些。当然，不能拿得太多，除非把额外货物当作礼物来送。从长远看来，这种买卖的价格不比城镇里的市场价格高，因为如果买家发现小贩的价格确实比城里的市场价格高，

next time. Probably the price will also not be lower than the town price, for if the gross return obtained by the seller is less than he could obtain from selling to the stores in the town, eventually he will not come to the village. But this leaves a large margin for fluctuation in particular transactions.

There are two regular pedlars from the town: one sells tailoring and toilet articles and the other sells sweets for the children. The women in the village go to the town less frequently than the men, since they have duties in household work and care of the children. Tailoring and toilet articles are solely for women consumers. Moreover, these goods are connected with personal tastes. Women will not trust their agent or their husbands to buy for them, and it is this which gives the pedlar his market. Bargaining with such a pedlar takes a different form from that described above. The buyer will not accept the price offered and then ask for extra pieces but will try to reduce the price for a fixed amount of goods. Thus the transaction may not take place if a price satisfactory to both parties cannot be arrived at. The lowest price which the pedlar will take is determined by the amount he paid for the goods, and the amount of profit necessary to maintain his living. Since the goods are not perishable, he can wait for better terms.

The pedlar selling sweets follows another method. The demand for such goods must be artificially created by the seller. A loud bugle is used to attract children. Usually not all the children possess petty cash. Many have to ask adults to buy for them. The pedlar thus often causes dramatic domestic scenes. Children's cries and mothers' curses are mixed with the transaction of buying and selling. Bargaining is not keen because the buyer is either the child who does not know how to hide his real interest or the mother whose main purpose is to get rid of the nuisance. Part of the sweets are made in the pedlar's own house. The raw material is cheap. The price is thus determined largely by the living expenses of the pedlar.

Each of these pedlars has a customary area of peddling which includes several villages, and the area of which is determined by the distance the pedlar can walk and the profit he can make. The frequency of his visits is also thus determined. The pedlar selling tailoring and toilet articles comes to the village every two or four days, while the pedlar selling sweets comes nearly every day.

卖者下次将不易出售他的货物。可能价格也不低于城镇的商品，因为如果卖家的利润比他把商品卖给城镇的店铺要少，最后他就不到农村来卖货了。但在某些具体交易中价格上下的界限是比较宽的。

从城镇来的有两名固定的小贩：一个卖缝纫和梳妆用品，另一个卖小孩吃的糖果。女人由于有家务在身，还需照顾孩子，因此到城里去的机会比男人少。缝纫和梳妆等用品是专为妇女的消费品。此外，对这些商品的需求与个人喜好有关。妇女不愿托别人或丈夫替她购买，这才使小贩有他的市场。与这种小贩议价的形式和上述有所不同，买主不是先接受小贩的要价然后拿取额外的商品，而是先还价。因此价格如不能使双方满意时便不能达成交易。小贩要的最低价格取决于他买货时付的价钱和维持他的生活所需的利润。货物是经放的，他可以等待好一些的价钱。

卖糖果的小贩用另一种方式。对这种货物的需求必须通过卖者人为的创造。小贩用一个很响的喇叭来吸引孩子。通常孩子们不是都有零钱用的，很多孩子必须要求大人买给他们。因此，小贩常常会引起戏剧化的家庭场面。孩子的吵闹和母亲的呵责往往与买卖糖果声混杂在一起。这种买卖，讨价还价并不厉害，因为买主或是不懂得隐瞒自己真正兴趣的那些孩子，或者是一心想摆脱麻烦的孩子母亲。部分糖果是在小贩自己家里做的，原料便宜。因此糖果的价格主要取决于小贩的生活费用。

每一个小贩都有一个习惯卖货的地区，有时是几个村，范围的大小取决于小贩能走多少路，能赚多少钱。售货的次数也取决于上述因素。卖缝纫和梳妆用品的小贩每隔两天或四天到村里一次，而卖糖果的则几乎每天都来。

❹ Retail Stores

Pedlars do not live in the village. They visit the consumers periodically. Retail stores, on the other hand, are located at permanent places and attract buyers to the stores. This gives rise to a group of people who specialize in trading. They do not produce the objects which they sell, but buy them from the town and sell them to the villages. The following table shows the number of stores in their respective trades:

Grocers	3
Meat sellers	3
Bean cake sellers	2
Medicine seller	1
Brick seller	1
	—
TOATAL	10

The three groceries are located near the three bridges. They sell mainly cigarettes, matches, sweets, paper, candles, paper-money and other religious articles. I was not able to assess the total amount of their stock. Neither was I able to discover their average sales each day. The main difficulty is that they do not keep accounts. According to their information their daily sale varies from one dollar to twenty cents, and it is obvious that they are not able to supply the whole village with daily necessities of miscellaneous types. As we shall describe presently, the majority of purchases are made from the town by means of the agent boats. Chou described to me the function of these groceries, "We go to the groceries to buy cigarettes when we have guests." In other words, they are only supplements of the agent boats. The agent boats take a whole day to fulfil their customers' orders, and in urgent cases, people cannot wait until their return. They will then go to the stores. Religious articles are never needed at a very short notice, but are used at definite periods which can be foreseen. These appear in the retail stores because of the difficulty of transporting them in the agent boats. The paper-money is made of tin foils in the shape of old silver ingots. It is empty inside and so cannot be compressed. A larger space is therefore required for its transport than is available in the agent boats.

Meat is an important article of diet in the village. This is supplied by the butchers in the town through the meat dealers who go to the town at midnight and bring back to the village the amount needed in the morning.

四、零售店

小贩不住在村里。他们定期到消费者那里去。而零售店则坐落在一个固定的地方吸引顾客到店里来。这就产生了一群专门从事商业的人。他们出售的东西并不是自己生产的，而是把从城镇里买来的东西再卖给村庄。下表说明了各行业的店铺数目：

杂货店	3
肉　店	3
豆腐店	2
药　店	1
砖瓦店	1
总　共	10

三家杂货店在三座桥附近。它们主要出售香烟、火柴、糖果、纸张、蜡烛、纸钱及其他带宗教色彩的物品。我未能估计他们的存货数量。我也无从计算他们每天的平均销售量。主要困难是他们不记账。按他们所说，每天销售额两角至一元不等，很明显，他们不能供应全村以各种日用必需品。我即将谈到，大多数货物是靠航船从城里购运来的。周向我描述了杂货店的功能："我们有客人时，便到杂货店去买纸烟。"换句话说，这只是航船的一种补充。航船为了满足顾客的订货，需要花一整天的时间在城里购买，紧急需要时，顾客等不及它们回来，便到店铺里去买。带宗教色彩的东西不属于紧急需要，但在预期的某一时间内使用。又由于这些东西用航船运输有一定困难，所以人们常常可在零售店里见到这些东西。纸钱是用锡箔做成旧的银锭形，里面是空的不能受压，航船无法提供如此大的空间来运输它。

在村里，肉类是重要食物之一。肉贩在半夜去到城镇屠夫那里购买第二天早晨需要的猪肉后，将其运回村里。消费者到中午煮饭时就

Consumers are thus able to get their meat when they cook their meal at noon. Since there is no means of preserving fresh meat, the dealer will not bring more than he is certain to sell. This is often exhausted before the last buyer comes to the store, and if one wishes to make sure of the supply one must order it the evening before.

Bean cake is used as fertilizer on the farm. This is heavy and takes up much space like bricks. The agent boat cannot be cumbered with this type of goods. Thus there are special stores for them in the village. The medicine store sells Chinese herbal medicines. These are usually sold at high retail prices and are often needed at a moment's notice, therefore the store finds a place in the village.

❺ Agent Boats as Consumers' Buying Agent

The village stores cannot meet all the daily needs of the villagers. For instance, there is no place in the village from which such essential goods as salt and sugar can be bought. These must be fetched by agent boats. The agent boats offer a free daily service to purchase necessities from the town and derive their income from acting as selling agents of the villagers. They play an important function in the village economy. This institution is common in the region round the Lake Tai, and it has led to a special development of the neighbouring towns.

Every morning, about seven o'clock, the agent boats begin to be active. There are four boats in the village; two plying on Stream A and two on Streams B and C (II–4). As the boats move along the stream, the villagers give their orders to the agent, "Twenty coppers of oil for this bottle and thirty coppers of wine in that container, please." The agent collects the bottles and money. Without counting he throws the money on the floor of the hinder part of the boat. He will talk freely with his clients on other topics. When the boat reaches the west end of the village, from where it proceeds directly to the town, the agent has collected a few dozens of bottles and a large number of coppers.

The people going to the town board the boat as it passes their houses. They do not pay any fare.

Each boat has its own regular clients. The village can be divided into two areas each served by two boats. The two boats plying on the same stream draw their clients from the same area. Thus they are in competition with one another. But it is friendly competition. If there are few passengers in one boat, it will wait for the other and all the passengers

能有肉。由于没有保存鲜肉的手段，所以卖肉的商人根据他能卖出多少来买进。最后一个主顾去买肉时往往就销售一空，如果有人一定要买到肉，必须在前一天傍晚订购。

豆饼是农田的肥料，份量重，像砖一样，也占地方。航船不能运这类货物。所以村里有专门出售砖和豆饼的店铺。药店出售中草药，零售价格较高，又常常是急需的，所以药店在村里有一席之地。

五、航船，消费者的购买代理

村庄店铺不能满足农民全部日常的需求。例如村里没有地方卖盐和糖这样的重要物品。这些东西必须由航船去买。航船提供免费的日常服务，从城里购买日常必需品，同时充当村民的销售代理，从中赚得一些收入。他们在乡村经济中起着重要的作用。这种制度在太湖周围地区非常普遍，它促使附近城镇有了特殊的发展。

每天早晨约 7 时许，航船开始活跃起来。村里共有 4 条船，两条往返于河 A，两条往返于河 B 与河 C（第二章第四节）。船沿着河划出村时，农民们便向航船主订货。"请在这个瓶里打 20 个铜板的油，在那个坛里打 30 个铜板的酒。"航船主收了瓶和钱，数也不数，他把钱扔在船尾的底板上，便和顾客随便交谈起其他的话题来。船到了村的西端，从这里就可以直接到城里，那时他已经收了数十个瓶子和很多铜板。那些要到城里去的人，船经过他们的家门口时便搭上船，他们不用付船费。

每一条船有它自己固定的顾客。村子可分为两个区域，每个区域有两条船为他们服务。在一条河里的两条船，它们的顾客是同一区域的。这两条船互相就有竞争，但是友好的竞争。如果一条船上的乘客很少，它就会等另一条船，把乘客都合到一条船上。摇船的

will be transferred to the one boat. The boat is rowed by the young men passengers. The agent will classify the bottles and containers according to the orders and collect the coppers on the floor, he will join the passengers in talking or will help them to bind the silk in a proper form for selling.

From the village to the town takes two and a half hours. The boat arrives there at about ten o'clock. Each boat has connections with several stores in the town, and from these the agent will buy the articles ordered by the villagers. Salesmen in the stores come down to the boat to fetch the bottles and containers and to receive their orders from the agent. Before he returns to the boat in the afternoon, the agent will visit the stores and pay the bills. The boat begins to return at about two in the afternoon, and reaches the village between four and five. Villagers wait at their door to receive their goods as the boat passes.

One of the four boats had begun its service only about two months before I reached the village; the other three have run for many years. One of the agents, now an old man, himself inherited this profession from his father. Thus we can see that it is a very old institution.

Theoretically anyone can start an agent boat. There is no formal qualification for the agent. He has only to announce to the public that he will be an agent and will receive orders. But once started, he must carry on the business regularly every day regardless of how many orders he has received. One agent, Chou Fu-sen, was very sick when I was there, but he could not stop his service because all the clients depended on him for their daily supply. The new agent, Chou Chi-fa, often went to the town without a single order. This means that the agent must devote his whole time to his job, and this is a requirement which most of the villagers who have land to cultivate cannot fulfil. Moreover, the agent must be connected with the stores in the town, especially when he acts as the selling agent. To acquire the knowledge and custom of the trade takes time and practice.

The number of agents in an area depends on the number of orders and personal ability of the agent. An unusually able man like Fu-sen could, in the past, monopolize the whole area around Stream A, more than a hundred and fifty households. Personal ability consists of clear-mindedness and a good memory which enables an agent not to make mistakes in the numerous oral orders. It is unbelievable at first sight that anyone can manage so many orders without the help of written notes. It is in fact possible only through a slow process of becoming familiar

是年轻乘客。航船主按照顾客订货把瓶子和容器分类，把船板上的铜钱收起来，一面与乘客聊天，或帮助他们把蚕丝按照出售的要求捆起来。

从村庄到城里需要两个半小时。船约于 10 点到达。每条船与城里的一些店铺有联系，航船主就向这些店铺购买农民订购的东西。店里的学徒下船来拿瓶子和容器并接受订货。下午航船主回到船上以前，要到店铺去结账。下午两点，航船开始返回，约四五点钟到达村里。船经过时，村民都在门口等待，接受他们托买的东西。

其中有一条船在我到村子以前约两个月才开始做此项经营，另三条船已做了多年。有一个航船主，现在已年老，这一职业是从他父亲处继承的。因此，我们可以了解到，这是一个存在已久的制度。从理论上讲，任何人可以经营航船，航船主没有正式的资格，他只要向公众宣布，他将做航船这行业，接受别人委托买东西即可。但一旦开始了这个行业，他必须每天有规律地继续下去，无论他接受多少委托。有一个航船主名叫周福生，我在村里时，他病得很厉害，但他无法停止他的服务工作，因为所有顾客都靠他供应日常必需品。有一个新经营这行业的叫周志法，他有时到城里去，连一家订户都没有。这意味着，航船主必须把全部时间和精力花在经营这个行业中，大多数有地种的农民是不可能达到这种要求的。此外，航船主必须与城里的店铺有关系，特别是作为一个销售代理人。要懂得商业上的知识和习惯，需要时间和实践。

一个地区有多少航船，要看有多少居民及航船主个人有多大能力。一个像福生这样有非凡能力的人，过去垄断沿河 A 的整个地区，约 150 多户。个人能力即脑子清楚，记忆力好，不会记错各种口头的委托。一眼看去，不借助任何记录，能处理这么多瓶瓶罐罐，简直是使人无法相信的。实际上，只有经过一个缓慢的过程，

with the particular bottle or container of each client, and through training the powers of memory. Mistakes are sometimes made. Once a client claimed that he had given Fu-sen a dollar but Fu-sen could not remember the order. Although Fu-sen bore the responsibility for returning the money, the client complained. As Fu-sen's powers were thus gradually failing, Chi-fa was able to look forward to succeeding him in his area.

The agent does not ask for any commission from his clients for his service, nor make any profit therefrom, except the periodical gifts and entertainments which the stores in the town offer him. Therefore the price of articles does not rise in passing through the hands of the agent. If the villagers go to purchase directly from the town, they may sometimes get worse and less goods than if they buy through the agents. The traders in the town may cheat the individual buyers, but he cannot so treat the agents. This is not due so much to the personal ability of the agent as to the competition among the town traders to secure constant customers. Most of the stores in the town depend on the agent boats for their wide market in the villages. Losing a single boat will mean a lot to the traders. They try to keep old customers and attract new. Thus the agents gain a favourable position in the transaction.

The existence of the agent boats has put the village stores into a supplementary position. Village stores cannot compete with the agent boats. They are too small to order goods directly from big wholesale stores in the cities, as the town stores do. They buy from the town stores like the agent boats. But the agent boats offer free services in buying while the village traders have to make a profit from retailing. As shown above, the village stores can only find a market in articles which are urgently needed and those which are too heavy to be transported by the agent boats.

The agents do not keep written accounts. I therefore found it rather difficult to assess the amount of their transactions. Fu-sen gave me his estimate as about ten to twenty dollars a day. The highest record was forty dollars a day near the end of the year. This seems to be a reasonable estimate, because it can roughly be checked with the general amount of goods that the village obtains from outside. According to the estimate given in the analysis of household expenditure (VII–8), this is about 80,000 dollars every year. If we exclude from this amount the expenses for clothing, vegetables, heavy tools, and mulberry leaves, which are not purchased through the agent boats, it amounts to 30,000 dollars, and this gives an approximate average similar to the above estimate.

才能逐渐熟悉每一个顾客的瓶子或罐头，记得每个顾客经常的需要。有时也会记错，有一次一个顾客说，给了福生一元钱，但福生不记得他这件事了。虽然福生毫不犹豫地负责还了他一元钱，但顾客还是埋怨。当福生的能力逐渐衰退时，志法已能够在他这地区开始接替他了。

航船主为顾客服务并不向顾客索取佣金，也不从中赚钱，城里的店铺定时送他一些礼物或招待他。货物通过航船主的手，价格并不提高。如果农民自己直接到城镇商店去买，他们可能得到更少或更坏的东西，城里的商人可能欺侮个别来的买主，而他不敢欺侮航船主。这并不光是因为航船主个人能力比城里的商人强，更是由于城镇商人竞争需要保持经常的主顾。大多数城里的店铺依赖航船来得到农村这个广阔的市场。对商人来说，失去一条船即意味着很大的损失。他们力图保持旧主顾，吸引新主顾。因此行贩在交易中是处于有利地位的。

航船的存在使村庄的店铺处于一种辅助性的地位。村庄店铺无法与航船竞争。它们太小，不能像城镇商店那样直接向城市里的大批发商店订货。它们也像航船一样向城镇店铺购货。但航船代客买东西免收服务费，而村庄的商人零售时要赚钱。如上所述，村庄小店里只有那些急需品以及航船不能运输的货物才有买主。

航船主不记账，所以我无从估计他们的交易额。福生作了一个估计，每天约 10 ～ 20 元。快到年底时，最高记录为每天 40 元。看来，这一估计是可靠的，可以从农民向外购货的总金额来核对一下。按农户开支的分析（第七章第八节），估计每年约为 8 万元。如果我们从这一数字减去衣服、蔬菜、重型工具和桑叶的费用，这些东西不是通过航船购买的，约为 3 万元，这与福生的估计大致相似。

I was not able to make a complete list of articles that the agent boats buy from the town. The list must be a very long one because all goods that can be bought in the town and can be transported by boat are ordered from the agent. Small quantities of those things such as bean cakes, bricks, and paper-money, during the time when the boat is not crowded, are also orderable. The most common goods found in the agent boats are food and ingredients for cooking.

To complete the description of the buying process, it is necessary to mention again the direct purchase by the consumers in the town market or from other villages. For instance, not enough mulberry leaves, the essential raw material for the silk industry, are grown in the village. The villagers must buy them from the other villages near the Lake Tai. The buyer goes personally and transports the goods himself. Every time people come to the town they will do some shopping. The amount of trade through this process is difficult to estimate. But as the villagers do not go to the town very often, it is thus limited.

❻ Agent Boats as Producers' Selling Agent

One important feature of the agent boat is that it does not make any profit as a buying agent of the consumers. Similarly passengers do not pay any fare (except that the young men are obliged to row the boat). The gift given by the town stores are far from enough to provide the agent with a living. The agents obtain their reward by acting as the selling agents of the producers.

The process of selling requires much skill and knowledge of the market which the villagers do not necessarily possess. When they sell their produce, they rely on the agents. The agents are constantly in touch with the collectors in the town and know every detail about the different collectors. Because the collectors are connected with different traders or weaving factories they have particular preferences in what they purchase. It is essential for the producers to get in touch with the right collector for his particular produce. Moreover, in collecting silk, there is an accepted practice by which the producer is allowed to add a certain amount of cotton and water to the silk in order to increase its weight. But if the conventional limit is exceeded the collector will deduct from his payment more than the weight of the cotton and the water added. Therefore the expert advice of the agent is needed.

我不能把航船从城镇购买的商品开列一个清单。这个清单一定会很长，因为所有从城镇购买的、航船可以运输的商品都可以委托航船去购买。船不挤的时候，少量的豆饼、砖、纸钱一类的商品也可代购。委托航船购买最多的东西是食品和烹调用的配料或调料。

为了对购买过程进行全面的描述，必须重提一下消费者从城镇市场或其他村庄直接购买的商品。譬如，村里桑叶不够，这是蚕丝工业的重要原料。村民必须从太湖附近的其他村庄购买。买主自己去购买和运输，每次他们进城，都要买些其他东西。通过这一渠道进行的贸易额就难以估计。但由于村民不常进城，所以买的东西也有限。

六、航船，生产者的销售代理

航船的一个重要特点是作为消费者的代购人，是不赚钱的。同样，乘客也不付船费（年轻人得出劳力划船除外）。城镇店铺给航船主的礼物远远不足以维持他们的生活。他们只有在充当生产者的销售代理人时才得到报酬。

销售货物需要更多的技巧和有关市场的知识，农民不一定具备，因此他们出售产品时需要依靠航船主。后者经常与城镇里的收购商品的行家保持联系。他了解各个行家的情况。行家与不同的商人或纺织厂相联系，他们收购货物是有挑选的。生产者为了出售他们的某种产品应该知道与那些有关的收购人保持联系，这是很重要的。此外，在收购生丝的时候，有一种已经被收购者接受了的习惯做法，即允许生产者在丝里加一定量的棉花和水以加重分量。但如果超过惯常的限量，收购者便要扣钱，扣的数量比外加分量的钱更多。因此，生产者需要就这方面的业务与内行的代理人商量。

The agent will help the producer to bind the silk in a proper way so that the same amount and quality of silk will yield the highest possible return. The producer goes with the agent to the collector. But the collector will recognize only the agent whose name appears on his account. If the producer does not accept the price, he is free to withdraw his produce. But generally he will follow the advice of the agent whom he trusts. When the producer sells 100 Liang (11.3 lbs.) of silk, about 25 dollars at the present price, he will pay the agent 1 dollar commission. In other words, the agent will get 4 per cent. commission from the amount of silk sold. The amount of the reward does not change according to the price. So when the price is high, the rate of commission is much lower. In the case of rice, the commission is 5 cents for 3 bushels, which will yield about 7 dollars for the producer. The percentage of commission is about 0.7. The total production of silk in this village is about 90,000 Liang which will give 900 dollars for the agents' commission. The total exported rice is about 7,000 bushels which will give a total commission for the agents of about 650 dollars. If this amount is equally divided among the four agents, each will get about 400 dollars a year. That amount will provide them with a fairly good living.

Those who have paid commission to the agents on the sale of their produce are entitled to use the boats for communication and to order goods through them. The payment for this service is thus distributed according to the amount of production but not to the amount of consumption of the clients.

The sheep raising recently introduced has added a new source of income to the agent; but I do not know the exact system of commission for selling sheep.

The change in the silk industry had challenged the very existence of the institution. The new silk factory does not make use of the selling agents in the town market. The produce is sold directly to Shanghai. At the start, the agent appealed for compensation. The reformers regarded the agent boats as a useful institution in the village and decided to support it by giving compensation according to the traditional amount of commission. Each member of the co-operative society receives a card on which the amount of his cocoon supply is recorded. The producer can give the card to the agent whom he uses as his buying agent. The agent in return receives compensation according to the total amount of cocoons recorded on the member's card. In this way the institution of the agent boat has been saved.

　　航船主还帮助生产者按照购买者的要求来包装蚕丝，以便使同样数量、质量的丝能卖到较高的价钱。生产者与航船主一起到收购人那里去，但收购人只认识航船主，他的账上有航船主的户头。如果生产者不接受对方的价格，他可以不出售他的产品。但在一般情况下，他听从他所信任的航船主的忠告。生产者如果出售100两蚕丝，约合当前的市价25元，他便付给航船主1元钱佣金。换句话说，航船主按生产者出售蚕丝的数量拿4%的佣金。佣金数不随蚕丝价格的变化而变化。因此，蚕丝价格高时佣金率反而低。每出售3蒲式耳米要给佣金5分，生产者收益约合7元，佣金百分率约为0.7%。这个村庄的蚕丝总生产量约为9万两，航船主可得900元佣金。大米的总出口量为7,000蒲式耳，航船主可得总数约为650元的佣金。如果四个航船主平分这个数额，每人一年约得400元。有这样一笔数目，生活可以过得不错了。

　　那些卖出产品后付给航船主佣金的人，有权把船当作交通工具使用，而且可委托航船主购买货物。因此，此项服务的支付额是根据生产量来定，而不是根据顾客的消费量来定的。

　　新近的养羊工作为航船主增加了一项新的收入来源，但我不知道卖羊收佣金的确切办法。

　　蚕丝业的改革对航船制度的存在提出了挑战。新的丝厂不利用航船到城镇市场去代销蚕丝，产品直销上海。开始时，航船主要求补偿。改革者考虑到航船是村里一种有用的制度，因此决定根据传统的佣金额给他们补偿。合作社的每一个社员收到一张卡片，上面记录着他供应蚕茧的数量。生产者可以把卡片交给他委托购买东西的航船主。根据合作社社员卡片上记载的蚕茧供应数量，航船主可收到一定数量的补偿费。这样才把航船制度保存了下来。

❼ Other Types of Collecting

The staple rural products are collected by the town through the agent boats or by the city through the factory. But for minor objects—and waste goods—such as old clothes, the ashes of paper money and old metal objects, there is yet another manner of collection. Sometimes this takes the form of barter, that is, direct exchange of objects. The collector carries with him porcelain articles or a special type of sweets to exchange for old clothes and metal objects. Ashes of paper-money, which contain tin, are exchanged for sheets of tin foil from which the paper-money is made.

❽ Marketing Areas and the Town

The size of a marketing area is determined by the system of transport—the cost and time involved in the movement of persons and goods. The primary market, in which the consumers buy their goods directly, is limited to an area in which the buyer can get his goods without spending so much time as to hamper his other activities. In this village we can distinguish two primary marketing areas. The people living near the bridge on Stream B will not make purchases from the stores near the bridge on Stream A. For instance, barbers, meat sellers, groceries, and temples are all segregated in these two areas, roughly corresponding to the areas divided by the activities of the agent boats. But the silversmith, the shoemaker, and the medicine store are located near the west bridge on Stream A, the centre of the intra-village route system (II–4). These are the only stores of their kind in the village. To this extent, the village is also a primary market.

The secondary market is that from which the retail dealers in the primary market draw their goods at wholesale prices. In this region, the agent boat cannot be considered as a retailer. It makes purchases on behalf of the consumers, but, as we have seen, without making a charge for this service. The agent boat thus restricts the function of the primary market in the village and enables the distant town to be the centre of primary purchase of the consumers.

The agent, specializing in this function, can spend all his time in this activity. Thus the distance between the buyer and the seller is lengthened to that practicable for a daily return trip. The actual distance depends on the rate of movement of the boat, which is estimated at about 1.6 miles per hour. The farthest village that is able to send its agent boat to

七、其他收集方式

大宗的农村产品由城镇通过航船或由城市通过工厂收购。但对一些零星物品和废品——如旧衣服、纸钱灰、废铜烂铁等还有另一种收购方法。有时候是以货易货的形式出现，即货物直接交换。收购者带着陶瓷器或一种特别的糖果来换取旧衣服和金属器皿。纸钱灰含锡，可换叠纸钱的锡箔。

八、贸易区域和集镇

贸易区域的大小取决于运输系统——人员及货物流动所需的费用和时间。消费者直接购买货物的初级市场局限于这样一个区域，即买者不需要花很多时间以致妨碍他的其他活动便可在其中买到货物。在这个村里我们可以看出来，有两个初级购销区域。住在河 B 的桥附近的人们不会到河 A 的桥附近的商店去买东西。例如，理发店、肉店、杂货店和庙宇都分设在两个地区，大致与航船活动分工范围相当。但银匠、鞋匠和药店坐落在河 A 的西桥附近，这里是村内道路系统的中心（第二章第四节）。这些行业在村里各自只有这一家店。从这个意义上说，这个村子也是一个初级市场。

中级市场就是初级市场的零售商用批发价格购买货物的地方。在这个地区，航船不能被看作是一个零售商。它代替消费者买货，但正如我们知道的，这项服务不收费。这样，航船便限制了村里初级市场的作用，并使远处的城镇成为消费者初级购买的中心。

专门从事这项工作的航船主能把他所有的时间用于这一活动。因此，购买者和出售者之间的距离便延长到适于当日往返的旅程。实际距离取决于船的速度，估计每小时为 1.6 英里。能够派出航船到镇上代购货物的村子，其最远的距离不能超出 5 英里以外。

the town cannot lie farther than 5 miles distant. The diameter of such a marketing area is thus between 8 and 10 miles.

At the centre of each marketing area is a town, the essential difference of which from the village lies in the fact that the population in the town is mainly occupied in non-agricultural work. The town is for villagers the centre of exchange with the outside world. The villagers buy most of their manufactured goods from the middlemen in the town and supply their produce to the collector there. The development of the town depends on the number of customers that can be attracted to it. As we have seen, the institution of the agent boat enables the town in this region to concentrate the primary purchase from its tributary villages and thus reduce the function of the village traders. The size of the marketing area of this type is much larger than that found in North China, where land transport is predominant and the agent system is not developed. A study by C. K. Yang[49] showed that the marketing area, above that of the primary village market, typical in North China, is about $1\frac{1}{2}$ miles to 3 miles in diameter. The marketing area of a higher order, consisting of six basic marketing areas, is about 8 to 12 miles in diameter. The latter type is comparable in size to the town market in the region we are investigating.

The town on which the village depends—that is, the town to which the agent boats go daily—is called Chên Tsê, about 4 miles south of the village. It is true that the town does not monopolize all the marketing activities of the village. There is another town in the north, called Tai Miao Chiung, about $1\frac{1}{2}$ miles from the village on the bank of Lake Tai (Map II). This is a small town specializing in trade with the islands in the lake. Near the town is a temple of the God of Lake Tai from which the name of the town is derived. When the people visit the temple they usually do some shopping in the town. To walk there takes about $1\frac{1}{2}$ hours. But trade between the village and Tai Maio Chiung is insignificant as compared with that with Chên Tsê.

In the process of collecting rural produce, Chên Tsê monopolizes nearly all the rice trade of the village. But it has never completely monopolized the silk produce, and since the establishment of the silk factory in the village, manufactured silk has been directly transported to Shanghai. Even in former times, when the village supplied a large quantity of raw silk for the weaving industry in Sheng Tsê, a town about 12 miles east of the village, there was a boat which plied direct to that town. It was too far for a daily return trip, and the service was irregular,

因此，这样一个购销区域的直径是 8～10 英里。

每个贸易区域的中心是一个镇，它与村庄的主要区别是，城镇人口的主要职业是非农业工作。镇是农民与外界进行交换的中心。农民从城镇的中间商人那里购买工业品并向那里的收购的行家出售他们的产品。城镇的发展取决于它吸引顾客的多少。正如我们已经了解的，航船的制度使这一地区的城镇把附属村庄的初级购买活动集中了起来，从而减弱了农村商人的作用。这一类购销区域的范围比中国北方的购销区域大得多，中国北方主要是陆路运输，代购或代销体系不发达。杨庆堃的研究 [49] 说明了在村庄初级市场之上的典型的中国北方购销区域的直径约为 1.5～3 英里。更高一级的购销区域，包含 6 个基本购销区域，其直径约为 8～12 英里。后者与我们现在正在研究的城镇市场规模相仿。

这个村庄所依托的城镇，就是航船每天去的镇，叫做震泽，在村庄以南约 4 英里的地方。其实，这个镇没有垄断这个村庄的全部贸易活动。在北面，还有一个镇，叫大庙港，离村庄约 1.5 英里，在太湖边上（见地图 II）。这是一个专门与太湖里的岛屿进行贸易的小镇。镇附近有一座太湖神庙，镇由此而得名。人们去庙宇的时候，通常在这个镇里购买物品。徒步走去需要约 1.5 小时。但这个村庄和大庙港之间的贸易同这个村庄和震泽镇的贸易相比是无足轻重的。

在收购农产品的过程中，震泽镇垄断了这个村庄全部大米的贸易。但它从未完全垄断蚕丝产品，而且自从村中丝厂成立以来，加过工的蚕丝被直接运到上海。即使在过去，这个村庄也供应大量生丝给村东约 12 英里处的盛泽镇丝织工业，那时还有一条航船直接往返此镇。路程太远，不能当天往返，班次也不定期，所以只管售货。

so the boat was only engaged in selling. It ceased to run more than ten years ago owing on the one hand to the decline of the weaving industry of the town, and on the other to the reform of the silk industry in the village.

An interesting study might be made of the competition of the towns to secure tributary territories. But a detailed analysis of this problem requires a wider investigation of the whole region than the present study could afford.

❾ Marketing and Production

Silk and sheep are produced entirely for selling. We have already seen how the price has affected the production in these industries. The low price of native silk stimulated the reform programme. As a result of the reform, the amount of the production of native silk was greatly reduced. But in recent years, the amount has not declined in proportion to the decline of price. On the contrary there are signs of an increase. As explained, this is due to the lack of other work to absorb the surplus female labour in the village. Sheep raising was started because of the new demand of the market. But the amount of production cannot be increased while supply of grass is limited as at present. Price is thus not the only factor determining the volume of production.

Rice is produced partly for selling and partly for consumption. The amount of reserve does not necessarily fluctuate according to the price. Each household will try to reserve enough rice for a year's consumption. A high market price of rice will not induce the producer to sell his reserves, because the future price level is uncertain. But a low price will force people to sell more rice to the market; this is because the amount of money income needed by each household is more or less known at the time of harvest when the tenants are required to pay their rent in terms of money. This fact is important for the rice collectors. They usually try to force down the price in order to increase the volume of trade. The villagers' total reserve is frequently so reduced as to be insufficient for their own consumption. In the following summer the villagers will be dependent on outside supply (XV–3). This also is to the benefit of the trader.

The fluctuation of price does not affect the total production of rice. The total amount is determined by the size of the land, the technique of production, and last, but not least, the supply of rainfall. These are matters over which the people have little control. Change of occupation is difficult and even change of crop seldom comes to the minds of the villagers.

十多年前，一方面由于该镇丝织工业衰落，另一方面由于这个村庄的蚕丝业改革，此船就已经停止了。

关于城镇之间如何竞争以保持它们的附属村庄，将是一个有趣的研究。但是对这一问题的详细分析，需要对整个地区作更广泛的调查，这不是目前的研究所能达到的。

九、销售与生产

丝和羊完全是为出售而生产的。我们已经看到，在这些行业中，价格是如何影响生产的。土产生丝的价格低廉，催生了改革计划。改革结果是土产生丝产量大大下降。但近年来，其产量并未按其价格下降的比率下降，相反，还有一些增加的迹象。正如已经解释过的，这是由于缺乏其他工作来吸收村里剩余的妇女劳力的缘故。村里开始养羊，这是因为市场有新的需要。但目前缺乏草的供应，产量不可能增加。因此，价格不是决定产量的唯一因素。

生产大米，部分是为出售，部分是为消费。储备粮的数量不一定根据价格的波动而升降。每一户都要准备够一年消费的储备粮。市场大米价格上涨不会诱使生产者出售他的存粮，因为未来的大米价格不确定。但大米价格低会迫使农民出售更多的大米。这是因为收割的时候要求佃农用钱交租，那时每户所需要的货币收入或多或少都已知道。这一事实，对大米收购者来说很重要。他们通常为了增加贸易额而压低大米价格。农民的总储备量往往就这样被减少到不够他们自己消费。来年夏季，他们就只得靠外界供应（第十五章第三节）。这样商人也有利可图。

价格波动不影响大米的总生产量。总生产量取决于土地的大小、生产的技术以及最终取决于降雨量的多少。这些都是人们几乎不能控制的事。改变职业是困难的，甚至改变农作物，村民都很少想到。

Thus the structure of production is a rigid one and does not react elastically to the demand of the market. When changes take place, they are gradual and far-reaching.

Let us take the silk industry as an example. The adjustment between the new demand of the market and the productive system has taken nearly ten years in spite of a well-planned programme and special efforts. From our analysis of the changing process (XII), we have seen that the effectiveness of supply and demand depends on a knowledge of the market which villagers do not always possess. Without some special agents to affect a change, the people would hardly understand the cause of the decline of price and still less define the type of goods that would meet the new demand of the market. To bring about a change in the industry, special knowledge and social organization are needed. All these factors delay an immediate and automatic adjustment of supply and demand in the rural economy.

Change of occupation in the village is more difficult than reform of an existing industry. No serious attempt has yet been made to find out the possibility of introducing new industries to the village besides sheep raising. Even the latter is only a supplement to the existing productive system and not a change of occupation. Villagers can change their occupation only by leaving the village. In other words, occupational mobility under the present situation means a mobility of population from the village to the town. In the village, those who go out to find new occupation are mostly young girls who have not yet entered into a fixed social place in the community. Even in this group, such mobility has already challenged the traditional kinship relation and the stability of the domestic group (XII–9). The reaction against the disruptive forces in social stability becomes a force to counteract the present mobility. It is difficult to say at the present stage how far the traditional forces will give way in the novel situation. But on the whole the slow mobility of population, especially of the male population, indicates the slow effect of the outside demand for labour and the rigidity of the traditional productive system in the village.

Nevertheless it is clear that the market affects production strongly. It has led to various changes which are not limited to economic life only. The reaction of the productive system to market conditions does not take a simple course but is a long and involved process which requires investigation in a wider perspective than that of a purely economic inquiry.

因此，生产结构是受到严格限制的，它不能随着市场的需求作出灵活的反应，变化是缓慢而长远的。

让我们以丝业作为例子。尽管在蚕丝业方面有很好的改革计划，计划者对改革也作出了特殊的努力，但市场的新需求与生产系统之间的调整过程经历了几乎十年的时间。从我们对变迁过程的分析（第十二章），我们看到供应和需求的有效性取决于对市场的了解，这是农民不具备的。如果没有特殊的力量来影响并促使变革，人们几乎不理解蚕丝价格下跌的原因，更不明白什么样的货物类型才能满足市场的新需求。为了实现蚕丝改革，需要专门的知识和社会组织。所有这些因素都会延误乡村经济在供求方面的及时自动调整。

在农村，改变职业比改革现有作业更加困难。除养羊以外，没有发现人们想在村里发展新的职业。甚至养羊也仅仅是现有生产系统的一种补充，而不是职业的改变。农村居民只有离开农村才能改变他们的职业。换句话说，在目前情况下，职业流动意味着人口从农村流向城镇。在村里，出去找新职业的大多数是女青年，她们在这个社区里尚未进入一个固定的社会位置。甚至在这个群体里，这种流动已经向传统亲属关系和家庭群体的稳定性提出了挑战（第十二章第九节）。反抗破坏社会稳定的力量变成了一股阻碍当前人口流动的力量。目前很难说，在新的情况下，传统力量会作多少让步。但总的来说，人口流动是缓慢的，特别是男性人口流动得很少，这说明了外界对劳动的需求不大和村里传统生产系统的僵化。

尽管如此，市场强烈地影响着生产，这一点是显而易见的。它导致了各方面的变化，这些变化不仅仅局限于人们的经济生活。生产系统对市场情况的反应不是一个简单的过程，而是一个长期复杂的过程，要了解这一过程需进行范围更广泛的调查研究，单纯从经济方面研究是不够的。

CHAPTER XV   FINANCE

The problem of credit rises when, in the process of exchange, the return either in the form of goods and services or of money is delayed. Credit, in its simple sense, is the trust by one party in another for an eventual return after a certain lapse of time.

In this sense non-immediate forms of exchange such as mutual obligation, mutual accommodations, and gift-making, are forms of credit. The return of these types of credit is secured by the principle of reciprocity inherent in the social institutions and is bound up with the ties of kinship and friendship. For transactions outside the group thus related, the time for repayment has to be explicitly agreed upon and credit can only be received by the economic benefits of the transaction.

The loan may be used for any purpose or may be limited to certain uses prescribed by the agreement. But the term credit cannot be limited to refer only to advances for future production. In the village, credit is in most cases for consumption or for payment of tax and rent which is only indirectly related to the process of production. Similarly it is difficult to regard (except in a very metaphorical sense) the money borrowed to finance a marriage ceremony as a help to the borrower's productive ability.

Professor Tawney, in his discussion on the problem of the credit system in rural China, says, "The characteristic feature of the system... is that neither borrower nor lender appears to make any clear distinction between loans needed to finance the business of farming, and loans sought to eke out the domestic budget. Everything goes down, so to speak, in a common account, with the result that there is no discrimination in the mind of either debtor or creditor between the borrowing and advancing of money for productive purposes, which should yield a return sufficient to meet the interest, and household expenses which ought, in the absence of exceptional misfortune, to be met out of income."[50]

In this chapter, I shall use the term credit in its broad sense.

❶ Saving and Deficiency

Credit is possible only when there is saving on the one hand and deficiency on the other. Saving is the surplus of income over expenditure in an economic unit, in the village the Chia. Income is the total production of the Chia. It may or may not be converted into money.

拾伍 资金

在交换过程中，以货物、劳务或现金不能及时偿还时便发生了信贷。简单地说，信贷就是一方信赖另一方，经过延迟一段时间，最后偿还。

在这一意义上讲，相互之间的义务、互相接待留宿、互赠礼物等非即刻交换的形式也是信贷的形式。这些信贷的偿还是通过社会制度中固有的互惠原则来保证的，并与亲属关系及友谊有密切关系。对于有这种关系的群体之外的交易，偿还的时间必须有明确的协议，并且信贷只有对贷方有利才能被接受。

贷款可以作任何用途，或可能限于协议中规定的某种用途。但信贷一词不能仅限于指对未来产品的预先付款。在这个村里，信贷在多数情况下是用于消费或付租付税，租和税与生产过程仅有间接的关系。同样地，也很难把借来办婚事的钱看作是对借钱人的生产能力有所帮助（除非是隐喻的意义）。

在讨论中国农村的信贷体系时，托尼教授写道："这个体系的特点……是借钱人和出借人对用于农业生产的信贷和补助家庭开支的借款两者之间的区别看来都不清楚。这就是说，把一切都记作一笔笼统的账，结果，在欠债人或债权人的脑海中对借贷来作生产用途或家庭用途的钱无所区别。他们不明白：用于生产的钱最后应该产生利润并足以偿还利息，家庭开支在没有意外的不幸事故的情况下，应能以收入偿付。"[50]

在本章，我将从信贷的广泛意义上来使用这一术语。

一、积蓄与亏空

信贷只有在一方面有积蓄、另一方面亏空时才可能产生。积蓄是指村里的经济单位家庭的收入超过支出时的剩余。收入指家庭的全部产品。它可以转换为钱，也可以不转换为钱。支出则包括家庭的成员

Expenditure includes all the goods, produced by the unit or purchased on the market, used by the members for consumption, for fulfilment of social obligation and for production.

The amount of production of each Chia in the village does not vary much because the groups are very similar in size, and in their technique of production. There is also uniformity in the amount of consumption among them (VII–1). The inequality in the distribution of wealth is, apart from special reasons in individual cases, mainly due to the system of land tenure. A tenant has to bear a heavy burden of rent. Two-thirds of the land in the village is now in the hands of absentee landlords. Each year the villagers pay in total 4,800 bushels of rice for rent. This burden is not shared equally by the villagers, but is spread over about 70 per cent. of the people. Among these again the burden is not equal (XI–5). The system of land tenure has resulted in an annual outflow of a large quantity of wealth from the village to the town and an unequal distribution of wealth in the village.

When the silk industry was prosperous the villagers, in spite of high rents, were able to enjoy a sufficient standard of living and could in consequence save. This saving was usually hoarded. The opportunity for investment in the village is limited and there is no other means, except in rent, for the town to absorb its accumulated wealth. The goods or money hoarded were used firstly for a reserve against recurrent disaster and secondly for financing expensive ceremonies. The elaborate ceremonies in connection with individual life crises or periodical religious meetings of the local groups were in fact an important outlet for the hoarded wealth of the rural district. On ceremonial occasions the idea of thrift gives place to competitive display. Wealth was lavishly expended in burials, on marriage gifts, on dowries and feasts, and especially in inter-village parades (VII–7).

The depression of the silk industry has caused a decline of one-third of the average income of the village (XII–2). On the side of expenditure, consumption and social obligations have remained largely as they were. The only elastic item that can be reduced or suspended is ceremonial expenditure; and according to my estimate, the minimum amount of such expense at present is only one-fifth of the total money expenditure (VII–8). With the rapid decline of the income level, accompanied by a rigid level of expenditure, deficiency is the result.

用于消费、用于完成社会义务和用于生产而由自家生产或从市场购买的全部物品。

村里每家的生产量相差不大，因为这种群体的大小大致相仿，生产技术亦基本相同。它们的消费量也有一致性（第七章第一节）。除个别情况有特殊原因外，其财产分配不平等的原因，主要是土地占有制问题。佃农必须负担很重的地租。村里三分之二的土地为不在地主掌握。村民每年交付租米总额为 4,800 蒲式耳。这一负担并不是平均分摊在村民身上，而是由约 70% 的人分担。在这些人中间，负担又不同（第十一章第五节）。土地占有制的这种情况导致了每年大量财富从村里外流到城镇，以及村中财富分配不均的情况。

蚕丝业兴旺时，尽管地租很高，但村民仍可维持足够的生活水平，并且尚可有所积蓄。这种积蓄通常被储藏起来。在村里，很少有投资的机会，除交租以外，城镇没有其他手段吸收积累的财富。农民储藏的货物或金钱首先是用作储备以对付经常发生的灾难，其次是供昂贵的礼节性开支。与人生大事相关的繁重礼节或当地群体定期的宗教集会实际上是农村地区所积蓄的财富的重要出路。在礼节性场合，炫耀财富的思想替代了勤俭节约。在丧葬、结婚聘礼、嫁妆、宴席等方面，特别是举行村际游行时，财富挥霍严重（第七章第七节）。

蚕丝业的萧条使村里的平均收入减少了三分之一（第十二章第二节）。在开支方面，消费和社会义务仍然像过去一样。唯一可以缩减或暂缓的款项是礼仪性开支，据我估计，目前这种开支占总货币开支的五分之一（第七章第八节）。由于收入迅速降低，支出依然不变，结果是亏空。

Deficiency may be urgent or may not be urgent. Urgent deficiency calls for immediate measures. It is found in such situations as food shortage, lack of capital goods, and inability to pay rent and tax. Unless financial aid in these cases is forthcoming there will be disastrous consequences to the individuals concerned. Owing to the unequal distribution of rent obligations, deficiences of this urgent kind are confined to a part of the villagers. There is still a small group which, even in present circumstances, is able to save and another group which is able to meet all the minimum requirements of subsistence. But deficiency of a less urgent nature, such as inability to pay for ceremonial occasions, is more common even among the better-off group. I have already described how the villagers have suspended their annual meeting, delayed their marriages, and reduced their ceremonial expenses.

The decline of the ability to save has caused an increasing need for outside financial help. The internal credit system functions only as a means to cope with the unequal distribution of wealth within the community. It cannot meet the situation of general insolvency. Thus external aid has become the urgent financial problem in the village.

In the following sections, I shall describe the working of various internal and external credit systems. But the present material is not sufficient to define their relative importance in quantitative terms. Such data, important as they are, require more extensive inquiries than I was able to make.

❷ Financial Aid Society

As with goods and services, small sums of money can be borrowed from relatives or friends for a short term without interest. This system of mutual allowance is found chiefly in cases of temporary deficiency, and the creditor is confident in the ability of the debtor to repay within a short time. But the term of such allowance may extend over a period of months. Such relatively long-term credit is frequently found among brothers after division of the Chia. Although they may have separate houses and properties, they are still bound by social ties to look after each other's welfare. To demand interest from a brother for any small loan is considered to be impossible.

But when a large sum is needed, it is difficult to borrow from one individual and to repay in a short time. Here the mutual help among brothers or other relatives becomes inadequate. Hence there is the financial aid society.

亏空可以是紧急的或非紧急的。紧急亏空需要立即采取措施。食物不足、资本货物缺少、无能力付租付税等属于这种情况。除非给以资助，否则对有关个人会产生灾难性结果。由于付租义务并不是人人都有的，这种紧急亏空限于一部分村民。一小部分人，即使在目前情况下，仍能有些积蓄，还有另一些人则可以维持最低限度的生活。非紧急亏空，例如无力支付礼仪所需的费用，即使在比较有钱的人中间也比较平常。我已经描述过村民是怎样推迟婚期、暂停每年的团聚、缩减礼仪性开支等情况。

积蓄减少造成了对外界资金支援的需求增加。内部借贷系统只能对付这个社区内部财富分配上的不平等，不能解决普遍无力偿付债务的问题。因此外界资金援助便成为村里紧急的金融问题。

以下各节，我将描述各种内部和外部的信贷系统。但目前掌握的材料不足以从定量分析方面来阐明它们相对的重要性。这种数据很重要，但需要比我现在所能做到的更广泛的调查研究。

二、互助会

物品、劳务和少量的钱可以不付利息，短期地向亲戚朋友借用。这种补贴的办法主要见于遇有暂时性亏空时，债权人相信借款人有能力在短期内还债。此类借贷可能延续数个月。这种相对较长期的信贷在分家后的兄弟之间常见。他们虽然有各自的房子和财产，但仍然有社会纽带把他们联系起来，照顾彼此的福利。为少量借款向兄弟要利息，被认为是不可能的。

但需要大笔款项时，向个人商借并在短期内归还常有困难。因此，兄弟之间或其他亲戚之间的互相帮助便不能满足需要。这样才产生了互助会。

The financial aid society is a mechanism for collective saving and lending. It consists of a number of members and lasts for a number of years. The members meet several times a year. At each meeting, each subscribes a share. The total subscription of the members is collected by one of the members who can thus use the money to finance his activities. Each member in turn collects the sum. The first collector is the organizer. From the very beginning, he is a debtor to the society. He repays his loan bit by bit during the whole course with a certain amount of interest. The last collector is a depositor. He collects at the end the sum of his deposit and its interest. Other members change from depositor to debtor as they collect the sum. The order of collection is determined either by contract or by lot, or by auction. The system of calculating the amount of subscription of each member in each meeting is sometimes complicated by various factors which will be described later.

Such a society is organized on the initiative of the person who needs financial help. Members who join the society are considered as having rendered help to the organizer. According to the system described above, it would appear that all the members in turn would profit by the society. But we must remember that, with the limited opportunity of investment, to raise a loan and to pay interest on it may be uneconomical. Moreover, owing to the uncertainty of time of the collection, it may be difficult for the collector to find a profitable use for the money collected. Therefore, the organizer cannot appeal to members on economic grounds only. He must state his need of aid and ask for help. Membership is thus usually limited to certain groups of persons who are obliged to help the organizer and those who are willing to join for other purposes.

The usual purpose of organizing such a society is to finance marriage ceremonies. Repayment of a debt incurred for such proper reasons as the financing of a funeral ceremony may also be regarded as acceptable ground. But productive purposes, such as starting a business or buying a piece of land, are not so regarded.

Given a proper purpose, the organizer will approach his relatives: father's brother, brother, sister's husband, mother's brother, wife's father, etc. These have an obligation to join the society. Even when they are unable to subscribe, they will find some of their relatives to take their place.

The number of members varies from eight to fourteen. In the village the kinship circle, in which intimate relations are maintained, is sometimes smaller. Membership may then be extended to relatives' relative or friends. These are recruited by appealing, not to social

互助会是集体储蓄和借贷的机构，由若干会员组成，为时若干年。会员每年相聚数次。每次聚会时存一份款。各会员存的总数，由一个会员收集借用。每一个会员轮流收集使用存款。第一个收集人即组织者。一开始，他是该会的借债人。他分期还款，交一定量的利息。最后一个收集人是存款人。他最后收集自己那笔存款和利息。其他成员则依次收集存款，从存款人变为借债人。收款次序按协议、抽签或自报公议的办法决定。每次聚会时，每一会员存款数目的计算往往由于各种因素而变得较为复杂，我将在以后描述。

这种互助会，经常是由于某人需要经济援助而发起组成的。参加互助会的会员被认为是对组织者的帮助。按以上描述的办法，每个人似乎都轮流得到好处。但我们必须记住，投资的机会有限，借一笔款并付利息，可能是不经济的。此外，由于收钱时间不定，收款人可能难以把收来的钱用于最适当的需要。所以组织者对会员不能只强调他们在经济上会得到什么好处，而必须说他自己需要经济上的帮助。因此，会员通常只限于某些有义务帮助组织者的人或一些为了其他目的自愿参加的人。

通常组织这种互助会的目的是为办婚事筹集资金、为偿还办丧事所欠的债务。这些也是可以被接受的筹集资金的理由。但如为了从事生产，譬如说要办一个企业或买一块土地，人们往往认为这不是借钱的理由。

有了一个正当的目的，组织者便去找一些亲戚，如叔伯、兄弟、姐夫、妹夫、舅父、丈人等。他们有义务参加这个互助会。如果他们自己不能出钱，他们会去找一些亲戚来代替。

会员的人数从 8 ～ 14 人不等。在村庄里，保持密切关系的亲属圈子有时较小。因此，会员可能扩展至亲戚的亲戚或朋友。这些

obligations but to mutual benefits. If someone needs financial help which does not justify organizing a society by himself he will join a society formed by others. Those who are known in the community to be rich will respond to a justifiable appeal for help in order to show generosity and to avoid public criticism. For example, Chou has gained much prestige by subscribing to more than ten societies.

But the nucleus of such a society is always the kinship group. The person who has a larger sphere of relatives has a better chance of gaining support in a financial crisis. In this connection we can see that institutions such as the *siaosiv* (III–8), which diminish the kinship circle, will in the long run produce unfavourable economic consequences. On the other hand, the widening of kinship relation, even through such means as pseudo-adoption, has an important economic significance (V–3).

In theory the organizer will be responsible for any default by the members, and will pay the share of the defaulters. But since he is usually in need of financial help himself, his responsibility does not give a real guarantee of security. Default is prevented not by legal sanction but by the acknowledged social obligations between relatives. The possibility of default is again diminished by the supplementary system of mutual allowance. It is easy for a person to raise an allowance in such a situation, especially when he has the prospect of collecting a sum from the society. Reciprocity is also an essential consideration. The defaulter will find it difficult to organize his own society in case of need. Nevertheless defaults do occur, and have done so especially during the past few years. As I have mentioned, the efficiency of the local credit system depends on the general saving ability of the villagers. The economic depression has caused defaults to be increasingly frequent, and these have threatened the local credit system. This has had far-reaching consequences in disrupting the existing kinship ties. But as I did not make a detailed study of this problem, I can only leave it for further investigation.

There are three types of financial aid societies. The most popular one is called Yao Hui. In this the organizer gathers fourteen members, each of whom subscribed 10 dollars. The organizer thus gets 140 in all. The society will then meet twice a year: first in July or August when the silk industry is completed, and again in November or December, when rice is reaped. At each meeting, the organizer will repay to the society 10 dollars

人不是凭社会义务召集来的而必须靠互利互惠。如果一个人需要经济上的帮助，但他没有正当的理由来组织互助会，他将参加别人组织的互助会。社区公认的有钱人为了表示慷慨或免受公众舆论的指责，也会响应有正当理由的求援。例如，周加入了十多个互助会，他的声誉也因此有很大提高。

但这种互助会的核心总是亲属关系群体。一个亲戚关系比较广的人，在经济困难时，得到帮助的机会也比较多。从这一点来说，我们可以看到，像"小媳妇"（第三章第八节）这样的制度，使亲属圈子缩小，最终将产生不利于经济的后果；另一方面，扩大亲属关系，即使是采取名义领养的方式，在经济上也有重要的意义（第五章第三节）。

在理论上，组织者将对会员的任何违约或拖欠负责，他将支付拖欠者的一份款项。但由于他自己需要别人的经济援助，因此他的负责是没有实际保证的。拖欠或违约并不是通过法律的制裁来防止，而是通过亲戚之间公认的社会义务来防止。拖欠的可能性又因互相补贴的辅助办法的存在而减少。一个人在这样的环境中，很容易提出要求补贴，特别是他届时有从互助会中收集存款的机会。相对的后果也是一项重要的考虑。拖欠人会发现，他需要帮助时便难于组织起他所需的互助会。然而事实上还是有违约或拖欠的，尤其是以往数年来，有这种情形发生。正如我已提到过，当地信贷系统的有效程度取决于村民普遍的储蓄能力。经济萧条使拖欠人数增加，从而威胁着当地的信贷组织。这对现存的亲属联系起着破坏的作用。但由于我对此问题没有详细的调查，只好将它留待以后作进一步的研究。

有三种互助会，最流行的一种叫"摇会"，在这个会中，组织者召集 14 个会员，每人交纳 10 元。组织者总共得 140 元。摇会每年开两次会：第一次在 7 月或 8 月，那时蚕丝生产告一段落，第二次在 11 月或 12 月，水稻收割完毕。在每一次会上，组织者偿还摇会

of capital and 3 dollars of interest. He will thus clear his debt at the end of the fourteen meetings.

At each successive meeting, one of the members will collect a sum of 70 dollars. The one who has collected this sum is a debtor to the society and will repay at each succeeding meeting 5 dollars of capital and 1.5 dollars of interest. The system of calculation is complicated by the fact that the member's sum is reduced to half of the organizer's own. Thus half of the organizer's annual subscription will be equally divided among the members ($\frac{13}{2} \div 14 = 0.464$), this being called the organizer's surplus. The actual member's sum is 70+0.464, and the actual debtor's annual subscription is 6.036 (6.5−0.464).

The organizer's and the debtors' annual subscriptions and the member's sum of collection are constant. Those who have not collected the member's sum are depositors of the society. Since at every meeting there is a member who collects the sum, the number of debtors increases and the number of depositors decreases accordingly. The depositors' subscription at each particular meeting is determined by the following formula: Member's sum (70.464)−{Organizer's subscription (13)+[Number of debtors×Debtor's subscription (6.036)]}÷Number of depositors.

The total amount of the depositor's subscriptions decreases at every meeting.[51] For each individual member, the total amount of subscription decreases according to the order of collection. Since the amount of collection is constant, the difference between the amount of subscription and the amount of collection is the interest either paid for the loan or received from the deposit. The rate of interest fixed for the debtor is 4.3 per cent. per annum. But owing to the combination of deposit and loan as well as the two kinds of surplus, the actual rate of interest is different among the members and from each year.[52] The collector at each meeting is determined by lot. Each member throws two dice, and the one who scores the highest points is the collector. A feast is prepared at each meeting by the organizer and paid by the collector of that particular meeting. Lot drawing comes after the feast, when all the subscriptions, having been collected, are in the hand of the organizer.

This system is rather complicated. But it has its merits—

(1) The members who join the society have no definite prospective use for the sum collected. By reducing the member's sum, the burden of the members is reduced. Thus it diminishes the risk of default. (2) To determine who is to be the collector by lot gives every depositor an equal hope of collecting. This induces subscription by those who are in need of financial help.

10 元本钱和 3 元利息。这样，在第十四次会结束时，他可以把债还清。

在相继的每一次会上，有一个会员收集 70 元钱。收这笔钱的人就是摇会的借款人，他在以后的每一次会上应还 5 元本钱及 1.5 元利息。由于会员只拿相当于组织者一半的钱，所以计算时稍为复杂。组织者每年交款的半数将在会员中平分（$\frac{13}{2} \div 14 = 0.464$），这叫组织者的余钱。会员拿的实际数为 70 + 0.464，借款人每年交款为 6.036 元（6.5 − 0.464）。

组织者和借款人每年交的钱和会员收的钱数均为恒定。没有收款的那些人为摇会的存款人。由于每一次会有一个会员收款，所以借款人逐步增加，存款人随之减少。在每一次会上，存款人存款数目根据以下公式计算：会员的款数（70.464）−｛组织者的存款（13）+［借债人数 × 借债人存款（6.036）］｝÷ 存款人数。

在每一次会上存款人存款总数减少。[51] 对每一个会员来说，存款总数，按照收款的次序逐步减少。由于收款数不变，存款和收款数目之间的差即借债人付的利息或存款人收的利息。借债人的利率规定为年利 4.3%。但由于存款和借款以及两种余额混在一起，因此，会员之间以及每年的实际利率不同。[52] 每次会的收款人根据抽签的办法决定。每个会员掷两颗骰子，点数最高者为收款人。组织者为每次摇会准备了宴席，由各次摇会的收钱人负担宴席费用。席后，组织者收齐了会员交纳的款项，再进行抽签。

摇会的办法比较复杂，但有它的优点：

（1）参加会的会员对收来的钱没有预计肯定的用处。减少会员交纳的钱数，会员的负担减少，从而也减少了拖欠的危险。（2）用抽签办法决定收款人，每个存款人都有收款的均等希望。这促使需要

(3) The rapid decrease of subscriptions of the depositors compensates their delayed collection. (4) The rich feasts attract the members. Some people had modified the system by offering the feast once a year in the winter, and the collector for the next period was determined beforehand. It has been found that collection of the shares in the spring was very difficult. Therefore the practice was given up.

Order of Meeting	Number of Depostiors	Amount of Subscription of Each Depositor
1st	13	4.420
2nd	12	4.286
3rd	11	4.126
4th	10	3.936
5th	9	3.702
6th	8	3.410
7th	7	3.035
8th	6	2.535
9th	5	1.838
10th	4	0.785

The complexity of this system is too difficult for every ordinary villager to understand. In fact, very few persons in the village know the system of calculation. They have therefore to invite the village heads to instruct them. To meet this difficulty, another and simplified system was introduced a relatively short time ago. This is called Hui Hui, because it is supposed to have originated in Anhwei Province. According to this system, the order of collection and the amount to be subscribed by each member is fixed in advance.[53]

The total collected at each meeting is constant. This is 80 dollars, including the collector's own share. This system is convenient for calculation, and each member can foresee his turn of collecting and adjust it to his need.

A third type is called Kwangtung Piao Hui, an auction system supposed to be originated in Kwangtung. All depositors will offer a sum expected to collect from the meeting. The one who offers the lowest bid will be the collector. The surplus of subscription, after the sum for the collector is deducted, will be equally divided among the members, both the debtors and the depositors. This type is not popular in the village because, as my informant put it, there is too much gambling.

经济援助的人去交款。(3)存款人交款数迅速下降弥补了他们延期收款的不足之处。(4)丰盛的宴席吸引会员。有些人把宴席改在冬天，每年一次，下一阶段的收款人预先决定。人们发现春天收款极为困难，所以放弃了这种办法。

摇会次序	存款人数	每个存款人的存款
第一次	13	4.420
第二次	12	4.286
第三次	11	4.126
第四次	10	3.936
第五次	9	3.702
第六次	8	3.410
第七次	7	3.035
第八次	6	2.535
第九次	5	1.838
第十次	4	0.785

这种会的办法比较复杂，普通农民很难理解它。事实上在村子里，懂得这种计算办法的人很少，所以必须请村长来教。为了解决这一困难，不久以前，有人提出一个比较简单的互助会办法，叫徽会，因为据说这是从安徽传来的。这个会的收款次序及每个会员交纳的款数，均事先规定。[53]

每次会收款总数不变，规定为80元，包括收款人自己交纳的一份。这一借贷办法便于计算，每个会员能预知轮到他收款的时间并纳入他自己的用款计划。

第三种互助会称广东票会，来源于广东，采取自报的方式。所有存款人自报一个希望在会上收款的数目，报数最低的人为收款人。存款余钱减去收款人的款数后，在会员中平分。在村子里，此种会不很普遍，向我提供材料的人告诉我，这种方式的赌博性质太重。

❸ Agent Boats as Credit Agent

Kinship ties between the village and the town are very limited. The number of villagers living in the town is small. Those who have been resident in the town for some generations, have allowed kinship ties with their clansmen in the village to become very loose. As I have mentioned, the clan is usually divided when the members disperse (V–1). Marriage between village and town is rare, except in the case of maid servants in the town who may return to the village upon marriage. It appears to me that the relation between the town people and the villagers is mainly of an economic nature. It may, for example, be the relation between landlord and tenant, which under the present system of land tenure, is impersonal. More intimate relations are found between the master and the servant who temporarily works in the town; but on the whole, the social relation between townsmen and villagers is not strong enough to maintain a system of mutual allowance or the financial aid society. When the villagers need external financial help, they usually resort to the system of rice-lending and usury.

Deficiency of food supply is extraordinary in a village where rice is the staple produce. It is a result of the decline of price of rural produce. To receive the same money income as formerly, the amount of output must be increased. As a result, the rice reserve of the villagers is sometimes exhausted before the new rice is ready. In this connection the agent boat plays an important function in the village economy.

The villagers sell their rice to the town collectors through the agent boat. The collector deals with the agent, not with the real producers. To secure a constant supply, especially against the competition of the town market, the collector must maintain good relations with the agent. On the other hand, the agent is indispensable to the producers. They rely upon him for selling and buying. These relations enable the agent to bring the collector and the villagers into financial relationship in case of need.

The agent will ask the collector on behalf of his clients to lend rice and he will guarantee the return when the new rice comes to market. His guarantee is effective because the rice produced by the debtor will pass through his hand. Moreover, by extending credit, the collector can not only make a profit, but ensures his future supply.

The rice borrowed from the collector is valued at 12 dollars per 3 bushels, which is higher than the market price. The debtor repays an amount of rice equivalent to 12 dollars at the market price (which during

三、航船，信贷代理

村庄和城镇之间亲属关系非常有限。住在城镇的农民很少。几代在城镇居住的人，他们与村子里同族的关系已经比较疏远。我已提到过，族人分散后，族就分开了（第五章第一节）。城镇与农村通婚也很少，除了在城里的女佣嫁回村里这种情况。在我看来，城里人和村民的关系主要是经济性质的。例如，他们可能是地主和佃农的关系，在目前的土地占有情况下，他们之间的关系不是个人的关系。主人和暂时在城里当女佣的妇女，他们之间的关系较密切。但就整体来看，城里人和农民之间的社会关系不密切，不足以保持一个在经济上互相补贴或互助会的系统。当村民需要外界资助时，他们通常只得求助于借米和高利贷系统。

在稻米是主要产品的农村里，粮食供应不足并非常态。这是农产品价格下降的结果。要使收入与过去一样不变，产量必须增加。结果是村民的稻米储备往往在新米上市以前便消耗尽，以致需要借贷维持。从这方面讲，航船在村庄经济中起着重要的作用。

村民通过航船出售稻米给城镇的米行。米行与航船主联系，而不是与真正的生产者联系。为了能得到经常不断的供应，特别是为对付城镇市场的竞争，米行必须与航船主保持友好的关系。另一方面，航船主对生产者来说也是不可缺少的。生产者依赖航船主进行购销。这些关系使航船主在需要时建立起米行和村民之间的借贷关系。

航船主代表他的顾客向米行借米，并保证新米上市后归还。他的保证是可靠的，因为借米人生产的米将通过他出售。此外，收购人出借大米不但可以获利，而且也有利于保证未来的供应。

向米行借米的价格为每 3 蒲式耳 12 元，比市场价高。借债人将以市场价格偿还相当于 12 元钱的大米（冬天，3 蒲式耳米约为

the winter is about 7 dollars per 3 bushels). The rate of interest works out at about 15 per cent. per month if the term is two months. This rate is comparatively low. It is made possible because the creditor does not run much risk owing to the institution of the agent boat and the economic value for the collector of insuring his future supply. The existence of a number of collectors on the market makes the supply of credit more elastic and gives the debtor a better position in negotiation.

This credit system is comparatively a recent one. It has not been developed beyond the sphere of rice-lending. But by the same principle it might be gradually extended to money-lending through rice and silk collectors as a payment in advance for produce which is relatively stable and can be counted on beforehand.

❹ Usury

Money-lending from the town to the village is indispensable when the village finance is in distress. Villagers borrow money from wealthy people in the town with whom they have relations. The interest on such a loan varies according to the closeness of the personal relation between the debtor and the creditor. But, as I have mentioned, the personal relation between villagers and townsmen is limited, and the townsmen with whom the villagers have personal relations may be unable to lend money. As a result there emerge professional money-lenders in the town. Professional money-lenders advance money to the villagers on very high rates of interest. This traditional institution we may term usury.

A person who finds himself unable to pay land tax, for instance, and is not prepared to spend the whole winter in prison, has to borrow money. The usurer's door is open to him. The money from the usurer is expressed in terms of an amount of mulberry leaves. At the time of the transactions, there are no mulberry leaves at all and a market price does not exist. The price is arbitrarily set at 70 cents per picul (114 lbs.). For instance, a loan of 7 dollars will be regarded as a loan of 10 piculs of mulberry leaves. The term of the loan expires at Ch'ing Ming (April 5th), and it must be repaid not later than Ku Yü (April 20th). The debtor has to pay an amount of money according to the market price of mulberry leaves, which at that time is about 3 dollars per picul. Thus a loan of 7 dollars or 10 piculs of mulberry leaves, concluded in October, yields a return of 30 dollars to the creditor in April. During these five months, the debtor is paying an interest of 65 per cent. per month. This system of money-lending is called "living money of mulberry leaves."

7 元）。如果借期两个月，每月利率约为 15%。这一利率比高利贷还算低些。这是因为一方面有航船主作为中保，另一方面对米行来说，可以保证其未来的大米供应，出借人所担的风险不大。由于镇上存在好几家米行，出借大米的价格并不划一，有利于借米人以较低的利息借进大米。

这是一种比较新的信贷系统。它尚未超出借米的范围。但用同样的原则，这种系统可逐步扩展至通过米行和丝行借钱，作为对收购产品的预先支付。这种产品相对来说比较稳定，而且是可以预计的。

四、高利贷

当农村资金贫乏时，从城镇借钱给农村是必然会发生的。农民向城镇里有关系的富裕人家借钱。其利息根据借债人与债权人之间关系疏密而异。然而，如我已经提到过的，农民和城里人之间的个人关系有限，而且与农民有个人关系的人也可能没有钱可出借。结果城镇里便出现了一种职业放债者。职业放债者以很高的利息借钱给农民。这种传统制度，我们可称之为高利贷。

例如，无力支付地租并不愿在整个冬天被投入监狱的人，只得向别人借钱。高利贷者的门是向他敞开的，出借的钱按桑叶量计算。农民借钱时并没有桑叶，也没有桑叶的市场价格。价格是人为制定的，每担（114 磅）7 角。譬如，借 7 元钱，可折算成 10 担桑叶。借期在清明（4 月 5 日）结束，必须在谷雨以前还款（4 月 20 日）。借债人必须按照当时桑叶的市场价格归还相当于 10 担桑叶的钱，那时每担桑叶为 3 元。因此，如 10 月份借 7 元钱，到第二年 4 月必须还高利贷者 30 元。在这五个月中，借债人每月付利息 65%。这种借贷办法被称为"桑叶的活钱"。

At the time of Ch'ing Ming the people are just starting their silk industry. This is a financially vulnerable period in the village. Persons who were unable to pay their rent in the winter are not likely to be able to pay the amount back to the creditor. In the previous five months, they have been engaged on no major productive enterprise, except trade ventures. In these circumstances, the debtor may ask the creditor to renew the loan in terms of rice. This process is called "changing to rice." The price of rice is counted, irrespective of the market, at 5 dollars per 3 bushels. The term is extended to next October. Repayment will be made according to the highest market price of the rice, which is about 7 dollars per 3 bushels. The person who borrowed 7 dollars in one October will thus repay 48 dollars in the next October. The rate of interest is thus about 53 per cent. per month on the average.

If the debtor is still unable to clear up his debt, no prolongation of the term will be allowed. The debtor must settle by handing the legal title of his land to the creditor. In other words, he will transfer the right of ownership of the subsoil of the land to the creditor. The price of land is counted as 30 dollars per *mow*. From then on, he is no longer a debtor but a permanent tenant. Instead of paying interest, he will pay an annual rent (XI–4).

The rent is 8 pints (2.4 bushels) of rice or about 4.2 dollars per *mow*. If we take Professor Buck's estimate of the average rate of interest from the investment in rural land as 8.5 per cent.,[54] we find that a *mow* of land has a money value of 56 dollars. Thus a loan of 7 dollars will ultimately in one year yield as return to the creditor a piece of land worth 89 dollars.

Through the usurer, the ownership of the subsoil is transferred from the hand of the cultivators to the absentee landlords who buy the land titles from the usurer. Upon this financial institution, the system of absentee landlordship is based (XI–4).

Usury is an extra-legal system. According to law, if the rate of interest agreed upon exceeds 20 per cent. per annum, the creditor is not entitled to claim any interest over and above 20 per cent.[55] Therefore, the contract must be enforced by other means than legal force. The usurer employs his own collector to force the debtor to pay when the term has expired. If payment is refused, the collector will use violence and take off or destroy anything at his disposal. In one case, I know, on the death of the debtor, the creditor took off a girl of the deceased to town as his slave. The debtor is usually too ignorant to seek the protection of the law and

清明时节，人们正开始从事养蚕业。在村里，这是经济上最脆弱的时期。冬天付不起地租的人，也不见得有能力还钱给债权人。在前五个月中，人们除了做一些生意外，不从事大的生产活动。在这种情况下，借债人可以向债权人续借贷款，按米计算。这种方式被称作"换米"。不论市场米价如何，借米的价格为每 3 蒲式耳 5 元。借期延续至这一年 10 月。偿还时按市场最高米价计算，每 3 蒲式耳约 7 元。一个人在 10 月借 7 元，到第二年 10 月应还 48 元，利率平均每月 53%。

借债人如果仍无力还清债务便不允许再延长借期。借债人必须把手中合法的土地所有权交给债权人。换句话说，他将把田底所有权移交给债权人。土地价格为每亩 30 元。从此以后，他再也不是一个借债人而是一个永佃农。他每年须付地租（第十一章第四节）而不是利息。

地租为每亩 2.4 蒲式耳米或约 4.2 元。如果我们按巴克对农村土地投资所估计的平均利率 8.5% 计算，[54] 我们发现每亩地值 56元。因此，7 元钱的贷款一年之后使债权人最终得利为一块价值89 元的土地。

通过高利贷者，田底所有权从耕种者手中转移到不在地主手中，不在地主系从高利贷者手上购得土地所有权。不在地主制便是以这种金融制度为基础的（第十一章第四节）。

高利贷是非法的制度，根据法律，约定年利率超过 20% 者，债权人对于超过部分之利息无请求权。[55] 所以，契约必须用其他手段来实施而不是法律力量。高利贷者雇用他自己的收款人，在借债满期时迫使借债人还债。如果拒绝归还，收款人将使用暴力并拿走或任意损坏东西。我知道一个实例，借债人死的时候，债权人便抢走死者的女儿，带到城里作他的奴婢。借债人通常无知，不懂得寻求法律

the community gives him no support. He is actually at the mercy of the usurer. If the debtor really has nothing to pay the debt with, and possesses no subsoil of land, the creditor will find it to be wiser to let him continue farming and reserve his claim on the future produce. In the worst situation, the debtor may commit suicide at the house of the usurer. The usurer will then face the revenge of the spirit and also the pressure of public resentment which will force him to forfeit his claim. This drastic means, though rarely used, is, to a certain extent, effective in preventing the usurer from going too far.

Usurers live in the town. Each has a nickname. The one connected with the village of our study is Sze, the Skin-tearer. This nickname indicates the public hatred. But he is an important source available to the villagers in case of urgent need. The supply of credit is very limited while the demand is urgent. The consequence of being imprisoned or losing the entire silk crop is more immediate and irreversible. To borrow money from the usurer at least leaves open the possibility of repaying when the time comes.

I was not able to calculate the total amount of loans from usurers outstanding in the village. Since there are few, if any, other ways for the ownership of the subsoil to pass out of the village, the extent of tenancy might be an indication of the extent of the usury system (XI–5).

The existence of the system is due to the lack of a better financial organization between the town and village. Under the present system of land tenure, the villagers supply an increasing amount of produce to the town in terms of rent while there is no means for the villagers to draw back an equivalent amount from the town. Formerly when the chief textile industries in China, such as silk and cotton, were developed in rural districts, the villagers were able to offset the outflow of rural wealth by the profit made from the industrial export. The rapid de-industrialization of the rural district has dislocated the financial balance between town and village. The rural problem, broadly speaking, originated in de-industrialization, finds its concrete expression in financial insolvency and is crystallized in the issue of land tenure. In the village, effort for an immediate solution has been directed to the rehabilitation of the silk industry. The partial success of this industrial reform is significant also as a factor relieving the acute land problem.

保护，社区也不支援他。他完全受高利贷者的支配，如果借债人既没有钱还债，也没有田底所有权，债权人认为比较巧妙的办法还是让借债人继续耕种，这样可以保留他向借债人未来产品提出要求的权利。借债人被逼得毫无办法时，可能在高利贷者家里自尽。高利贷者便面临着鬼魂报复，也会引起公愤而被迫失去债权。这种极端的手段虽然很少使用，但在某种程度上，对防止高利贷者贪得无厌的做法是有效的。

高利贷者住在城里，每人有一外号。同我调查的这个村庄有关系的一个高利贷者，姓施，叫剥皮。这一外号说明了公众的愤恨。但他却又是农民急需用款时的一个重要来源。可供借贷的款项极为有限，而需求又很迫切。入狱或者失去全部蚕丝收益的后果更加不可逆转。向高利贷者借款至少到一定的时候，还可能有一线偿还的希望。

我未能计算出村里高利贷者放债的总数。因为田底所有权转移到村外的其他方式即使有的话，也是很少的。租佃的范围可能就说明了高利贷制度的范围（第十一章第五节）。

高利贷的存在是由于城镇和农村之间缺乏一个较好的金融组织。在目前的土地占有制下，农民以付租的形式，为城镇提供了日益增多的产品，而农民却没有办法从城镇收回等量的东西。从前，中国的主要纺织工业，例如蚕丝和棉织工业在农村地区发展起来，农民能够从工业出口中取得利润以补偿农村的财富外流。农村地区工业的迅速衰退打乱了城镇和农村之间的经济平衡。广义地说，农村问题的根源是手工业的衰落，具体地表现在经济破产并最后集中到土地占有问题上来。在这个村子里，为了解决当前的问题，曾致力于恢复蚕丝业。这种努力的部分成功是很重要的，它也是在尖锐的土地问题下减轻农民痛苦的一个因素。

❺ Co-operative Credit Society

In this connection I should also mention the well-intentioned measure by the government for stabilizing rural finance through the co-operative credit system. The co-operative credit system, introduced into the village, in fact, is not an organization of the villagers themselves but a means for them to borrow money from the national bank at low interest rates. A sum was allotted by the Provincial Peasant Bank for credit to the villagers. This system promised a fundamental solution of the problem of rural finance. But the success of this system depends on its administration, and the capacity of the government to afford the credit. In our village, I found that a few thousand dollars had been borrowed by the people from the "co-operative society." But owing to the financial insolvency of the debtors, they were not able to repay their debt when the term expired. The creditor does not possess the same extraordinary means as the usurer to compel the debtor to pay, and the small interest on the loan is not enough to finance an elaborate administration. When the small sum allotted was exhausted, the society ceased to function and had a full list of black debts.

The present failure of the experiment, at least in the village, teaches the importance of a full knowledge of the local financial organization. It might be better if the government could use the existing system, such as the agent boat and the financial aid society, to finance the people. To introduce a new credit system requires a new system of sanctions. In the local credit system, sanctions are ready. There seems better chance of success if the traditional channel can be utilized and improved by governmental effort.

五、信贷合作社

关于信贷问题，我也应该提一下政府为稳定农村金融而采取的措施。农村的合作信贷系统实际上不是农民自己的组织，而是农民用低利率从国家银行借钱的一种手段。江苏省农民银行专拨一笔款项供农民借贷。这一措施指望基本解决农村资金问题。但它的成功与否取决于它的管理水平和政府提供贷款的能力。在我们这个村里，我知道这个"合作社"借出了数千元钱。但由于借债人到期后无能力偿还债务，信贷者又不用高利贷者所用的非常手段来迫使借债人还债，借款利息又小，不足以维持行政管理上的开支。当这笔为数不大的拨款用完后，信贷合作社也就停止发生作用，留下的只是一张写得满满的债单。

目前，至少在这个村里，这种实验的失败告诫我们，对当地的信贷组织有充分的了解是很重要的。如果政府能利用现有的航船、互助会等系统来资助人民，效果可能要好一些。建立一个新的信贷系统需要有一个新的约束办法。在当地的信贷系统中，对到期不还者有现成的约束办法。如果能利用传统的渠道，再用政府的力量将其改进，似乎成功的机会会大一些。

CHAPTER XVI   AGRARIAN PROBLEMS IN CHINA

The above account of the economic life of a Chinese village is the result of a microscopic examination of a specimen. The phenomena observed in this confined area undoubtedly are of a local character. But they also have wider significance because this village shares a common process with most other Chinese villages. Hence we can learn some of the salient features of the agrarian problems in China.

The essential problem in Chinese villages, putting it in the simplest terms, is that the income of the villagers has been reduced to such an extent that it is not sufficient even to meet the expenditure in securing the minimum requirements of livelihood. It is the hunger of the people that is the real issue in China.

In this village, the immediate cause of the present economic depression is the decline of domestic industry. The present depression is not due to a deterioration of quality nor to a decrease of the quantity of production. Had the villagers produced the same type and the same amount of silk, they could not get the same amount of money from the market as before. The cause of depression lies in the relation between the village industry and the world market. It is the lack of adjustment between production and demand that accounts for the fall in the price of silk.

In view of the decline of domestic industry, the only alternatives open to the peasants are to improve their produce or to give up the industry. To improve the produce, as I have shown, is not only a matter of technical improvement but also a matter of social reorganization. Even this is not enough. A successful reorganization of rural industry depends ultimately on the prospects of industrial development in China. The present analysis is a warning to reformers who tend to underrate the force of international capitalist economy.

If there is no immediate recovery of rural industry, the peasants will be forced to adopt the second alternative. They will in despair give up their traditional source of income, as has already happened in the weaving industry. If the labour released from the doomed domestic industry could be used in other productive activities, the situation would not be so desperate. It must be recognized that in industrial development there are certain industries which it may not be advisable to retain in the village. But in so far as there is no new occupation to take the place of the old, the waste of labour will mean a further reduction in family income.

拾陆 中国的土地问题

上述一个中国村庄的经济生活状况是对一个样本进行微观分析的结果。在这一有限范围内观察的现象无疑是属于局部性质的。但他们也有比较广泛的意义，因为这个村庄同中国绝大多数的其他村子一样，具有共同的进程。由此我们能够了解到中国土地问题的一些显著特征。

中国农村的基本问题，简单地说，就是农民的收入降低到不足以维持最低生活水平所需的程度。中国农村真正的问题是人民的饥饿问题。

在这个村里，当前经济萧条的直接原因是家庭手工业的衰落。经济萧条并非由于产品的质量低劣或数量下降。如果农民生产同等品质和同样数量的蚕丝，他们却不能从市场得到同过去等量的钱币。萧条的原因在于乡村工业和世界市场之间的关系问题。蚕丝价格的降低是由于生产和需求之间缺乏调节。

由于家庭手工业的衰落，农民只能在改进产品或放弃手工业两者之间选择其一。正如我已说明的，改进产品不仅是一个技术改进的问题，而且也是一个社会再组织的问题。甚至于这些也还是不够的。农村企业组织的成功与否，最终取决于中国工业发展的前景。目前的分析对那些低估国际资本主义经济力量的改革者来说，是一个警告。

如果农村企业不立即恢复，农民只得被迫选择后者。他们将失望地放弃传统的收入来源，正如在纺织工业中已经发生的那样。如果从衰败的家庭手工业解除出来的劳动力能用于其他活动，情况还不至于如此严重。必须认识到工业发展中，某些工业并不一定适合留在农村。但就目前来说，尚无新的职业代替旧职业，劳力的浪费将意味着家庭收入的进一步减少。

As their income is diminishing and as there is no hope of immediate recovery, the peasants can naturally only resort to a corresponding reduction of expenditure. In expenditure, as the Chinese peasants are concerned, there are four categories: necessary daily account, periodical ceremonial expenses, capital for production, and interest, rent, and tax. As we have seen, the villagers have already suspended ceremonies as far as possible, and even sold their rice reserve when necessary. It appears that the most rigid category is the last one. If the people are not able to pay their ever-increasing interest, rent, and tax, they will be threatened by brutal treatment from the usurers, and rent and tax collectors, and by legal enforcement through imprisonment. But when hunger is stronger than the fear of being shot, peasant revolts take place. Perhaps, this is the situation that has resulted in the disturbance of the Red Spear Club in North China and the Communist movement in Central China. If the author of *Red Star Over China* is right, the main force that drove millions of peasants in the heroic long march was nothing but hunger and its derived hatred of landowners and tax collectors.

In the present study, I have tried to show that it is incorrect to condemn landowners and even usurers as wicked persons. When the village needs money from outside to finance their production, unless there is a better system to extend credit to the peasants, absentee-landlordism and usury are the natural products. Without them, the situation might be still worse. At present, owing to the insecurity of rent, there is already a tendency for urban capital to move into the treaty-ports instead of into rural districts, as seen in the recurrence of crises in Shanghai speculative enterprises. The scarcity of capital available in rural districts encourages the development of usury in the town. The more depressed is the country, the less capital is available, and the more active is the usury—a vicious circle which saps the life of the peasants.

There was another dilemma in the Chinese land problem. The national government with all its promises and policies on paper was not able to carry out any practical measures owing to the fact that most of the revenue was spent in its anti-communist campaign, while, as I have pointed out, the real nature of the communist movement was a peasant revolt due to their dissatisfaction with the land system. Despite all kinds of justification on either side, one thing is clear: that the conditions of the peasants are getting worse and worse. So far no permanent land reform has been accomplished in any part of China since the recovery of the Red Area by the government.

当他们的收入不断下降，经济没有迅速恢复的希望时，农民当然只得紧缩开支。中国农民的开支有四类：日常需要的支出，定期礼仪费用，生产资金，以及利息、地租、捐税等。正如我们已经看到的，农民已经尽可能地将礼仪上的开支推迟，甚至必要时将储备的粮食出售。看来，农民的开支中最严峻的一种是最后一种。如果人民不能支付不断增加的利息、地租和捐税，他不仅将遭受高利贷者和收租人、税吏的威胁和虐待，而且还会受到监禁和法律制裁。但当饥饿超过枪杀的恐惧时，农民起义便发生了。也许就是这种情况导致了华北的"红枪会"和华中的共产主义运动。如果《西行漫记》的作者是正确的话，驱使成百万农民进行英勇长征的主要动力不是别的，而是饥饿和对土地所有者及收租人的仇恨。

在现在这个研究中，我试图说明单纯地谴责土地所有者或甚至是高利贷者为邪恶的人是不对的。当农村需要外界的钱来供给他们生产资金时，除非有一个较好的信贷系统可供农民借贷，否则不在地主和高利贷是自然会产生的。如果没有他们，情况可能更坏。目前，由于地租没有保证，已经出现一种倾向，即城市资本流向对外通商口岸，而不流入农村，上海的投机企业危机反复发生就说明了这一点。农村地区资金缺乏，促使城镇高利贷发展。农村经济越萧条，资金便越缺乏，高利贷亦越活跃——这个恶性循环耗尽了农民的血汗。

中国的土地问题面临的另一个困境是：国民党政府在纸上写下了种种诺言和政策，但事实上，它把绝大部分收入都耗费于反共运动，所以它不可能采取任何实际行动和措施来进行改革，而共产主义运动的实质，正如我所指出的，是由于农村对土地制不满而引起的一种反抗，尽管各方提出各种理由，但有一件事是清楚的，农民的境况是越来越糟糕了。自从政府重占红色区域以来到目前为止，中国没有任何一个地区完成了永久性的土地改革。

It must be realized that a mere land reform in the form of reduction of rent and equalization of ownership does not promise a final solution of agrarian problems in China. Such a reform, however, is necessary and urgent because it is an indispensable step in relieving the peasants. It will give a breathing space for the peasants and, by removing the cause leading to "revolt," will unite all forces in finding the way to industrial recovery.

A final solution of agrarian problems in China lies not so much in reduction of expenditure of the peasants but in increasing their income. Therefore, industrial recovery, let me repeat once more, is essential. The traditional industry of China was mainly rural; for example, the entire textile industry was formerly a peasant occupation. At present, China is, in fact, facing a rapid decay of this traditional industry directly due to the industrial expansion of the West. By arresting this process, China comes into conflict with the Western Powers. How this conflict can be solved peacefully is a question I would like to leave to other competent scientists and politicians.

But one point connected with the future industrial development in China must be stressed here. Being a late comer in the modern industrial world, China is in a position to avoid those errors which have been committed by her predecessors. In the village, we have seen how an experiment has been made in developing a small-scale factory on the principle of co-operation. It is designed to prevent the concentration of ownership of means of production in contrast with the capitalist industrial development in the West. In spite of all difficulties and even failures, such an experiment is of great significance in the problem of the future development of rural industry in China.

Finally, I would like to emphasize that the above-mentioned problems have not disappeared since the present Japanese invasion. The tragedy is unavoidable in building our new China. It is a part of our international adjustment that sooner or later we must face. Only by going through it, can we hope for a real reconstruction of our country. During the struggle, the agrarian problems in fact have become more vital. Our victory against foreign aggression can be insured only by removing internal conflicts through relieving the peasants by a reasonable and effective land reform. Now Japan has offered us an opportunity to break our old vicious circle in the land problem. It is true that thousands of villages have already,

　　我们必须认识到，仅仅实行土地改革、减收地租、平均地权，并不能最终解决中国的土地问题。但这种改革是必要的，也是紧迫的，因为它是解除农民痛苦的不可缺少的步骤。它将给农民以喘息的机会，排除了引起"反叛"的原因，才可以团结一切力量寻求工业发展的道路。

　　最终解决中国土地问题的办法不在于紧缩农民的开支而应该增加农民的收入。因此，让我再重申一遍，恢复农村工业是根本的措施。中国的传统工业主要是乡村手工业，例如，整个纺织工业本来是农民的职业。目前，中国实际上正面临着这种传统工业的迅速衰亡，这完全是由于西方工业扩张的缘故。在发展工业的问题上，中国就同西方列强处于矛盾之中。如何能和平地解决这个矛盾是一个问题，我将把这个问题留待其他有能力的科学家和政治家去解决了。

　　但是有一点与中国未来的工业发展有关，必须在此加以强调。在现代工业世界中，中国是一名后进者，中国有条件避免前人犯过的错误。在这个村庄里，我们已经看到一个以合作作为原则来发展小型工厂的实验是如何进行的。与西方资本主义工业发展相对照，这个实验旨在防止生产资料所有权的集中。尽管它遇到了很多困难甚至失败，但在中国乡村工业未来的发展问题上，这样一个实验是具有重要意义的。

　　最后，我要强调的是，上述问题自从日本入侵以来并未消失。这种悲剧在建设我们的新中国过程中是不可避免的。这是我们迟早必然面临的国际问题的一部分。只有经历这场斗争，我们才有希望真正建设起自己的国家。在斗争过程中，土地问题事实上已经成为一个更加生死攸关的问题。只有通过合理有效的土地改革，解除农民的痛苦，我们与外国侵略者斗争的胜利才能有保证。现在日本入侵，给我们一个机会去打破过去在土地问题上的恶性循环。成千个

like Kaihsienkung, been destroyed by the invaders, but in their ruin our internal conflicts and follies should find their last resting-place. From the ruin, a new China will emerge. The coming generation will, I sincerely hope, credit us with facing the problems of our age in a spirit of understanding and sympathy; our sacrifices and the hardship we are undergoing shall stand vindicated only if we look forward to the future with oneness of purpose and clarity of vision.

村庄，像开弦弓一样，事实上已经被入侵者破坏，然而在它们的废墟中，内部冲突和巨大耗费的斗争最后必将终止。一个崭新的中国将出现在这个废墟之上。我衷心希望，未来的一代会肯定我们以理解和同情的态度正视我们时代的问题。我们只有齐心协力，认清目标，展望未来，才不辜负我们所承受的一切牺牲和苦难。

APPENDIX   A NOTE ON CHINESE RELATIONSHIP TERMS

In view of the special interest in anthropology on the problem of relationship terms, I would like to add an appendix to the present book as a supplement to the chapter on kinship extension.

It is essential to make clear that a structural analysis of relationship terms, at best, covers only a part of the whole problem of kinship system and that a mere presentation of a chart of terms is of little use by itself because it fails to show their sociological implications. Such a treatment, which most of the previous studies have followed, from the old work of Morgan and Hart up to the recent publication of H. Y. Feng,[56] is resulted from the unsound conception of language which views words as representations of reality. Therefore it is believed that an analysis of the relationship terms will be enough to understand the organization of kinship.

Relationship terms, like all other linguistic data, should be studied in their contexts. They are used for pragmatic purposes in establishing claims, in expressing affectional attitudes and, in short, as a part of the behaviour of the speaker towards his relatives. An adequate analysis must be carried out by direct observation of how the terms are actually used.[57] But in the present note it is not possible to treat the problem in detail; I only intend to suggest an outline for further investigation.

Chinese relationship terms can be classified into four categories based on the general contexts of speech: (1) the context in which a person addresses his relatives directly, (2) the context in which a person refers his relative indirectly, (3) the context in which a person describes the relationship as such in colloquial language, and (4) that in literary language.

❶ Terms of Address

Terms of address are the first set of relationship terms used in individual life. A child is taught to name different persons in contact by relationship terms. The first group of persons whom the child will come into contact and whom he will address are his fellow members in the Chia—his parents, father's parents, sometimes father's brothers and their wives and children, and father's unmarried sisters. Most of the time the child is in the arms of its mother, but when the mother is busy in her household work, she will put it in the arms of other persons.

附录 关于中国亲属称谓的一点说明

由于对人类学中亲属称谓问题具有特殊的兴趣，我想为本书增写一个附录，作为"亲属关系的扩展"这一章的补充。

必须弄清楚亲属称谓的结构分析至多只能作为研究整个亲属系统问题的一部分，如果仅仅提供一个称呼表是没有什么用处的，因为这不能说明它们的社会意义。过去的有关研究都用这种方法处理，从摩尔根和哈特的旧著直至冯汉骥最近的出版物[56]都是如此。这是由于对语言的概念谬误，把词语看作是表现现实的结果，因此才相信对亲属称谓的分析就足以了解亲属关系的组织情况。

像其他一切语言资料一样，亲属关系的称谓应该结合其整个处境来研究。它们被用来表示某人身份或对某物享有某种权利，表达说话人对亲属的感情和态度，总之是说话人对亲属的部分行为。我们必须直接观察称谓究竟是如何使用的，然后才能充分地分析。[57] 但在本说明中不可能详尽地研究这一问题，我只想为今后的进一步调查研究提供一个提纲。

中国亲属称谓从语言处境来说大致可分为四类：（1）某人直接与亲属说话；（2）某人说话时间接提到亲属；（3）某人用通俗口语描述亲属关系；（4）用书面语表达亲属关系。

一、对话时的称呼

对话时的称呼是个人生活中最早使用的一套亲属称呼。人们教孩子用亲属称谓称呼他所接触的不同的人。孩子最先接触要称呼的人便是家里的人——父母、父亲的双亲，有时父亲的兄弟和他们的妻子、孩子以及父亲的未婚的姐妹等等。在多数情况下母亲抱孩子，母亲的家务繁忙时，她便把孩子交给别人抱。

The child's grandmother, father's sister, own elder sister, and wives of father's brothers are candidates to take up the mother's function.

Male members of the Chia have less direct a duty in caring for the child. But when it grows up, the father as a source of discipline becomes more and more important. (The relation of the child with its relatives, *cf.* III–4 and V–1, 2). Terms used for this group of fatherside relatives are given in the following table.

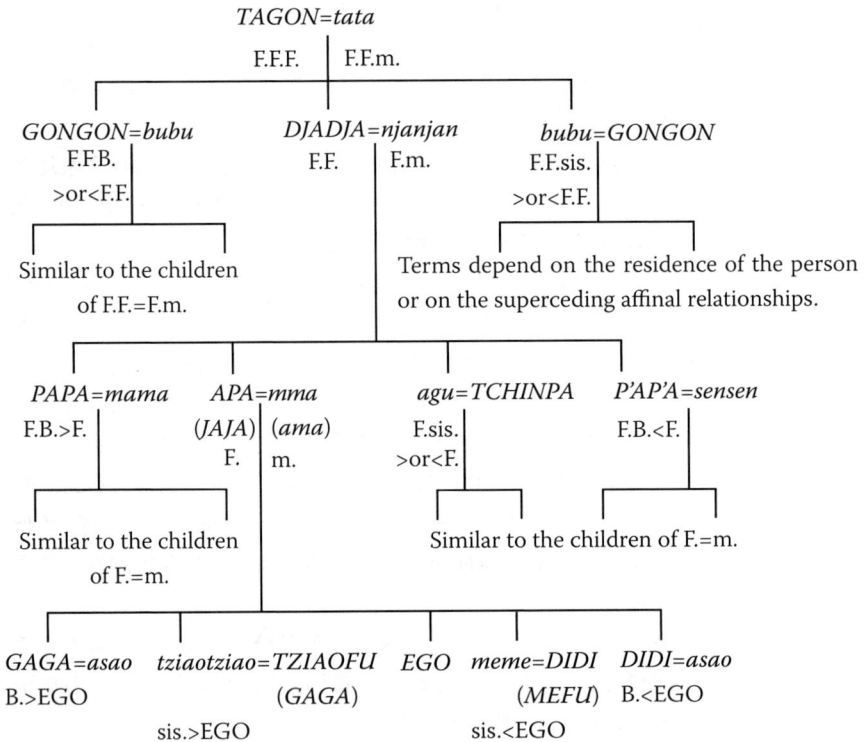

TAGON=tata
F.F.F. | F.F.m.

GONGON=bubu DJADJA=njanjan bubu=GONGON
F.F.B. F.F. | F.m. F.F.sis.
>or<F.F. >or<F.F.

Similar to the children   Terms depend on the residence of the person
of F.F.=F.m.   or on the superceding affinal relationships.

PAPA=mama APA=mma agu=TCHINPA P'AP'A=sensen
F.B.>F. (JAJA)| (ama) F.sis. F.B.<F.
F. | m. >or<F.

Similar to the children   Similar to the children of F.=m.
of F.=m.

GAGA=asao tziaotziao=TZIAOFU EGO meme=DIDI DIDI=asao
B.>EGO (GAGA) (MEFU) B.<EGO
sis.>EGO sis.<EGO

All the relatives of descending grade are called by their personal name or by simple numbers.

Terms for males in capitals, for females in small type, = for marriage bond, F. for father, m. for mother, B. for brother and sis. for sister, > for elder and < for younger, ( ) for the terms recently introduced.

这时孩子的祖母、父亲的姐妹，孩子的姐姐以及父亲兄弟的妻子将代替母亲担任起照看孩子的功能。

家中的男性成员对照看孩子负较少的直接责任。但当孩子长大时，父亲作为孩子的纪律教育者，他的作用便逐渐显得重要起来（孩子与亲属的关系，参看第三章第四节和第五章第一、二节）。父亲方面的亲属称谓见下表。

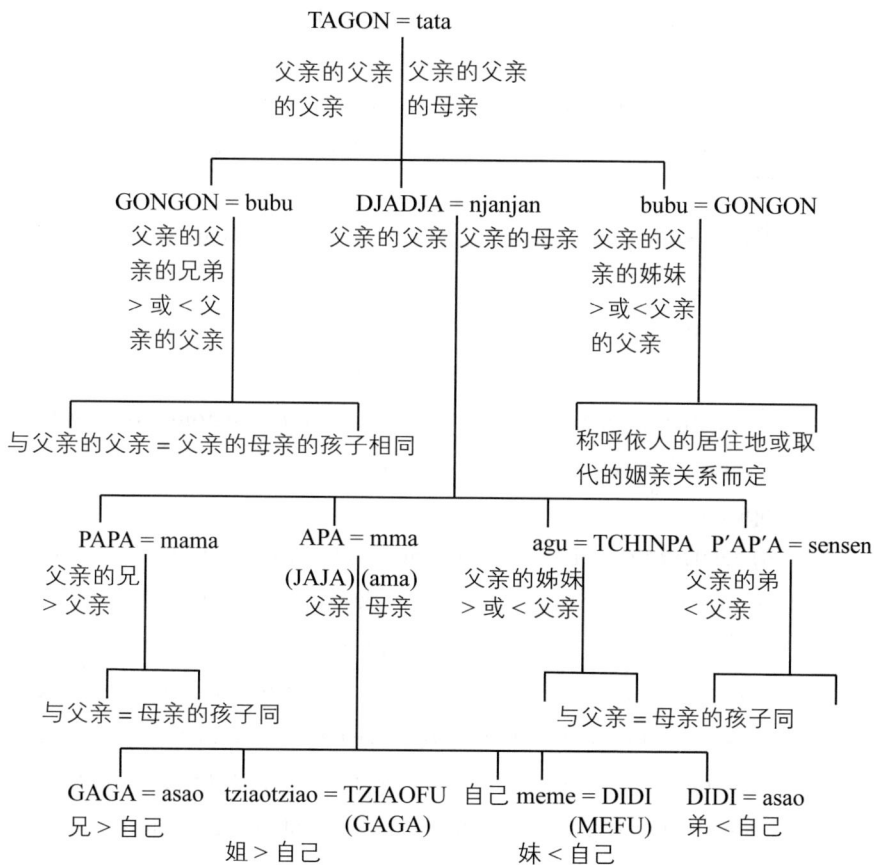

TAGON = tata

父亲的父亲　父亲的父亲
的父亲　　　的母亲

GONGON = bubu　　DJADJA = njanjan　　bubu = GONGON
父亲的父亲的兄弟　父亲的父亲　父亲的母亲　父亲的父亲的姊妹
> 或 < 父亲的父亲　　　　　　　　　　> 或 < 父亲的父亲

与父亲的父亲 = 父亲的母亲的孩子相同　　称呼依人的居住地或取代的姻亲关系而定

PAPA = mama　　APA = mma　　agu = TCHINPA　P'AP'A = sensen
父亲的兄　　　(JAJA)(ama)　　父亲的姊妹　　父亲的弟
> 父亲　　　　父亲　母亲　　　> 或 < 父亲　　< 父亲

与父亲 = 母亲的孩子同　　　　　　与父亲 = 母亲的孩子同

GAGA = asao　　tziaotziao = TZIAOFU　　自己　meme = DIDI　　DIDI = asao
兄 > 自己　　　　　　　　　(GAGA)　　　　　　(MEFU)　　　弟 < 自己
　　　　　　　　　姐 > 自己　　　　　　妹 < 自己

所有下代的亲属均用个人名字或以简单数字称呼。

= 代表婚姻关系；> 代表年长的；< 代表年幼的；( ) 表示近来用的称谓。下同。

The terms recorded in the table are sometimes only radicals of the terms actually used. For an addresser, each term stands for a definite person. If there are two or more persons bound with him in a similar relationship, such as two elder brothers of his father, modifiers will be added to the radicals for particularization. He will call the eldest as *DA PAPA* (*DA* meaning large or elder) and the second as *N'I PAPA* (*N'I* meaning the second). Modifiers are of two types: numbers and personal names. As a rule, in reference to intimate and senior relatives, such as father's brother and sister, elder brother and sister, numbers are used, while for remote relatives and younger brother and sister personal names are used.

Several principles in classifying paternal relatives can be seen in the above list:

(*a*) Distinction of sex: No exception of this principle is found. The correlation between linguistic distinction and sociological distinction is high in this case. Sex differentiation in the household work and in other social functions, privileges and duties has been shown in above description.

(*b*) Distinction of kinship grade:[58] The differentiation of social obligations and privileges according to kinship grade is well expressed in kinship sociology. The grandfather, for instance, does not exercise authority very often as the father over the child but very frequently indulges him and acts as mediator between the father and son. The grandson has no specific economic obligation towards his grandfather so long as his father is living. But the terms for male relatives of the second and third ascending grade, except father's father, have the same root, *GON*; *TA* being a modifier meaning great. In fact, the term *TAGON* is very seldom used in direct address because it is rarely seen that four kinship grades exist in the same group.

(*c*) Distinction between consanquinity and affinity: Relatives resulted from marriage are always distinguished from relatives resulted from procreation. For instance, father's sister is differentiated from father's brother's wife. This distinction is maintained in daily life. Father's brother's wife, does not live very far if not in the same house, while father's sister after marriage usually lives in another village. The former is available to take up the mother's function in case of need while the latter is met mostly in occasional visitings.

　　表中所记载的有时只是实际生活中所使用的称谓的基本词。对讲话的人来说，每一个称呼代表一个确定的人。如果与讲话人有同样关系的有两个以上的人，例如他父亲的两个哥哥，则须在基本称呼词前面加修饰词，以表示特指的关系。他将称父亲的大哥为 DA PAPA（DA 意思是年纪大的或年长的）。称父亲的二哥为 N'I PAPA（N'I 意思是第二）。修饰词有两种：数词和个人名字。一般说来，对近亲或亲属中年纪大的，如父亲的兄弟姊妹及自己的哥哥、姐姐加数字。对远亲和弟弟妹妹则加个人的名字作为称谓前的修饰词。

　　对父系亲属分类时可从上表看出几个主要规则：

　　（a）性的区别：这一规则没有发现例外。在这一页中，语言区别与社会关系方面的区别两者之间的相关关系大。在家务劳动、其他社会功能、权利和义务方面的性的区别在上面已有描述。

　　（b）亲属关系级别的区别[58]：根据亲属关系级别而分化的社会义务和权利，在亲属关系社会学中已有很好的表述。例如，祖父对孙子往往不像父亲对儿子那样行使他的权威，相反还经常姑息孩子，在父亲和儿子之间充当调停者。只要父亲还活着，孙子对祖父没有特定的经济义务。但上两代、上三代的男性称谓，除父亲的父亲外有同一个基本称谓词 GON；TA 是修饰词，意思是辈份高的。实际上，TAGON 这个称呼在直接对话中很少用，因为罕见有四代同堂的。

　　（c）血亲关系与姻亲关系之间的区别：由于婚嫁而产生的姻亲与由于生育而产生的血亲总是有区别的。譬如，父亲的姊妹与父亲的兄弟的妻子有区别。在日常生活中就保持这种区别。父亲的兄弟的妻子即使不住在一所房屋内，也住得不远，而父亲的姊妹出嫁后通常便住到另一个村子里。前者在需要的时候便接替母亲的任务，后者则多数在逢年过节、走亲戚时才见面。

(*d*) Distinction between the elder and younger relatives in reference to ego or ego's direct ascending male relatives: This distinction holds good only in ego's own grade and the first ascending grade. But in the latter, it is not so pronounced because father's elder and younger brothers are distinguished only by a slight change in articulation of the sounding *PA*, shorter for the younger and longer for the elder although such difference is always distinguishable. Father's sisters are called by the same term without distinction of elder and younger and similarly their husbands.

The distinction between elder and younger brothers may be correlated with the special privilege and obligations of the eldest son (IV–3). The less differentiation in social relation with the relatives of higher grade also reflects in the fusion of terminology.

(*e*) Distinction of family groups. This principle does not effect ego's own grade. In the first ascending grade, the term for father has the same root, *PA*, as found in the terms for father's brothers. Only recently, a new term *JAJA* has come into use. *JA* is the term for father used in the context of describing the relationship as such. Terms for mother and father's elder brother's wife have also the same root ma. Nevertheless, the maintainence of the distinction shows the same fact as indicated above that the family nucleus is not entirely submerged in the larger kinship unit Chia.

From this examination, we can see there is a rough correlation between kinship language and kinship sociology. This correlation is found only in the general principle of classification but not in specific terms.

The second group of relatives come from the child's mother's kindred who usually live in some neighbouring village. Although his mother's mother assists his mother in child delivery, she does not stay long in the house; this is one of the few occasions when the mother of a daughter-in-law will spend a night in her daughter's husband's house. The child will however very often go to his mother's parents' house with his mother and will stay there several times a year for periods of ten days or more. In his mother's parents' house, he is a guest and enjoys indulgences (V–2). He learns the relationship terms for his mother-side relatives in a context which is different from that in which he learns the terms for his own kindred. The sentiments attached to these terms are thus different.

（d）自己同代中，年长的或年幼的亲属的区别或自己直接的男性上代中，年长的和年幼的亲属的区别：这种区别只存在于自己的一代或自己的上一代。但称呼后者，发音区别不大，因为父亲的哥哥和弟弟都用 PA 这个音，只是称呼哥哥的音长一些，称弟弟的音短一些，然而区别还是有的。对父亲的姊妹用同样称呼，大小没有区别，称呼她们的丈夫，也是如此。

哥哥和弟弟称呼的区别可与长子的特殊权利和义务联系起来（第四章第三节）。上代亲属的社会关系区别较少，从称谓的融合来看也反映了这一点。

（e）家庭群体的区别。这一规律不影响自己这一代。自己的上一代，父亲这个称谓与称呼父亲的兄弟用同一个主要词素 PA。而近来又有一种新的称谓 JAJA。用于描述这种关系时，JA 是父亲的称谓。母亲和父亲兄长的妻子用同一个主要词素 ma。虽然如此，保持的区别说明了同样一个事实，即在较大的亲属关系单位的家中，家庭核心并未完全被淹没。

从上述情况，我们可以看出亲属关系的语言与亲属社会学之间大体上是相关的。这种关系只能在分类的普遍规律中找到，而不能在具体称呼中找到。

第二类亲属是孩子母亲方面的亲属，他们通常住在邻近的村子里。虽然，孩子的外婆在他母亲生孩子时就来帮忙，但她呆得不长；女儿出嫁以后，母亲只是在这种情况下偶尔在女婿家呆一夜。但是孩子却常常和母亲一起到外婆家去，每年数次，每次住十天或十多天。在外婆家，他是客人而且是受娇宠的（第五章第二节）。他在这个环境中学到了母亲一方的亲属称谓，这个环境不同于父亲一方的环境，他在那里学到自己的亲属称谓。因此，他对这些称谓的感情也不同。

The list of maternal relatives is given in the following table:

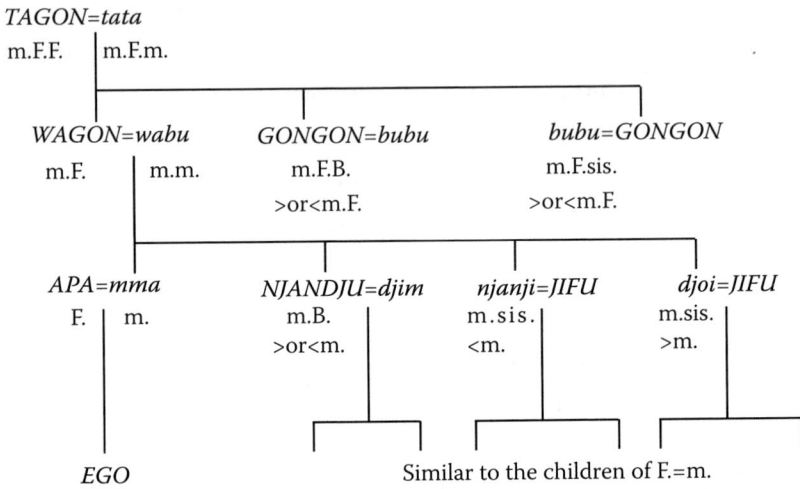

TAGON=tata
m.F.F. | m.F.m.

WAGON=wabu	GONGON=bubu	bubu=GONGON
m.F.	m.m.	m.F.B.	m.F.sis.
		>or<m.F.	>or<m.F.

APA=mma	NJANDJU=djim	njanji=JIFU	djoi=JIFU
F.	m.	m.B.	m.sis.	m.sis.
		>or<m.	<m.	>m.

EGO   Similar to the children of F.=m.

Special terms used for maternal relatives as distinguished from paternal relatives are found mostly in the first ascending grade, except mother's own parents. As I have shown above, those maternal relatives who have intimate association with ego are limited to mother's parents, mother's brothers and sisters and their children. Special terms are limited to them too, except the relatives of ego's own grade. The distinction of elder and younger is found only in the terms for mother's sisters and this distinction is made by different modifiers. No difference in social relation with ego is found between them.

Usually a person will learn the whole set of relationship terms during childhood except sometimes those terms for younger brothers and sisters. Few new terms are added after one gets married.

A married woman is introduced to her husband's relatives soon after the wedding ceremony. In the introduction, she addresses them in the same manner as does her husband, except her father-in-law, who she calls TCHINPA, and the wife of her husband's brother, whom she calls by the same term as her own sister. At the beginning of her married life she is a newcomer and refrains from making intimate and frequent contacts with her husband's relatives. She does not even address her husband.

母系亲属称谓见下表：

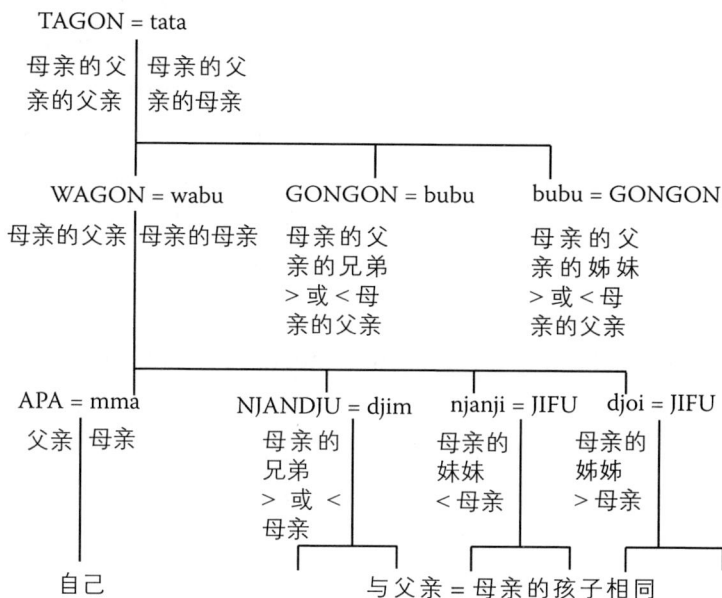

TAGON = tata

母亲的父亲的父亲	母亲的父亲的母亲

WAGON = wabu　　　GONGON = bubu　　　bubu = GONGON

母亲的父亲	母亲的母亲	母亲的父亲的兄弟 > 或 < 母亲的父亲	母亲的父亲的姊妹 > 或 < 母亲的父亲

APA = mma　　NJANDJU = djim　　njanji = JIFU　　djoi = JIFU

父亲	母亲	母亲的兄弟 > 或 < 母亲	母亲的妹妹 < 母亲	母亲的姊姊 > 母亲

自己　　　　　　　　与父亲 = 母亲的孩子相同

母系亲属与父系亲属在称呼上的区别主要存在于上一代，母亲自己的父母例外。正如我已在上面说明的，与自己有亲密关系的母系亲属限于母亲的父母、母亲的兄弟和姐妹以及他们的儿女。特殊的称谓也限于他们，与自己同一代的亲属除外。年长的和年轻的区别仅在对母亲的姊妹的称呼。这种区别是在称呼前加修饰词来表示。他们和自己在社会关系方面没有区别。

通常一个人在童年时便学会了全部亲属称谓，有时弟弟妹妹的称呼除外。成婚后再加上的新称谓很少。

已婚妇女在她的婚礼结束后，人们便把他丈夫一方的亲戚介绍给她。在介绍时，她同她丈夫一样称呼他们，公公除外，她称公公为 TCHINPA（亲爸）。称丈夫的兄弟的妻子，同她称自己的姊妹一样。结婚初期，她是一个新来的人，不便于同她丈夫一方的亲属有过多密切的接触。她甚至不称呼自己的丈夫。

There is in consequence no special term used by them for one another. For instance when she has prepared the dinner, she simply calls the whole house as *tagale*, meaning all come here. This is the accepted manner of annonymous address. When she wishes to refer to her husband, a simple pronoun is enough. But when she must address the relatives, she uses her husband's system of terms. When a child is born to her, her contacts with her husband's relatives increase on behalf of her child. She also has the obligation to teach her child, who is constantly attached to her. Kinship terminology is a part of this education. On these occasions, when making inquiries for or about her child and teaching her child to recognize relationships, she uses the terms that should be used by her child. For instance, she will call her father-in-law *DJADJA* the term for grandfather, in this context. But this does not mean the abandonment of the special term *TCHINPA*, which is used on other occasions. In fact, she has a choice of her own special term, her husband's term and her child's term, according to the context.

A man will call his wife's father as *TCHINPA* and mother as *tchinm*. The term *TCHINPA* is also used for father's sister's husband. Since it is also used by a daughter-in-law to call her father-in-law, it indicates both types of cross-cousin marriage—the up-hill type and the reverting type (III–8). In practice the reverting type is not preferable. Therefore, the identification of terms cannot be interpreted only by the married system.

The other relatives of his wife will be addressed by the term used by his wife or his children, according to the appropriate contexts.

The number of terms actually used depends on the size of the kinship groups. In the village, the size of the Chia is small, therefore, the number cannot be large. Moreover, for the child of a mother who had been married through the institution of *siaosiv*, the entire group of mother-side relatives may be eliminated.

If a person talks about a certain relative to another person, what term will he use for that relative? There are three persons involved: A the speaker, B the person A speaks to, and C the person A and B talk about.

因此，彼此间没有特别的称呼。例如，她烧好了饭，便招呼"大家"，意思是大家来吃饭。这种无名的称呼是大家认可的做法。她要提起丈夫时，用一个简单的代名词就足够了。但如果她必须称呼亲戚时，她用丈夫所用的称谓。生下了孩子后，她代表着孩子，与丈夫一方亲属的接触增多。孩子常常和她在一起，她也有义务教育孩子。亲属关系称谓是这种教育的一个组成部分。代孩子问询或问到孩子并教孩子认识亲属关系时，她用孩子应该用的称谓。例如，在这种情况下她叫孩子的祖父为 DJADJA。但这并不意味着，放弃在别的场合用 TCHINPA 的称谓。事实上她可以根据不同情况选择她自己专用的、她丈夫用的以及孩子用的称谓。

一个男人称他妻子的父亲为 TCHINPA，称妻子的母亲为 tchinm。TCHINPA 的称呼也用于父亲的姊妹的丈夫。它既然也被媳妇用来称呼公公，这表明了两种表亲婚姻——"上山"型和"回乡"型（第三章第八节）。在实际生活中"回乡"型不受欢迎。因此，称谓的识别不能只用婚姻方式来理解。

对于他妻子的其他亲戚，根据不同的场合用他妻子或孩子用的合适的称呼。

实际使用的称谓，其数目取决于亲属关系群体的大小。在农村，家的规模小，所以称谓数目不会大。此外，一个孩子的母亲如果是通过"小媳妇"制度成婚的，则整个母系亲戚群可能就消灭了。

二、间接称谓

如果一个人对另一个人谈起某一个亲戚，对这个亲戚用什么称呼呢？这牵涉到三个人。A，说话人；B，同 A 谈话的人；C，A 和 B 谈及的人。

A may refer C to B

(I) by the term he uses to address C, or

(II) by the term which B uses to address C, or

(III) by the term used to describe the relationship between A and C or
B and C in colloquial or in literary language (see next section), or

(IV) by the terms referring to the non-relatives (see V–4).

Application of these principles depends on the relation existing among A, B, and C—whether they belong to the same kinship group and who is senior in kinship grade and in social status.

The general rules can be formulated as follows but space does not allow me to give examples of each case and to qualify them with exceptions.

(1) A, B, and C are of the same Chia:

        (*a*) C<A and B—personal name of C

        (*b*) C=A and B—I

        (*c*) C>A and B, A<B—I

                A=B—I

                A>B—II

(2) A, B, and C are of the same extended kinship group:

        (A) C is in A's Chia:

            (*a*) —III or personal name,

            (*b*) —III or personal name,

            (*c*) A<B—I or III

              A=B—III

              A>B—II

        (B) C is in B's Chia:

            (*a*) —personal name of C

            (*b*) —II, III, or IV

            (*c*) A<B—I

              A=B—I or III

              A>B—II, III, or IV

(3) A and B have no kinship relation (seniority is counted according to age and social status):

A 对 B 谈及 C 时可用：

(I) 他招呼 C 时所用的称谓，或

(II) 用 B 招呼 C 时所用的称谓，或

(III) 用口语或书面语描述 A 和 C 之间的关系或 B 和 C 之间的关系时所用的称谓（见下节），或

(IV) 用提及非亲属时所用的称谓（第五章第四节）。

应用这些原则还须视 A、B 和 C 之间存在的关系而定——他们是否属于同一亲属群体，在亲属级别和社会地位方面哪一个是尊者。

一般的规则可列公式如下，但没有篇幅一一举例说明并描述特殊例外。

(1) A、B 和 C 属于同一家：

(*a*) C<A 和 B，用 C 本人的名字

(*b*) C=A 和 B，用 (I)

(*c*) C>A 和 B，A<B，用 (I)

      A=B，用 (I)

      A>B，用 (II)

(2) A、B 和 C 属于同一个扩大了的亲属群体：

(A) C 在 A 的家中：

(*a*) 用 (III) 或个人名字，

(*b*) 用 (III) 或个人名字，

(*c*) A<B，用 (I) 或 (III)

   A=B，用 (III)

   A>B，用 (II)

(B) C 在 B 的家中：

(*a*) 用 C 的个人名字

(*b*) 用 (II)、(III) 或 (IV)

(*c*) A<B，用 (I)

   A=B，用 (I) 或 (III)

   A>B，用 (II)、(III) 或 (IV)

(3) A 和 B 之间没有系属关系（哪一个是长者系按年龄大小和社会地位高低来计算的）：

(A) C is a relative of A,

     (*a*) —III or personal name,

     (*b*) —III or personal name,

     (*c*) A<B—I or III

          A=B—III

          A>B—III or IV

(B) C is a relative of B,

     (*a*) —III or personal name,

     (*b*) —III or personal name,

     (*c*) A<B—IV

          A=B—III or IV

          A>B—II, III or IV

In the contexts listed above, A and B are in direct conversation while C is indirectly referred to. There is another type of context in which A addresses C taking B as the centre of reference. I have already pointed this out in the case of a child for whom somebody else is acting as spokesman. His mother addresses her father-in-law as *DJADJA*, grandfather, for the child. In these contexts, A is speaking not as himself or herself but for somebody else. But this must not be confused with the terms used in direct address.

❸ Terms to Describe Relationships

Terms of this type differ from those of the above types in that the latter refer to particular persons and the former refer to relationships as such. A child calls his mother *mma* but the relationship between them is described as *NITZE* (son) and *njian* (mother).

These terms are also used, as shown in the above section, in indirect reference. For instance, a child may be asked by a senior, "How is your *njian*?" or "Is his *njian* well?" In such a case, a pronoun is usually added, unless in a context no confusion can be made.

The general term for describing relationship may be "classificatory," because there may be a group of persons related to ego in similar relationships. For example, if there are two father's younger brothers, the relationship existing between them and ego are the same, that is, *SOSO* (father's younger brother) and *ADZE* (brother's son).

　　　　　(A) C 是 A 的亲属，
　　　　　　　(*a*) 用 (III) 或个人名字，
　　　　　　　(*b*) 用 (III) 或个人名字，
　　　　　　　(*c*) A<B，用 (I) 或 (III)
　　　　　　　　　A=B，用 (III)
　　　　　　　　　A>B，用 (III) 或 (IV)
　　　　　(B) C 是 B 的亲属，
　　　　　　　(*a*) 用 (III) 或个人名字，
　　　　　　　(*b*) 用 (III) 或个人名字，
　　　　　　　(*c*) A<B，用 (IV)
　　　　　　　　　A=B，用 (III) 或 (IV)
　　　　　　　　　A>B，用 (II)、(III) 或 (IV)

　　在上述情况中，A 和 B 是直接对话，C 是间接地被谈及。另一种情形是 A 和 C 对话，B 作为涉及的中心。我已经在孩子由别人作为代言人的例子中指出过这种情况。孩子的母亲代孩子说话称公公为 DJADJA，即祖父。在这种情况下，A 并不是作为他或她自己在说话，而是替别人说话。这不能同直接对话时用的称呼混淆。

三、描述亲属关系用的称谓

　　这类称谓与上述称谓不同，后者指特定的人，前者指这种关系。一个孩子叫母亲 ma，但两者之间的关系被描述为 NITZE（儿子）和 njian（娘）。

　　如上节所示，这种称谓在间接提到时也使用。例如，一个大人问小孩"你的 njian 怎么样了？"或"他 njian 好吗？"在这种情况下，除非完全不可能混淆，一般要加一个代名词。

　　描述关系用的一般称谓是可以"归类的"，因为可能有一群人与自己有同一类关系。例如，父亲有两个弟弟，他们同自己的关系是一样的，即 SOSO（叔叔——父亲的弟弟）和 ADZE（阿侄——兄弟的儿子）的关系。

The classification of relatives expressed in using the same radical in the terms of address may be different from the classification given in the terms to describe relationships. For instance, mother's brother's son is called by the same term used for brother. But the former is described as *PIAOGA* and the latter as *AGA*. All the relatives of descending grades are called by personal names or by numbers, but they are classified by the terms to describe relationship, one's own son is *NITZE*, brother's son *ADZE*, sister's son *WASEN*, etc.

In this type of terms, decrepencies may be found between colloquial and literary languages. A general distinction between colloquial and literary language is that the former is spoken by local people and the latter is written by all the literate Chinese. Indeed, both of them can be spoken and written, but in actual usage the distinction is on the whole maintained. Although recently there is an attempt to develop colloquial literature, in other words, to write in spoke form, nothing has been done besides the Pai-hua actually the "Peking dialect." On the other hand the literary language, which has been used through thousands of years and by all the literate Chinese, are expressed in system of written characters which can be read differently according to local phonetic peculiarities. It remains on paper and ready to be read. Since the grammar of the literary language is different from that of the colloquial language, the former cannot be understood by ordinary people in its reading form. The literary terms enter in the spoken language only in special context. The literary term for a thing or a relation may be different from the colloquial term for the same thing or relation. This difference may be illustrated by the relationship terms. Take the term describing the relationship of father as an example: the literary term is *FU*, but the colloquial term in the village is *JA*. Moreover, the classes of relatives made in literary language may be undifferentiated in colloquial language; for instance, the relationships of father's brother's son and father's father's brother's sons' son are all described in colloquial terms as *Z-ZOSHONDI* (brothers of my clan) but are distinguished in literary terms as *TONSHON* and *ZETONSHON* respectively.

I cannot in my present note discuss in full on the problem of the relation between the literary and colloquial relationship terms. I have given elsewhere a summary of my view. "In the written system the theorists had systematically and throughly carried out those principles of classification, which had been noticed by them empirically in the process of change in the relationship system. Each generation is designated by

对话时用同一个基本称谓表述的亲属分类与描述亲属关系时用的称谓的分类不同。例如，称母亲的兄弟的儿子与称父亲的兄弟的儿子用同样的称呼。但在描述关系时，前者为 PIAOGA（表哥）后者为 AGA（阿哥）。称呼所有下代的亲戚用个人名字或用数字，但描述关系的称谓则分类了，自己的儿子叫 NITZE（儿子），兄弟的儿子叫 ADZE（阿侄），姊妹的儿子叫 WASEN（外甥）等。

在这一类称呼中，口头语言和书面语之间可能不一致。口语和书面语的总的区别在于前者系当地人口说的，后者为所有有文化的中国人写的。当然两者都可以口头说和用文字写，在实际运用中，总起来说，一直保留着这种区别。虽然近来有一种发展口头文学的尝试，换句话说，就是写成口说的形式，即白话，实际上是"北京话"。另一方面，几千年来有文化的中国人用的书面语言是以书写的文字表达的，可以根据地方的特有语音，读法不同，但总是写在纸上，随时可以读它。由于书面语的语法与口语语法不同，将前者读出来，普通人听不懂。书面的词语仅在特殊的情况出现于口语中。书面表示一件东西或一种关系与口头表达所用词语可能不同。这种区别可以用亲属称谓举例说明。例如，描述父亲的关系：书面词用 FU（父），但口语，在村庄中用 JA（爷）。此外，在书面语中分类别的亲属在口语中可能就没有区别。例如，父亲的兄弟的儿子这一亲属关系和父亲的父亲的兄弟的儿子的儿子，在口语中都叫 Z-ZOSHONDI（自族兄弟——我本族的兄弟），但在书面则分别称 TONSON（堂兄）和 ZETONSHON（族堂兄）。

我不能在此充分阐述书面的和口头的亲属称谓之间的关系问题。我已在别处扼要发表了我的观点："在称谓的书写系统中，理论家系统地、完全地实现了分类原则，这些分类原则是他们在亲属关系系统变化的实际过程中注意到的。每一代用同一主干定名，

the same stem, vertically split into two groups of older and younger, and then the family group is distinguished, by using modifications of the terms, from the other groups which are again differentiated according to their closeness to the family group. Such logical construction has not only over-shadowed the existence of the senior-junior classification, especially the fact of the absence of special terms of address for the junior class, but also misrepresented the relative working influence of these principles. As a result of such a construction, the literary system went too far from the actually practised systems. Of course, the process of change in the above mentioned direction has been greatly helped by the literary system. However, new changes in the Chinese social organization, such as the partial disintegration of the clan organization, the growing importance of the mother clan, and the change of the social status of the females, as shown in the analysis of the Wukiang system, has resulted in a direction of change which was not foreseen by the old theorists and is not to be found in the codified written system. Thus, the new social change will carry the actual practice still further from the written one." [59]

垂直分裂成两组，年长的和年轻的，然后在这个'家庭'（父母子女这个团体）的称谓前加修饰词以此表示它不同于其他'家庭'；其他'家庭'又根据其与这个'家庭'的亲疏加以区别。这种逻辑结构不仅模糊了年长和年轻的类别的存在，特别是年少的一类失去了特殊的称呼，而且还错误地表述了这些原则实际应用时的现实性。这种结构的结果是，书面语的称谓系统与实际上实行的称谓系统相去甚远。当然，上面提到的变化方向曾受到了书面称谓系统的很大影响。然而中国社会组织的新变化，如族的部分瓦解、母系亲属的日益重要、妇女社会地位的变化等，正如对吴江情况分析中所显示的，已经形成了一种变化的趋向，这些是过去的理论家所未预见到的，同时也是在已编纂的书面称谓系统中找不到的。故新的社会变化将促使实践中的称谓系统更加远离书面的称谓系统。"[59]

NOTES 注释

[1] The work already completed, mostly in Chinese, includes such subjects as: *The Marketing System in Shangtung*, by C. K. Yang; *Litigation in a Village Community of Hopei*, by Y. S. Hsu; *Peasant Custom in Hopei*, by S. Huang; *A Clan-Village in Fukien*, by Y. H. Lin; *Chinese Rural Education (in Shangtung) in Change*, by T. C. Liao; *The Social Organization of Hua Lan Yao (in Kwangsi)*, by Dr. and Mrs. Fei. Further studies are now being made of Land Tenure in Shansi, by Y. I. Li; and problems of emigrant relations between Fukien and overseas outpost, by A. L. Cheng.

这些已经完成的作品大多用中文写成，有下列诸题：《山东的集市系统》，杨庆堃著；《河北农村社区的诉讼》，徐雍舜著；《河北农民的风俗》，黄石著；《福建的一个氏族村》，林耀华著；《变动中的中国农村教育》，廖泰初著；《花蓝瑶社会组织》，费博士及夫人著。正在进行研究的有李有义的"山西的土地制度"，及郑安仑的"福建和海外地区移民的关系问题"。

[2] Professor A. Radcliffe-Brown gave a lecture in Yenching University, Peiping, in 1935 on the problem of intensive study of Chinese villages. Following this lecture, Dr. Wu Wen-tsao has published a series of articles on the problem in *Social Research Weekly, Yih Shih Pao*, Tientsin. Recently Dr. Raymond Firth has discussed the problem in his article, "Stability in North China Village Life," *The Sociological World*, Vol. X, in Chinese.

A. 拉德克利夫－布朗教授于 1935 年在北平燕京大学就深入研究中国农村的问题作了讲演；接着，吴文藻博士在天津《益世报》的《社会研究》周刊上就这个问题发表了一系列文章。近来，雷蒙德·弗思博士在"华北农村社会团结性的研究"一文中讨论了这个问题。此文刊登在《社会学界》第十卷中。

[3] *Op. cit.*, English Abstract, p. 435.

同前引文，英文摘要，第 435 页。

[*] Chinese terms are transcribed in this book following the conventional Wade system. But for special local terms, broad phonetic transcriptions are used, and printed in italics. In phonetic transcription, I adopt *j* as sign for jetisation.

[4] *China's Geographical Foundation*, 1934, p. 283.

《中国地理概况》，1934 年，第 283 页。

[5] *Op. cit.*, p. 295.

同前引书，第 295 页。

[6] Arnold Wright, ed. *Twentieth Century Impressions of Hongkong, Shanghai and Other Treaty Ports of China*, p. 291.

阿诺德·赖特编：《香港、上海及中国其他通商口岸二十世纪印象记》，第 291 页。

7 D. K. Lieu, *The Silk Reeling Industry in Shanghai*, 1933, p. 9.

刘大钧：《上海缫丝工业》，1933 年，第 9 页。

8 *Op. cit.*, p. 9.

同前引书，第 9 页。

9 *The Chinese Year Book*, 1935-36, "Foreign Trade," p. 1094.

《1935—1936 年中国年鉴·对外贸易》，第 1094 页。

10 *Land and Labour in China*, p. 24.

《中国的土地和劳动》，第 24 页。

11 Law Governing the Population Registration, December 12, 1931.

《人口登记法》，1931 年 12 月 12 日。

12 The following table gives the number of each type of Chia :

I. Those which do not include a married couple		99
(*a*) Without extended relatives	62	
(*b*) With extended relatives	37	
II. Those containing a single married couple		223
(*a*) Corresponding exactly to "family"	85	
(*b*) With extended relatives	138	
III. Those with more than one married couple		37
(*a*) Parents with one married son and his wife	25	
(*b*) One of the parents with two married sons and their wives	9	
(*c*) Parents with two married sons and their wives	3	
Total (excluding the priest)		359

下表列出了各类不同的家的数字：

I. 不包括一对已婚夫妇 ·············· 99
   (a) 没有远亲 ············· 62
   (b) 有远亲 ············· 37
II. 包括一对已婚夫妇 ·············· 223
   (a) 完全与家庭一致 ········· 85
   (b) 有远亲 ············· 138
III. 有一对以上的已婚夫妇 ·········· 37
   (a) 父母和一个已婚儿子及其妻子 ···· 25
   (b) 父母之一，和两个已婚儿子及其妻子 ·· 9
   (c) 父母及两个已婚儿子及其妻子 ···· 3
总计（不包括和尚）·············· 359

[13] R. H. Tawney, *Land and Labour in China*, p. 43, note 1.

R. H. 托尼：《中国的土地和劳动》，第 43 页，注 1。

[14] *Chinese Rural Education in Change*, Yenching University, 1936 (in Chinese).

《动变中的中国农村教育》，燕京大学，1936 年。

[15] A Chinese dollar equals in English currency about 1s.–1s. 3d. in normal exchange rate.

按正常兑换率，中国币制一元等于英国货币约一先令至一先令三便士。

[16] Lin Yueh-hwa, *Clan Village in Foochow*, unpublished monography, Yenching University (in Chinese), also Kulp II, *Country Life in South China*, p. 167–168.

林耀华：《福州的族村》，未出版的专著，燕京大学（汉文），及葛学溥：《中国南方的农村生活》，第 167–168 页。

[17] Chinese Civil Code, article 1, 147. The term succession to property is used in English translation of the code (C. L. Hsia, etc., Kelling and Walsh, Ltd., 1930). I follow the definition given by W. H. R. Rivers: inheritance for the transmission of property and succession for transmission of office (*Social Organization*, p. 87).

《中华民国民法》（以下简称《民法》）第 1,147 条。《民法》译本（C. L. 夏等，凯林及沃尔什有限公司，1930 年）用 succession to property 这一术语。我沿用 W. H. R. 里弗斯的定义：用 inheritance 一词表述财产的继承，用 succession 一词来表述职位的继承（《社会组织》第 87 页）。

[18] R. H. Lowie, *Primitive Society*, pp. 243–255.

R. H. 洛伊：《原始社会》，第 243–255 页。

[19] Villagers explained the meaning of this term as yellow (*wan*) muddy (*ni*) leg (*pon*). But they did not know why he should be so called. Afterwards I found that a similar expression "muddy leg" is used in the Northern Chinese dialect, for example, in the classical novel *Red Chamber Dream*, chapter 45, referring to those wandering vagabonds. But another literary explanation of this term was given to me by the literate people in the town as "to prevent the wildness or lack of the child." The word for prevent, Fang, is pronounced by the local people as *ban* which has been changed as *wan* in this term. The word for child, Er, is pronounced as *ni* in the local dialect. The word for wild or lack, Huang, is pronounced as *whan*, and is changed here to *pon*. The phonetic changes such as *b* to *w* and *wh* to *p* are observed in other instances. The literary explanation gives the function of the substitute while the local explanation gives the nature of the substitute. They are both useful in understanding the practice.

村里的人解释方言"黄泥膀"这个词的意思为黄泥腿。但他们并不知道为什么要这样称呼他。后来我发现中国北方方言也有同样的叫法——"泥腿光棍"，例如在古典小说《红楼梦》第 45 回中，指那些无业单身汉。但城镇里识字的人告诉我这个词的另一种书面的解释是"防儿荒"。"防"，当地人念 ban，在此词中变音为 wan。

"儿"，当地方言念作 ni。"荒"，读作 whan 在这里变成 pon。语音变化如 b 变成
w，wh 变成 p，在其他例子中也常见。书面的解释说出了替代人的功能，而当地人
的解释说明了替代人的性质。两种解释对了解这种习俗都有用处。

20 Code Nos. 1,000, 1,002, 1,059, and 1,060.

《民法》第 1,000、1,002、1,059 及 1,060 条。

21 The average percentage for grave land in the farm is 2.6 in Eastern Central China
(Buck, *Chinese Farm Economy*, p. 33). The absence of special grave land, except the
tombs for the rich in the town who bury their dead in the village, indicates the
particularly high population pressure on land.

在华东中部，坟地占农田面积的平均百分比为 2.6%（巴克：《中国农村经济》，第 33
页）。除城镇里的富人把死者埋藏在农村以外，没有其他专门的坟地，这说明了人
口对土地的压力极大。

22 The Chinese Civil Code, Article 1,138: "Heirs to property other than the spouse
come in the following order : (1) Lineal descendants by blood; (2) Parents; (3) Brothers
and sisters; and (4) Grandparents." Lineal relatives are defined in Article 967 as "His
relatives by blood from whom he is descended or those that are descended from
him." They include both son and daughter and their lineal descendants.

《民法》第 1,138 条："遗产继承人，除配偶外，依下列顺序定之。一、直系血亲卑亲
属。二、父母。三、兄弟姊妹。四、祖父母。"直系亲属在第 967 条中的定义为："称
直系血亲者，谓已身所从出，或从己身所出之血亲。"他们包括儿子、女儿以及他们
的直系后裔。

23 This summary is supplied by Mr. H. P. Li, Barrister-at-law at Shanghai.

这一条综述由上海高等法院律师 H. P. 李先生提供。

24 "Kingship," *Encyclopædia Britannica*, 14th ed.

《不列颠百科全书》第 14 版，"亲属关系"条目。

25 From the legal point of view, however, an individual not related in kinship but
living permanently in the group is recognized as a member of the Chia (Code,
No. 1,122–1,123). But this has not been accepted by the villagers. Even those who
have lived a long time in the Chia are regarded as distinct from members of the
Chia.

从法律观点来看，一个人虽然无亲属关系，但永久地住在此群体内者，亦应视为
"家"的一员（《民法》第 1,222—1,123 条）。但此规定并未被村民所接受。甚至那些
在"家"中居住了很长时间的人还是被认为与"家"的成员有区别的。

26 *Decree Governing District Administration*, Article 7, June, 1928.

《区自治施行法》第七条，1928 年 6 月。

27 *Chinese Farm Economy*, pp. 416–417.

巴克：《中国农村经济》，第 416–417 页。

[28] S. D. Gamble, *How Chinese Families Live in Peiping*, 1933, p. 200.

甘布尔：《北平的中国家庭是怎样生活的》，1933 年，第 200 页。

[29] "Lunar and Seasonal Calendar in the Trobriands," *Journal of the Royal Anthropological Institute*, Vol. LVII, pp. 203–215.

《特罗布里恩德群岛的阴历和季节历》，载《皇家人类学会杂志》，第 57 卷，第 203–215 页。

[30] The translations follow Derk Bodde, *Annual Customs and Festivals in Peking*, 1935, p. 107.

翻译依照卜德所译的《燕京岁时记》，1935 年，第 107 页。

[31] Theory of magic and science: see Professor B. Malinowski, "Culture," *Encyclopœdia of Social Sciences*.

巫术与科学的理论，见布·马林诺夫斯基教授的 "Culture" 条，载《社会科学百科全书》。

[32] *Coral Gardens and their Magic*, 1935, p. 318.

《珊瑚园和它们的巫术》，1935 年，第 318 页。

[33] *Ibid.*, p. 320.

同前书，第 320 页。

[34] Chen Han-seng, *Agrarian Problem in Southernmost China*, Lingnan University, Canton, 1936, p. 4, and Chapter III.

陈翰笙：《华南土地问题》，岭南大学，广东，1936 年，第 4 页及第三章。

[35] It is also observed in South China that the land right is transferred through the intermediary step of mortgage. Chen Han-seng says, "Sometimes one-half of the peasant families have mortgaged their lands, as in many villages of Wung-yuen and Mei-hsien, where the percentage of land owning peasants is relatively high. The mortgaged price is from 50 to 60 per cent. of the land price, very rarely 80 or 90 per cent. Of course, only a very few peasants would like to sell their lands, most of them prefer to mortgage in the hope of recovering them. But once the peasants have stepped into the sepulchre of usury, they are led to descend down the inescapable staircase with only a remote chance of coming out again. At least 70 or 80 per cent. of the landless peasants in Kwangtung have lost some of their land possessions through mortgage."…"According to the statistics of ten representative villages in the district of Pan-yu, the peasants there have mortgaged and sold 5 per cent. of their land area within five years." *Op. cit.* p. 96.

在华南还可以看到，土地的移交是通过抵押这个中间步骤来完成的。陈翰笙说："有时，半数的贫农家庭抵押了他们的土地，如在翁源和梅县的许多村子中那样。在那个地方，拥有土地的农民比例相对地较高。抵押的价格为土地价格的 50% 至 60%，很少有 80% 到 90% 的。当然，只有极少数的贫农愿意出售自己的土地，多数人抱着赎回来的希望抵押自己的土地。但是，一旦贫农踏入了高利贷之墓门，他们就会被不容逃脱的阶梯一步步引入墓穴深处，再次离开坟墓的机会渺茫。在广东，至少有 70% 或 80% 的无地贫农在抵押中失去了一部分地产。"……"根据统计，在番禺县的 10 个有代表性的村子中，贫农在 5 年内抵押和出售的土地占他们土地面积的 5%。"同前书，第 95—96 页。

36 Code Nos. 846 and 847.

《民法》第 846 及 847 条。

37 The system of permanent tenancy seems to be a protection of the peasant against a quick process of losing land rights owing to the financial needs of the rural industry. It should be studied not as a historical survival but as an adjustment of the interests of cultivator and financier, an integral part of the absentee landlord system. This can be illustrated also by observation in South China. "It is a remarkable fact," says Chen Han-seng, "that nothing is ever heard of permanent tenancy in the south-western part of Kwangtung, just the sort of region where one would expect some such reminder of the old economy, because here, so far, the influence of modern commerce has been comparatively little felt. On the other hand, the custom does obtain, where it would least be expected, namely, in the extreme eastern part of the province, up and down the Han River where not only junks and barges but also modern steamers and a local railway ply a lively trade, emerging the modernizing influence of the Swatow business world far into the interior. Indeed, in the region there are not merely remnants of a system of permanent tenancy but a considerable part of the cultivated area is actually under this form of lease," *op. cit.* p. 52. Chen tends to solve the system by an historical explanation, p. 51, although, as the above quotation shows, the present fact does not fit in with his expectation. To me the historical explanation may be interesting by itself but is not important if we are trying to understand the function of the system in the institution of land tenure. Without his ungrounded expectation, Chen may be able to realize the importance of the financial problem in relation to the land problem which he has very rightly pointed out on several occasions in his analysis but not been able to emphasize.

永佃制似乎保护了贫农不致因乡村工业需要资金而迅速失去土地权。不应把永佃制当作历史遗存来研究，而应把它作为耕种者与投资者利益的调节来看待，是不在地主制整体的一个部分。这也可以用在华南所作的观察来说明。陈翰笙说道："一个明显的事实是，在广东的西南部尚未听说过永佃制，这里恰是那种人们预料会有旧经济陈迹的地方，因为至今这里还较少受到现代商业的影响。另一方面，在一些料想不到的地方，却见到了这种惯例。就是在广东省的最东端，韩江上来来往往的不仅有帆船、驳船，而且还有现代的轮船，以及一条地方铁路，经营得生意兴隆，汕头商业界的现代化影响出现在内地。在这个地区，的确不只是有永佃制的遗迹，而是已耕地的相当一部分实际上以这种形式出租。"（同前书，第 52 页）陈倾向于用历史观点来解释永佃制（第 51 页）。尽管上面的引语表明，目前的事实与他的期望并不吻合。对我来说，作历史的解释，其本身可能很有意义，但如果我们试图理解永佃制在土地占有中的作用，则这种解释并不重要。若不怀无根据的期望，陈就可能会意识到金融问题与土地问题关系的重要性。他在分析中，曾几度非常正确地指出了这一关系，但未能加以强调。

[38] *Land and Labour in China*, p. 67–68.

《中国的土地与劳动》，第 67–68 页。

[39] *Op. cit.* p. 36. The present material seems to confirm the general point suggested by Professor Tawney that the problem of tenancy is a function of the financial relation between village and city. "Occupying ownership," says he, "is least prevalent in the proximity of great cities where urban capital flows into agriculture—in the Canton delta 85 per cent. of the farmers, and in the neighbourhood of Shanghai 95 per cent., are said to be tenants—and most generally in the regions but little affected by modern economic developments. The provinces of Shensi, Shansi, Hopei, Shan-tung, and Honan, where some two-thirds of the farmers are stated to be owners, are the original home of Chinese agriculture. They have been little touched as yet by commerce and industry. The yield of the soil is too low to make it an attractive investment to the capitalist, while the farmer has not the resource to rent additional land. In the south, where the soil is more productive, agriculture yields a surplus, the commercialization of economic relations has proceeded further and both the inducement and the ability to invest capital in land are accordingly greater. It is reasonable to expect that, with the expansion of modern industry and financial methods into regions as yet unaffected by them, similar conditions will tend to establish themselves in other parts of the country. In that case, the struggle which has so often taken place in Europe between the customary rights of the peasant, farming largely for subsistence, and the interest of the absentee owner in making the most of his speculation is likely, it may be anticipated, to be repeated in China. In parts of the country, it is being repeated already," *op. cit.* pp. 37–38.

同前引书，第 36 页。目前的材料似乎肯定了托尼教授提出的观点。租佃制问题是城乡间金融关系的职能。他说："自耕所有制在大城市附近极不流行。在那里，城市资本流入农业，据说，在广东三角洲，85% 的农民是佃农，在上海附近，95% 是佃农。但在很少受到现代经济发展影响的地区自耕所有制却普遍盛行。陕西、山西、河北、山东、河南等省是中国农业的发源地，那里约有三分之二的农民据称是土地占有者。他们与工商业几乎没有什么接触，土壤的产量太低，不足以吸引资本家在那里投资，而农民也无能力租种更多的土地。在南方，土壤具有较高的生产率，农业产生了盈余，经济关系的商业化得到了发展，对土地进行投资的诱因和能力相应较强。可以合理地设想，随着现代工业和财务方法扩展到那些尚未受其影响的地区，中国的其他部分也会逐步产生类似的情况。在这种情况下欧洲经常发生的那种农民的习惯权利，为生存而耕作，同不在地主唯利是图地做投机生意这两者之间的斗争很可能在中国重新出现。在中国的某些地方，这种斗争已经发生了。"同前书，第 37–38 页。

[40] *Cf.* Chen Han-seng, *op. cit.* Chapter II, 24–41.

参照陈翰笙，前引书，第二章，第 24–41 页。

[41] In the Preface to the *Annual* of the land Bureau of Chung-shan Hsien, a follower of Dr. Sun Yat-sen wrote, "The agrarian problem is fundamental to our national livelihood. If this problem were to be rightly solved, naturally there would be a

proper way out for our national livelihood. Only by the solution of this problem can mankind gradually get rid of war. Equality in land ownership has been the principle advocated by the Kuomintang. Our chief purpose is to prevent the monopoly by a few, and to provide equal rights and equal opportunity of land utilization for all the people." Quoted in Chen Han-seng, *op cit.* p. 23.

Declaration of the First National Congress of the Kuomintang, 1924, contains the following statements: "The principle of the People's livelihood—This principle of the Kuomintang contains two fundamental aspects. The first is the equalization of land and the second is the control of capital. In as much as the greatest cause of the inequality of economic organization lies in the fact that the right of land is controlled by the few, the Kuomintang proposes that the State shall prescribe the law of land, the law for the utilization of land, the law of the taxation of land, the law for the taxation of the value of land. Private landowners shall declare its value to the government, which shall tax it according to the value so declared with the option of buying it at the price in case of necessity. This is the essence of the equalization of land....

"China is an agricultural country, and the peasants are the class that have suffered most. The Kuomintang stands for the policy that those peasants that have no land and consequently have fallen into the status of mere tenants should be given land by the State for their cultivation. The State shall also undertake the work of irrigation and of opening up the waste land so as to increase the power of production of land. Those of the peasants that have no capital and are compelled to borrow at high rates of interest and are in debt for life should be supplied by the State with credit by the establishment of rural banks. Only then will the peasants be able to enjoy the happiness of life." T. C. Woo, *The Kuomintang and the Future of the Chinese Revolution*, Appendices C, pp. 255–6.

在中山县土地局《年鉴》的前言中，孙中山先生的一名拥护者写道："土地问题是关系到我们国计民生的根本问题。如果这个问题能得到正确的解决，我们国计民生的问题也就自然会迎刃而解。只有解决了这个问题，人类才能够逐渐摆脱战争。土地所有制中的平等权利是国民党提倡的原则，我们的首要目的是防止少数人的独占，为所有的人提供利用土地的平等权利和同等机会。"引自陈翰笙前引书，第 23 页。

在 1924 年《国民党第一次全国代表大会宣言》中有下列陈述："民生主义——国民党之民生主义，其最要之原则，不外二者：一曰平均地权，二曰节制资本。酝酿成经济组织之不平均者，莫大于土地权之为少数人所操纵，故当由国家规定土地法、土地使用法、土地征收法及地价税法。私人所有土地，由地主估价呈报政府，国家就价征税，并于必要时依报价收买之，此则平均地权之要旨也……

"中国以农立国，而全国各阶级所受痛苦，以农民为尤甚。国民党之主张，则以为农民之缺乏田地，沦为佃户者，国家当给以土地，资其耕作，并为之整顿水利，移殖荒徼，以均地力。农民之缺乏资本，至于高利借贷以负债终身者，国家为之筹设调剂机关，如农民银行等，供其匮乏，然后农民得享人生应有之乐。"伍朝枢：《国民党以及中国革命之前途》，附录 C，第 255–256 页。

[42] The method of three-column analysis is devised by Professor B. Malinowski to study cultural contact. The theorical basis of this method is expounded in his "Introductory Essay on the Anthropology of Changing African Cultures," *Memorandum XV of the International Institute of African Languages and Cultures*, 1938.

三栏分析法是布·马林诺夫斯基教授创始，用以研究文化接触。这种方法的理论根据在他的《变化中的非洲文化人类学概论》一文中已有解释，载国际《非洲语言和文化研究所备忘录之十五》，1938 年。

[43] *Cf.* Karl Mannheim, *Ideology and Utopia, and Introduction to the Sociology of Knowledge*, 1936.

参阅卡尔·曼海姆《意识形态与乌托邦以及知识社会学概论》，1936 年。

[44] *Past Three Years of the Co-operative Factory*, 1931, in Chinese.

《过去三年的合作工厂》，1931 年。

[45] *Past Three Years of the Co-operative Factory*.

《过去三年的合作工厂》。

[46] "Reconstruction in China," Ed. Tang Leang-Li, reprinted in *The Chinese Year Book*, 1935–6, p. 859.

汤良礼编：《中国的重建》，转载于《中国年鉴》，1935–1936 年，第 859 页。

[47] "The Co-operative Movement," Wang Chih-hsien, *The Chinese Year Book*, 1935–1936, p. 881–2.

王志莘：《合作运动》，载《中国年鉴》，1935–1936 年，第 881–882 页。

[48] D. K. Lieu, *The Silk Industry in Shanghai*.

刘大钧：《上海的蚕丝工业》。

[49] *Marketing System in Chuping, Shantung*, Unpublished monograph of the department of Sociology, Yenching University, China.

杨庆堃：《山东邹平的贸易系统》，中国，燕京大学社会学系，未出版的专著。

[50] *Land and Labour in China*, p. 62.

《中国的土地和劳动》，第 62 页。

[51]

Order of Meeting 集会次数	Number of Depositors 存款人数	Amount of Subscription of Each Depositor 每个存款人交纳的数额
1st	13	4.420
2nd	12	4.286
3rd	11	4.126

（续表）

Order of Meeting 集会次数	Number of Depositors 存款人数	Amount of Subscription of Each Depositor 每个存款人交纳的数额
4th	10	3.936
5th	9	3.702
6th	8	3.410
7th	7	3.035
8th	6	2.535
9th	5	1.838
10th	4	0.785

At the eleventh meeting, the sum of subscription of the organizer and the debtors has already exceeded member's sum of collection. The depositors need not pay anything but share the new surplus. The principle of distributing the surplus is that, excluding the organizer and the collectors of first four meetings, all the members will have a share in proportion to the order of their collection. For instance, in the eleventh meeting the collector of the fifth meeting will get a share of 0.11 dollars or 5/110 of the total surplus (2.432). But the three depositors in that meeting, whose orders of collection are still not certain, will have an equal amount of 13/110 of the surplus. The total amount of surplus of each meeting from the eleventh is:

在第 11 次会上，组织者和借债人交纳的钱数已经超过会员的集款数。存钱人不需要再交付任何款项而可以分享新的余款。分配余款的原则是：前四次会的组织人和收款人除外，其余会员根据他们集款的次序按比例均可得一份。例如，在第 11 次会上，第 5 次会的集款人将得 0.11 元或总余款（2.432）的 5/110。但这个会上的三个存款人，其集款次序尚未确定，他们将各得余款的 13/110。从第 11 次会后的每次会的总余款为：

11th	第11次	.	.	.	.	.	2.432
12th	第12次	.	.	.	.	.	8.004
13th	第13次	.	.	.	.	.	14.968
14th	第14次	.	.	.	.	.	21.004

52

Order of Collection 收款次序	Amount of Subscription 交款数	Amount of Collection 收款数	Average Rate of Interest per Half Year (in Per cent.)® 每半年平均利率	
			For Loan 借款	For Deposit 存款
Organizer 组织人	182.00	140.00	2.2	—
1st 第一人	88.47	70.47	2.1	—
2nd 第二人	86.85	70.47	2.3	—
3rd 第三人	85.10	70.47	2.6	—
4th 第四人	78.96	70.47	2.0	—
5th 第五人	74.71	70.47	1.5	—
6th 第六人	71.99	70.47	1.0	—
7th 第七人	69.06	70.47	—	2.0
8th 第八人	65.62	70.47	—	3.4
9th 第九人	62.70	70.47	—	2.8
10th 第十人	57.08	70.47	—	3.1
11th 第十一人	51.41	70.47	—	3.4
12th 第十二人	44.91	70.47	—	3.6
13th 第十三人	38.43	70.47	—	3.8
14th 第十四人	31.06	70.47	—	4.0

®平均利率是这样计算的：把交款数与收款数的差被收款数加存款与还款次数之间的差除。

Average rate of interest is calculated by dividing the total difference between subscription and collection by the amount of collection and the difference between the numbers of times of deposit and repayment.

53

Order of Collection 收款次序	Amount of Subscription for Each Meeting 每次会的交款数
Organizer 组织者	13.5
2nd 第二人	12.5
3rd 第三人	11.5
4th 第四人	10.5
5th 第五人	9.5
6th 第六人	8.5
7th 第七人	7.5
8th 第八人	6.5

[54] *Chinese Farm Economy*, p. 158.

《中国农村经济》，第 158 页。

[55] The Civil Code, Article 205.

《民法》第 205 条。

[56] My criticism on the historical-literary method in studying Chinese kinship system, *cf.* "The Problem of Chinese Relationship System," *Monumenta Serica*, Vol. II, 1936–37, Fac.1; and my review of H. Y. Feng's *The Chinese Kinship System, Man*, August, 1938, p. 135.

我对用历史书面语言研究中国亲属制度的批评，参见《中国亲属关系制度问题》，载《华裔学志》，第 II 卷，1936–1937 年；我对冯汉骥的《中国亲属制度》的评论，载《人类》，1938 年 8 月，第 135 页。

[57] Theory of language, *cf.* Malinowski, *Coral Gardens and Their Magic*, Vol. II.

语言理论，参见马林诺夫斯基：《珊瑚园和它们的巫术》，第 II 卷。

[58] Kinship grade, following Raymond Firth, differs from generation in the sense that "the former implies a biological classification, based upon birth; the latter is of the sociological order, based upon genealogical ranking." *We the Tikopia*, p. 248.

根据雷蒙德·弗思，亲属关系级别在下述意义上与世代不同，即"前者根据出生，含有生物学上分类的意思；后者根据家谱等级，属于社会学上的次序"。参见《我们提科皮亚人》，第 248 页。

[59] "The Problem of Chinese Relationship System," p. 148. In the above quotation, the actual practised system refers to the colloquial terms while the written system the literary terms. A full list of literary terms can be found either in Chen and Shryock, "Chinese Relationship Terms," American Anthropologists, N.S., Vol. 34, No. 4, 1932; or H. Y. Feng, *op. cit. Harvard Journal of Asiatic Studies*, Vol. 2, No. 2, 1937.

《中国亲属关系制度问题》，第 148 页。在上述引语中，实际上实行的称谓系统指口语的称谓，书写的称谓系统指书面称谓。书面称谓的详单可见陈和施赖奥克：《中国亲属称谓》，载《美国人类学家》，1932 年，第 34 卷第 4 期；或冯汉骥，同前引文，载《哈佛亚洲研究杂志》，1937 年，第 2 卷第 2 期。

后记　重读《江村经济·序言》

去年在北大社会学人类学研究所召开的高级研讨班上我许下一个愿，要在 90 年代余下的几年里对自己一生中"已经写下的东西多看看，反思反思，结结账"。而且还说"我想结合《江村经济》写一篇关于马老师论社会和文化变迁的文章"。许下的愿还得及早还清。半年多来心上老是挂念着这篇欠账。人世纷扰，抽空下笔的闲暇不多。说实话，我送出该书中文版的清样以来的 10 年中，还没对这本书从头到尾重读过一遍。在 1986 年中文版发布会上，曾说"愧赧对旧作，无心论短长"，这种心理长期来尚未克服。这次为了已经当众许下了愿，不能不硬着头皮，重新读一遍。

——

重读旧作，开卷就是马林诺夫斯基老师为这本书写的序言。这篇短短 8 页的文章里触及到社会人类学里许多至今还应当反复琢磨的基本问题。我想就在这些问题中挑选一些出来，谈谈我经过 60 年的实践后的思考。我原想用《重读〈江村经济〉》作为本文的题目，现在既把范围缩小了，题目也得改为《重读〈江村经济·序言〉》。

关于我写这本《江村经济》和马老师为此书写序言的经过，我在 1962 年写的《留英记》（收入《芳草天涯》第一篇）中已有交代，在此不必再重复，于是发生了我这篇文章从何下笔的难题。正在踌躇中，我突然想起不久前有一位朋友送我一篇 1962 年伦院（L. S. E. 即伦敦经济政治学院）纪念马老师的演讲会上宣读的一篇讲词的复制件。讲员是英国人类学者弗里德曼（Maurice Freedman）教授，讲词的题目是"A Chinese Phase in Social Anthropology"。这篇讲词正好给了我一个下笔的入口。

先交代一下这位作者和这篇讲词。

我没有见过这位弗里德曼教授，但 80 年代我又获得出国访问的机会时，在国外一路听到许多同行朋友谈到关于弗里德曼的话。语气中都为我没有见到这位对中国社会文化研究具有突出热情的社会人类学家而惋惜，甚至有人听我说还没有读过弗里德曼的著作感到奇怪。事实是这样：我于1948年暑期离英返国后，由于战争的原因，我和国外的学术界已无法继续来往。大概在50年代末和60年代初这段时间里，弗里德曼在英国人类学界初露头角，而且名声日著，1962年已在高规格的伦院纪念马老师的会上发表讲话。听说后来1968—1970年曾一度当过伦院人类学系主任，成了马老师的接班人之一。他极力提倡研究中国社会文化，而且身体力行，做出成绩，获得"汉学人类学家"的名声。他培育了一批对中国社会文化有研究兴趣的社会人类学者，甚至有人认为他实现了马老师曾表达的愿望，开创了一代用社会人类学方法研究东方有悠久历史的国家的社会文化的风气。但不幸他在1975年过早逝世了，享年55岁。那时正在"文革"末期，我刚从干校回到北京不久，还戴着"脱帽右派"的帽子，尚未恢复正常的社交生活。如果他能增寿10年，有机会来华，想来我们双方都会感到知己难逢、相见恨晚了。但天不作美，良缘难得，交臂错失，只能说是天意了。

再说他在那篇讲词的题目坦率指出了社会人类学这门学科的"Chinese Phase"。这个提法怎样译作中文？据《英华字典》phase有两解：一是方面，一是时期。用方面来译，意思是在社会人类学中有研究中国的一方面，那是比较普通的译法，因为一门学科可以有多个方面。如果译作时期，意思就有中国研究可以成为这门学科在一定时期里的主流，那就有一点自负的味道，至于译成社会人类学的中国时代，那么这个味道更重了。我倾向于用"方面"，但用"时期"也不能说超越了弗里德曼的本意，因为我读了他的讲词，觉得他是有点想把马老师在序言里所提出的"社会学的中国学派"Chinese School of Sociology提高一下，把研究文明国家的社会文化作为社会人类学的奋斗目标。这是弗里德曼的"预言"。他们两人都寿命不够长，没有看到所预言的"学派"或"时期"实现于世，令人遗憾。

有人称弗里德曼为"汉学人类学家"，我也想加一点注释。这个名字是最近我从北大社会学人类学研究所副教授王铭铭同志的一篇《社会人类学与中国研究》一文（《人类学与民俗通讯》，第20—21期）看到的。原文是："后来，弗里德曼成为了研究中国的人类学家（或称"汉学人类学家"）共同推认的学术导师。"

　　汉学人类学的英文对译我没有见到过，这可能是由于我和外文资料接触太少所致，如果在英国此词现已流行，则弗里德曼所说的 Chinese Phase 确应译作"中国时期"甚至"中国时代"了。

　　这里插入一段有关掌故可能会有些启发。西欧各国学者研究中国文化已有好几个世纪，一般包括在东方学 Oriental Studies 之内，研究中国的东方学称 Sinology，这类学者称作 Sinologist。汉学或东方学来源于此。记得我在《留英记》里说过，我在接受博士考试时，有一位考官是罗斯（Sir Denison Ross），就是一位当时有名的东方学者。马老师事后曾为我解释说，关于中国社会文化的研究有需要得到东方学者的认可。可见直到 30 年代中国文化的研究在英国还属于东方学者的"领地"。但是马老师取得罗斯的同意把社会人类学跨进了这种学术王国里的传统界线。弗里德曼接着在 60 年代就在这块园地上撑起了"研究中国的人类学"甚至有人称之为"汉学人类学"这面旗子了。如果东方学者不出来抗议，就表明英国学术界里发生了变化。

二

　　弗里德曼是想紧紧抓住了马老师在《江村经济·序言》开始就说的该书"将被认为是人类学实地调查和理论工作发展中的一个里程碑"这句话作为在社会人类学的领域里开创一个新风气的根据。这个新风气就是从过去被囚禁在研究"野蛮人"的牢笼里冲出来，进入开阔庞大的"文明世界"的新天地。

　　不论在英国还是美国，社会或文化人类学在 30 年代前一直是以当时被欧洲人称为"野蛮人"作为研究对象的。他们把"人类学"实际上等同于"野蛮学"，但并不觉得这是对人类学的讽刺。马老师是在这陈旧的空气里熏染成长的，当他发表他的成名之作时，竟也把"野蛮人"这个我们现在听来十分刺耳的污辱人的名称用在他所著的书名里，但他醒悟得比别人早些，并公开发出了预言说："未来的人类学不仅对塔斯马尼亚人、澳洲土著居民、美拉尼西亚的特罗布里恩德群岛人和霹雳的俾格米人有兴趣，而且对印度人、中国农民、西印度群岛黑人、脱离部落的哈勒姆非洲人同样关注。"他在给《江村经济》写序言时，就引用了这句预言，并表示终于看到了这预言开始实现的喜悦。至于这句预言原来的出处，在序言中并未注明。

其实他这句预言是用了极为温和的口气表达的。只希望人类学对当时被划分为文野的两类人等同"关注"。这种口气相当于为人类学开阔一个研究的"方面"。60 年代弗里德曼用的 phase 一字就注入了"新时期"甚至"新时代"的意味了。这 30 年里怎样会发生这么大的变化呢？我不能不想起就在这 30 年里发生过震动全人类的第二次世界大战。这次大战使大英帝国瓦解了，世界各地被殖民主义压迫下的民族在不同程度上得到了解放。人类学者还想用过去那种气势凌人地到原来殖民地上的人民中间去进行所谓调查研究的田野作业，免不了要吃闭门羹了。这是大势所趋，人类学这门学科要能继续生存下去，就得另辟路径，开拓新的研究园地。这时自会有人想起马老师的预言。当时在伦院人类学系后来接班当主任的弗里德曼反应得比较迅速，跟着马老师指导的方向，看到了中国，想一举而抹掉"文野"之别。现在又过了 30 多年回头看，他未免急躁一点，在当时要树立起"社会人类学中国时代"或"汉学人类学"，条件似乎不够成熟，以致壮心未酬，赍志而殁。文野这条人为的鸿沟仍未填平。

马老师在序言里提到这预言时，心里明白要跨过这文野之别并不是那么轻松容易的。他在序言里接着说"这一段引语中包含着对现代实地调查和理论工作提出的重要基本要求，研究文化变迁、文化接触的现象、现代文化的传播"。他在写序的当时自己就在非洲研究现代各民族的关系、触及现代文明和土著文化中间这条文野鸿沟，也面对着一系列对他原有实地调查方法和理论的挑战。他也明白自己的探索就会在这条路子上爬上一个台阶，他要为人类学更上这层楼，从对野蛮人的研究过渡到对文明人的研究，筑好一顶楼梯。但是由于寿命的限制，只遗下了一大堆残稿，后来，虽经他的门生于 1945 年整理成了 *Dynamics of Culture Change* 一书，但他想建立的这顶楼梯还只是一个初步设计的图稿，留下许多空隙没有填实。

马老师看重《江村经济》的原因，到现在我才有了进一步的体会，可能是他在我这本书的骨子里看到了一些所希望培育的苗头。也许他曾考虑过，吴文藻老师所带领的这个小小队伍有可能就是实现他的宏图的一个先遣队，为人类学跨过"野蛮"进入"文明"进行一次实地探索。我当时实在不太能领会他说"社会学中国学派"时的期待心情。我曾多次坦白地说过，这本《江村经济》在我是一棵"无心种下的杨柳"。当时我哪里会有这种本领看出了马老师的用心？经过了30年的坎坷境遇之后，才如梦初醒，在1985年不自觉地吐出"愧赧对旧作"这句话。今天又过了10年才进一步发觉当时感到愧赧的原因是辜负了老师当时的这片心愿。能有此悟，还得感谢弗里德曼这篇演讲的启发。

三

弗里德曼在这篇演讲里，讲到了马老师离英后海外人类学者研究中国的企图和困惑。马老师这一代人在社会人类学里奠定了着重"田野作业"的传统，就是要从人们的实际生活中去观察他们的社会和文化。这个"田野作业"的调查方法虽不能说是从马老师开始，但他以后的社会人类学者都以他在特罗布里恩德岛上土人中的实地研究作为范本。马老师研究过的特罗布里恩德群岛上的土人是世世代代在这小岛上生活的人，为数不过几千人，长期和外界隔绝，往来稀少，有一点像陶渊明所描写的桃花源里的人物。像马老师这样有经验的人类学者在这岛上住上几年，用当地土语和当地土人亲密往来是不难做到的，可以说具备亲自接触和参与当地土人生活的条件，这就是为社会人类学者采取田野作业布置下的理想环境。马老师充分利用这些客观条件结合了主观的才能和努力，为社会人类学提升了一个阶段，走出书斋进入田野。

现在要从这种对过去曾被称过"野蛮人"的研究所用的田野方法去研究"文明人"行得通么？这是一个想把社会人类学再提高一个阶段必须解决的问题。马老师在《江村经济》的序言里一开始就列举若干他认为本书的优点，其中，第一点就是"一个土生土长的人在本乡人民中间进行工作的成果"。他加上一句提醒西方的读者说，中国是"一个世界上最伟大的国家。……本书的内容包含着一个公民对自己的人民进行观察的结果"。

上面的引语，我是用了中文版的译本。原文中前一句是"It is the result of work done by a native among natives"。他写完这篇序言后，特地打电话要我去他家吃便饭。在饭桌上边吃边谈，谈话中提到序里的这句话时着重说明"native"意思是指"本地人"。我当时觉得这位老人家心眼儿真不少。他怕我见怪，因为在西方 native 一词通常带着贬意，用来指殖民地上的野蛮人。当时我怪这位老师连这一点也值得要当面向我特地说明一下的么？随后我想起这次谈话时，发觉西方殖民主义确已深入民间的语言感觉之中。我觉得这位老师还不明白我们中国人的心态。我们也有野蛮这个词，不过只指粗鲁无礼，并不是人格的区别，更不触及人的尊严，不等于说"你不是人"。而西方把文野区别提高到了人和不是人的界线。在这一点上我们也许能看到至今还十分严重的西方种族矛盾的心态根源。说不定这个以种族绝灭到种族奴役为手段起家的现代西方文明会被这段历史在人们心态里的沉淀物所颠覆。天道轮回，报应说不定还是历史的规律。

话似乎说远了。但这次饭桌上的谈话，还是可以和社会人类学的发展主题联系起来。我在这次读这篇序言时，又深一层考虑到这位老人家既有用 native 这个词来指我和我所调查的家乡父老而怕我见怪之意，为什么偏要用这词，说这句话呢？看看前后文就不难明白这是有意说给有种族歧视的西方人听的，尤其是西方人类学者听的。这句话的前文是"作者并不是一个外来人在异国的土地上猎奇而写作的，本书的内容包含着一个公民对自己的人民进行观察的结果"。后文是"如果说人贵有自知之明的话，那么，一个民族研究自己民族的人类学当然是最艰巨的，同样，这也是一个实地调查工作者的最珍贵的成就"。重读生新意，联系着弗里德曼的演说来看，马老师死后，英国的人类学者中间对马老师这预言的反响就真使我另有一番滋味在心头了。

最令人深思的：马老师在上引这些话中明确反对的是"在异国的土地上猎奇而写作"，提倡的是"一个民族研究自己民族的人类学"。这样明确的态度却没有灌入他的一些学生耳中。由于我长期没有与国外社会人类学者有过深入接触，对国外文坛不应凭传说任意作出议论。事实是我实在还没有听说过国外的人类学家中有对自己民族或国家的人民进行过严肃的研究。我希望我这样说是出于我的孤陋寡闻。但是反对研究自己社会文化的人却是有的，比如利奇（Edmund Leach）教授在 1982 年出版的 *Social Anthropology* 里明白表示，他根本不赞成一个初学人类学的人从研究自己的民族入手，就是说他怀疑本民族的人从研究本民族能进入社会人类学的堂奥。我实在不明白他这种成见是否能说还是欧洲人的种族优越感在作弄他，连人类学者都跳不出这个魔掌？对此我们可以不去深究了。重要的是既然排除了自己的民族作为研究对象，而英美的人类学到他们这一代已面临过去出入无阻的"野蛮人世界"对他们关了门，除了回到书斋里去之外，还有什么地方可去呢？迫于无奈，这一代英美人类学者不能不转向自己国土之外的文明世界了。

四

弗里德曼在那篇讲演中提到了一系列在 30 和 60 年代研究中国的英美人类学者，这些都是 1938 年我离开伦敦之后所发生的事。当时我已是西方社会人类学界的局外人，看了弗里德曼这篇演讲的复制件才得知有些西方人类学者把研究对象指向了中国。

我特别注意到弗里德曼首先提到的是现在还和我通信问好的伦院的老师弗思（R. Firth）教授，现在已是雷蒙德爵士（Sir Raymond）了。他是最早赏识我这本《江村经济》的老师。我在《留英记》里已讲过，我初到伦院时，他是系里为我指定的导师。他和我商量写论文的内容时，我先提出"花蓝瑶的社会组织"，后来补充说我在来英之前又调查了一个家乡的农村。他看了我两篇节略后，建议我写《江村经济》，我一直不明白他作出这个选择时的考虑。现在联系了当时社会人类学的处境来说，可以猜测他已看到这门学科正面临从研究野蛮人转向研究文明人的起点上。他这个选择可以说是扭转方向盘的第一手。

弗里德曼的演讲里提到一段我过去不知道的事。他说 1938 年，应当是在我离英之后，弗思曾寄了一篇论文给燕京大学出版的《社会学界》，这一期还标明专门献给"L. S. E. 的人类学"。在这篇论文里他提出了"微型社会学"的概念，用来专指马老师所说"社会学的中国学派"的特点。马老师的那篇序言里曾说过"通过熟悉一个小村落的生活，我们犹如在显微镜下看到了整个中国的缩影"（中文版第 4 页）。六年后（1944），弗思又在伦院的讲坛上再一次说微型社会学是人类学在战后可能的发展方向。微型社会人类学是指以小集体或大集体中的小单位作研究对象去了解其中各种关系怎样亲密地在小范围中活动。他加重了口气说：我想社会人类学者可以做出最有价值的贡献或许依然就是这种微型社会学。他在 1952 年又强调了局限于小单位的观察有多种好处。关于这个问题我在下面还要提出来讨论。这里要指出的是，弗思把研究中国的社会人类学提高到了社会人类学发展方向上来了。从马老师的"社会学的中国学派"到弗思的"微型社会学"是一个飞跃，并为弗里德曼后来提出的"社会人类学的中国时期"开辟了道路。

弗思教授不但在理论上作出先导，而且就在这时候准备在行动上付诸实践，就是打算到中国来做"微型社会学"的试验。他开始学习汉文汉语，据说后来他发现汉文汉语不容易在短期内掌握，所以不得不改变计划，半途在马来西亚停了下来。1939 年他选择了马来半岛东北角沿海的吉兰丹（Kelantan）地方的一个滨海的渔村开始用社会人类学方法进行微型社会学的田野工作。弗思教授这次亚洲之行并没有同我和吴文藻联系，当时我国对外通信渠道已经断绝。他改变计划的原因可能并不完全是弗里德曼所说的在语言上的困难，而是当时的国际形势。他启程时日本侵略军已攻占了半个中国，前锋已到达桂黔边境，而日本还没有发动太平洋战争，马来西亚尚未进入战时状态。弗思教授就利用这短短一年多平静的时期取得研究一个亚洲的渔村的机会。他在日军进入马来西亚的 1941 年返回伦敦，编写他那本 *Malay Fisherman* 的初版。大战结束后，他于 1946 和 1963 年又两次重访这个渔村，改写了这本微型社会学的代表作，正是在弗里德曼发表那篇演讲的下一年出版。

说来也很有意思的是，一向不主张人类学者从微小社区入手研究一个文明的大民族文化的利奇教授，自己却利用参加英国军队进入缅甸的机会，大概在 1940 年前后，在中缅边境开始研究缅甸境内的景颇族的山官制度（所著的书是 1954 年出版的）。他在英军溃退时，靠我们的军队掩护，从滇缅路撤退，到达昆明时，我还在云南大学教书，他的临时住所就在翠湖边，和我只隔了一条街。可是他没有通知我，以致我们两人失之交臂，没有见面。

在弗里德曼的演讲中提到的西方人类学者在 1938 年之后到中国来研究

的还有牛津（Oxford）的纽厄尔（W. H. Newell），科内尔（Cornell）的斯金纳（C. W. Skinner），哥伦比亚（Columbia）的弗里德（M. H. Fried）和L. S. E. 的克鲁克（I. Crook）。在北京解放前不久，芝加哥（Chicago）的 R. Radfield 应邀来清华讲学。他是继 R. Park 和 A. R. Radcliffe-Brown 极力主张中国社会学和人类学者研究中国社会文化的有力支持者，不幸都没有看到他们所催生的婴儿的成长而逝世了。中国大陆解放之后，以上提到的这些西方学者除了克鲁克之外都离开了中国。直到 80 年代改革开放之后，才又有一些人类学者来华做研究工作。

令人遗憾的是弗里德曼在世时，至少在他发表这篇演讲前，并没有看到我 1945 年在美国芝加哥大学出版社出版的介绍我们抗战时期在云南内地农村调查的 *Earthbound China* 一书。在他这篇演讲里只能说到我返国后在左右两堵政治墙壁上撞破了头，似乎从此休矣。这怪不得弗里德曼，当时国际信息远不如当前这么发达，曾有一个时候西方曾盛传我已不在人世。但是马老师赞扬的研究自己民族的人类学在西方固然没有得到响应，我们中国学者却还守着他的遗训，而且有所发展。他如果在世时能看到我们在中国做出的探索，也许对他所主张的"社会人类学的中国时期"可以提供一些有力的支持。

我觉得抱歉的是在这篇文章中对弗里德曼本人用人类学方法研究中国社会文化的成绩不能多说几句。一是因为我们并无一面之缘，第二是因为除了这篇演讲的复制件外，我还没有机会读到过他的著作。我只能借上引王铭铭的文章里的话来说，他是现在英国"研究中国的人类学家（或称'汉学人类学家'）共同推认的学术导师。其影响至今不衰，他的后代现在已成为西方汉学人类学的中坚力量"。他在社会人类学历史上的地位，这几句话已足够定论了。希望有一天我还能向弗里德曼的原著认真学习，提高我对我自己的国家和民族的科学认识。

下面接着我想就我自己实践中得来的思考，对用人类学方法研究中国社会所需解决的几个理论问题发表一点意见，我倒并不急于和西方人类学者对话，更不想抬杠，还是为了推进我们中国人研究中国社会文化，用此余生作出一分努力。

五

马老师在《江村经济·序言》中重提他的预言，社会人类学的研究对象应当包括文明人，又鼓励本民族人研究本族的社会文化。如我在上节提到的，第一个在他指导下得到博士学位后来又成为他接班人的 Firth 教授曾依他所指出的方向，在马来西亚用马老师一贯强调的田野作业方法和功能主义理论，研究了一个海滨的渔村。他在实践中提出了"微型社会学"的概念。微型社会学是以一个人数较小的社区或一个较大的社区的一部分为研究对象，研究者亲自参与当地的社会活动，进行亲密的观察。在研究方法上还是等同于马老师在特罗布里恩德群岛土人中和弗思自己在提科皮亚（Tikopia）岛土人中所用过的田野作业方法。弗思的实践认为可以证明这种微型社会学是可行的。实际上他是想在人类学领域里一步直接跨过了我在上边所说的"文野之别"。

他这样一步跨越的试验，基本上消除了西方社会人类学的研究对象被困住在"野蛮人"里的传统桎梏。但是这也引起了许多值得注意的方法上和理论上的问题。这些问题的来源首先是出于"文野之别"的"别"在哪里。我们不应过于简单地以西方的种族成见一语把这区别予以抹掉。特罗布里恩德群岛土人和中国农民以及伦敦的居民存在着相同的一面是基本的，因为他们都是人，所以应当都是人类学的研究对象。这一点我在那篇讲马老师的文化论中已经说清楚了。我认为马老师和功能论就是要想以一切人类文化都是人类依据自己的生物需要和集体生活的需要而产生的这种基本认识，来消除人文世界中本质上文野的差异，比如他批判了把理知思考作为文明人所独具的特性等，就是为"文野一致"论找根据。但如果我们只讲文野一致也会导致文野无别的错觉，也就是忽视了人本身在文化上的演化，忽视了人的历史。所以我们既要根本上肯定人类的一致性，也要注意到人类本身还是处在自然的演化过程之中。这个过程首先表现在：人在发挥它生物遗传的底子上创造的人文世界，因处境不同存在着各种不同的选择。所以不同民族在社会文化上可以有差别，这种差别也是客观存在的，而且这种差别也曾引起了不同民族在过去的历史里产生了不平等的地位。我们不应当因为反对这种不平等而把差别也根本否定掉。我们既要承认文化本质的一致，也要重视文化形式上的差别。

我并不同意文化的发展是有一定不移的阶段，但也不同意完全是偶发的和无序的。从整个人类历史过程中看去，总的来说大体上是：一个社区里共同生活的人是由少而多，人所能支配的环境是由小而大，人和人的关系是由简而繁等等，这些基本上都是日常可见的实际情况。即以 Firth 自己研究过的 Tikopia 人和马来西亚渔民相比较，我想也会看到两者在这些方面的差异。

人口既有多少、社区既有大小、社会既有繁简，有人提出对"微型社会学"的责难就值得我们认真对待。责难是：一个包括人数众多、历史悠久、文化复杂的民族或国家，只研究其中的一个由少数人组成的小社区，能不能了解这个民族整体的社会文化？这正是利奇教授在 1982 年所写的 *Social Anthropology* 一书中向研究中国农村的社会人类学者提出的责难。

利奇教授责难我们从一个小小农村入手研究中国社会文化时提出了的这样一个问题，就是"中国这样广大的国家，个别社区的微型研究能否概括中国国情？"我在 1990 年所发表的《人的研究在中国》一文中答复了这个问题。我在当时的答复中首先承认他的"局部不能概括全部"的定式，即方法上不应"以偏概全"，而提出了用"逐渐接近"的手段来达到从局部到全面的了解。

后来我又提出在云南内地农村调查的实际中采用的"类型"的概念，和在 90 年代城乡经济发展的研究中提出了"模式"的概念，对局部和全面的关系作了进一步的修正。我认为："把一个农村看成是一切都与众不同、自成一格的独秀 Sui generis 也是不对的。一切事物都在一定条件下存在的，如果条件相同就会发生相同的事物。相同条件形成的相同事物就是一个类型。"（《人的研究在中国》，第 6 页）以江村来说，它虽然不能代表中国所有的农村，但是确有许多中国的农村由于所处条件的相同，在社会结构上和所具文化方式上和江村基本上是相同的，所以江村固然不是中国全部农村的"典型"，但不失为许多中国农村所共同的"类型"或"模式"。我这种思考，使我进一步摆脱了利奇的责难。我认为有可能用微型社会学的方法去搜集中国各地农村的类型或模式，而达到接近对中国农村社会文化的全面认识。

最近我在重温马老师的文化论时，又有所启发。在人文世界中所说的"整体"并不是数学上一个一个加起而成的"总数"。同一整体中的个体有点像从同一个模式里印刷出来的一个个糕饼，就是这个别是整体的复制品。生在社会里又在社会里生活的一个个人，他们的行为以至思想感情的方式是从先于他存在的人文世界里学习来的。学习基本上就是模仿，还加上社会力量对个人发生的规范作用，即所谓教育，社会用压力强制个人的行为和思想纳入规范中，一个社区的文化就是形成个人生活方式的模子。这个模子对于满足个人生活需要上是具有完整性的，每个人生活需要的方方面面都要能从这个人文世界里得到满足，所以人文世界不能是不完整的。关于这层意思我在关于学习马老师的文化论的体会那篇文章里已经说过，这里不再重复了。

这样看来，如果能深入和全面观察一个人从生到死一生生活各方面的具体表现，也就可以看到他所处的整个人文世界了。在实际田野作业里，要观察一个人从生到死一生的行为和思想是做不到的。所以实际研究工作是把不同个人的片断生活集合起来去重构这个完整的"一生"，从零散的情境中见到的具体镜头编辑成整体的人文世界。他所以这样做，是因为每个人在一定社会角色中所有的行为和感情都不应看作是"个人行为"，而都是在表演一套规范的行为和态度。我们都知道每个当父亲的人在他当舅舅时就不是一个面孔。社会人类学者首先要研究的对象就是规范各个个人行为的这个"模子"，也就是人文世界。从这个角度看去，人文世界里的"整体"必须和数学里的"总数"在概念上区别开来。这是"微型社会学"的基本理论根据。

利奇认为我们那种从农村入手个别社区的微型研究是不能概括中国国情的，在我看来，正是由于混淆了数学上的总数和人文世界的整体，同时忘记了社会人类学者研究的不是数学而是人文世界。其实利奇也明白这个道理。因为他在自己的 *Political Systems of Highland Burma* 一书里所分析的克钦人的社会结构时也只根据他在缅甸的一部分被称作克钦人的景颇族中所调查到的资料。他根本没有对跨越中缅两国的景颇族全部进行调查，而敢于下笔把在其中一部分克钦人中观察到的政治关系着手分析解放前在景颇族里广泛实行的山官制度。他在社会人类学研究实践中实际也是采用了

"微型社会学"的理论根据：只要在一部分克钦人中深入细致观察他们政治生活中所遵守的规范就可以用来概论跨越中缅边境的景颇族的整个山官制度了。如果他有机会在解放后看到在我国境内的景颇族实行了民族区域自治，他就可以说历史的条件变了，所以两地发生了不同的政治结构，而且进而可以用缅甸境内克钦人的山官制度来作了解我国境内景颇族区域自治的参考体系了。这种研究方法，我是可以赞同的。我也同意在人文世界里不必去应用"典型"这个概念，道理是在人文世界有它的特点。但是他在对待我们中国人研究农村时却忘记了这一条研究人文世界的基本原理。

六

既然我对利奇教授翻了一笔旧帐，对他提出的微型研究是否能概括中国国情的问题上发了一通议论，补充我在《人的研究在中国》一文中未尽之意，不妨接下去对他提出的另一个问题"像中国人类学者那样以自己的社会为研究对象是否可取？"也附带说几句。虽然不免是炒冷饭，炒炒热可能也有好处。

利奇公开认为中国人类学者不宜从本国的农村入手进行社会人类学的研究工作。这是他用委婉的语气反对马老师所赞赏的"本地人研究本地文化"的主张。他批评若干本中国学者出版的研究中国农村的著作用为例证之前，有一段他自己的经验之谈。他说："看来似乎是很可怪的，在亲自具有第一手经验的文化情境里做田野作业，比一个完全陌生的外客用天真朴素的观点去接近要观察的事物困难多得多。当人类学者研究他自己社会的一鳞一爪时，他们的视野似乎已被从公众的甚于私人的经验得来的成见所扭曲了。"（第 124 页）

他的意见简单地说是自知之难，知己难于知人。这一点可以说和我国常说的"贵有自知之明"颇有相同之处。但这是一般印象的总结，并不是经过了实证性的分析推考得出的定论。

利奇也许心里也明白他这样说不一定站得住脚，所以翻过几页，在他逐一批评过了中国学者的著作之后，又把已说过的调子收了回来。在第127 页最后一段里，语气改了，"尽管我对直接对本人自己的社会作人类学的研究采取消极的态度，我依然主张所有人类学者最重要的见识总是植根于自我的内省。研究'别人'而不研究'自己'学术上的辩解是虽则我们起初把别人看成是乖僻，但到头还得承认人们的'异相怪样'正是我们从镜子里看到自己的模样"。这段话我觉得他说到点子上了。利奇毕竟还是马老师的及门弟子，他尽管可以另有所好，但是功能派的一条基本"律令"他是丢不掉的，那就是"众出于一，异中见同"。

利奇说人类学者的见识根源还是在自我内省。我想就这句话补充一些自己实践的体会。我很赞同利奇从人类学者在田野作业切身的体会说起。我生平说得上人类学的田野作业，只有三次。第一次是在广西金秀瑶山，第二次是在江苏江村，第三次是在云南禄村。这三次都可以说是中国人研究中国社会文化。但是第一次我是汉人去研究瑶人。既不能说我是研究本土文化，又不能说完全是对异文化的研究。实质上我研究的对象是"我中有你，你中有我"，而且如果按我主观的估计，同多于异，那就是说汉人和瑶人固然有民族之别，但他们在社会文化生活上在部分已十分接近相同的了。这是中国少数民族研究的一个特点，各族间存在不同程度的相同和相异之处，似乎不能简单地以"本文化"和"异文化"的区别来定位。

江村离我出生的吴江松陵镇只有十多公里，同属一个县域，两地居民说是同乡，没人会提出异议。但是我和江村的"乡亲"们能不能说在社会文化生活上只有"同"而没有"异"呢？我觉得没有人会看不到"异"的存在，甚至江村的居民也并不真的感觉到我是他们所说的"自家人"。即以语言说，尽管都是吴语，但是他们讲的话我很多听不太懂。我所说的，他们更不容易一下就明白。若说《江村经济》是本土文化研究的代表作，我总觉得还不够格。这里所包的复杂性，在下文还要细说。

再说禄村。禄村是我一位燕京大学同学的家乡。他和禄村的关系有点近于我和江村的关系，但也不尽然。无论如何我和禄村居民又隔了一层，本村人间用本地话进行的亲谈杂语，我根本听不懂。他们和我说话时也要改口打"官腔"，异于他们日常的用语。《禄村农田》的本土性比了《江村经济》又少了些。所以严格说两者都还不能说是十足的"土生土长的人在本乡人民中间进行工作的结果"。

如果我自己把这三次田野工作互相比较，我对所接触到的人、事、物

425

能心领神会的程度确是不同的。在江村，基本上我不必通过第三者的帮助就能和对方交往，在禄村就不能那么随心所欲了，在瑶山里我离不开能说汉话的人的帮助。如果社会人类学的田野作业离不开语言作为取得认知的工具，我实在不能同意利奇所说的在熟悉的田野里工作比在不熟悉的田野工作更困难的说法。

更进一步来推考，我们怎样去认识一个和自己文化不同的所谓"异文化"的呢？我在学习马老师文化论的体会中已经讲过我怎样开始我在瑶山里的"田野工作"的情形。我曾说：我记得最初在瑶山里住下已是晚上，我们进入一间为我们准备下的小楼，顿时被黑黝黝的一群人围住了，我们进入了一个"友好但莫名其妙的世界"。这正是我们要认识的对象。怎样办？首先我们只有依靠在自己社区里待人的经验和他们作有礼貌的接触。在和他们接触中逐渐发觉这一群人对我们的态度、行为、感情都有差别。而且这群人之间相互对待也不相同。我们通过这些差别，用自己社会里看到过的关系，分辨出他们之间的社会关系，和他们在这群人中不同的地位。我们首先看出了他们之间也存在母子关系，从母子关系再看出了夫妇关系等等。我把这段回忆在此重述，目的是要说明，我是从比较自己熟悉的文化中得来的经验去认知一个不熟悉的文化的。这是我认为就是利奇所说"反省"的一种具体表现。

当然这个认知过程并不是套取已知的框架，而是依靠已有的经验和新接触的事物相比较，起着参考体系的作用。两者不同之处是作为参考体系的只引导在比较中注意新事物的特点，由相同引路，着重注意其相异，就是作为认知的依傍，而不作为范本。如果遇到轶出于已有经验范围的完全新鲜的事物，作为参考体系的已有经验正可肯定其为新事物，而作为完全新的经验来接受，扩大已有知识的范围。用已有经验作参考体系，在心理过程上我认为就是利奇所说的"反省"。如果把这种参考体系本身有系统地综合起来也可能就是马老师所说的"文化表格"。马老师是根据他本人的和其他人类学者的田野经验归综成一个可用以帮助田野作业的比较完整的参考体系。这个体系的原料是田野作业者的个人经验，个人经验要个人反省才能表达出来。

社会人类学田野作业的对象，以我以上的思路来说，实质上并没有所谓"本文化"和"异文化"的区别。这里只有田野作业者怎样充分利用自己的或别人的经验作为参考体系，在新的田野里去取得新经验的问题。我们提出"社会学中国化"或本土化是因为当时我们中国学者忽视了用田野作业的方法去研究我们自己的中国社会和文化。我们绝没有拒绝出生于异文化的学者来中国进行田野作业。如果要以研究者自己不同的文化出生来比较在工作上哪里方便，根据我的经验，只以传媒手段的语言来说，本土人研究本文化似乎占胜一些，当然还得看研究者掌握当地语言的能力。至于利奇所提出的"私人的"或"公众的"成见问题，我在《人的研究在中国》一文已经发表过我的意见。我认为这是个"进得去"——"出得来"的问题，在这个问题上双方各有长短。我不再重复申论了。

七

用微型社会学的方法去调查研究像中国这样幅员广阔、历史悠久、民族众多的社会文化，不应当不看到它的限度。拉德克利夫-布朗和弗思两位前辈鼓励我们的农村研究，以我现有的体会来说，其实不过是指出一条入手的门径，并不是说要了解中国国情，农村研究已经足够。这一点无需我多作说明。如果要加一条补充的话，农村研究实在是了解中国国情的基础工作，只从80%以上的中国人住在农村里这一事实就足够作为这句话的根据了，而且还可以说即是那小部分不住在农村里的人，他们的基本社会结构和生活方式大部分还是等同于农民或是从农民的型式中发展起来的。因之至少可以肯定研究中国社会文化应当从农村研究入手。到目前为止，对中国农村社区进行比较全面的研究还不多。这方面工作自应更认真地继续做下去。

如果再读一下马老师在《江村经济·序言》里所表达对"社会学的中国学派"所抱有的期待，就可以看到这种微型研究事实是存在着相当严重的不足之处。他说："这本书集中力量描写中国农民生活的基本方面。我知道，他打算在他以后的研究中说明关于崇祀祖先的详细情况以及在村庄和城镇中广为流传的关于信仰和知识等更复杂的体系。他还希望终有一日将自己的和同行的著作综合起来，为我们展示一幅描绘中国文化、宗教和政治体系的丰富多彩的画面。对这样一部综合性著作，像这本书这样的专著当是第一步"。

马老师心目中我这本《江村经济》只是一部综合中国国情的巨著的初步起点。他还为这部巨著的内容做出了一个启发性的提纲，就是除了我在《江村经济》所勾画的该村土地的利用和农户家庭中再生产的过程，也就是社会基层结构和经济活动之外，还应当包括文化、宗教、政治等等方面的社会规范和意识形态方面的叙述和分析，并且把这类研究成果综合起来，成为一幅"丰富多彩的画面"，其实他可能已看到要达到他的要求，当时我采用的微型研究的方法和理论是不够的，所以像这本书那样的著作只能是编写这样一部综合的有关中国国情的长卷的起步工作。

如果把马老师提出的要求作为我们的目标，我们不能不承认微型社会学的限度，承认限度并不是否定在限度内的成就和它的价值。以微型研究为"第一步"可以得到比较结实的基础。我们应当从这基础上走出去，更上一层楼。怎样走，怎样上，首先要在实践中去发现"微型"的限制在那里。

我在上面各节里已肯定了一个像农村一样的社区可以作为社会人类学的一个研究的适当对象，因为这个社区的人文世界是"完整"的，从功能上说能满足每一个社区居民生活各方面的需要。从这个意义上 Leach 说我这本《江村经济》不失为一本功能主义的著作，虽则我并没有把社会各方面的功能全面顾及，但是从整体出发有重点地叙述了这个社区的经济生活，也就是马老师所说的"农户家庭再生产的过程"。我后来用建立类型来补充这种研究方法，用以区别于通过数量上的增加以取得总体的认识。

抗战时期我在云南内地农村的研究工作中充分利用了类型这个概念，进行比较的研究工作。江村、禄村、易村、玉村等名称就表示了我的研究方法。我认为可以从发现各种类型的方法逐步接近认识中国全部国情的目的，也就是通过"微型社会学"累积各种类型，综合出马老师所要求我做的那部有关中国文化和社会的巨著。

直到 80 年代，我第二次学术生命开始时，才在总结过去的实践中，清醒地看到了我过去那种限于农村的微型研究的限度。我在 60 年代提出的"类型"概念固然可以帮助我解决怎样去认识中国这样的大国对为数众多、结构不同的农村的问题，但是后来我明白不论我研究了多少类型，甚至把所有多种多样的类型都研究遍了，如果把所有这些类型都加在一起，还不能得出"中国社会和文化"的全貌，因为像我所研究的江村、禄村、易村、玉村等等的成果，始终没有走出"农村社区"这个层次的社区。整个"中国文化和社会"却不等于这许多农村所加在一起的总数。农村不过是中国文化和社会的基础，也可以说是中国基层社区。基层社区固然是中国文化和社会的基本方面，但是除了这基础知识之外还必须进入从这基层社区所发展出来的多层次的社区，进行实证的调查研究，才能把包括基层在内的多层次相互联系的各种社区综合起来，才能概括地认识"中国文化和社会"这个庞大的社会文化实体。用普通所熟悉的现成概念来说就是中国文化和社会这个实体必须包括整个城乡各层次的社区体系。

在《江村经济》中我早已看到江村这个村一级的社区并不是孤立和自给的。在这方面和太平洋岛屿上的社区比较，江村这一类中国农村的社区居民固然在本社区里可以取得满足他们基本的需要，但这些都不是封闭的社区，或封闭性远没有特罗布里恩德群岛土人或提科皮亚岛土人那样强。当然当前世界上绝对封闭孤立的人群已经可以说不再存在了，或是只是极为个别的例外了，但在和社区外的联系程度各地方的情况可以差别很大。自从航海技术有了大发展以来，几个世纪海运畅通。全世界的居民已抛弃了划地聚居、互不往来、遗世孤立的区位格局，不同程度地进入了稀疏紧密不同的人和人相关的大网络。就在这个历史的变化中，在农村社区基础上发展出了若干农村间在生活资料上互相交换的集散中心的市镇。

传统市镇的出现在中国已有几千年的历史。在本世纪的近一百年里，特别是近几十年里，中国传统市镇发生了巨大的变动。城乡关系已脱颖而出，成了一个特别引人注意的理论和实际问题。

城乡关系不但把分散的自成一个社区的许多农村联系了起来，形成一种有别于农村的市镇社区。它的社会和文化内容可以说是从农村的基础上发展出来的，所以保留着许多基本相同的一面，但是又由于它作为一个社区的功能已不同于农村，因而也自有其不同于农村的一面，它属于与农村不同层次的社区。

在研究方法上说，在研究农村这种基层社区时，只要不忘记它是有许多方面和本社区之外的世界相联系这一点，然后集中注意力在本社区的自身，还是可以在既划定的范围内观察到社区居民社会生活各方面的活动，并把本社区和外界的关系交代清楚，还是可以在这既定的空间范围内把这个社区人文世界完整地加以概括。比如我在《江村经济》中把居民依靠区外供应日常所需的油、盐、酱、醋、糖、酒，在"航船"的一节里讲清楚了，在江村的经济体系中也不留下很大的缺漏。又比如在《禄村农田》里把当地农业里重要的劳力供应，说明是从附近各地集中到禄村来卖工的劳动市场里得到的，而并没有去追踪这些出卖劳力的人的来源是外村的少数民族，也可以交代过去了。这些例子说明，"微型社会学"虽则带来了限制，如果说明把研究的范围限于基层社区，这样做法还是可以说得通的。但也必须承认这些"微型"资料是不可能综合起来说明高一层次的社会情况。

如果我自己不满足于完成一本不失为"功能主义的著作"或是还想沿着马老师在该书序言中希望我能进一步完成一部有关中国社会和文化的综合性的著作，我就不能停留在这本《江村经济》的著作上了，而且也不能只走"云南三村"的老路，尽管这条路还应当走下去。为了更上一层楼，我就势必走出农村社区这个范围而从农村里发展出来、为农村服务的市镇社区拓展我的研究领域了。

至于我怎样从《江村经济》里走出来进入小城镇的研究，这一段叙述，我觉得已超出了对《江村经济·序言》的体会的范围，尽管这一步还是从《江村经济》的基础上走出来的。我在去年年初写了一篇《农村、小城镇、区域发展》，可以作为本节的参考，在本文里不再重复了。

八

"微型社会学"有它的优点，它可深入到人际关系的深处，甚至进入语言所难于表达的传神之意，但是同时有它的限制。我在上一节里指出了在空间坐标上它难于全面反映和该社区有密切的联系的外来辐射，如我已提到的一个农村所倚赖的市镇，和没有提到而同样重要的亲属和行政上的种种关系，这是因为社区是通过社会关系结合起来的群体，在这种人文世界里谋取生活的个人已不是空间的一个点，而是不断在扩大中的一堆堆集体的成员，就是在幅员可伸可缩的一堆堆集体中游动着的分子，这是很难用普通几何学图形予以表述的。

如果我们从空间转向时间，社区的人文世界同样是难用几何形象来加以表述的。这正是社会人类学和历史学争论已久的问题的根子。时间本身，以我们常识来看，日换星移总是在一条线上向前推进，以个人生命经历来说，从幼到老，不能倒流。这就是我们熟悉的过去、现在和未来后浪推前浪的程序。在西方拉丁语系的语言中的动词还要用这个三分法来定式。这三分法就成了我们一般认识历史的标尺。这种以时间里运行的一切事物总是按照先后次序一幕幕地层次井然地推演的认识框架在社会人类学里也就出现了所谓社会演化规律。把人类的历史看成和其它事物的历史一般像是一条流水线。这线又可以划成若干段，一段接一段，如野蛮、未开化、文明等等。一个人不论生在什么地方，都可以根据他生活上一部分的表现，划定他在历史框架里的地位，而推论他全部生活的方式和预测他的未来。这种方法的内容可以搞得很复杂，其实把人文世界看得太机械化和简单化了。

马老师对这种机械的社会演进论是深恶痛绝的，但也由于他反对这种错误的历史观，又由于他主要的田野作业是在特罗布里恩德这一个太平洋小岛上居民中进行的，这些小岛上的居民生活比较简单而且看来长期没有发生过重要的变动，以致他的著作给人一种印象就是研究这类居民的人文世界可以不必去追问他们的历史演变，甚至误解功能主义是非历史主义的。功能主义确是主张一件事物的功能是它对人生活发生的作用，这里所说的作用又被认为是这事物当地当时对个人需要的满足。个人的需要持续的时间和包括的范围也就成了人文世界的时间和范围。因而被认为功能主义的社会人类学可以不讲历史。我认为这是一种误解。马老师在他的著作里可以说确是没有历史的分析，但这是出于他所研究的对象首先是在他进行田野作业这段时间里社会变动不大，其次当地居民并没有文字去记下他们的历史和他们的历史还是靠个人的头脑里记下的上辈人口头传下来的传说。这就使过去的历史和现在的传说分不清，以致这两者之间在时间框架里互相融合了。传说有它当前的作用，满足当前的需要，并不一定符合已过去了的事物发生当时的实际。在了解当前的人文世界自应当把两者分开而着重在当前发生作用的功能。这就出现了他强烈否定所谓"遗俗"这一类"失去了功能的事物"，因而他被认为不注意在客观时间中发生过的一般所谓"历史"了。

以上是我个人的体会，就是说在功能的分析里，一件人文世界中的事物都可以存在时间框架上的多重性，即我们习以为常的过去、现在、未来结合在一起的情况。上面我已说过人们对过去的记忆可以因当前的需要而和实际上过去的情况不相符合，而且在当前决定个人行为的心理因素里还包含着对未来的希望和期待。早在《江村经济》一书的"前言"里我也说过以下一段话：

"任何变迁过程必定是一种综合体，那就是：他过去的经验，他对目前形势的了解以及他对未来结果的期望。过去的经验并不总是过去实事的真实写照，因为过去的实事经过记忆的选择已经起了变化。目前的形势也并不总是能得到准确的理解，因为它吸引注意力的程度常受到利害关系的影响。未来的结果不会总是像人们所期望的那样，因为它是希望和努力以外的其他许多力量的产物。……"

我全部引用 60 年前的话，因为这段话里我表明了我们习以为常的时间的三分法，不能简单地运用在分析变动中的人文世界。我当时所说的时间上的"综合体"，其实就想指出我们单纯常识性的时间流程中的三分法是不能深入理解人文世界的变动过程，我在《学习文化论的体会》一文中所说"三段直线的时间序列（昔、今、后）融成了多维的一刻"也就是这个意思。在这个问题上我总觉得不容易说清楚，所以反复地用不同说法予以表述。

马老师在《江村经济·序言》中已说明了他对历史的态度。"正因为那个国家有着最悠久的没有断过的传统，要理解中国历史还必须从认识中国的今天开始。这种人类学的研究方法对于现代中国学者和欧洲的一些汉学家所进行的以文字记载为依据的重要历史工作是一种不可缺少的补充。研究历史可以把遥远过去的考古遗迹和最早的记载作为起点，推向后世；同样，亦可把现状作为活的历史，来追溯过去。两种方法互为补充，且须同时使用。"

马老师当时已看到中国社会的特点是在它有考古遗迹和文字记载的悠

久文化传统。这是和殖民地上土人的重大的差别。但由于自己没有在像中国这样的地方进行过田野作业，所以他只能做出原则性提示，认为历史学和社会人类学应当是两门可以互为补充的学科。至于在具体研究工作上怎样合作和补充，他并没有详细说明。但这却直接涉及到是否能应用"微型社会学"的方法来研究中国农村的问题，或"从农村社区能否全面研究中国国情"的问题了。

以《江村经济》来说，我在关于历史材料方面应用得确实很少，而且很简单。像在江村经济中起重要作用的蚕丝副业，我只查了赖特（A. Wright）的一本关于20世纪对香港、上海等商埠的印象记，和用了他1908年在这本书里所写的有关"辑里丝"的一段话。有关江村的人口数字我只用了1935年的普查数字。当然我在许多地方讲到开弦弓的传统时，除了我从现场视察到实事外，也以我自己过去的生活经验来加以说明，而我的生活经验最早只能推到1910年。总括一句，我在这本书里并没有如马老师所说的结合了历史来进行的。我自己也多次说所写的这些记录今后将成为历史，时至今日这本书确可以说是一本记载了这个村子的历史。当时是活历史，现在只能是已过去了的历史，所以决不能说是结合了历史的社会学分析。

在实践中我不能不怀疑像《江村经济》一样的村一级"微型社会学"调查、社会学和历史学结合的田野工作是否切实可行？同时我是赞同马老师所说的话，要读这部历史得有历史学者和考古学者从文字和实物中得来的有关过去情况的知识作为补充。至少我认为今后在微型社区里进行田野工作的社会人类学者应当尽可能地注重历史背景，最好的方法是和历史学者合作，使社区研究，不论是研究哪层次的社区都须具有时间发展的观点，而不只是为将来留下一点历史资料。真正的"活历史"是前因后果串联起来的一个动态的巨流。

九

写完了上一节我总觉得意犹未尽，问题是在对马老师的"活历史"怎样理解。序言里的原文是"History can be read back, taking the present as its living version"。（原书 p. xxii）中文版的译文是"可把现状作为活的历史，来追溯过去"。我心里对这句话反复琢磨，想进一步体会马老师的原意。从我所理解的马老师对文化的分析中可以说他是着重从活人的生活中认识文化的。在活人的生活中他不能不看到很多行为和思想是从前人学来的，这里见到了文化有传统的一面。文化是在时间里积累而成的，并不是一切都是现在活着的人自己新创的。如果从上节里所说到的昔、今、后三段的直线延伸观念来说，就得承认今日的传统就是前人的创造和昔日传下的"历史"了。这样的思路就会给马老师一向反对的"遗俗"这个概念一个结实的基础。为了否认从今日文化里的传统拉出这条一线三维的时间序列，他提出了"活历史"的概念。"活历史"是今日还发生着功能的传统，有别于前人在昔日的创造，而现在已失去了功能的"遗俗"。传统是指从前辈继承下来的遗产，这应当是属于昔日的东西。但是今日既然还为人们所使用，那是因为它还能满足人们今日的需要，发生着作用，所以它曾属于昔，已属于今，成了今中之昔，至今还活着的昔，活着的历史。

历史学者和人类学者在这个今中有昔的问题上出现了分歧的态度。历史学者咬定历史是一线三维的序列，对于文化的传统必须回顾它本身的面目，那就是要追根求底。人类学者着眼于人们当前的生活，所以马老师主张到活生生的生活中去观察才能明白人们为什么这样生活。他不否认活生生的生活中有许多是从过去传下来的，但这些传下来的东西之所以传下来就因为它们能满足当前人们的生活需要。既然能满足当前人的生活需要，它们也就是当前生活的一部分，它们就还是活着。这也等于说一个器物、一种行为方式之所以成为今日文化中的传统是在它还发生"功能"，即能满足当前的人们的需要。凡是昔日曾满足过昔日人们的需要的器物和行为方式，而不能满足当前人们的需要时，也就会被人们所抛弃，成为死历史了。

当然说"死了的历史"并不正确，因为文化中的活和死并不同于生物的生和死。文化中的要素不论是物质的或是精神的，在对人们发生"功能"时是活的，不再发生"功能"时还不能说"死"，因为在生物界死者不能复生，而在文化界或人文世界里，一件文物或一种制度的功能可以变化，从满足这种需要转而去满足另一种需要，而且一时失去功能的文物、制度也可以在另一时又起作用，重又复活。人文世界里自有其"逻辑"，不同于自然世界。关于这一点，我在这里不去发挥和展开讨论了。总之马老师用"活历史"这个概念是值得我们进一步思考的。我在上一次研讨会上讲对马老师文化论的体会时曾提"三维一刻"时间观，可以参阅。

<h1 style="text-align:center">十</h1>

我接着想联系到在去年暑期召开的那一次研讨会上李亦园教授发表的关于"大传统"与"小传统"的讲话。我受到的启发是他对文化的层次分析。他指出了大传统和小传统的区别，因为他在田野作业中看到了中国文化的结构里有着具有权威的一套经典性的以儒家为代表的人生观和宇宙观，另外还有一套在民间流行，表现在民俗信仰的人生观和宇宙观。前者称之为大传统，后者称之为小传统，即伯格尔（Berger）教授所说的"李氏假设"。

我很赞赏李教授的分析，认为对中国文化宏观研究或微观研究都应当应用这个文化层次的分析，因为这种文化里存在着经典的和民间的区别，的确可以说在研究中国文化时表现得特别清楚，也影响得特别深刻。我想在这篇重读《江村经济·序言》文章后面加上我对这个问题的一些个人的体会，或说不成熟的假设，因为这也和上面我提到的马老师的"活历史"有关。

我认为这个特点在中国很可能和历史上很早就发生了文字而且是用图形作为符号，因而发展成一套和语言脱钩的文字体系有关。这个体系是怎样发生和发展的，是个历史问题，留给历史学家去讲更为适合。我着眼的是由于这个体系所发生的社会和文化后果。

这个体系对中国文化和社会的影响很大很深，我只举出其中一些特别引起我注意的方面。首先是由于它和语言脱了钩，冲破了地方性和民族性的限制。这个特点的意义只要和其它以语音为基础的文字体系相比较一下，就很容易看得清楚。我们普通所谓"方块字"在解放前后曾受到过很猛烈的冲击，提出所谓"拉丁化"或"世界语"的文字改革方案。尽管这种改革有权威性的支持，但是群众对此并没有积极的响应，结果只成为一种"注音"性质的符号，作为学习"方块字"发音的辅助工具。热心于文字和语音结合的人们没有注意到"方块字"在中国几千年文化中所起的积极作用，那就是阻挡了以语音差别为基础，由方言发展不同语言而形成分割为不同民族的历史过程。最清楚的例子是多语言和多民族的欧洲，到现在还不容易合成一体，在东亚大陆上我认为正因为产生了这个和语音脱钩的文字体系，汉族才能保存地方方言而逐渐统一成一个民族，而且掌握这"方块字"作为信息媒介的汉族才能起到不断吸收和融合其它民族的作用以成为当今世界上人口最多的民族，同时还起着形成多元一体的中华民族的核心作用。

"方块字"在中国文化上所起的积极作用是不应当忽视的，但也不能不看到它消极的一面，那就是和语音脱钩之后要学习这种文字是比学习文语合一的文字要困难得多。学会全部"方块字"需要相当长的时间，比学会拼音的字要多好几倍。而且如果不常使用这些"方块字"，就会所谓"返盲"。这已成为当前"扫盲"运动中的一个严重问题。识字的困难限制了文字的普及性。在一个以小农为基础的大国里，在这样长的历史过程，能掌握这个信息媒介的人数在开展扫盲运动和义务教育之前总是在全民中占很小的比例，这就引起一个很基本和很严重的社会现象，那就是文字被少数人所独占。直到目前，为了要消灭这种独占性还得付出很大的努力。

这些识字的人在中国历史上常有专称，"士"可能是最早的名称。从有文字以来直到我的幼年，20世纪初年，这种掌握文字的人在社会上还是占有比一般不识字的人民高一等的地位。读书门第是高出普通人一级，这一级的人在20世纪年代里被称作"知识分子"，在"文革"时期里被称作"臭老九"。这些称号都反映了他们在社会上具有一定的特殊地位。

我在30年代抗战时期在西南后方进行农村调查时曾注意到这种在社会上具有特殊地位的知识分子，曾想作专题研究，但这个愿望并没有完成。以我记忆所及，我曾把这种人看成是城乡之间的桥梁。这种人就是历来被称作士绅的人物，他们一般和基层农民是有区别的，但存在着血缘关系，许多是农民出身或和农民保持着亲属关系，而另一方面又大多走出农村，住入乡镇和城市，成为具有政治权力的统治阶级的一部分或和统治阶级相互沟通，特别是科举时期各级政府的领导人大多出于这种人。这种人长期以来被称为"士大夫"，士是指读书人，大夫是指当一官半职的人。在乡镇和城市里他们是头面人物，尽管没有官职，但是有社会名望，被称为缙绅先生。我曾根据初步的见解写成过一些文章，后来被译为英文，用 *China's Gentry* 的书名出版，在这本书里我曾表述过中国士绅在城乡间的桥梁作用。

这桥梁作用如果和"李氏假设"联系起来就找到了大传统的载体和大小传统之间的联系人物，或是把他们看作一个社会阶层。这些以掌握"方块字"的技能，把上下双方的文化嫁接调适在一起。我有一个假设，就是在这些士大夫手上，广大民间的基层思想和愿望整理和提高出了一个头绪，使它们能和过去在民间受到尊重的经验和教训，结合历史上各代掌握有权力的统治阶级所需要的维持其地位和扩大权势的需要，编制成一套行为和思想规范。其实就是在民间的实际习俗中通过选择使其能得到历代帝王的支持，用文字表达出来成为影响社会的经典。我这种想法是把小传统作为民间广大群众从生活的实践和愿望中形成的传统文化，它的范围可以很广，其中有一部分可以和统治者的需要相抵触的，在士大夫看来是不雅驯的，就提不到大传统中去，留在民间的乡风民俗之中。在我看来，大传统之所以能表现一部分中国文化的特点，正在于它是以小传统为底子的。它又不同于小传统，因为经过了一道选择和加工的过程。选择和加工过程就是司马迁所说的"其文不雅驯，荐绅先生难言之"。雅驯与否是选择的标准，也就是这些文人们看不入眼的风俗民情。孔子对鬼力乱神一字不提，因为他觉得这些民间信仰不雅驯，看不入眼。这些掌握着文字的人就通过"难言之"把这些不雅驯的东西排除在以文字为符号的信息系统之外，就是拔除在大传统之外；但并没有在民间把这些东西消灭掉，仍在民间用口头语言口口相传，这就成了"小传统"，还可以传给后来人。大传统在民间还是发生作用的，因为它仗着这可以超越时间的文字构成的消息系统，从识字的人传给识字的人。这些人又凭他能接触到历代传下来的经验保存了人们生活中有用的知识，利用这些传统知识能帮助别人适应生活环境，成为"人师"，取得社会的信誉名望和特殊地位，大传统也依靠他们影响着民间大众。

　　在小传统里还可以分出"地上"和"地下"两层。在民间的生活中有种种思想信仰和活动，士大夫是看不入眼的，认为不雅驯，而没有被采用，未成为大传统。这部分依旧在民间活动，凡是到民间去观察的人还能看得到，而且在民间是公开的，不受限制的，这些就是我所说地上的小传统。但有一部分是犯了统治阶级的禁例，不能公开活动，但是在民间的思想信仰里还是保留着，只在大人先生们不屑看或视而不见。这些我认为可以包括在地下的小传统里。

另外还有一部分由于受到社会上权势的镇压，不得公开露面，只能改头换面，设法在民间的私生活中存在下去，久而久之甚至已打入了人们的潜意识里，即本人也不自觉这种思想信仰的意义，只作为一种无意义的习惯盘踞在人们的意识里，这种东西不去发掘是不易暴露它的本来面目的，我觉得可以称之为潜文化。在被视为邪教等等名目下就有这种潜文化存在，而且当其发挥作用时，也常常以曲折和隐蔽的方式有力地暴发出来，所以更难捉摸和正视。

我这样的假设又暴露了《江村经济》这一类微型社会调查的又一种限制，可说这是文化的层次上的限制。农民的人文世界一般是属于民间的范围，这个范围里有多种层次的文化。它有已接受了的大传统，而同时保持着原有小传统的本身，有些是暴露在"地上"的，有些是隐蔽在"地下"的，甚至有些已打进了潜意识的潜文化。作为大传统载体的士绅在近代已有很多离乡入镇，而其社会活动和影响还在农村里发生作用。当前的情况又有很大的变动，士绅阶层可说已经解体，在农村里他的作用已由基层干部所取代，而基层干部的性质和过去的士绅阶层又有差别，这个演变现在我还没有追踪调查，说不出来。由于文化差别形成的社会层次的原则我觉得在文盲没有扫尽、现代知识没有普及之前还不会有很大的变化。因之如果以农村社区为范围进行微观研究，这方面的情况就难于作深入具体的观察了。如果要了解农村的社会结构，这个文化层次的问题单靠微型研究方法看来还是不够的，因之我把它列入微型社会学受到限制的一个方面。

十一

以上三节是想指出我认为"微型社会学"在空间、时间和文化层次上所受到的限制。我再回头一看，我发现我所指出的限制实在是出于我对自己所研究的要求超过了微观的范围。我一直想闯出微观的限制走出农村，逐步扩大我的研究范围和层次，因为它已不能满足我的要求。如果我像利奇教授一样安心于他对社会人类学的要求，自然可以安身立命于微型社区的观察了。

利奇教授代表了30年代英国人类学者的流行观点。他们认为社会人类学的目的是在理解或发现不同人群组合社会以谋取生存及发展的基本原则，组成社会的基本结构和结构中各部分有机配合的规范，即想从各地、各时、各类的个别人群中去找出集体生活的共同原理。如果以此目的来要求自己的研究工作，我想从任何一个正常活动的社区都可以作为取得这些原理的研究对象，因为它既然是个充满生机的社区，必然具备其所以能生存和发展的必需的条件和必需的结构以及各部分必需的配合。我们把任何一个标本仔细地予以观察和分析，都可以得出其所以能生存和发展的原理的。对一个单身进行田野作业的社会人类学者来说，为了观察得更精细和深入，要求他能接触到社区里的一个个人，观察他们的行为、感情、思想和希望，所选择的研究对象就贵在全而不在大了。我想这应当是强调个人进行田野作业的"微观社会学"的理论出发点。正如弗思教授（1951 年）所说微观社会学是"the microcosm to illumine the macrocosm, the particular to illustrate the general"，"以微明宏，以个别例证一般"。这句话引起后来社会人类学的疑问的就在"以微能否明宏，以个别能否例证一般？"

如果研究者的目的不是在发现一般的文化和社会结构原理，而是在认识一个具体国家、一个具体地方或一个具体村子，即一个具体社区的情况，那就不同了。这些研究者就需要运用一般原理工具去理解和说明一个或大或小的具体社区里人们的生存情况和发展的前景。前者也许可说是纯科学的研究，后者可说是应用科学的研究，我回头看我自己可能就属于后者。这一点，马老师在《江村经济》的序言里实际上已经点明。介绍我时首先是他说我是"中国的一个年轻的爱国者"，他同情我当时关心自己祖国"进退维谷"的处境，更同意我以我这个受过社会人类学训练的人来进行为解答中国怎样适应新处境的问题。从这一点出发我提出要科学地认识中国社会文化的志向，为此我走上了这一条坎坷的人生道路，一直坚持到暮年。实际上，真正了解我学人类学的目的、进入农村调查工作的，在当时——甚至一直到现在在同行中除了马老师之外，为数不多。我在西方的同行中长期成为一个被遗忘的人。我有一次在国际学术会议上自称是被视为在这个学术领域的一匹乱闯的野马。野马也者是指别人不知道这匹马东奔西驰目的何在。其实这匹四处奔驰的马并不野，目的早已在 60 年前由马老师代我说明白的了。

作为一个应用社会人类学者并不轻视纯学理的研究。如果不明白社会人类学的原理如何谈得上应用这门知识来为人民谋利益呢？如何谈得上来促进社会的发展呢？关于这一点我在《江村经济》的前言里已讲得很清楚，马老师在序言里引用了我的一段话来说明应用科学和纯粹科学的关系。

"如果要组织有效果的行动并达到预期的目的，必须对社会制度的功能进行细致的分析，而且要同它意欲满足的需要结合起来分析，也要同它们的运转所依赖的其他制度联系起来分析，以达到对情况恰当的阐述。这就是社会科学学者的工作。所以社会科学应该在指导文化变迁中起重要的作用。"

他接着在下页里说："他书中所表露的很多箴言和原则，也是我过去在相当一段时间里所主张和宣扬的，但可惜我自己却没有机会去实践它。"在这里他表白了内心的慨叹。我自以为能明白他慨叹的由来。可惜的是他生逢那个时代，他所出生的民族还没有摆脱被统治的地位，他对此连纸上谈兵的时代都没有。他接着说："我们中间绝大多数向前看的人类学者，对我们自己的工作感到不耐烦，我们厌烦它的好古、猎奇和不切实际，虽则这也许是表面上的，实际上并不如此。"

这是马老师写这篇序言来推荐这本我自认为还远没有成熟的果实的实在原因。他看到这书字后行外的意向，指向人类应当用知识来促进世人的幸福和美好社会的实现。这触及了马老师心中早已认识到的社会人类学的应用价值和它的使命。

我的"愧赧对旧作"也就是因为我并没有完成老师在这篇序言里表达的深厚的期待和明确的指向。我享受到的天年超过了我的老师，但是尽管生逢盛世，但在临近谢幕之前，所能回报于世的还只有这么一点说不上什么成就的一堆不成熟的残意浅见。可以告慰于自己的也许只是我这一生并没有忘记老师的教益和亲友的抚育，能在这条学以致用的道路，一直走到现在这垂暮之年。我更高兴的是 60 年前所记下的我姐姐费达生所开创的"工业下乡"的实验，现在已经开花结果，并在祖国的工业现代化的事业里作出了重大的贡献。我想还是用我在《江村经济》中文版发布会上即席写下的诗句最后两句作为本文的结语："阖卷寻旧梦，江村蚕事忙。"愿江村的乡亲们，继续不断从劳动中创造自己的光辉前途。

1996 年 3 月 25 日